Pride of Korean Saga

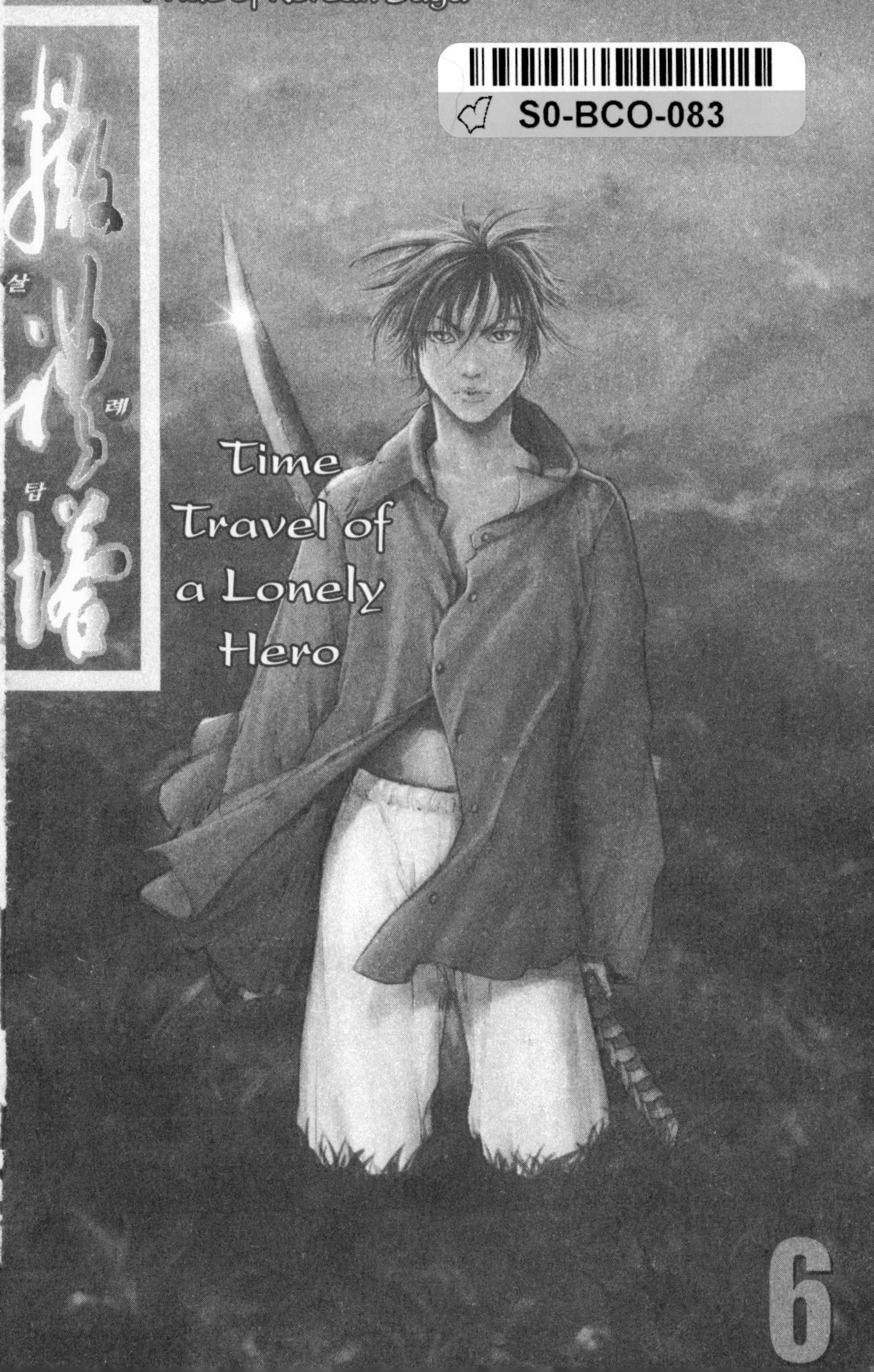
살
례
탑
Time Travel of a Lonely Hero
6

Threads of Time Vol. 6
created by Mi Young Noh

Translation - Jihae Hong
English Adaptation - Frank Marraffino
Retouch and Lettering - Erika Terriquez
Production Artist - Lucas Rivera
Cover Design - Kyle Plummer

Editor - Luis Reyes
Digital Imaging Manager - Chris Buford
Production Managers - Jennifer Miller and Mutsumi Miyazaki
Managing Editor - Lindsey Johnston
VP of Production - Ron Klamert
Editor-in-Chief - Mike Kiley
President and C.O.O. - John Parker
Publisher and C.E.O. - Stuart Levy

A  Manga

TOKYOPOP Inc.
5900 Wilshire Blvd. Suite 2000
Los Angeles, CA 90036

E-mail: info@TOKYOPOP.com
Come visit us online at www.TOKYOPOP.com

© 2002 MI YOUNG NOH, DAIWON C.I. Inc. All rights reserved. No portion of this book may be
All Rights Reserved. First published in Korea in reproduced or transmitted in any form or by any means
2002 by DAIWON C.I. Inc. English translation without written permission from the copyright holders.
rights in North America, UK, NZ, This manga is a work of fiction. Any resemblance to
and Australia arranged by Daiwon C.I. Inc. actual events or locales or persons, living or dead, is
entirely coincidental.
English text copyright © 2006 TOKYOPOP Inc.

ISBN: 1-59532-037-7

First TOKYOPOP printing: February 2006
10 9 8 7 6 5 4 3 2 1
Printed in Canada

Threads of Time ™

Volume 6

By
Mi Young Noh

HAMBURG // LONDON // LOS ANGELES // TOKYO

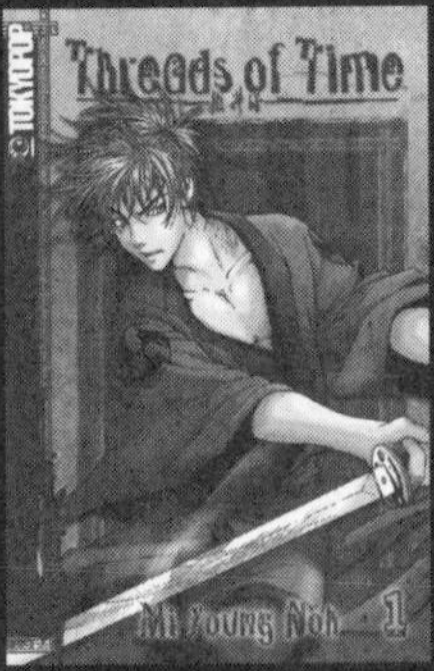
Threads of Time
TOKYOPOP
Mi Young Noh 1

Threads of Time Vol. 1

High school kendo champion Moon Bin Kim suffers from a recurring nightmare in which he lives as Sa Kyung Kim, the son of a prominent warrior family in 13th Century Korea (Koryo). After a freak accident at the school swimming pool, Moon Bin falls into a coma, but his modern-day personality resurfaces in the distant past when Sa Kyung revives miraculously after years of unconsciousness. As if being displaced in medieval Koryo isn't enough, Moon Bin finds himself at the very brink of war. From his deathbed, Genghis Khan decreed that Koryo should be conquered. Sali Tayi, the most brutal and feared general of the Mongol army, is appointed to lead the invasion into the peninsula. Opposing him is Moon Bin's 13th Century father, the legendary warlord Kim Kyung-Sohn.

Threads of Time Vol. 2

Using her clever wiles and substantial might, the stunning granddaughter of Genghis Khan, Atan Hadas, is made second-in-command to the ruthless Sali Tayi. Her first mission is to be sent into the heart of Koryo to gather intelligence on the defensive forces. In the woods near Ghu Zhu Palace, Moon Bin happens upon the princess while she is bathing in a waterfall, and is smitten immediately by her beauty. At the same time, Kim Kyung-Sohn discovers the true identity of Atan Hadas, and orders her arrest. Unaware that she is a princess and a spy of the enemy, the impetuous Moon Bin helps her escape capture. Returning to Sali Tayi, Atan Hadas learns that a full-scale invasion of Koryo has begun.

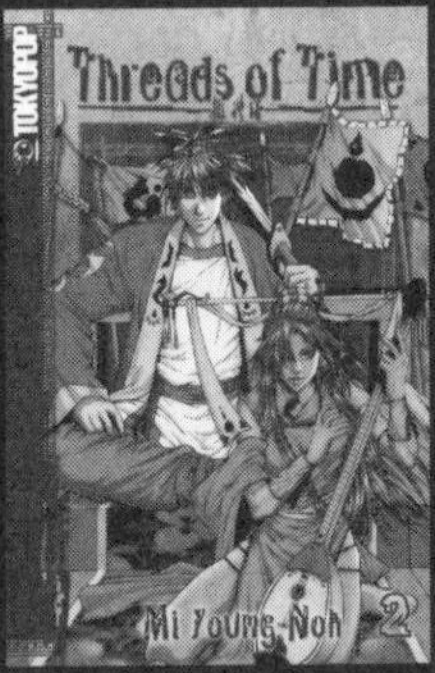
Threads of Time
TOKYOPOP
Mi Young Noh 2

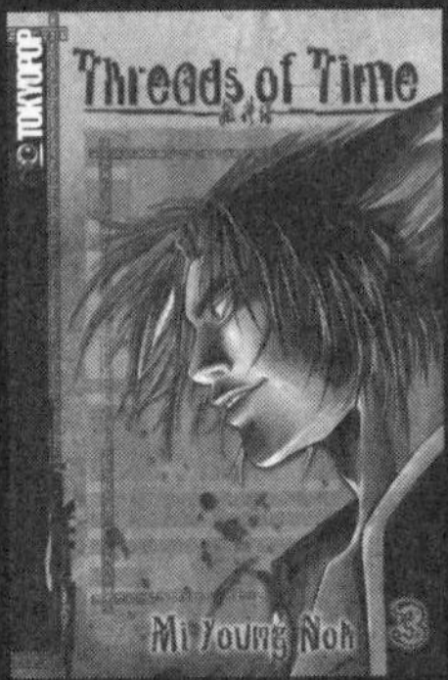
Threads of Time
TOKYOPOP
Mi Young Noh 3

Threads of Time Vol. 3

In an all-out assault, the Mongol army ravages the northern towns and outposts of the land. With their howling war cries, the invaders cut a bloody swath toward Ghu Zhu Palace, the stronghold of Koryo's defense. General Sali Tayi offers Koryo an ultimatum: surrender to the devastating ferocity of the Mongol army or go to war with it. With his valor unmoved by the Mongol's threats, Kim Kyung-Sohn upholds a remarkable resistance. Despite facing overwhelming enemy forces, the Koryo palace weathers the storm of a vicious Mongol siege. On the field of battle, the two commanders engage one another in personal combat and Kim Kyung-Sohn astonishingly perseveres—keeping the hopes of a successful resistance alive for one more day.

Threads of Time Vol. 4

Having had both his body and his pride injured, Sali Tayi vows to deliver death to not only Kim Kyung-Sohn, but to his entire family as well. Locating the defenseless village of Keh Kung, the crazed Mongol general orders the rape and massacre of his opponent's household. Witnessing the brutality of her fellow soldiers, Atan Hadas begins to doubt the glorified honors of the Koryo conquest. Walking again in the woods outside Keh Kung, she is reunited with the equally pensive Moon Bin. Seeking to repay Moon Bin for his earlier assistance, Atan Hadas warns of the slaughter and counsels that he should flee the land and save himself. Unable to abandon his 13th Century family, Moon Bin returns to his home to find that everything he knew in this new reality has been destroyed...

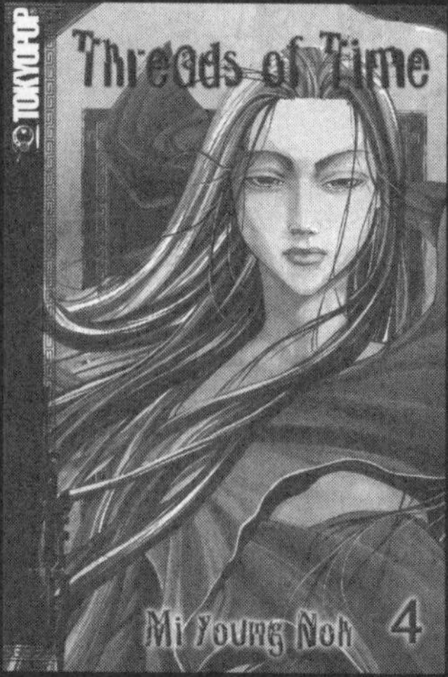
TOKYOPOP
Threads of Time
Mi Young Noh 4

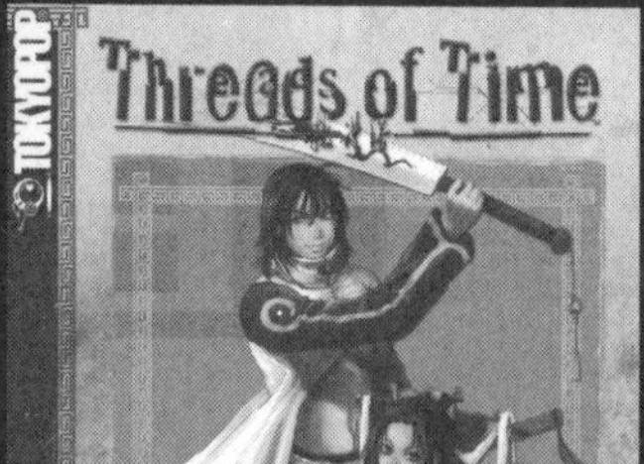
TOKYOPOP
Threads of Time
Mi Young Noh 5

Threads of Time Vol. 5

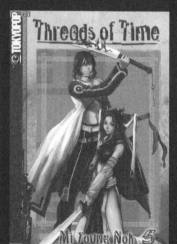

Still mourning the loss of his mother and the destruction of his home, Moon Bin Kim recalls the dream visions he had of his sister, calling for "revenge." Reacquainted with Chung-War, he is convinced to dress as a woman to better hide among the Koryo people and avoid the murderous clutches of the Mongols. Meanwhile, the Koryo ruler turns over control of the country to the Mongol hordes, much to the shocking surprise of General Kim Kyung-Sohn, who has fought fiercely for the preservation of his country only to be betrayed by its leaders. But this betrayal turns to nightmare when the Mongols present the brave general with the head of his wife. Thus stands a defeated but hardly beaten warrior atop the battlements of Ghu Zhu Castle.

contents

6

Threads of Time

24

A Father's Will....7

25

Death in Battle....41

26

To The North....89

27

A Distant Memory....129

Chapter 24
A Father's Will

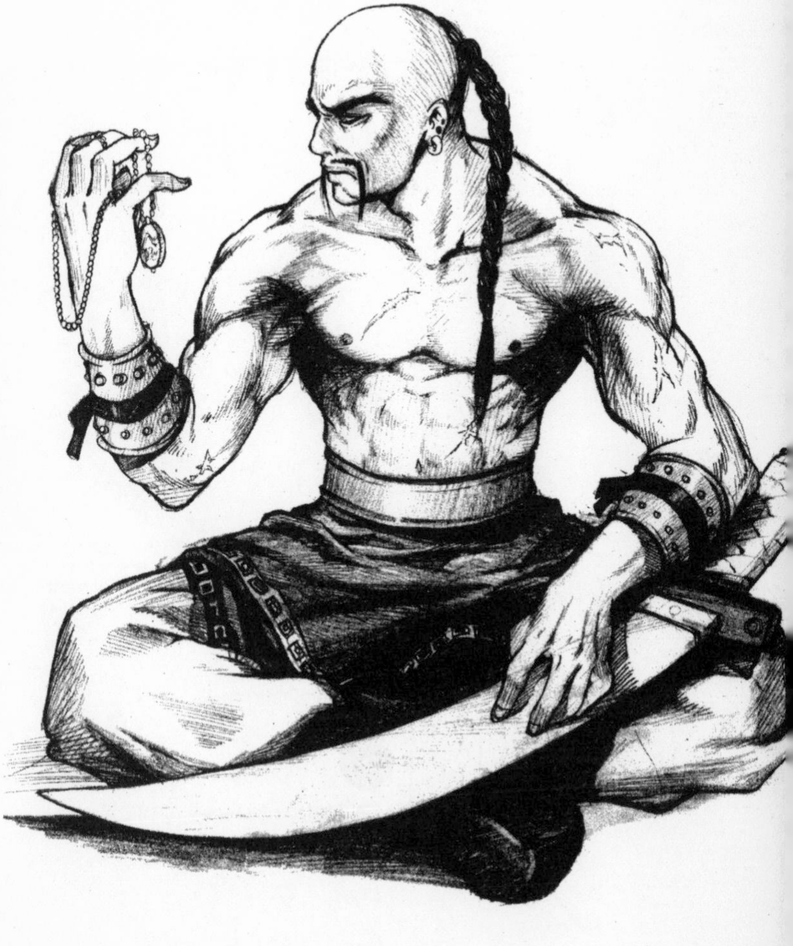

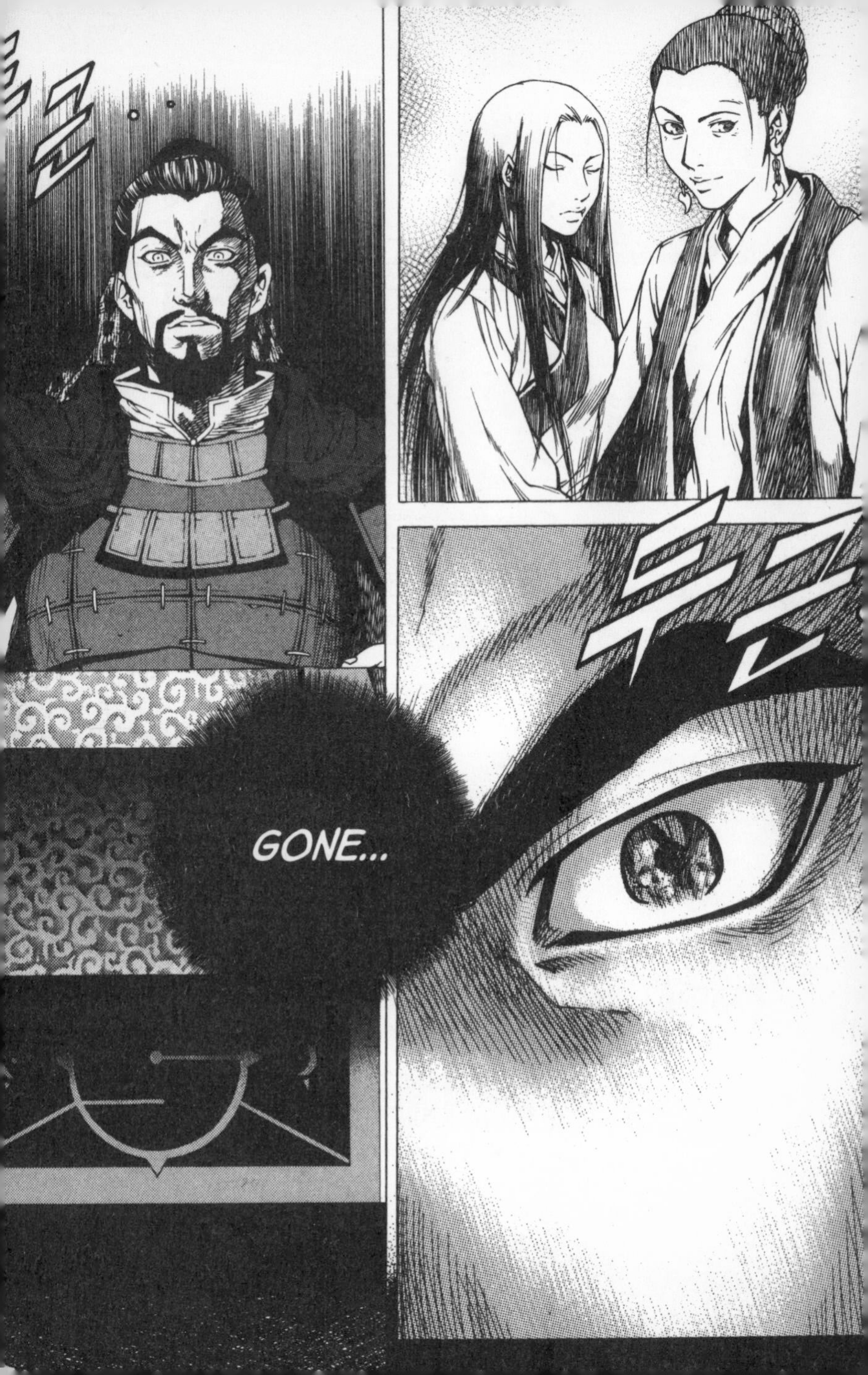
GONE...

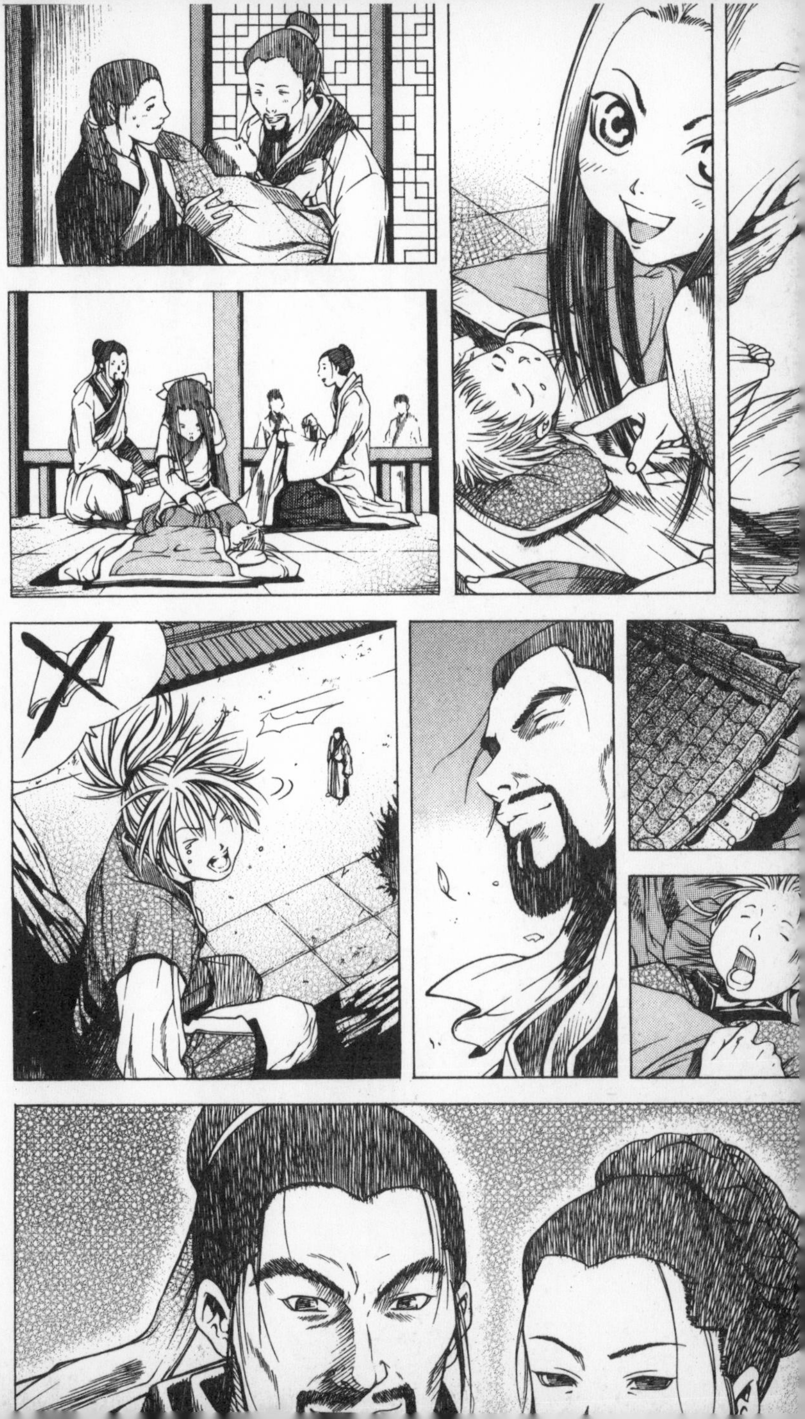

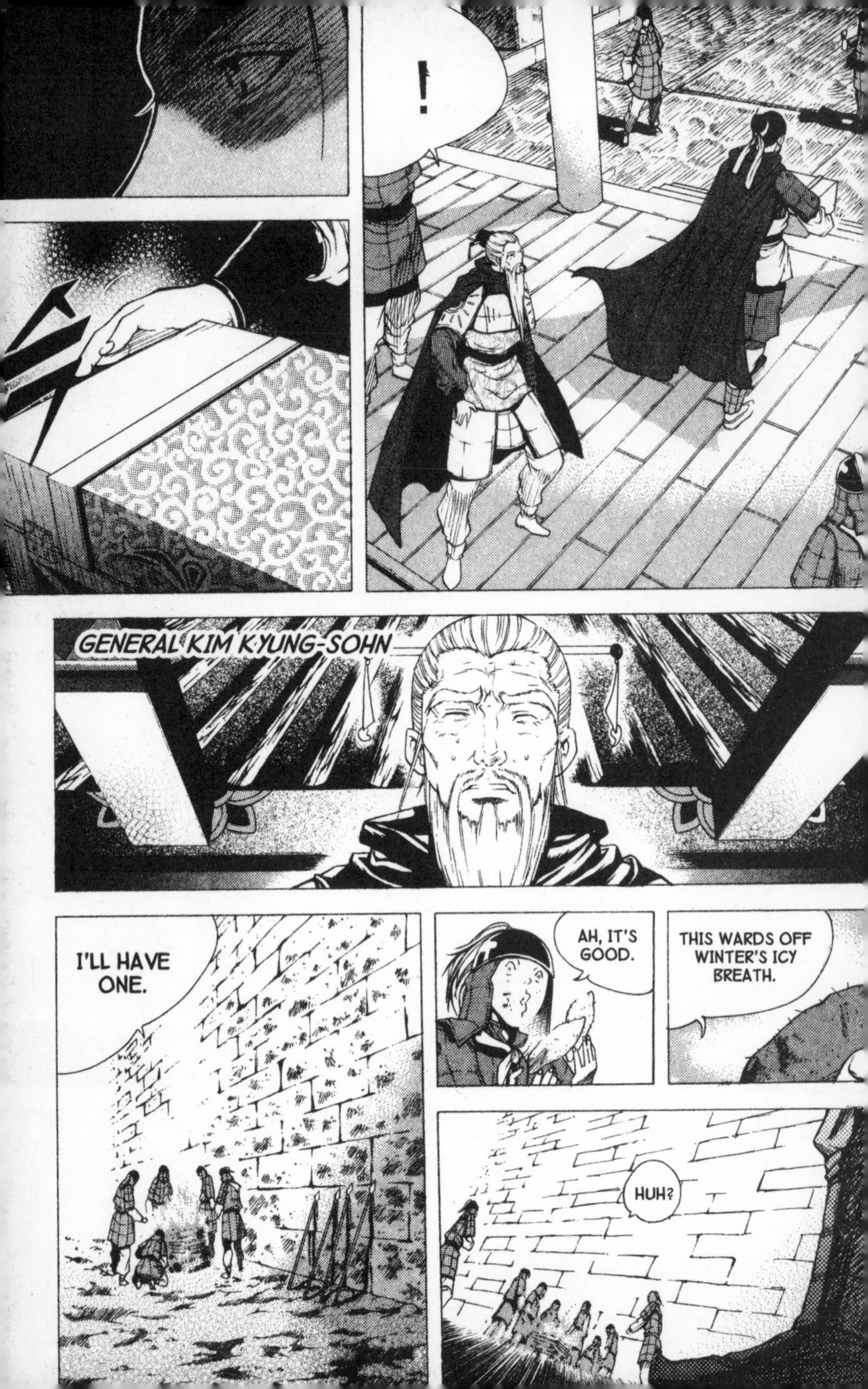
!
GENERAL KIM KYUNG-SOHN
I'LL HAVE ONE.
AH, IT'S GOOD.
THIS WARDS OFF WINTER'S ICY BREATH.
HUH?

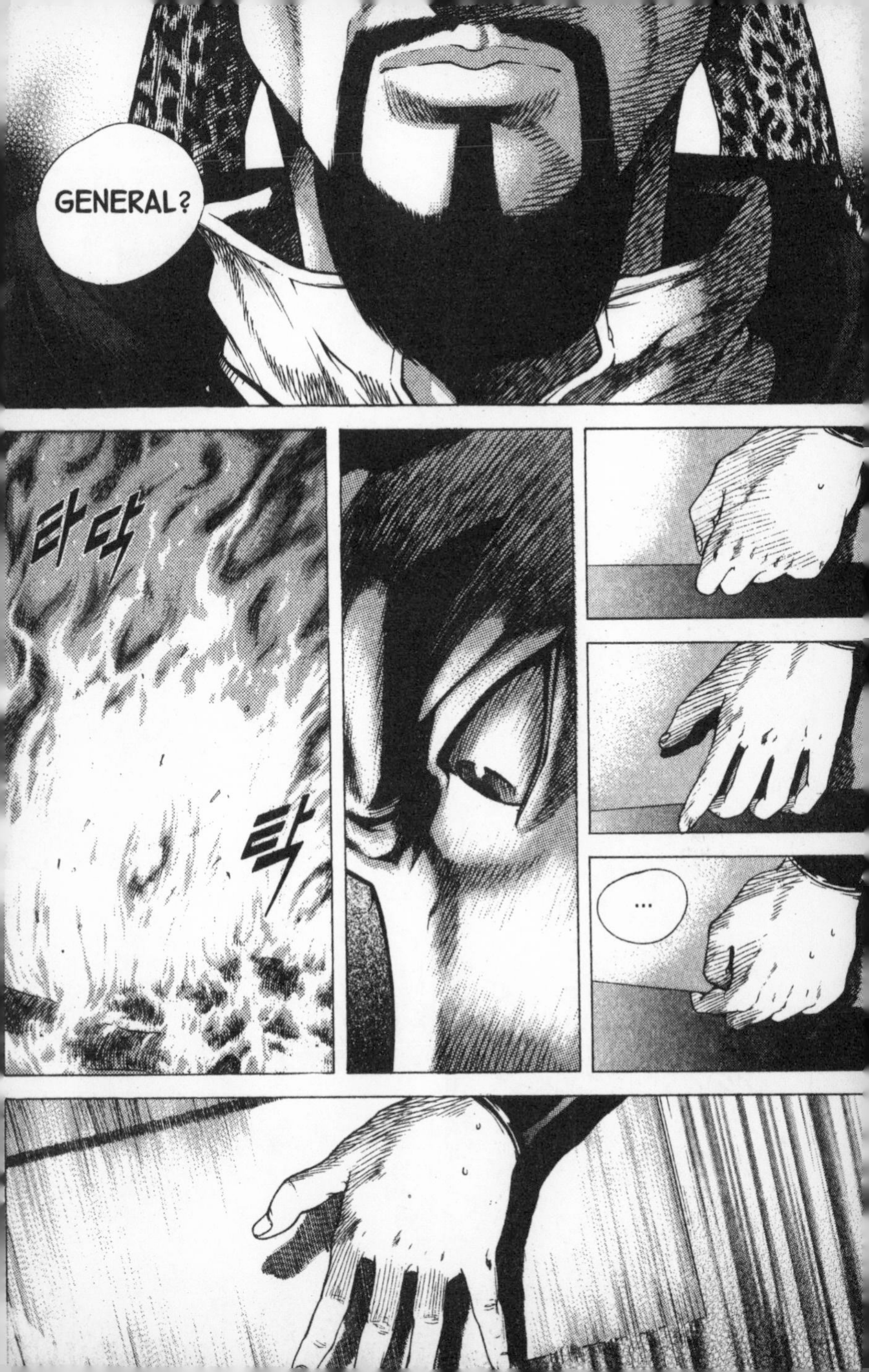
GENERAL?
타닥
탁
...

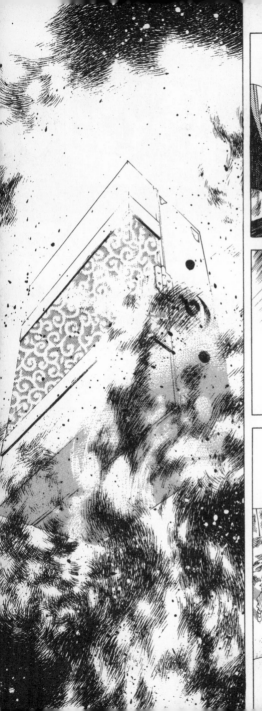

THAT LOOKS EXTREMELY VALUABLE, GENERAL.

WHY BURN IT?

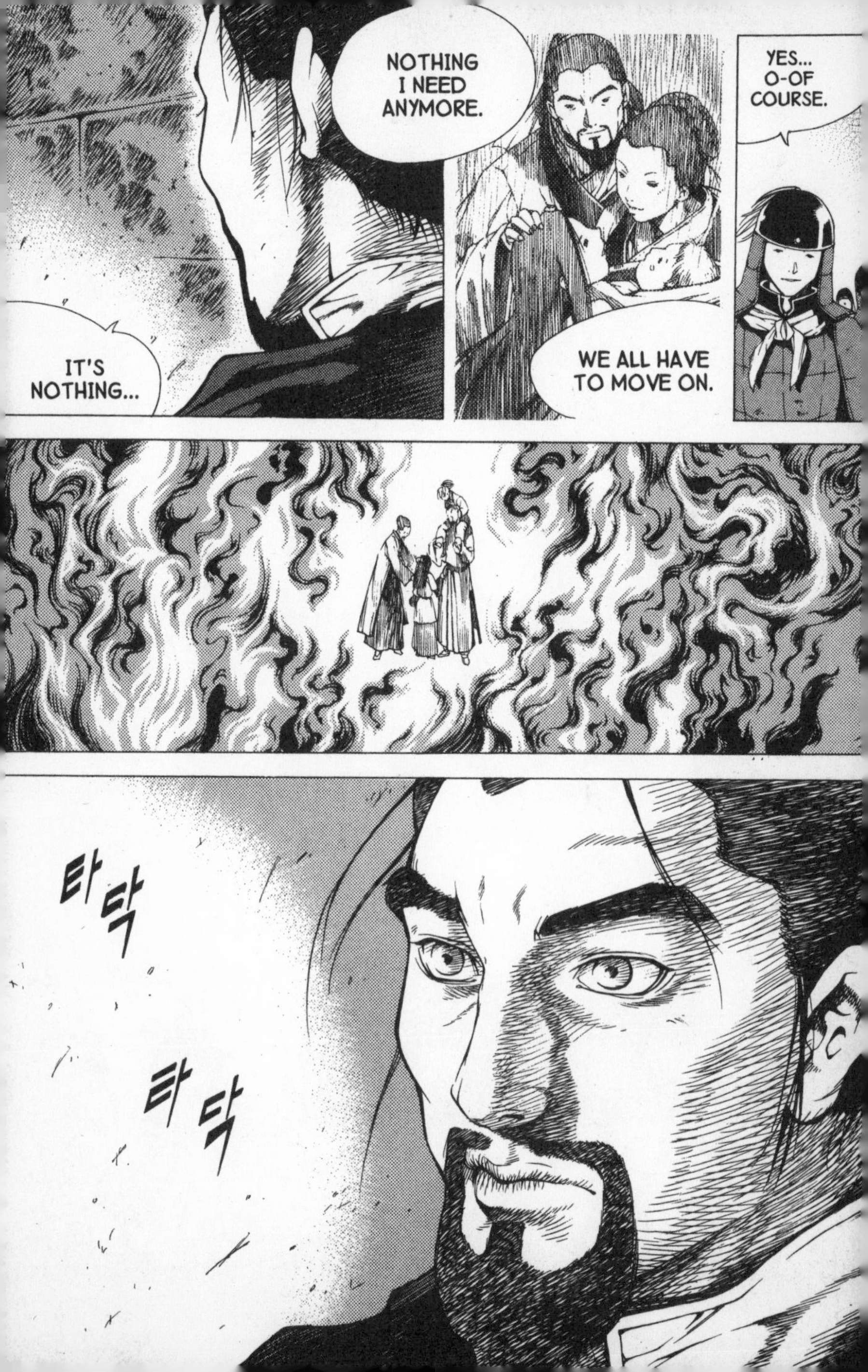
IT'S NOTHING...
NOTHING I NEED ANYMORE.
WE ALL HAVE TO MOVE ON.
YES... O-OF COURSE.
타닥
타닥

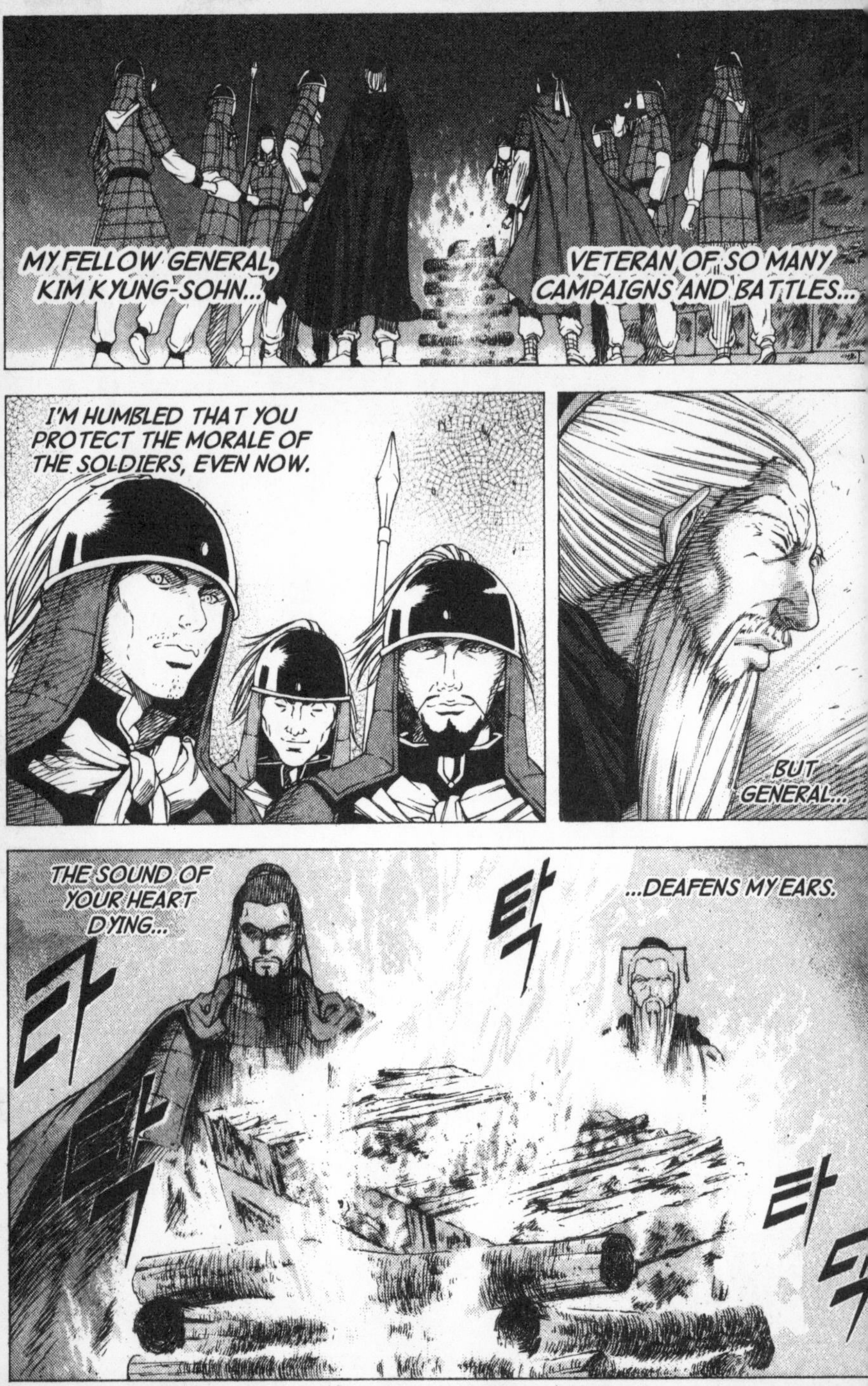
MY FELLOW GENERAL, KIM KYUNG-SOHN...
VETERAN OF SO MANY CAMPAIGNS AND BATTLES...
I'M HUMBLED THAT YOU PROTECT THE MORALE OF THE SOLDIERS, EVEN NOW.
BUT GENERAL...
THE SOUND OF YOUR HEART DYING...
탁
...DEAFENS MY EARS.

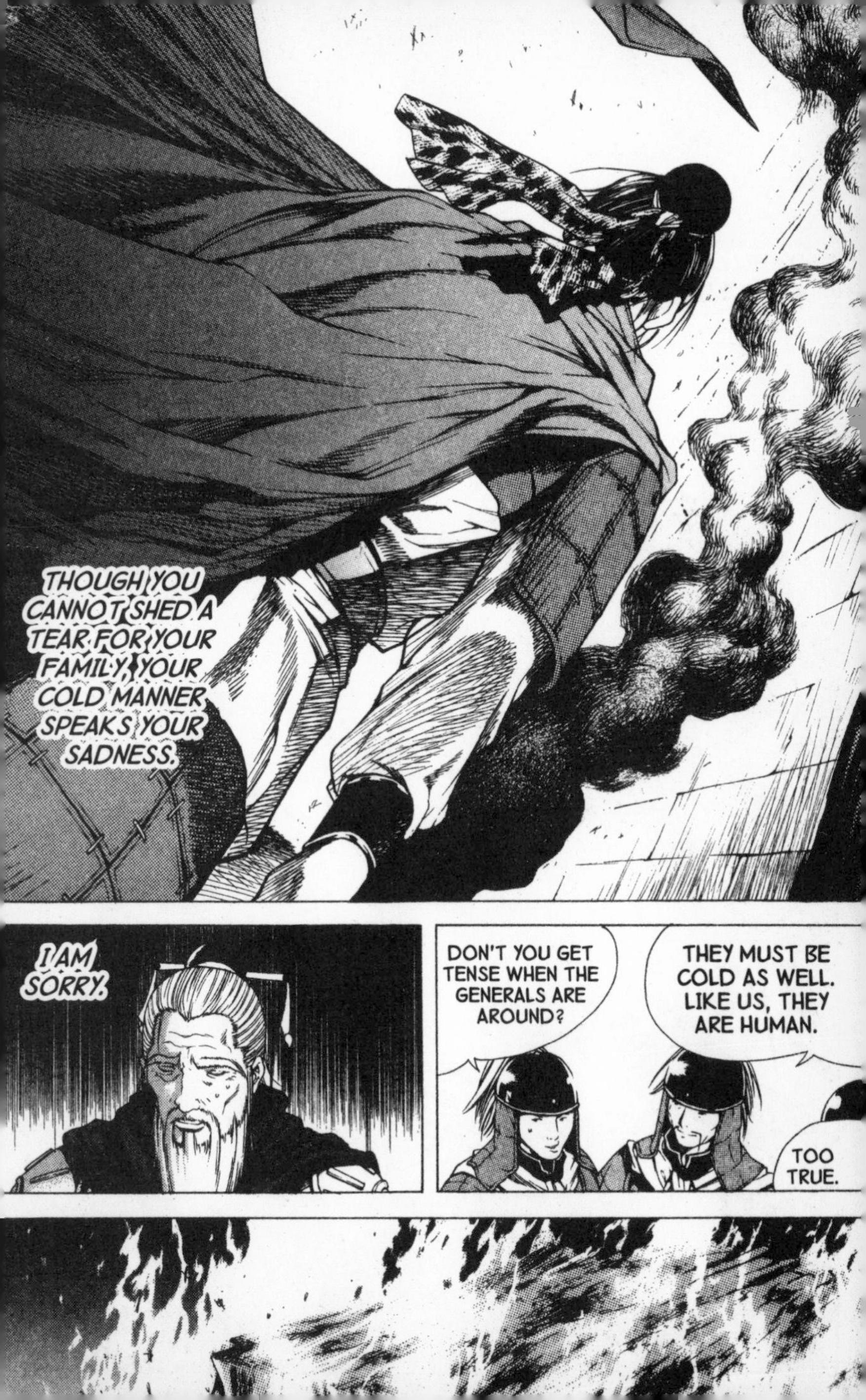
THOUGH YOU CANNOT SHED A TEAR FOR YOUR FAMILY, YOUR COLD MANNER SPEAKS YOUR SADNESS.
I AM SORRY.
DON'T YOU GET TENSE WHEN THE GENERALS ARE AROUND?
THEY MUST BE COLD AS WELL. LIKE US, THEY ARE HUMAN.
TOO TRUE.

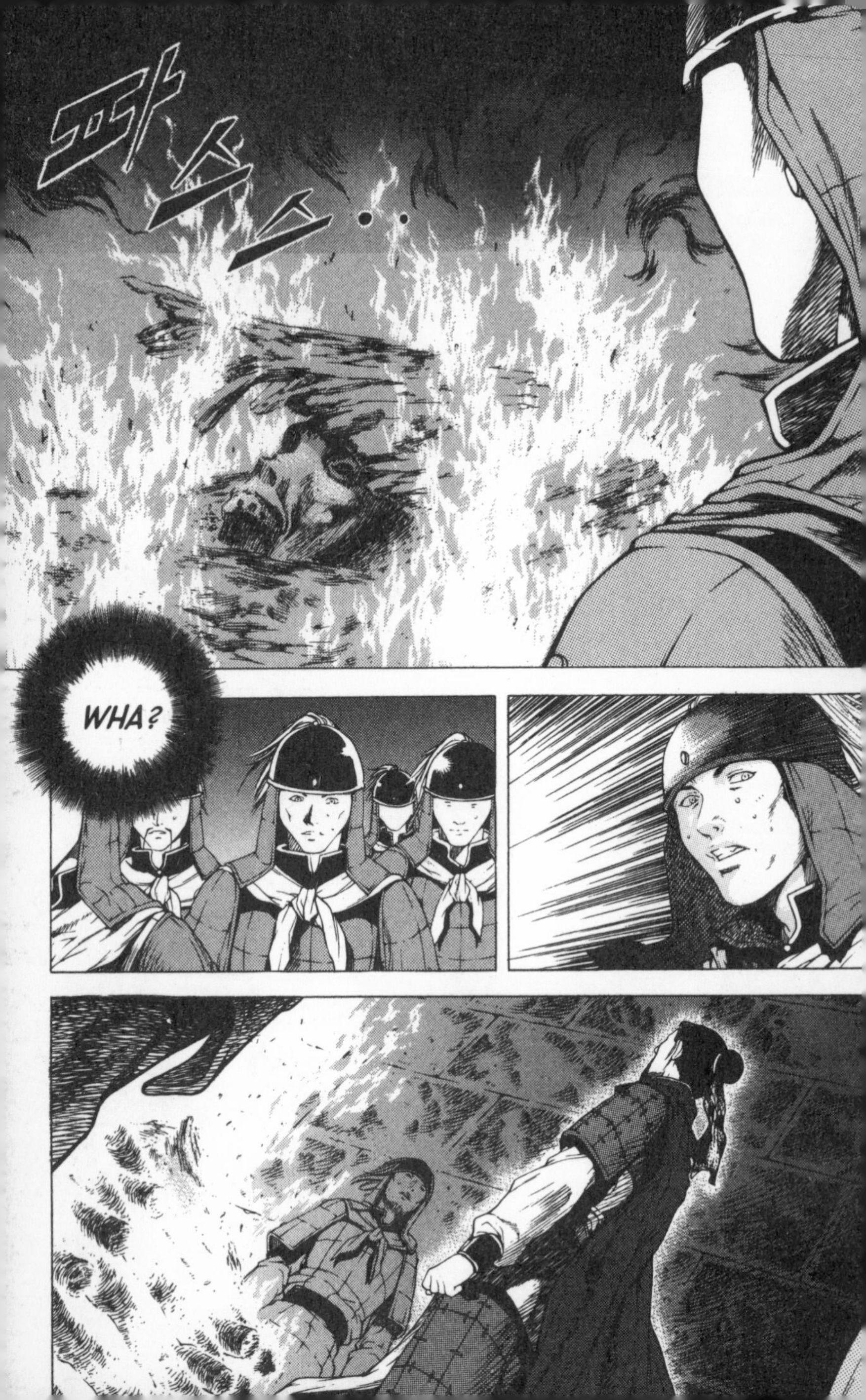
WHA?

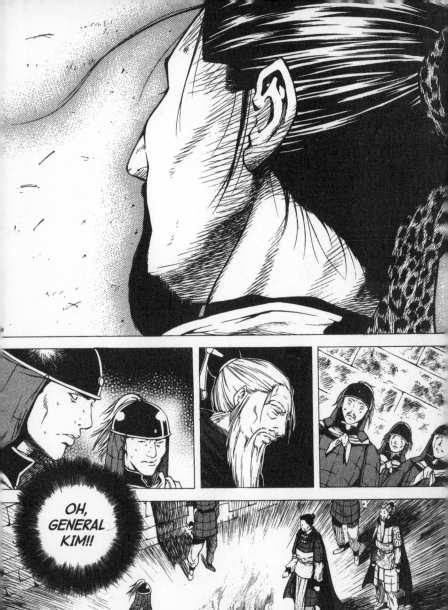

OH, GENERAL KIM!!

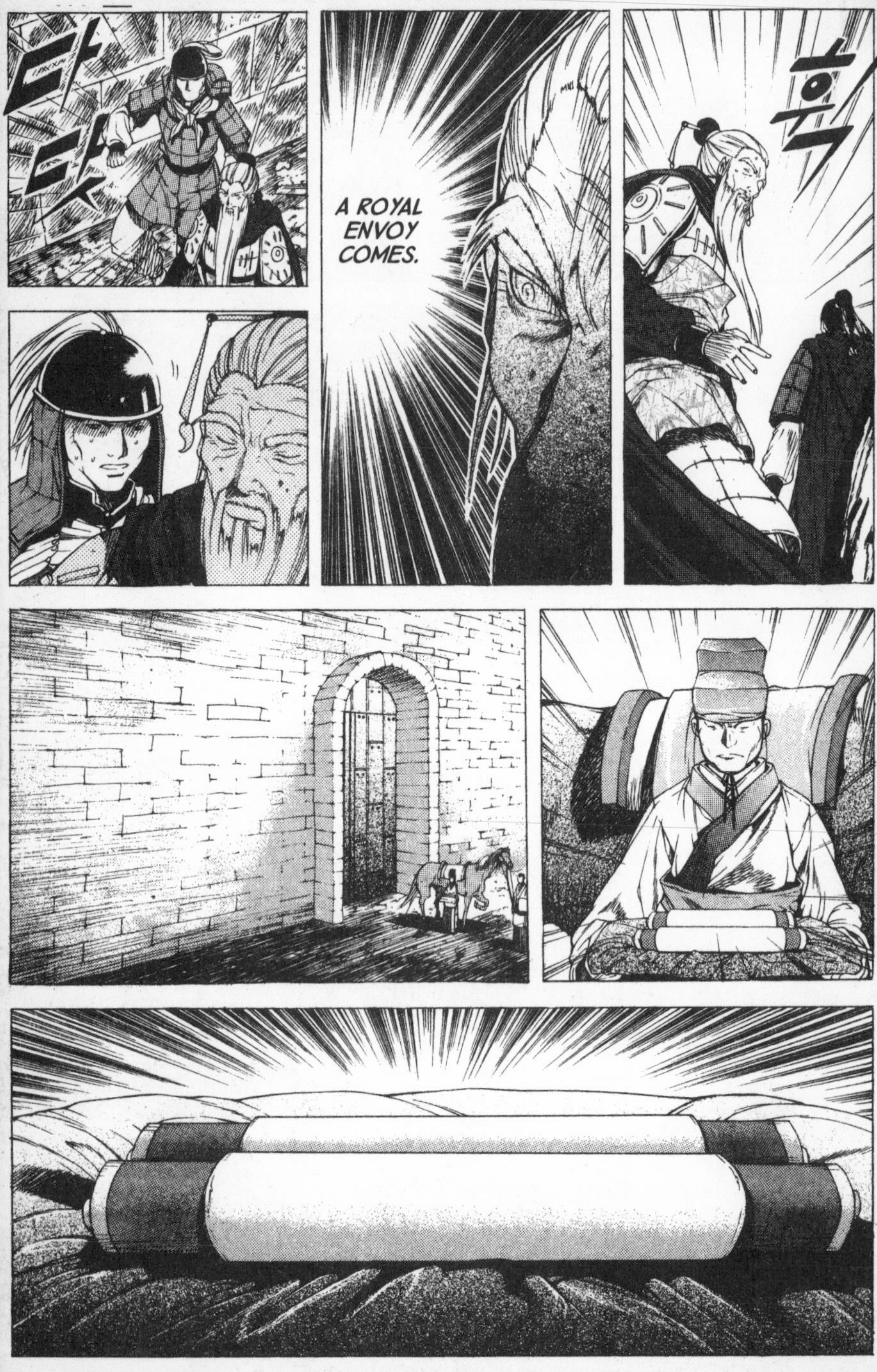
A ROYAL ENVOY COMES.

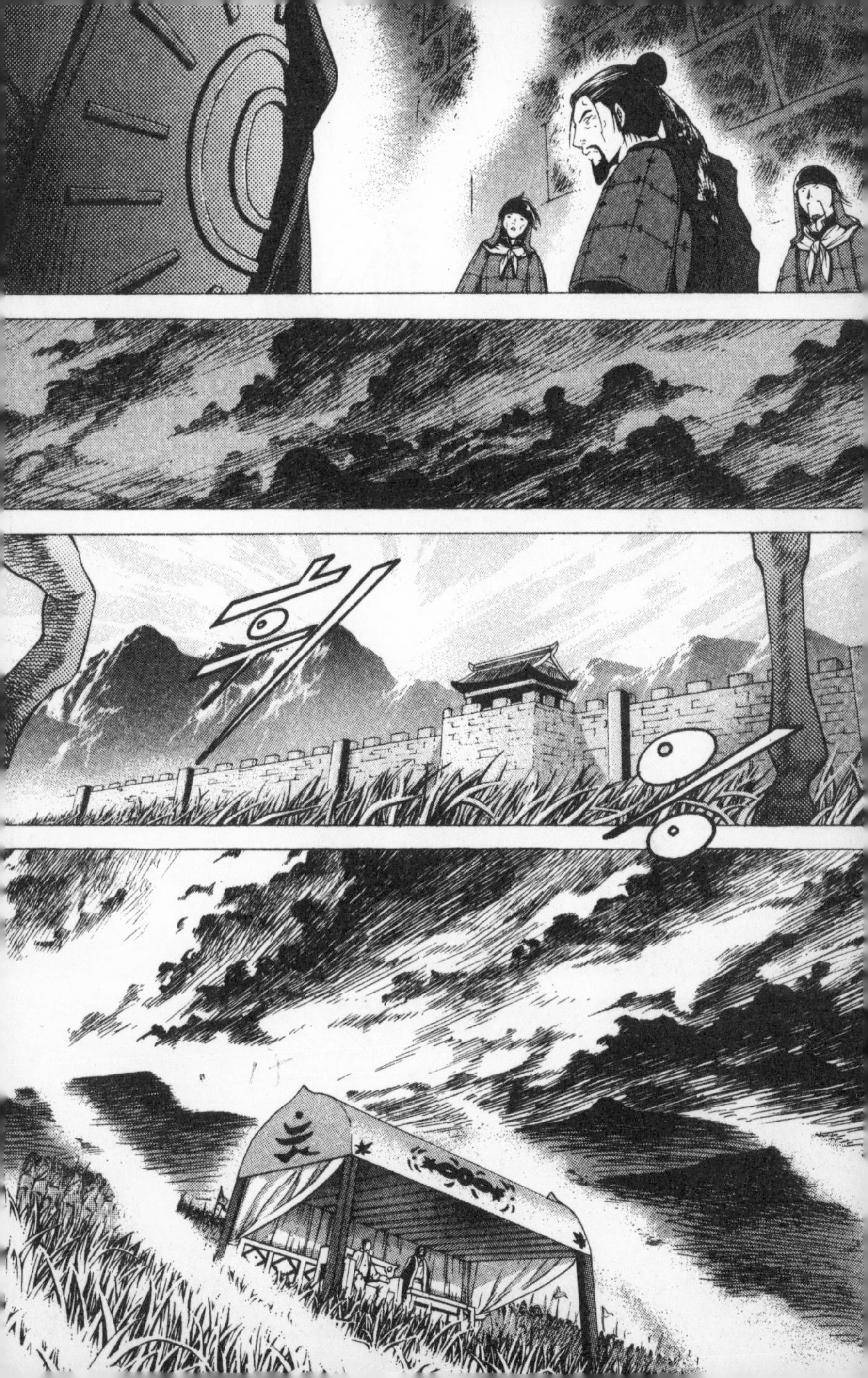

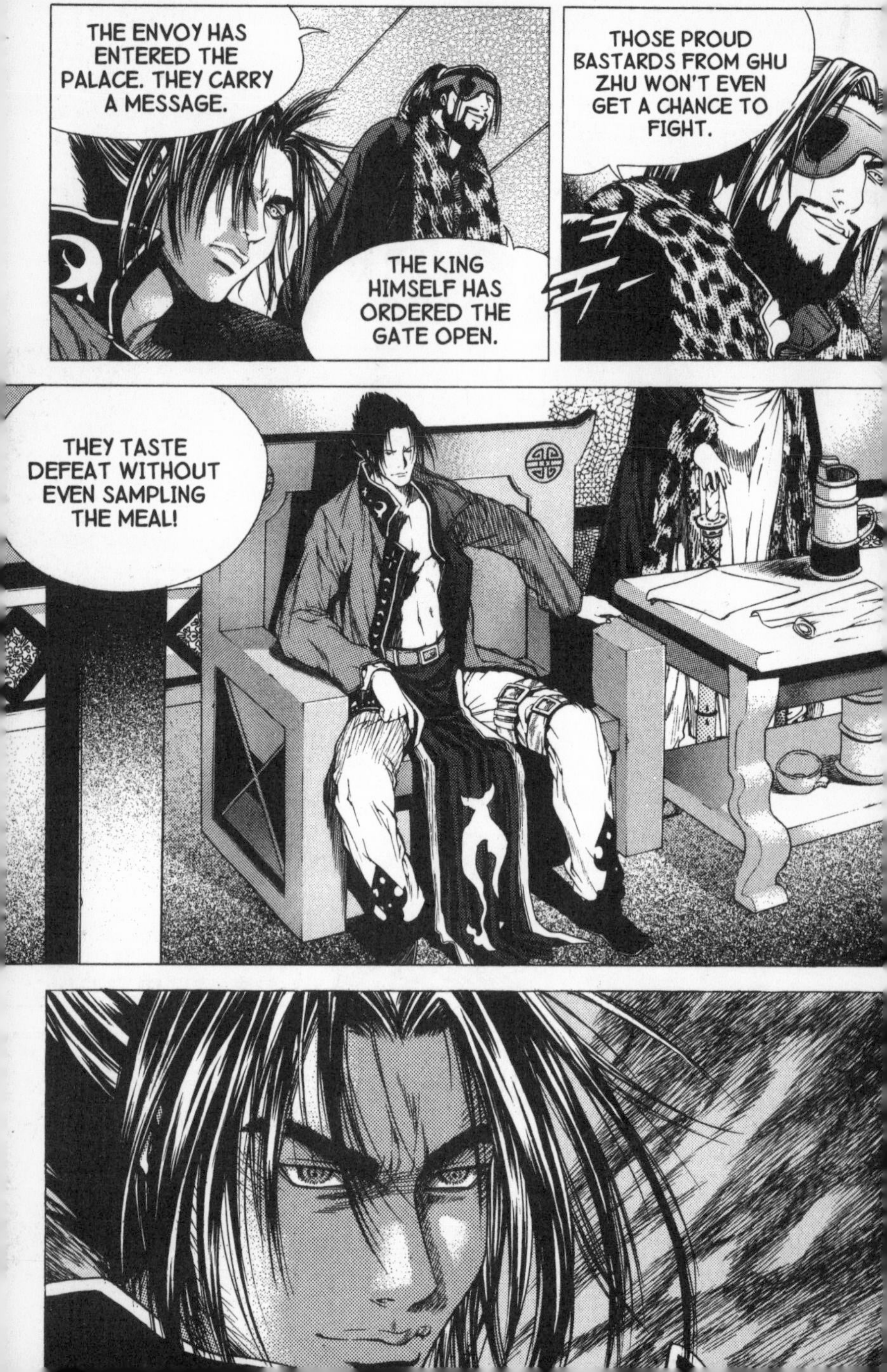
THE ENVOY HAS ENTERED THE PALACE. THEY CARRY A MESSAGE.
THE KING HIMSELF HAS ORDERED THE GATE OPEN.
THOSE PROUD BASTARDS FROM GHU ZHU WON'T EVEN GET A CHANCE TO FIGHT.
THEY TASTE DEFEAT WITHOUT EVEN SAMPLING THE MEAL!

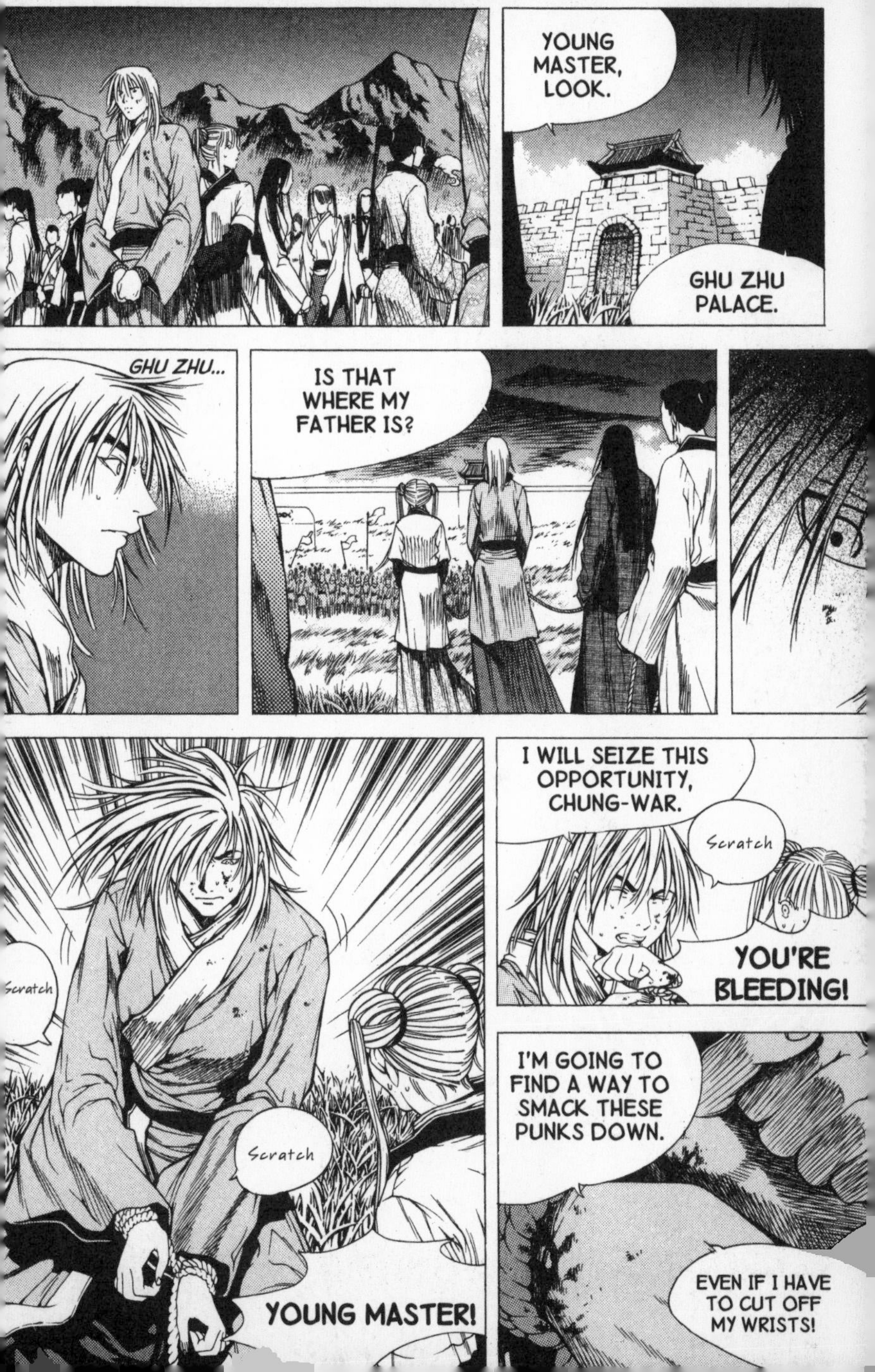
YOUNG MASTER, LOOK.
GHU ZHU PALACE.
GHU ZHU...
IS THAT WHERE MY FATHER IS?
Scratch
Scratch
YOUNG MASTER!
I WILL SEIZE THIS OPPORTUNITY, CHUNG-WAR.
Scratch
YOU'RE BLEEDING!
I'M GOING TO FIND A WAY TO SMACK THESE PUNKS DOWN.
EVEN IF I HAVE TO CUT OFF MY WRISTS!

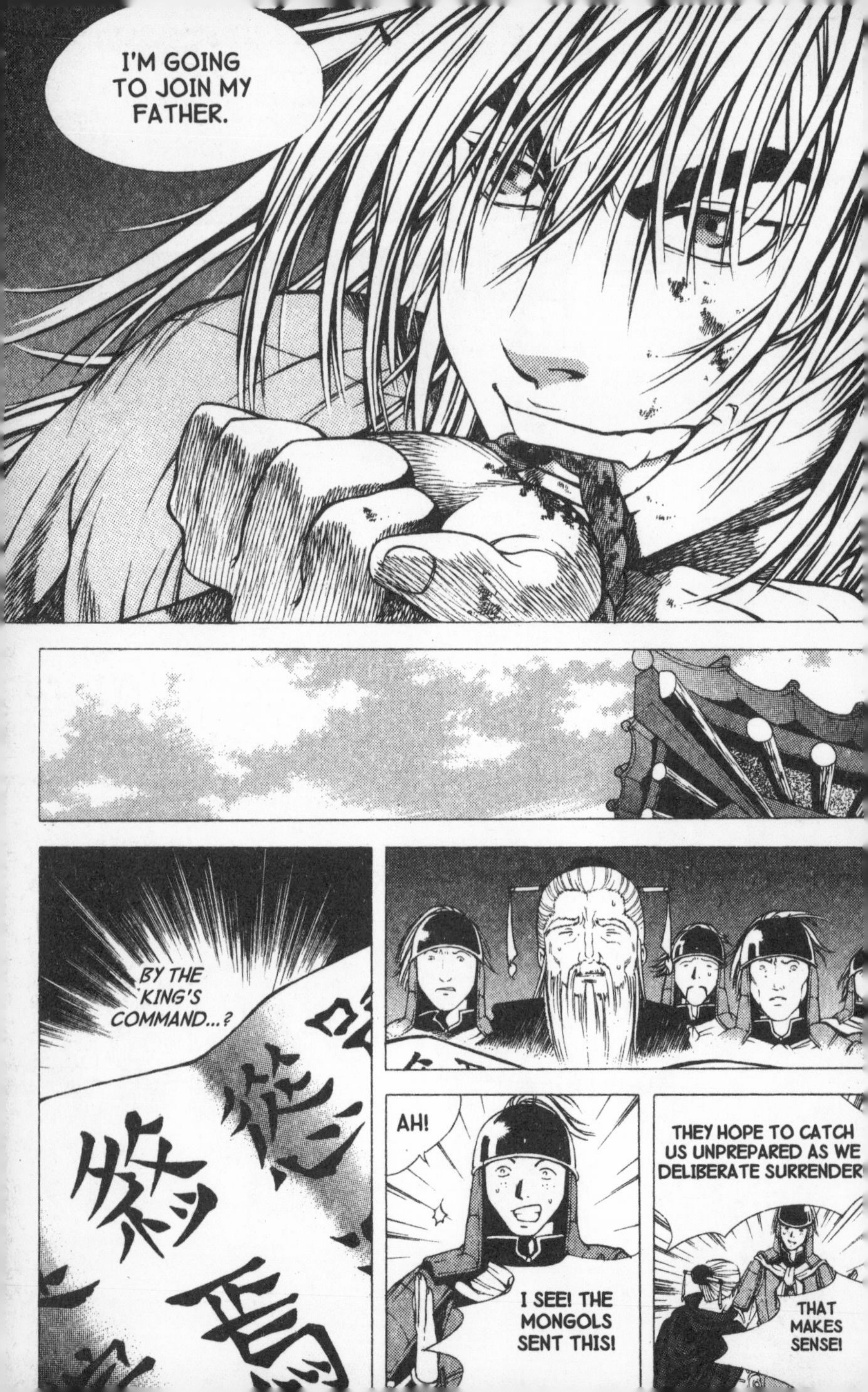
I'M GOING TO JOIN MY FATHER.
BY THE KING'S COMMAND...?
AH!
I SEE! THE MONGOLS SENT THIS!
THEY HOPE TO CATCH US UNPREPARED AS WE DELIBERATE SURRENDER
THAT MAKES SENSE!

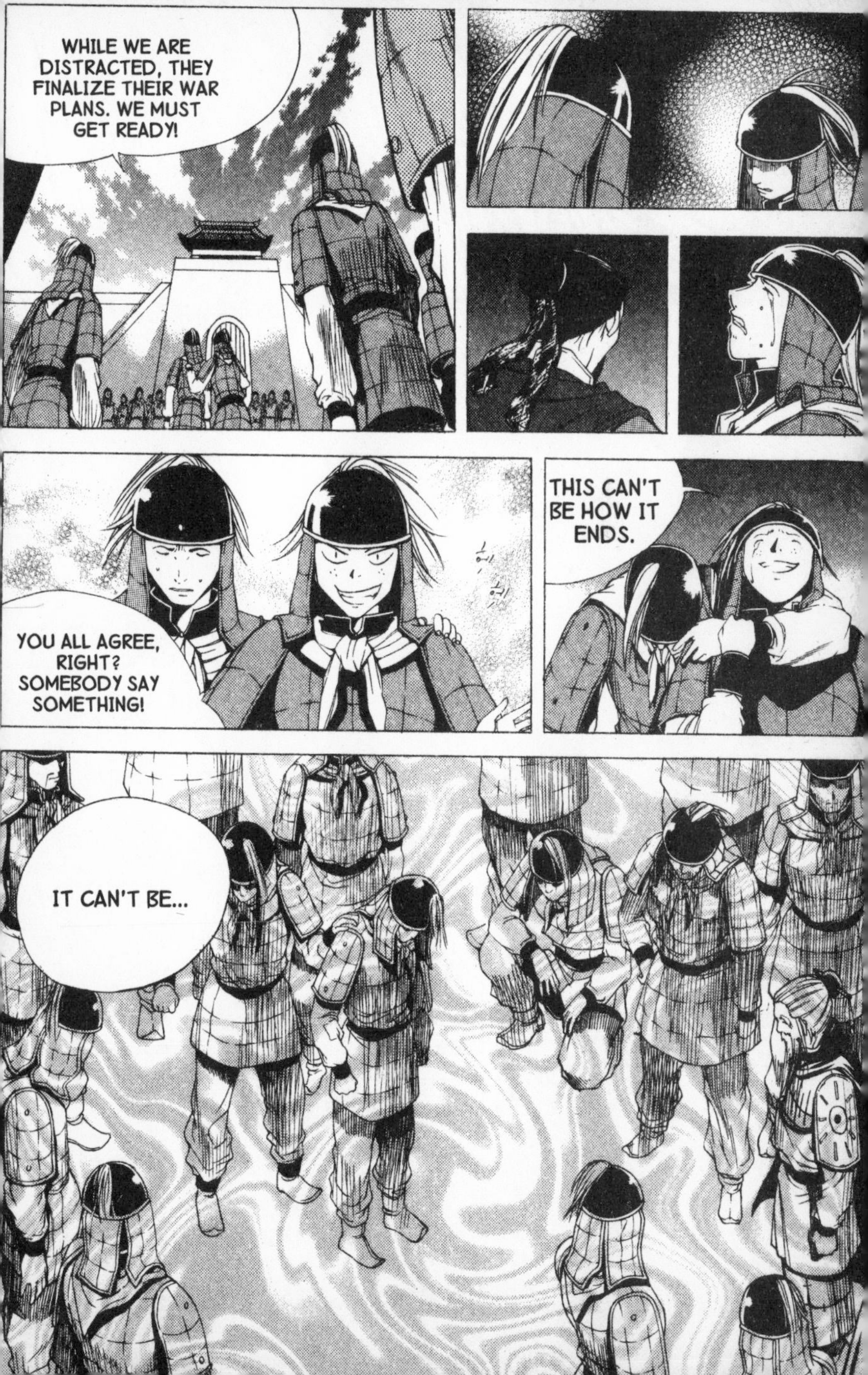
WHILE WE ARE DISTRACTED, THEY FINALIZE THEIR WAR PLANS. WE MUST GET READY!
YOU ALL AGREE, RIGHT? SOMEBODY SAY SOMETHING!
THIS CAN'T BE HOW IT ENDS.
IT CAN'T BE...

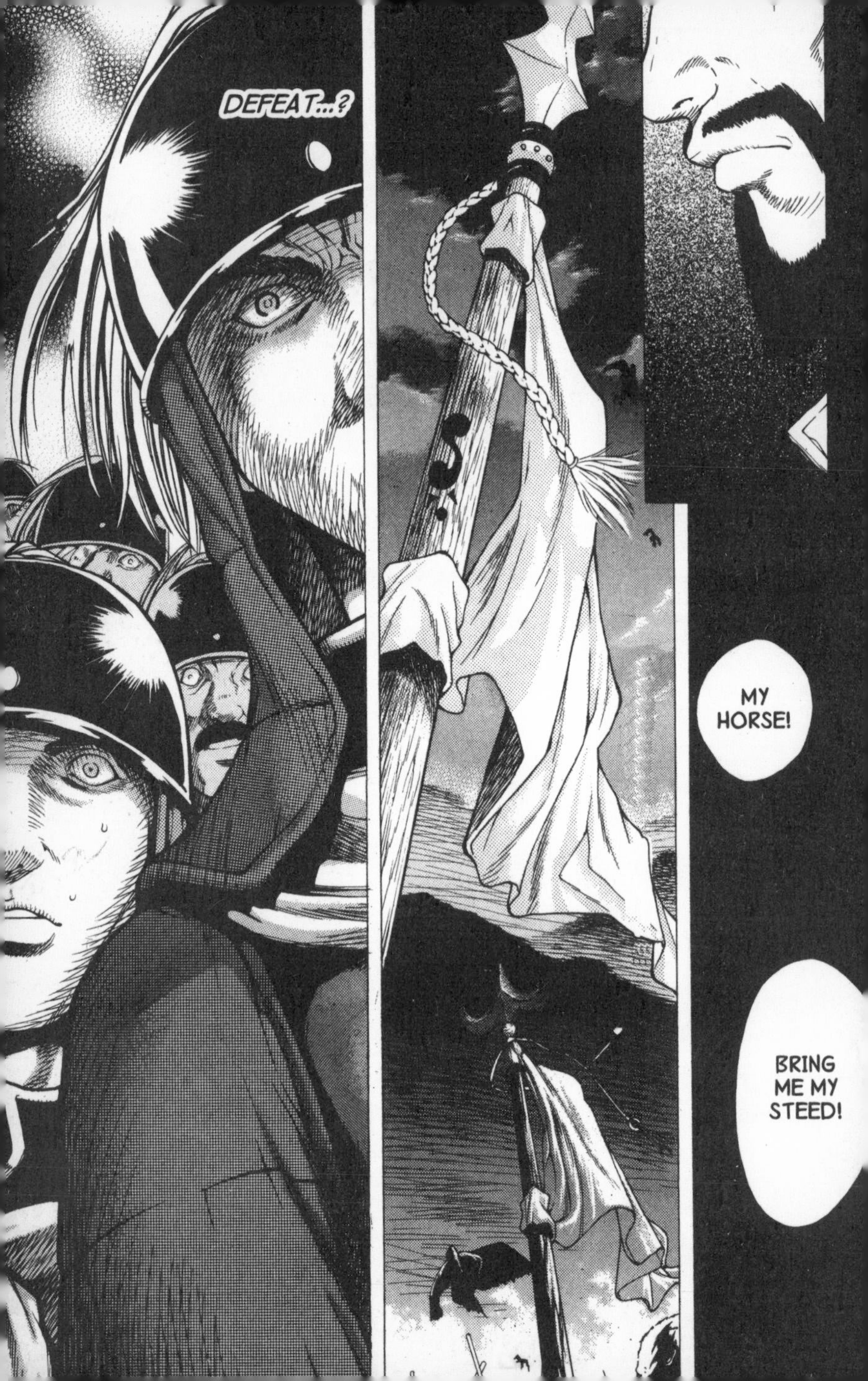
DEFEAT...?
MY HORSE!
BRING ME MY STEED!

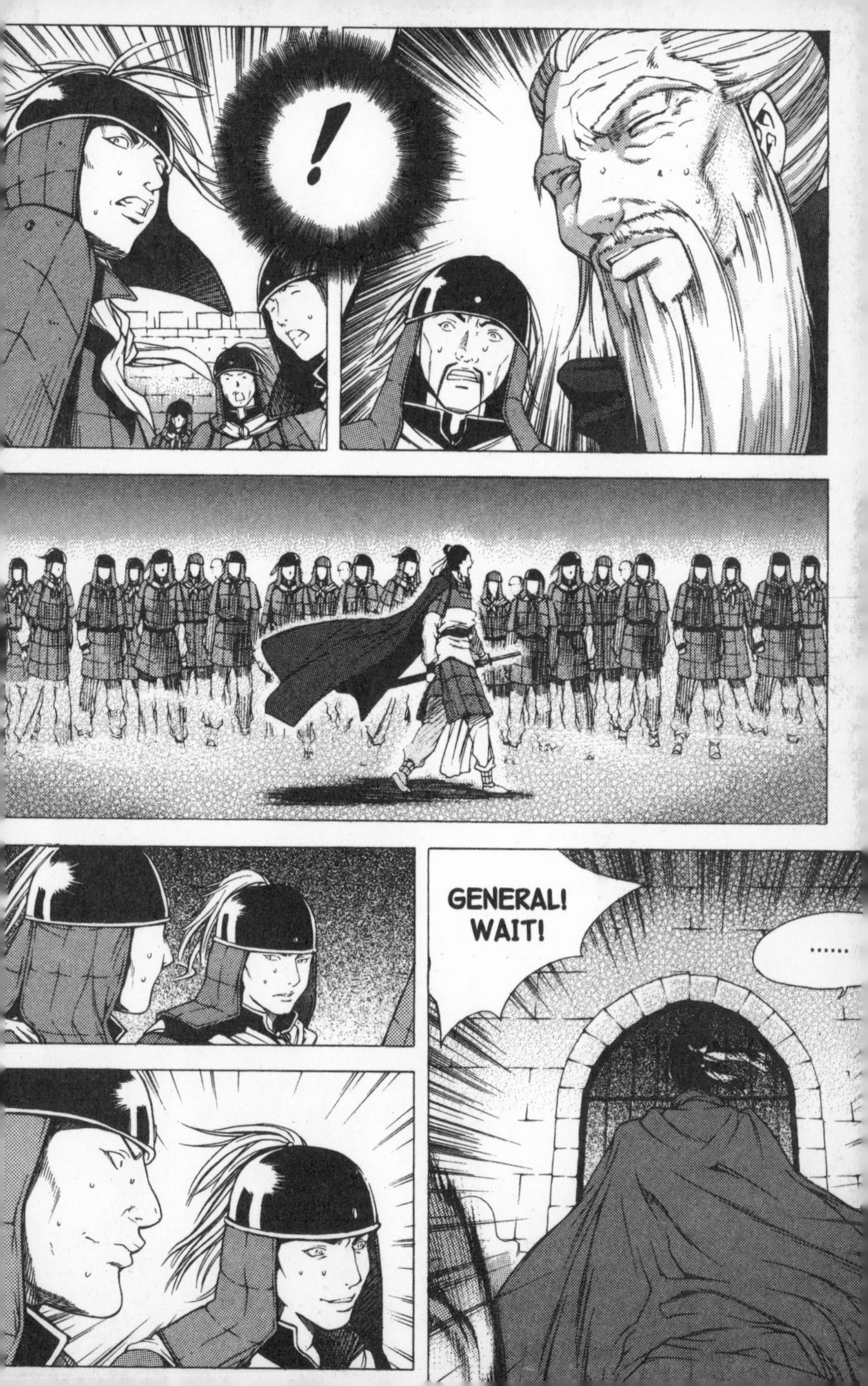
!
GENERAL! WAIT!
......

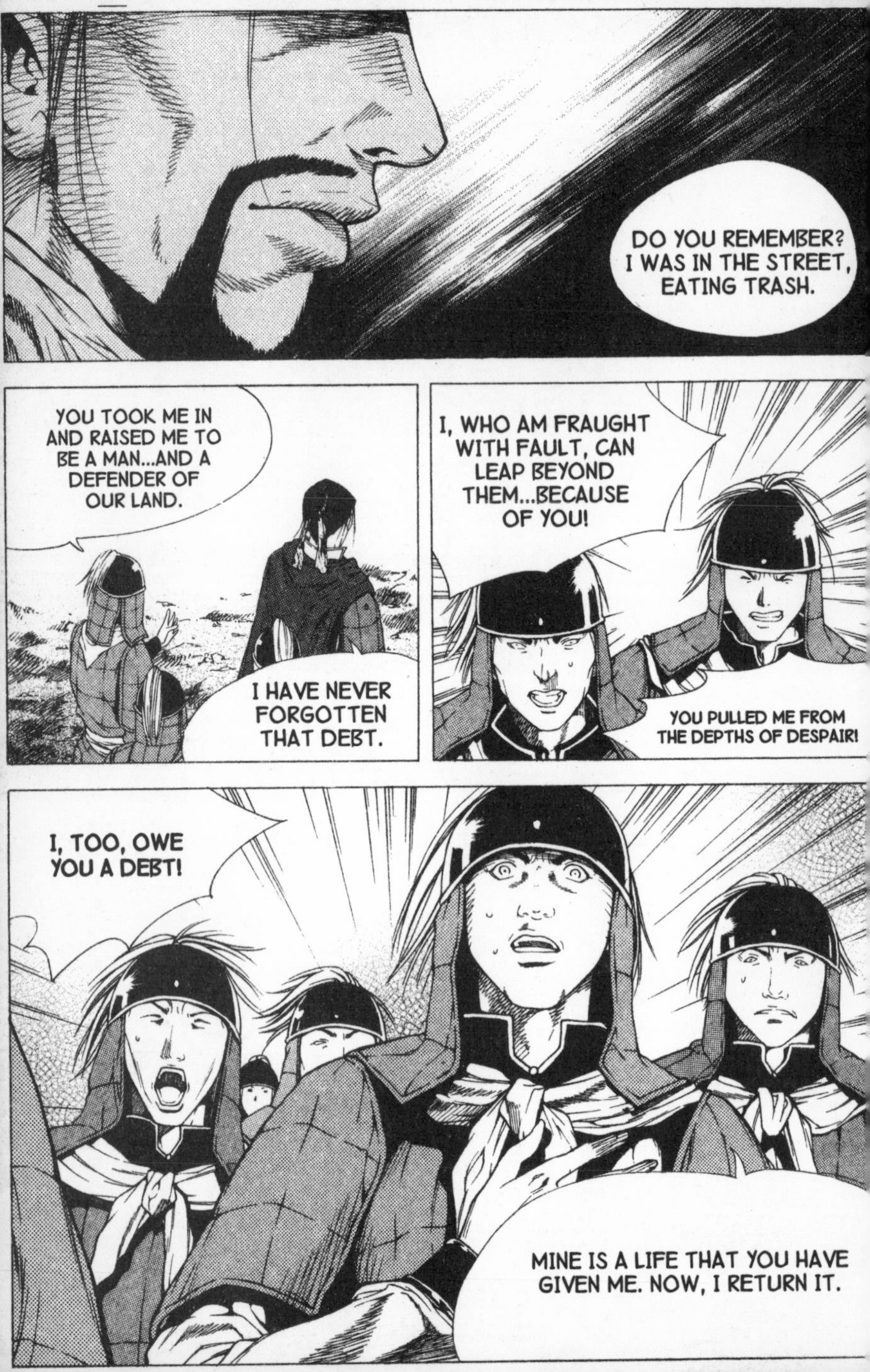
DO YOU REMEMBER? I WAS IN THE STREET, EATING TRASH.
YOU TOOK ME IN AND RAISED ME TO BE A MAN...AND A DEFENDER OF OUR LAND.
I HAVE NEVER FORGOTTEN THAT DEBT.
I, WHO AM FRAUGHT WITH FAULT, CAN LEAP BEYOND THEM...BECAUSE OF YOU!
YOU PULLED ME FROM THE DEPTHS OF DESPAIR!
I, TOO, OWE YOU A DEBT!
MINE IS A LIFE THAT YOU HAVE GIVEN ME. NOW, I RETURN IT.

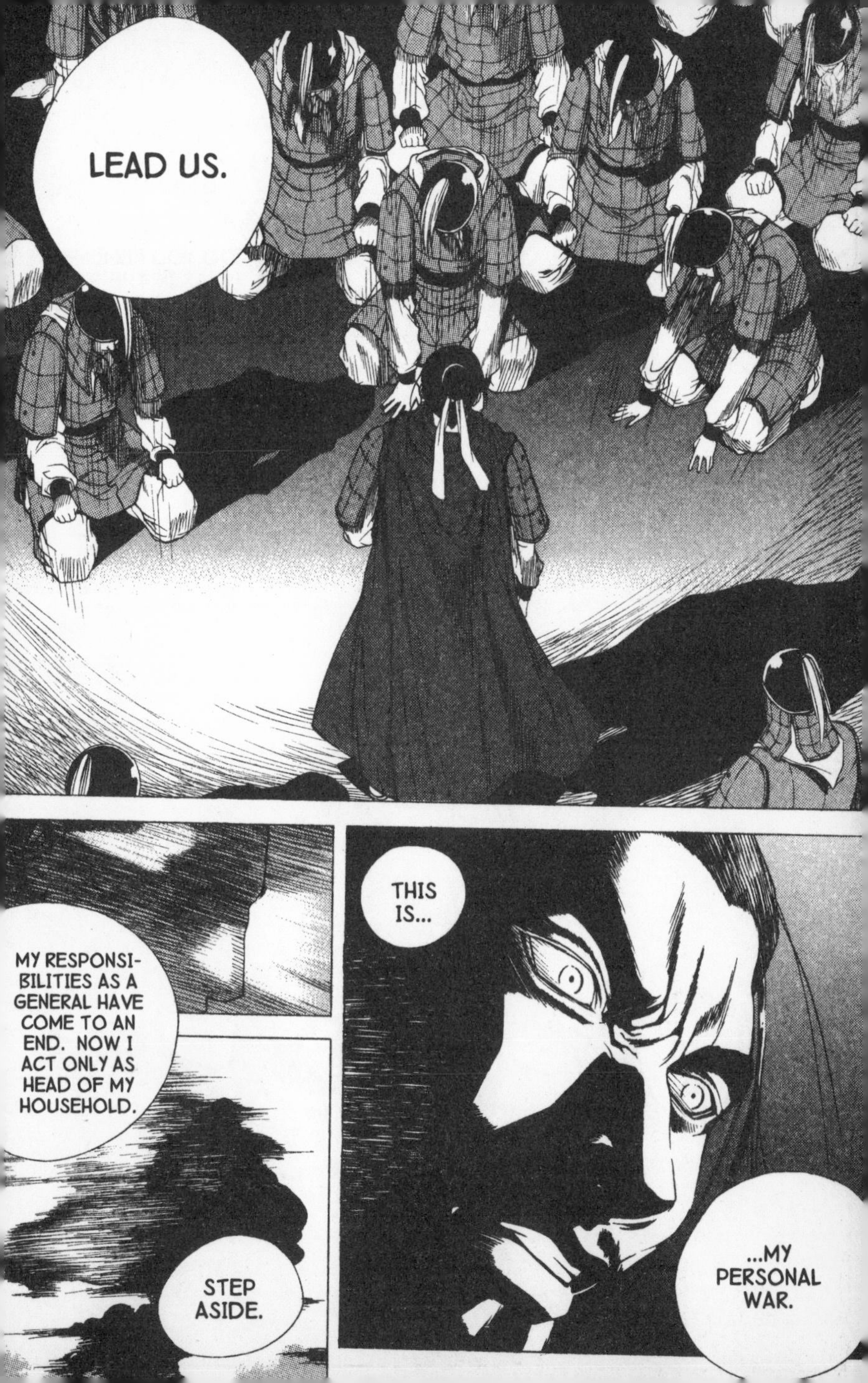
LEAD US.
MY RESPONSIBILITIES AS A GENERAL HAVE COME TO AN END. NOW I ACT ONLY AS HEAD OF MY HOUSEHOLD.
STEP ASIDE.
THIS IS...
...MY PERSONAL WAR.

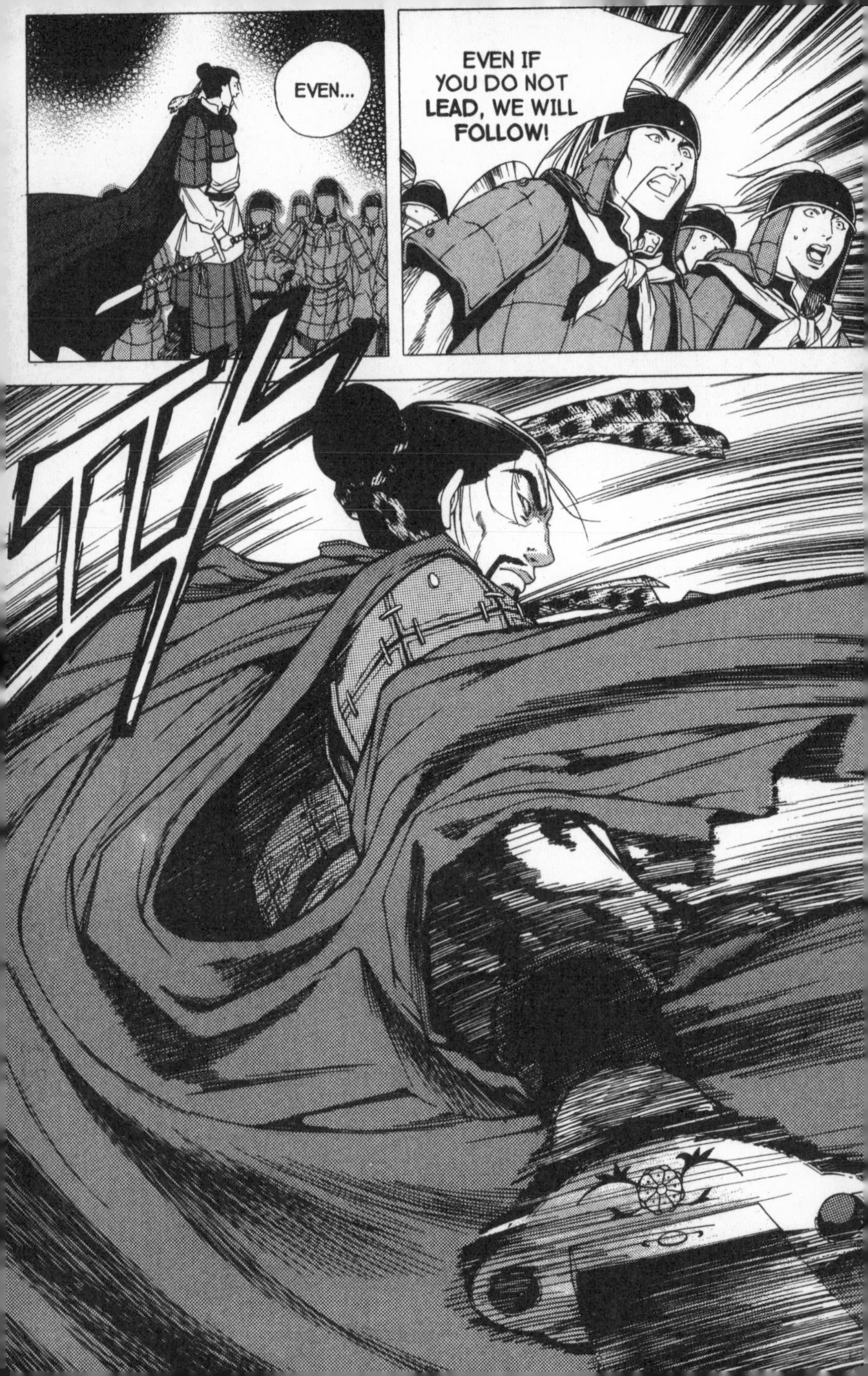
EVEN...
EVEN IF YOU DO NOT LEAD, WE WILL FOLLOW!

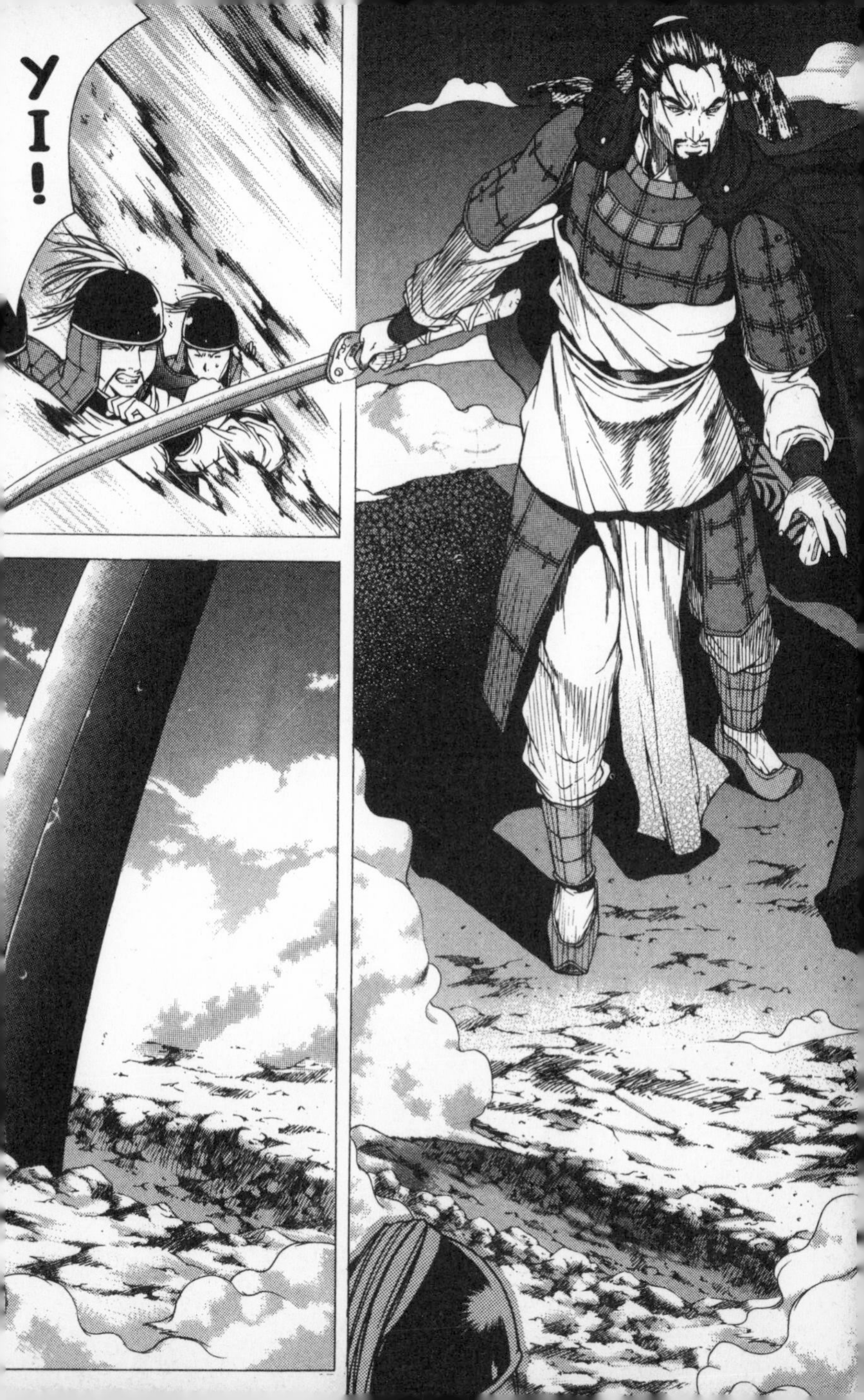
YI!

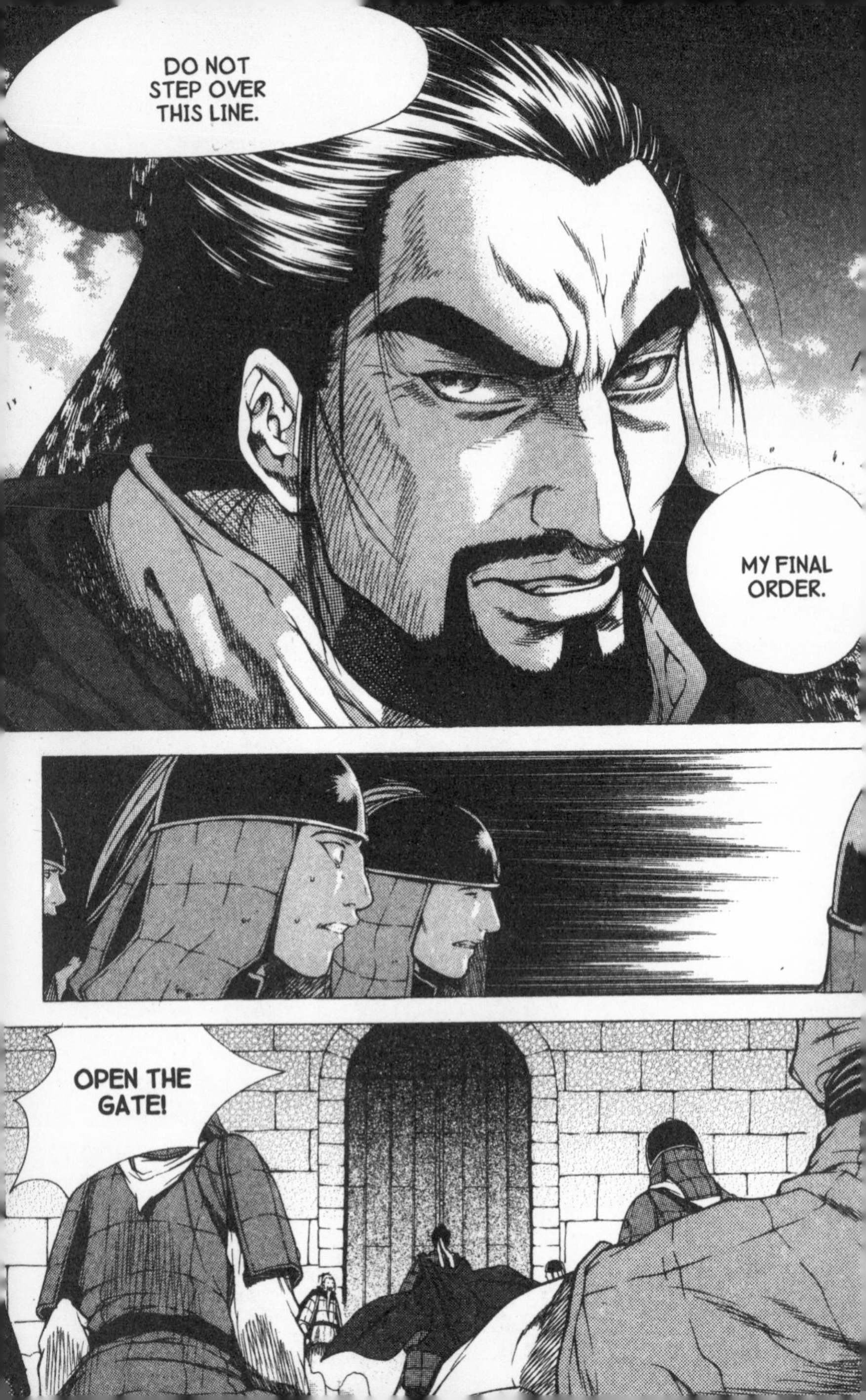
DO NOT STEP OVER THIS LINE.
MY FINAL ORDER.
OPEN THE GATE!

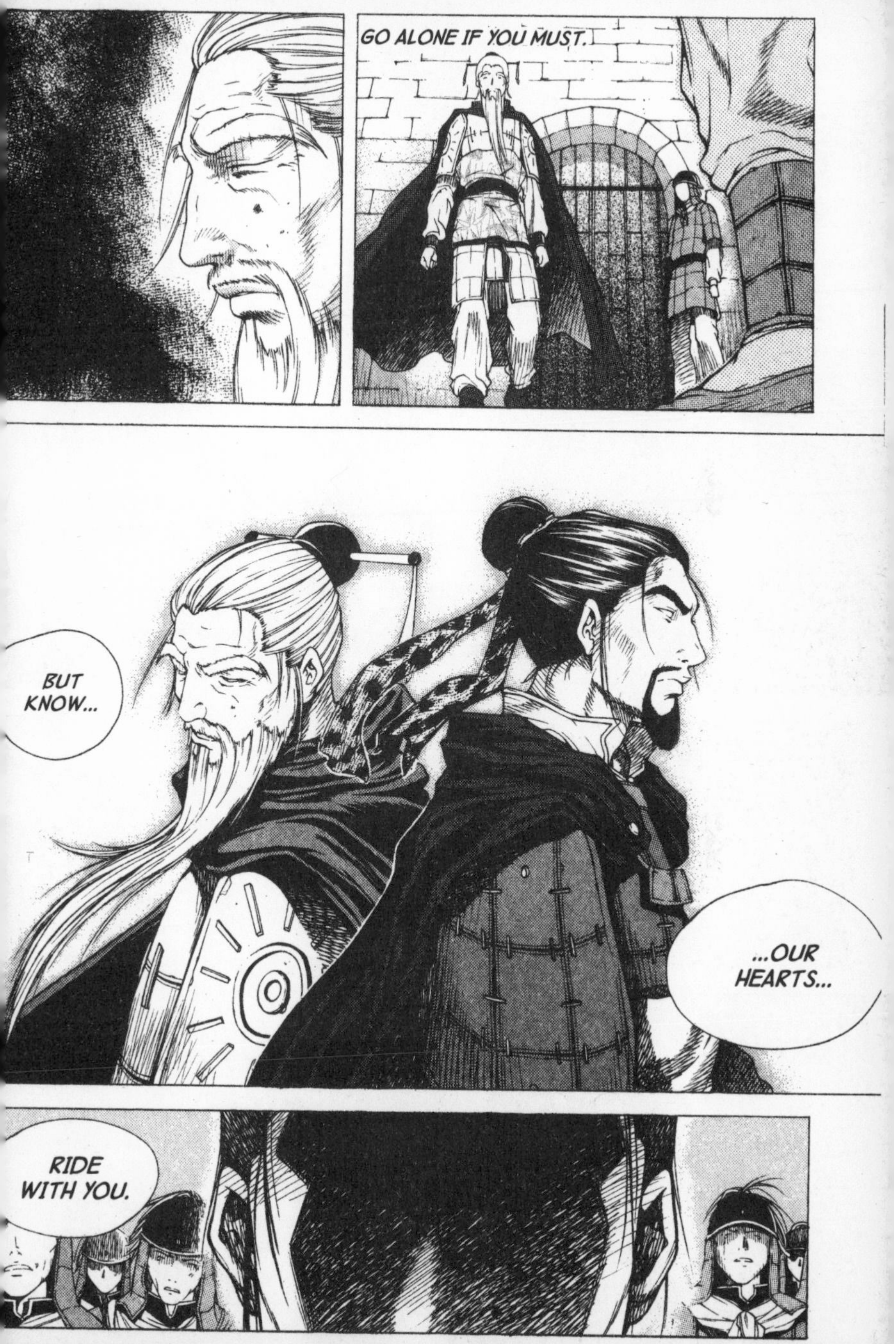
GO ALONE IF YOU MUST.
BUT KNOW...
...OUR HEARTS...
RIDE WITH YOU.

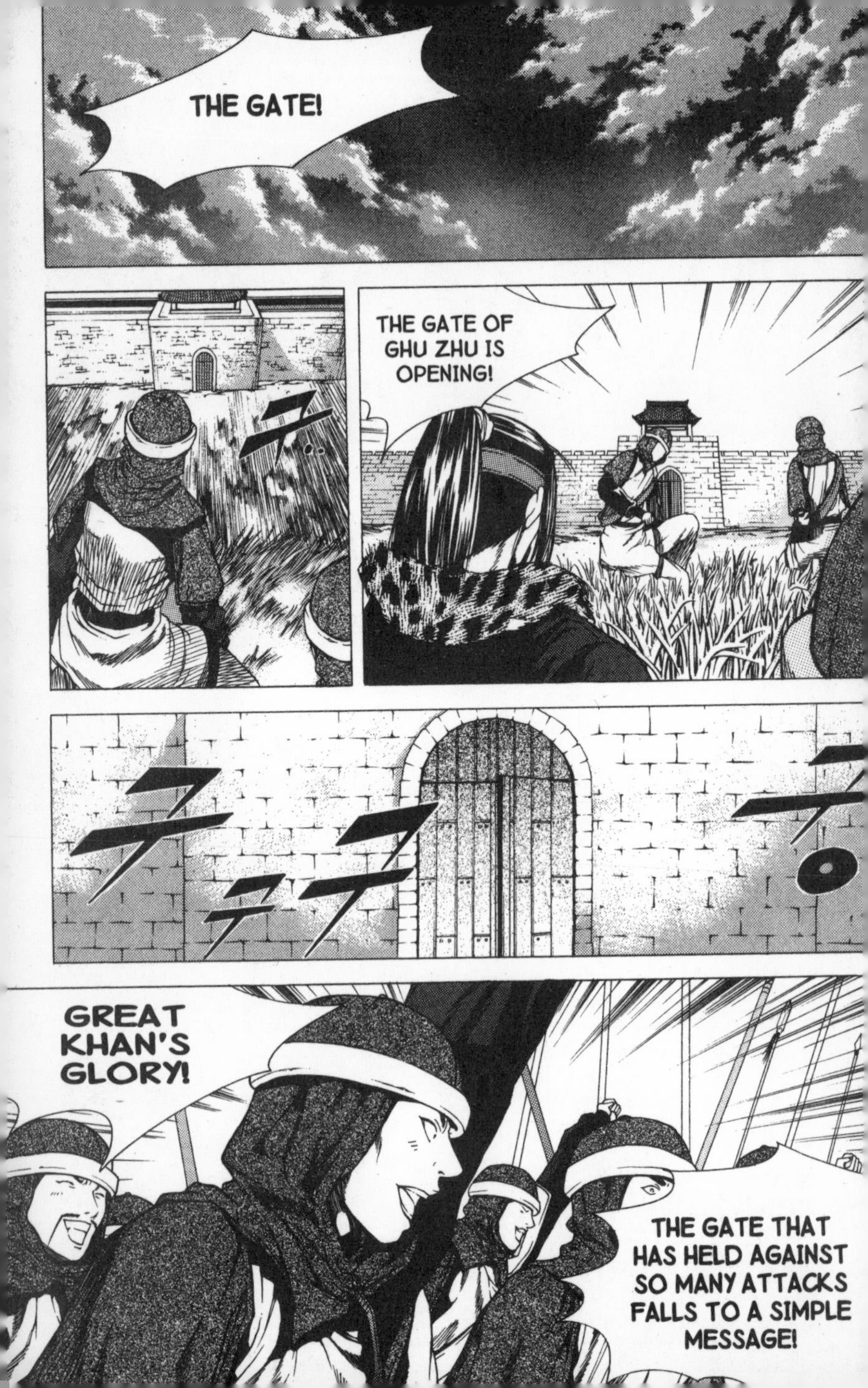
THE GATE!
THE GATE OF GHU ZHU IS OPENING!
GREAT KHAN'S GLORY!
THE GATE THAT HAS HELD AGAINST SO MANY ATTACKS FALLS TO A SIMPLE MESSAGE!

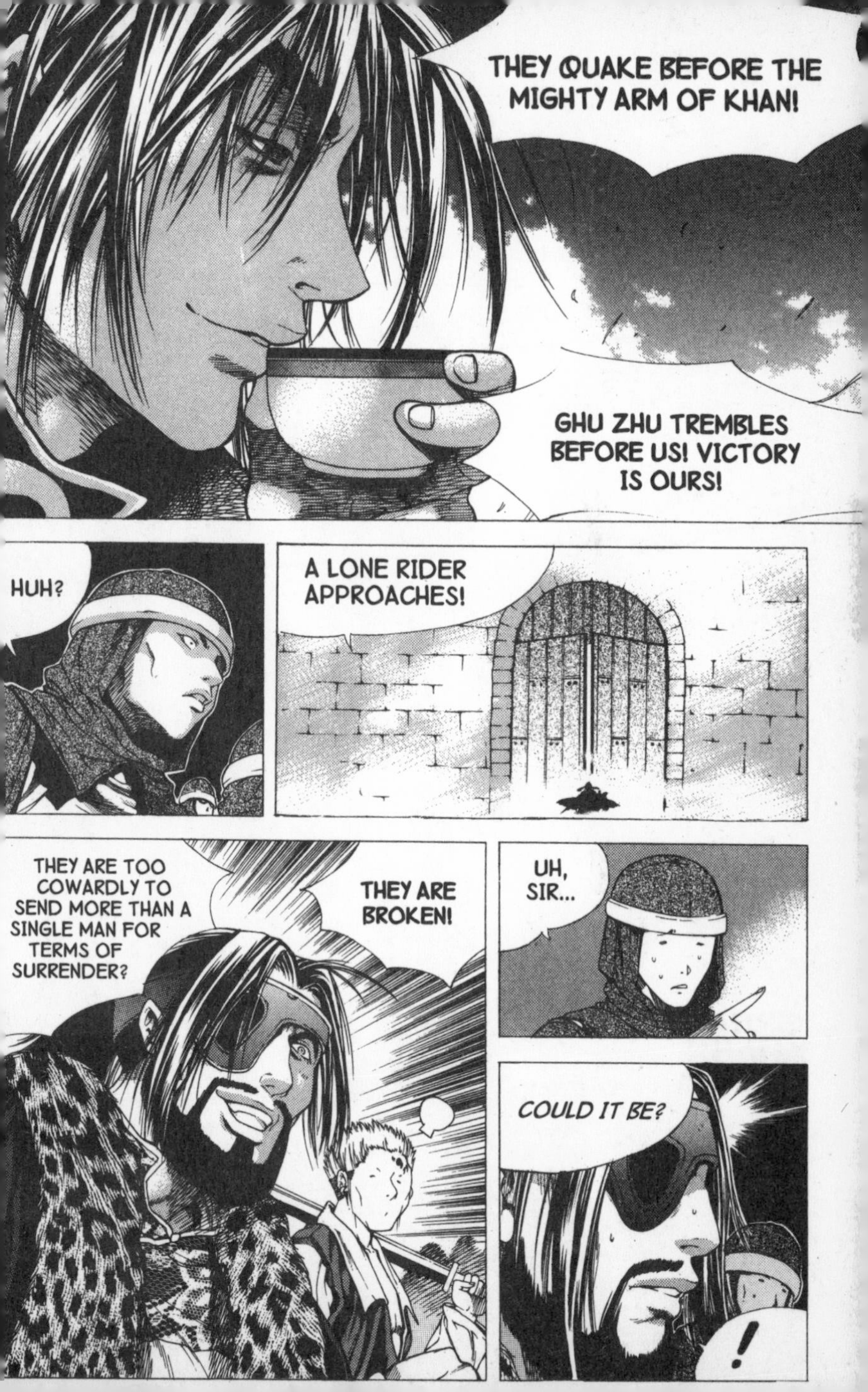
THEY QUAKE BEFORE THE MIGHTY ARM OF KHAN!
GHU ZHU TREMBLES BEFORE US! VICTORY IS OURS!
HUH?
A LONE RIDER APPROACHES!
THEY ARE TOO COWARDLY TO SEND MORE THAN A SINGLE MAN FOR TERMS OF SURRENDER?
THEY ARE BROKEN!
UH, SIR...
COULD IT BE?
!

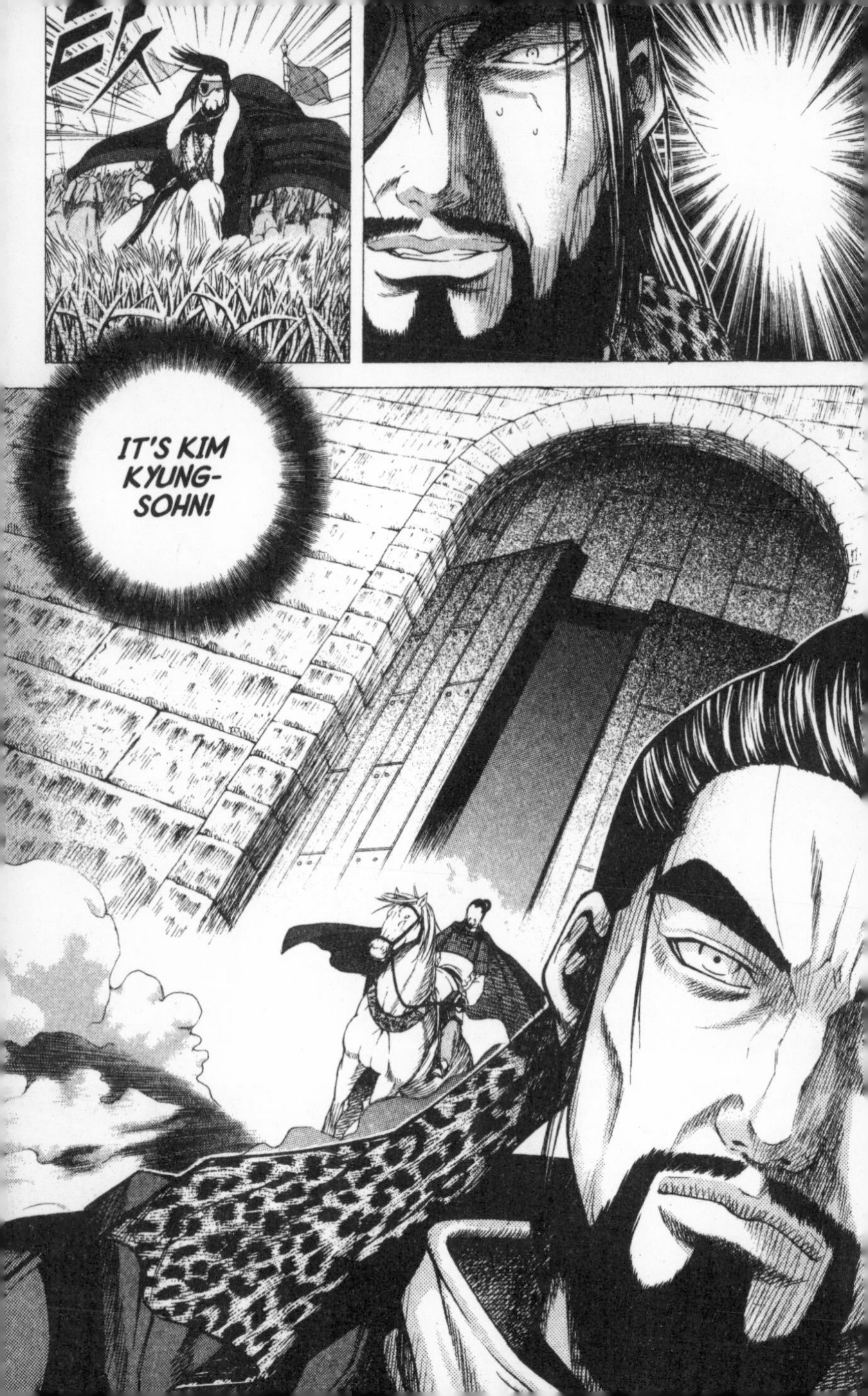
IT'S KIM KYUNG-SOHN!

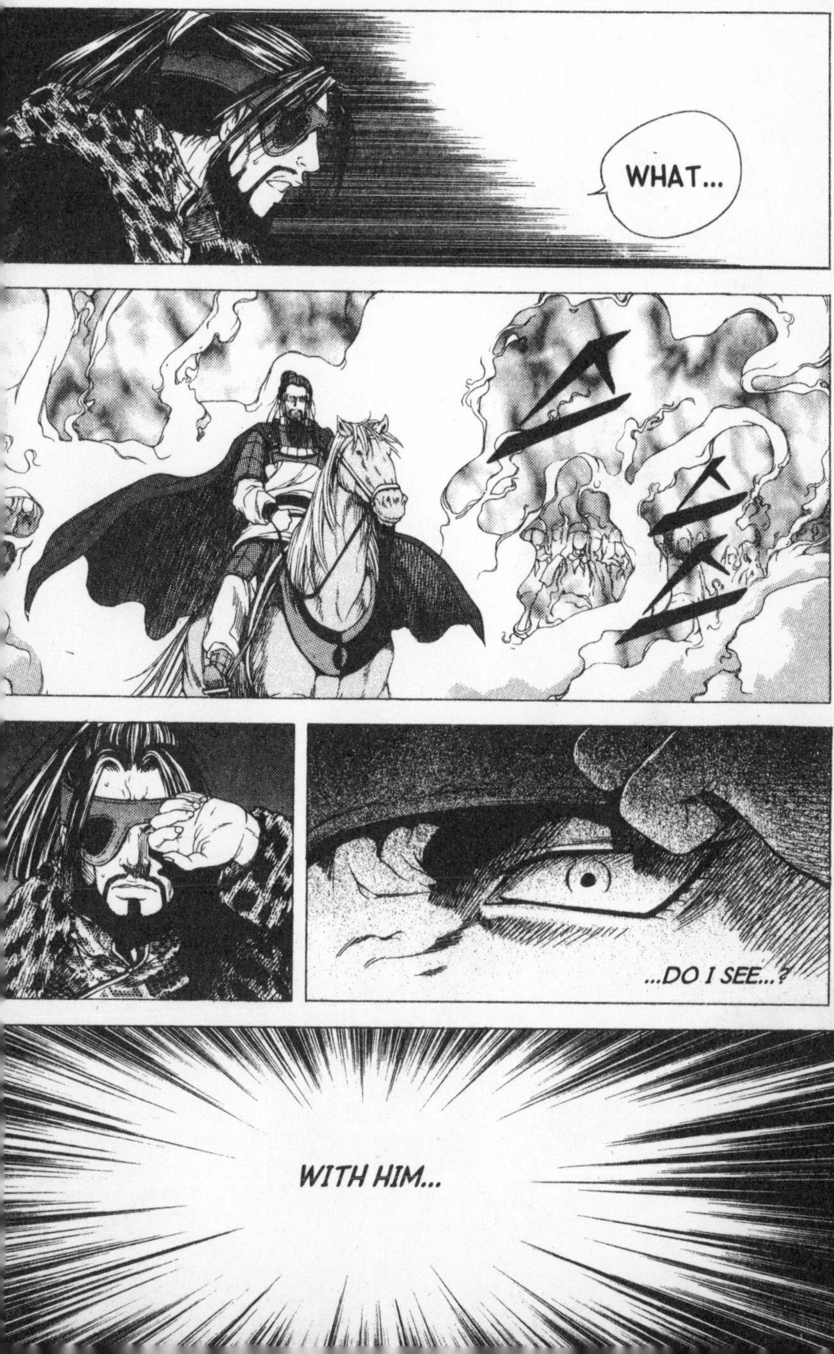
WHAT...
...DO I SEE...?
WITH HIM...

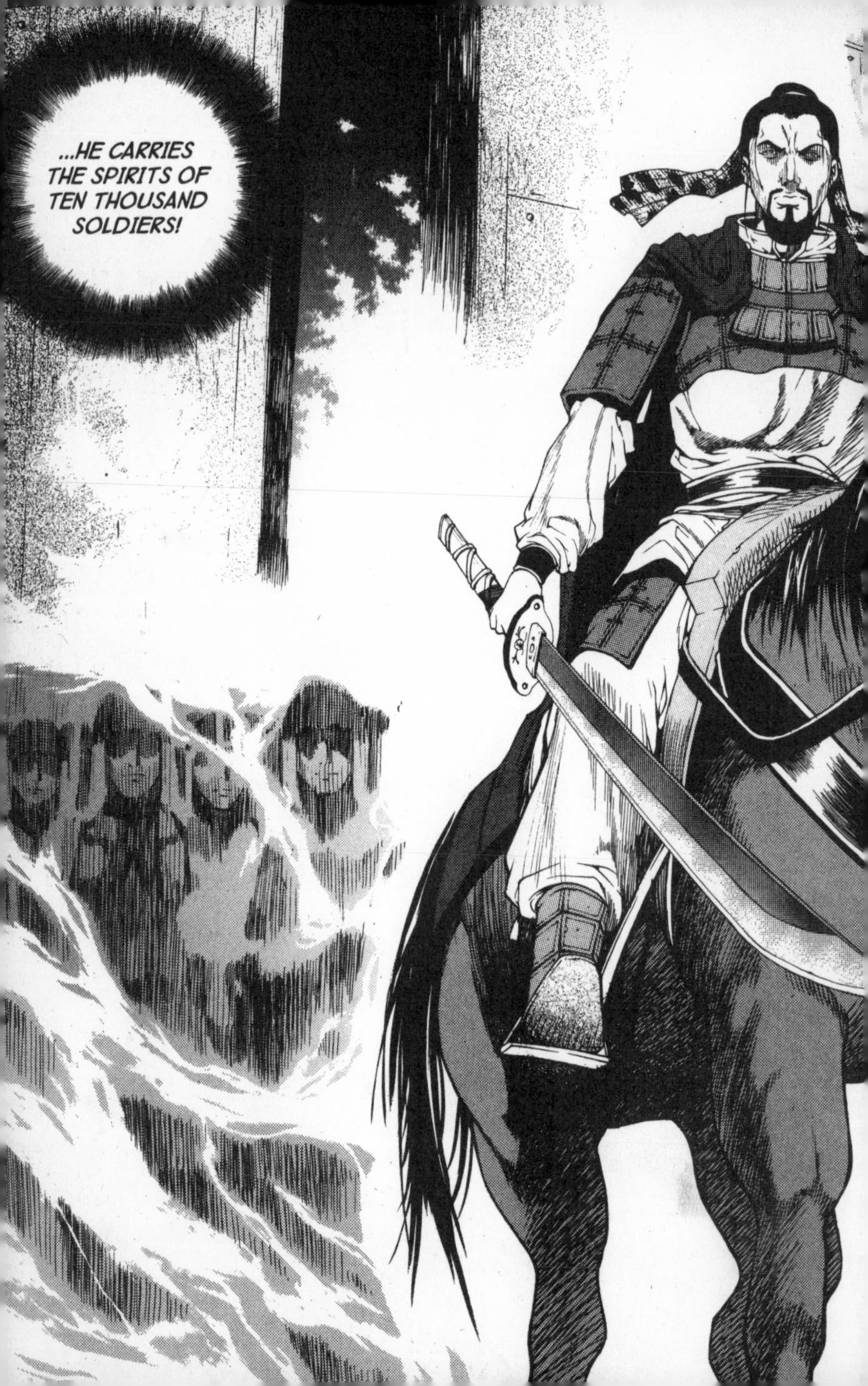
...HE CARRIES THE SPIRITS OF TEN THOUSAND SOLDIERS!

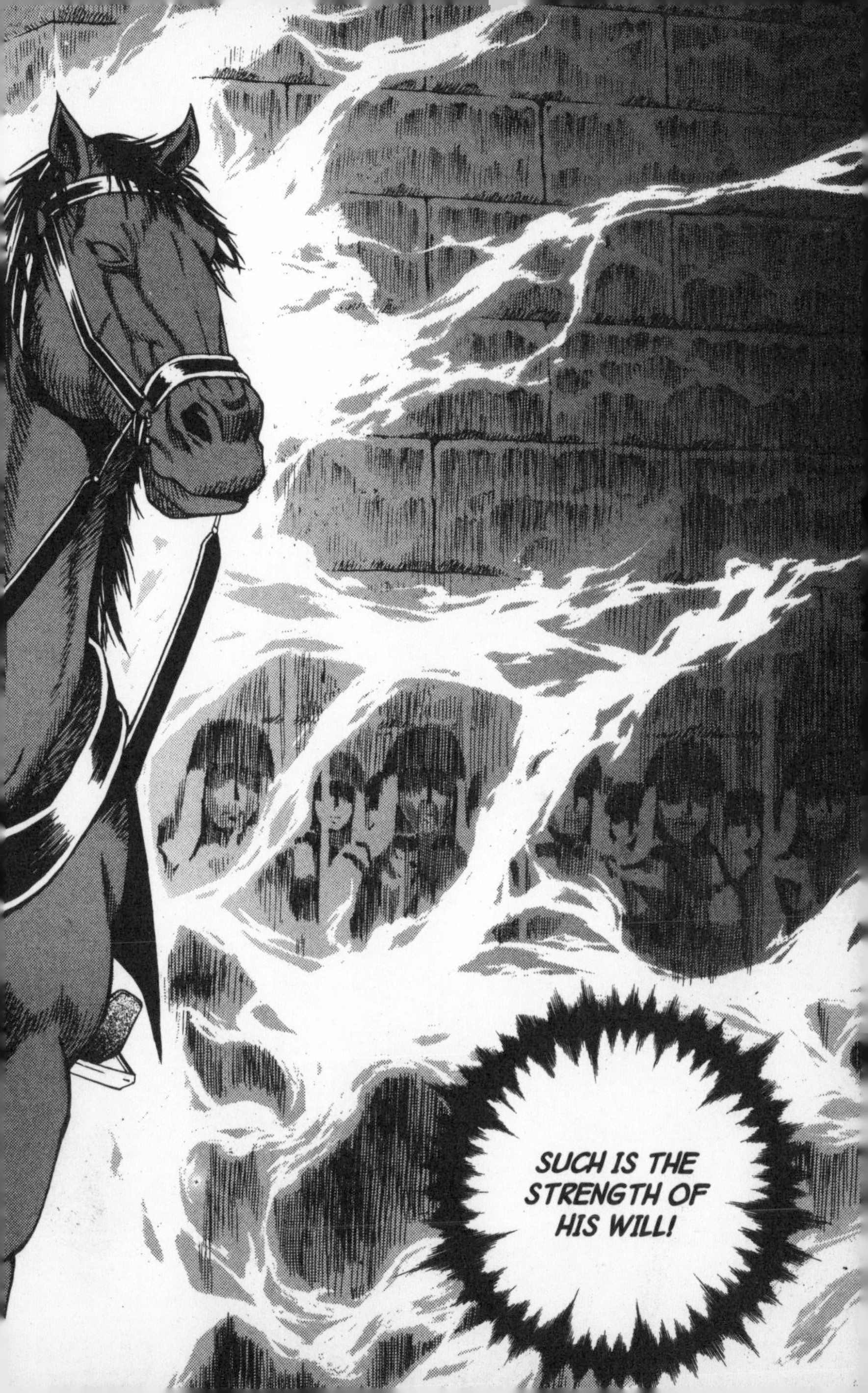
SUCH IS THE STRENGTH OF HIS WILL!

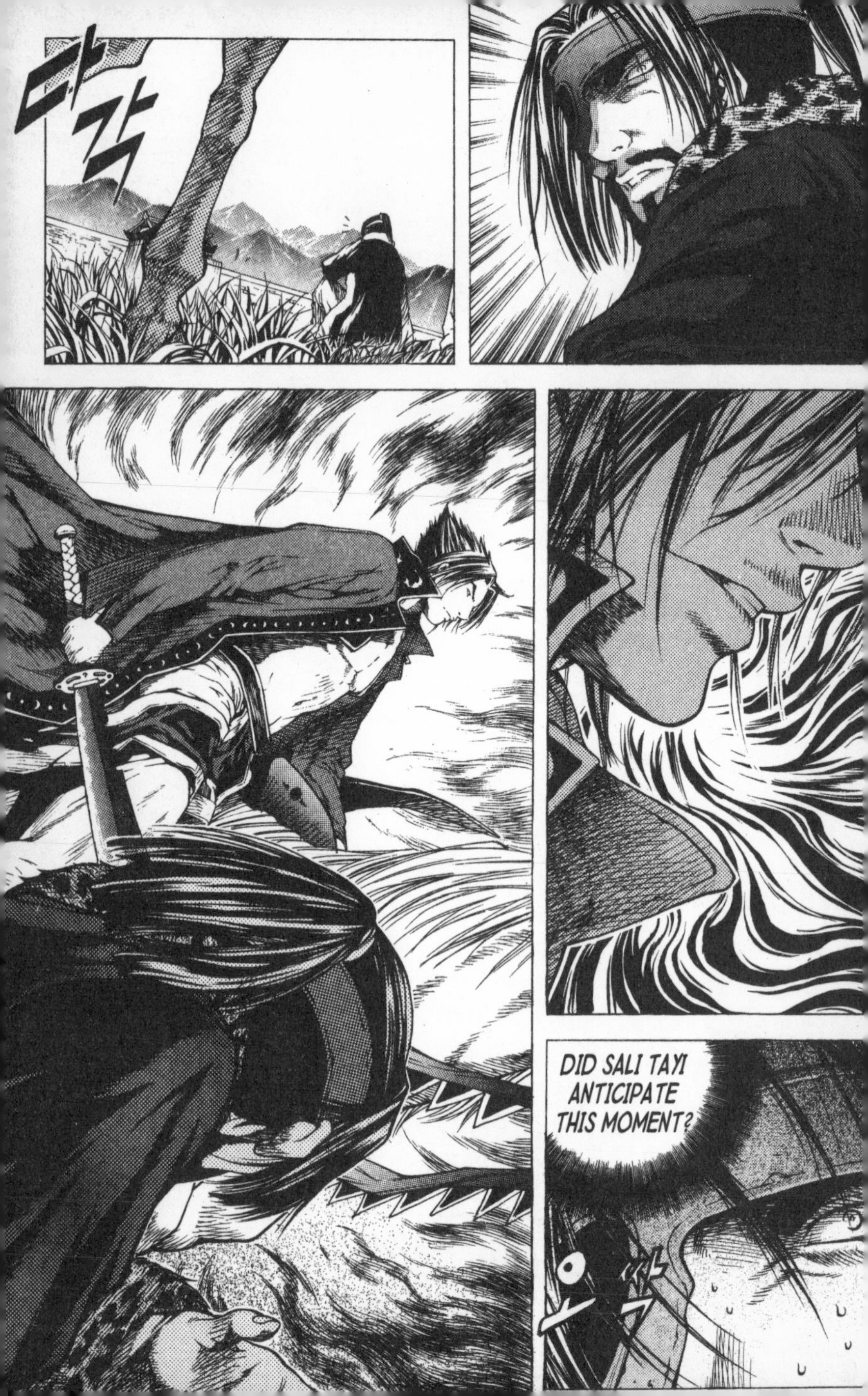
DID SALI TAYI ANTICIPATE THIS MOMENT?

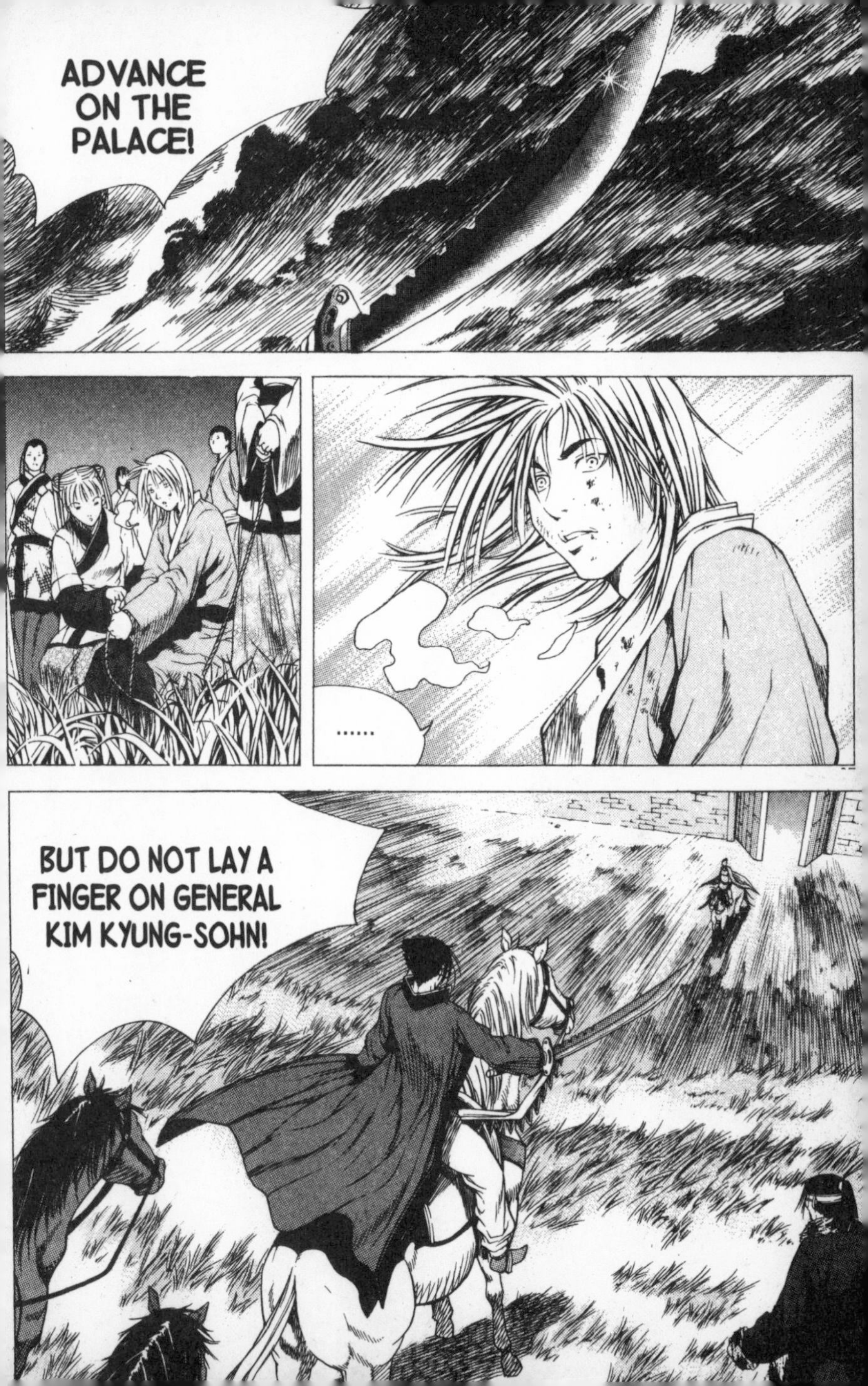
ADVANCE ON THE PALACE!
......
BUT DO NOT LAY A FINGER ON GENERAL KIM KYUNG-SOHN!

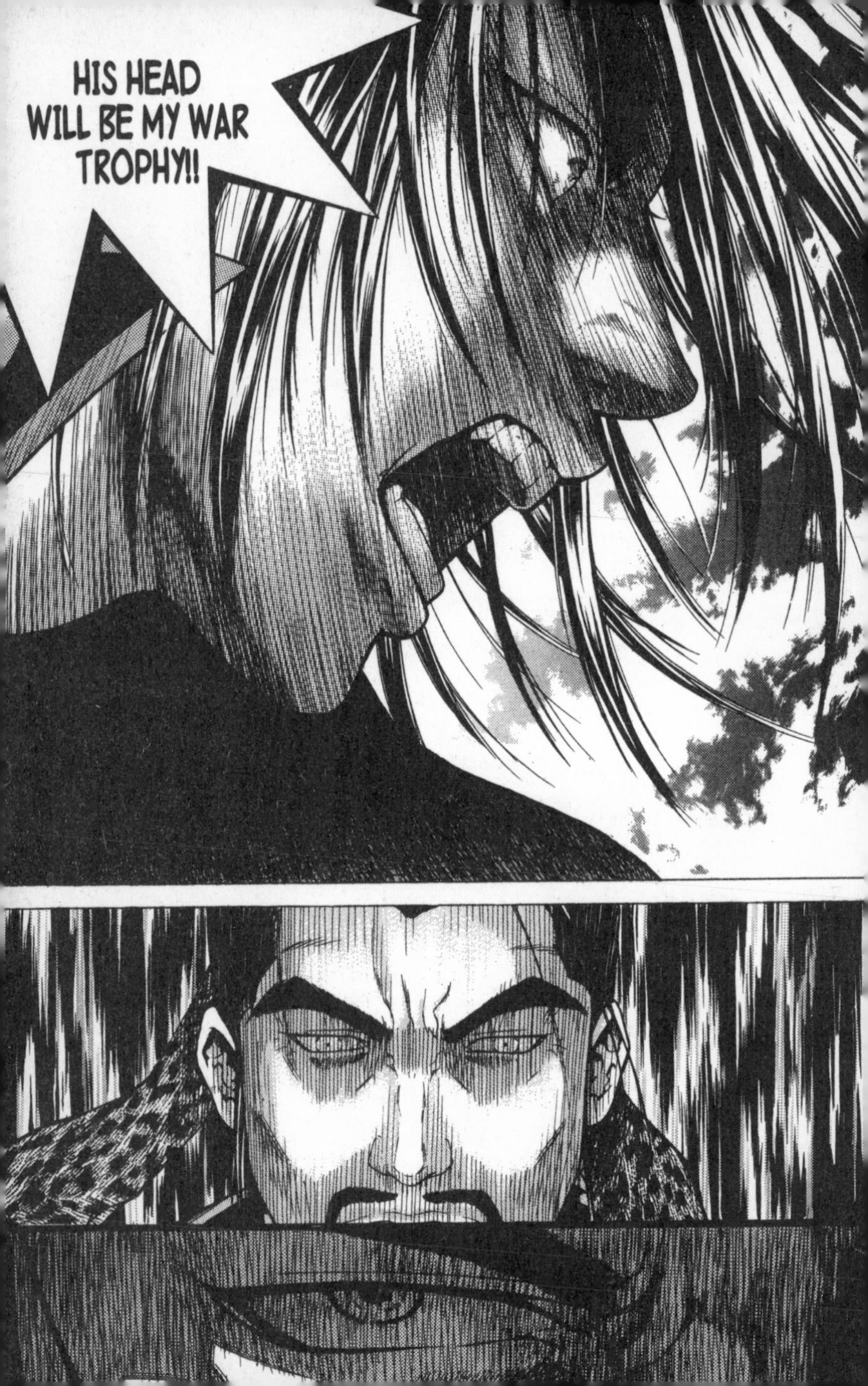
HIS HEAD WILL BE MY WAR TROPHY!!

Chapter 25
Death in Battle

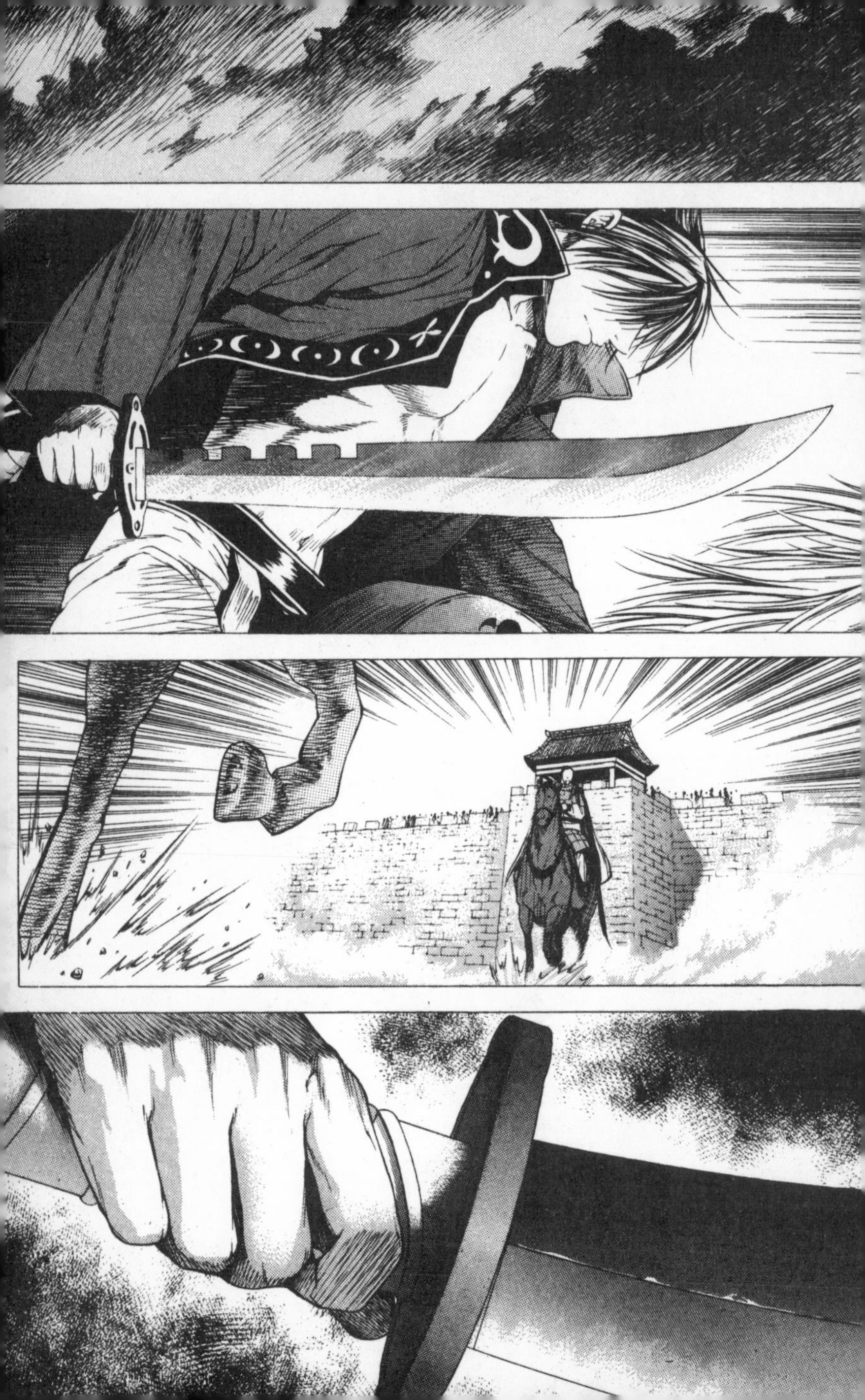

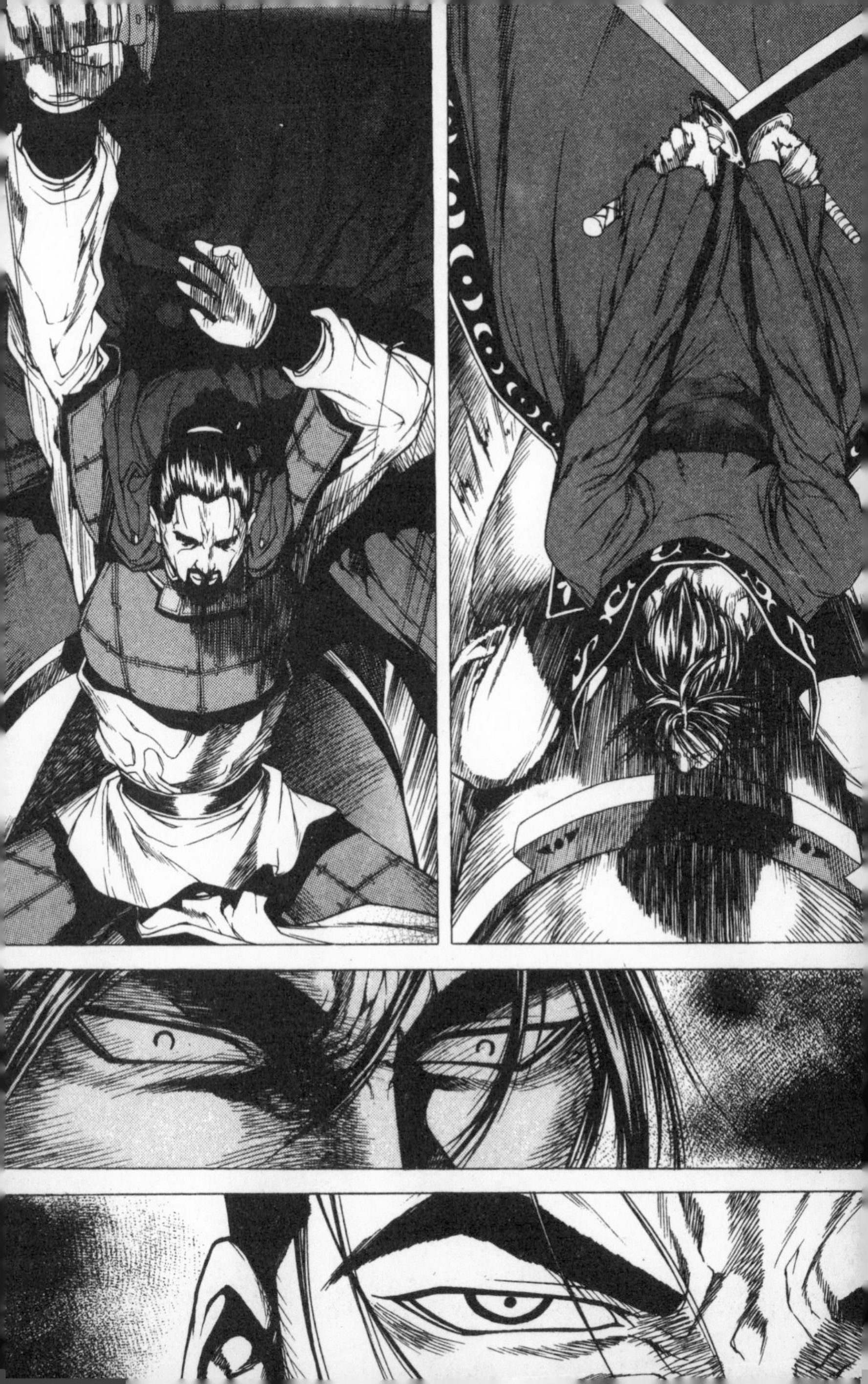

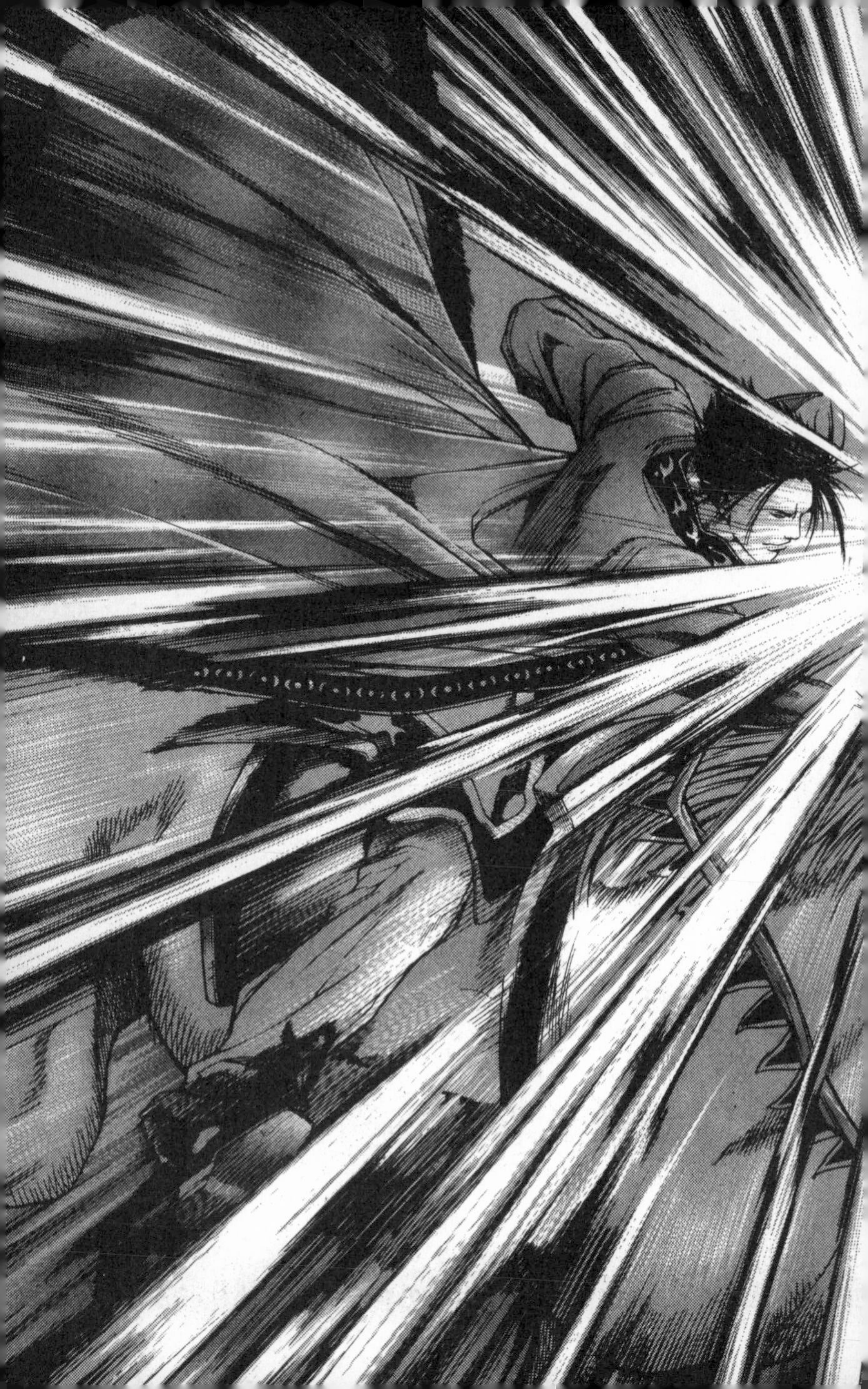

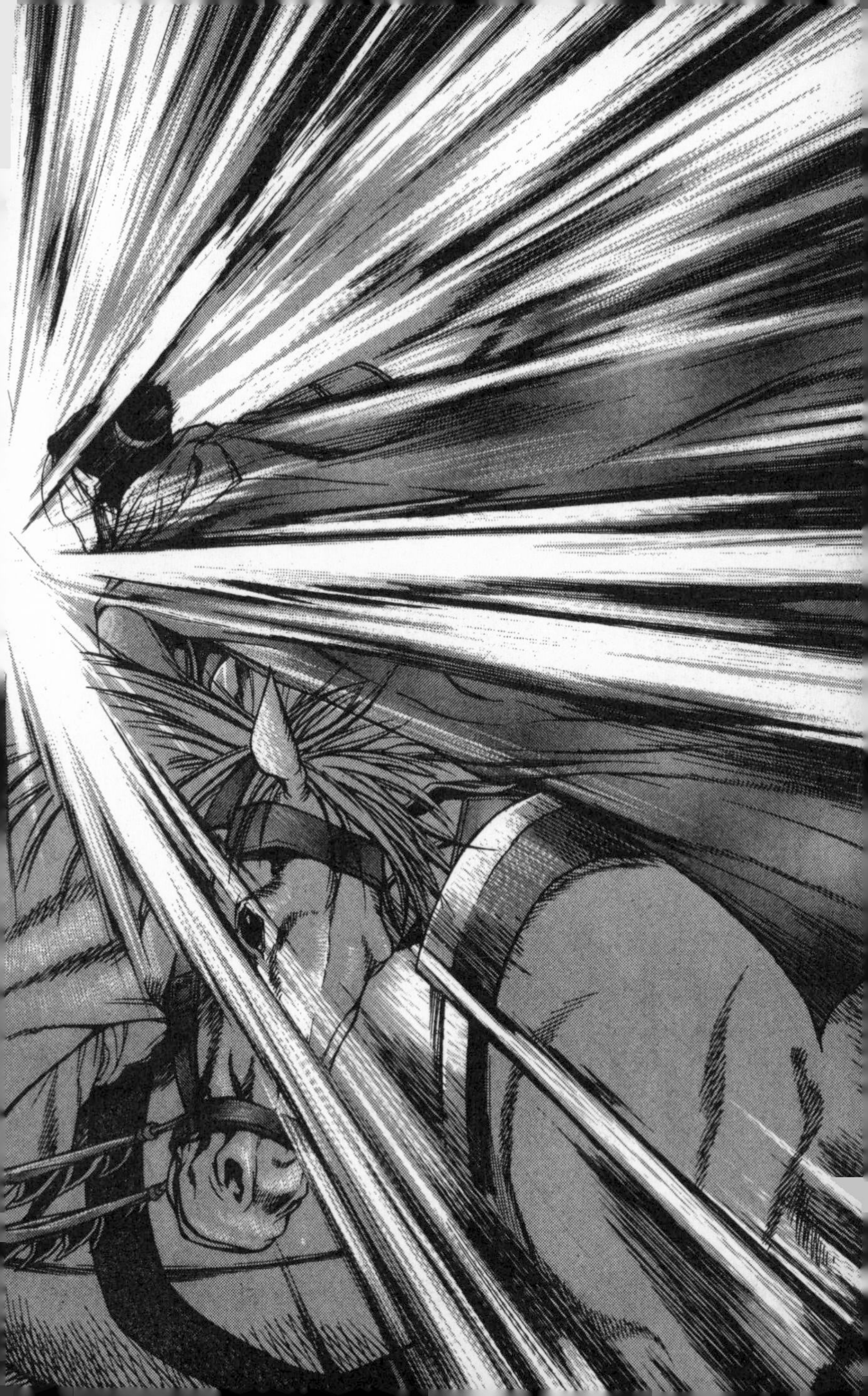

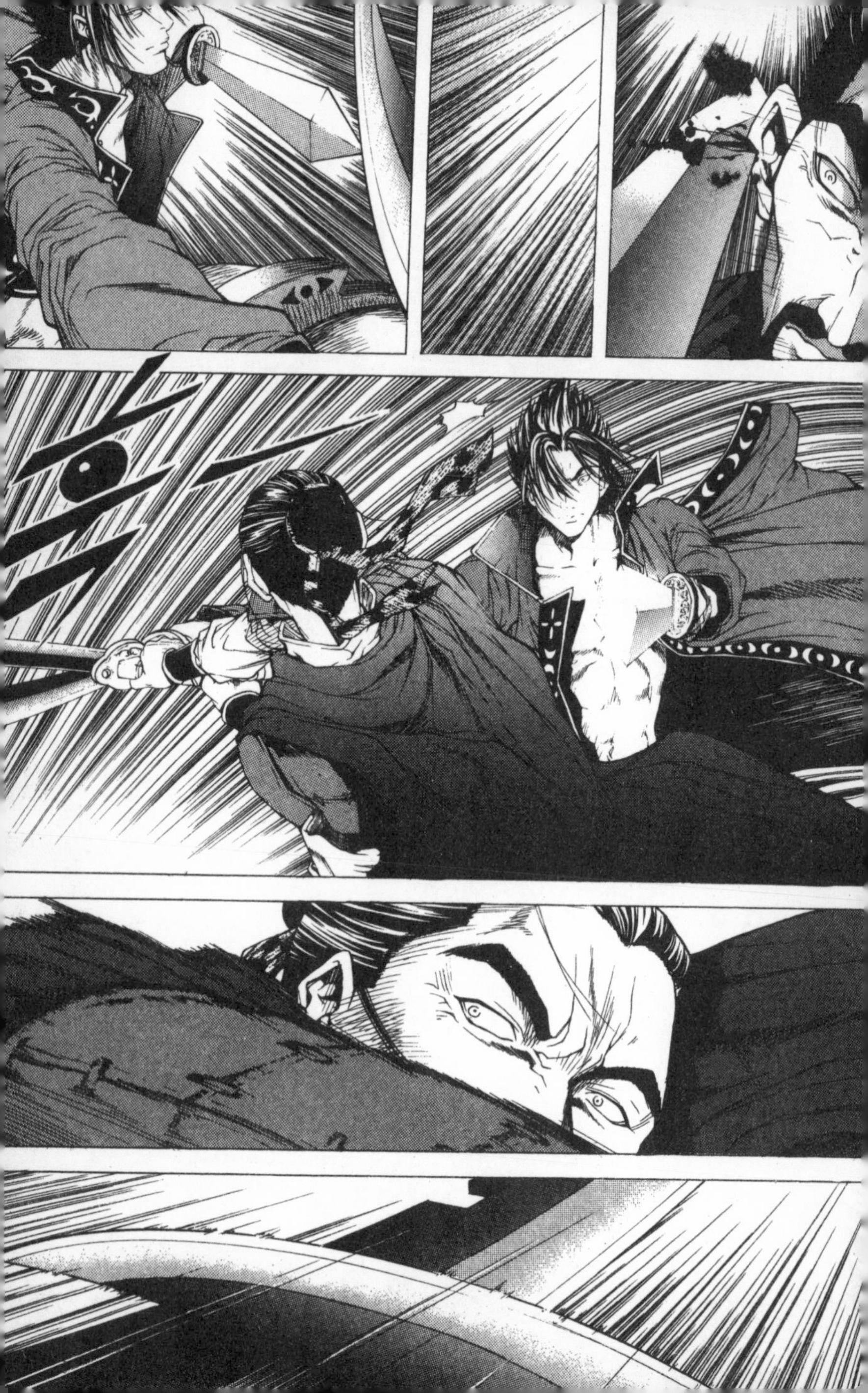

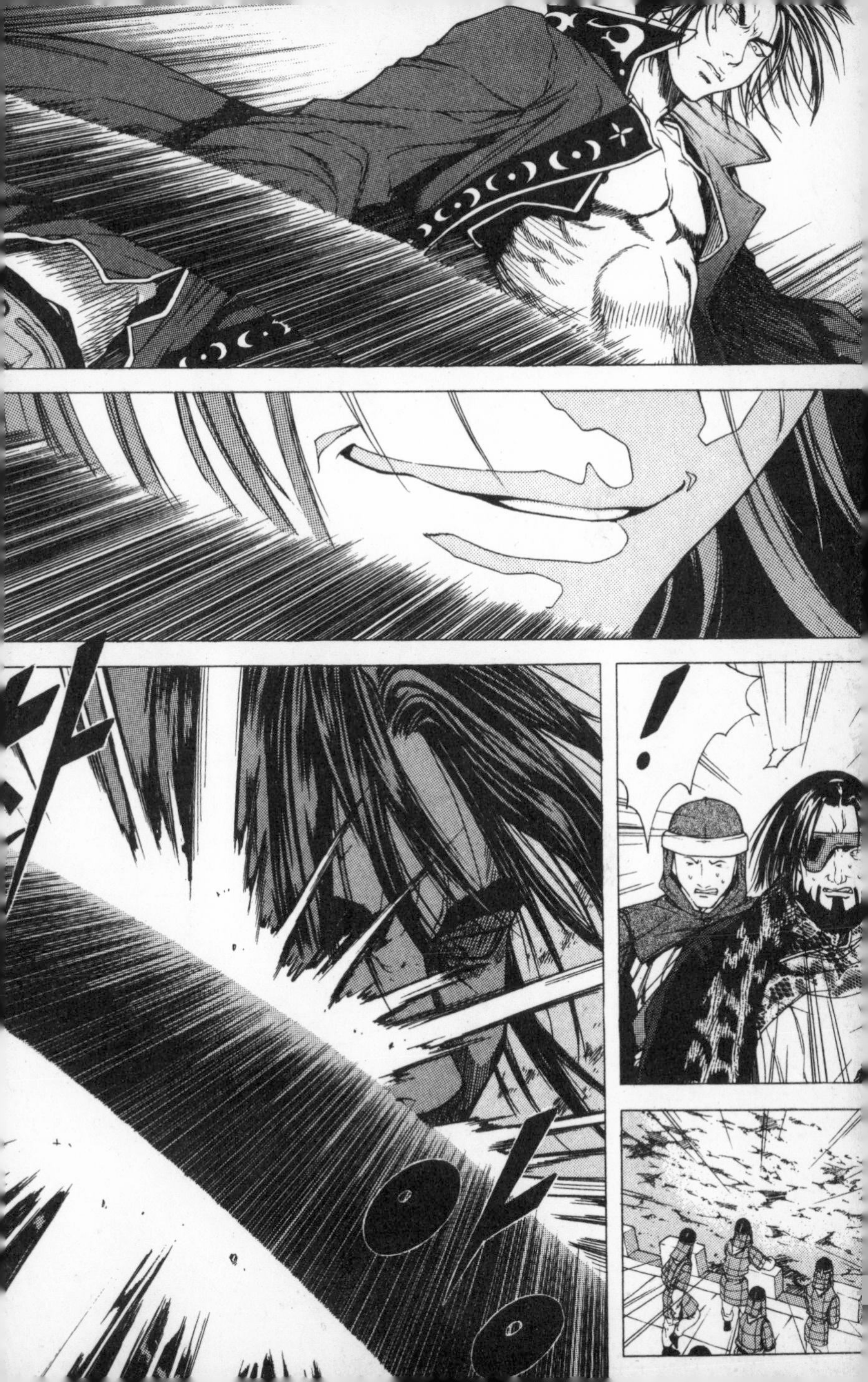
!

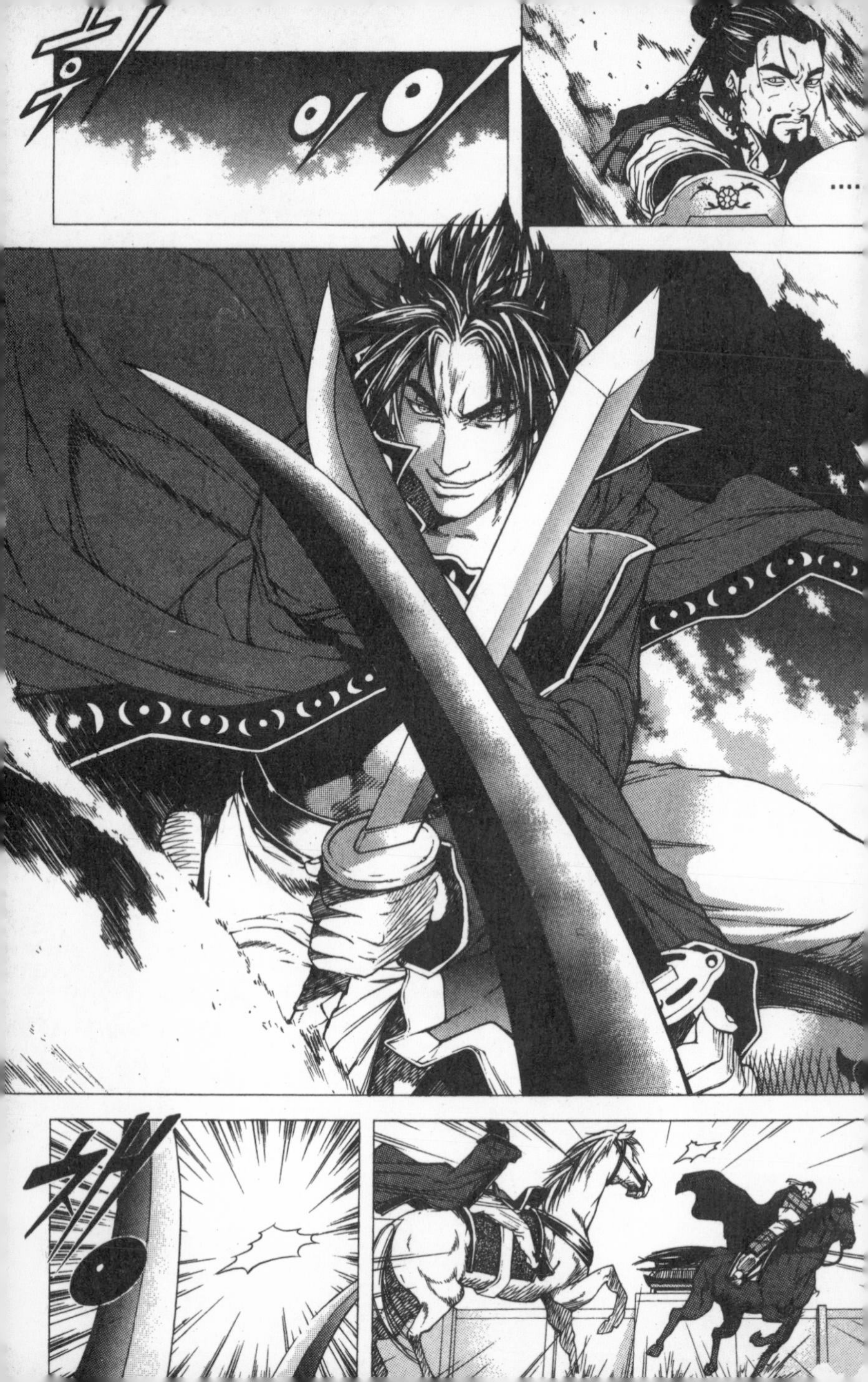
후이이
......
챙

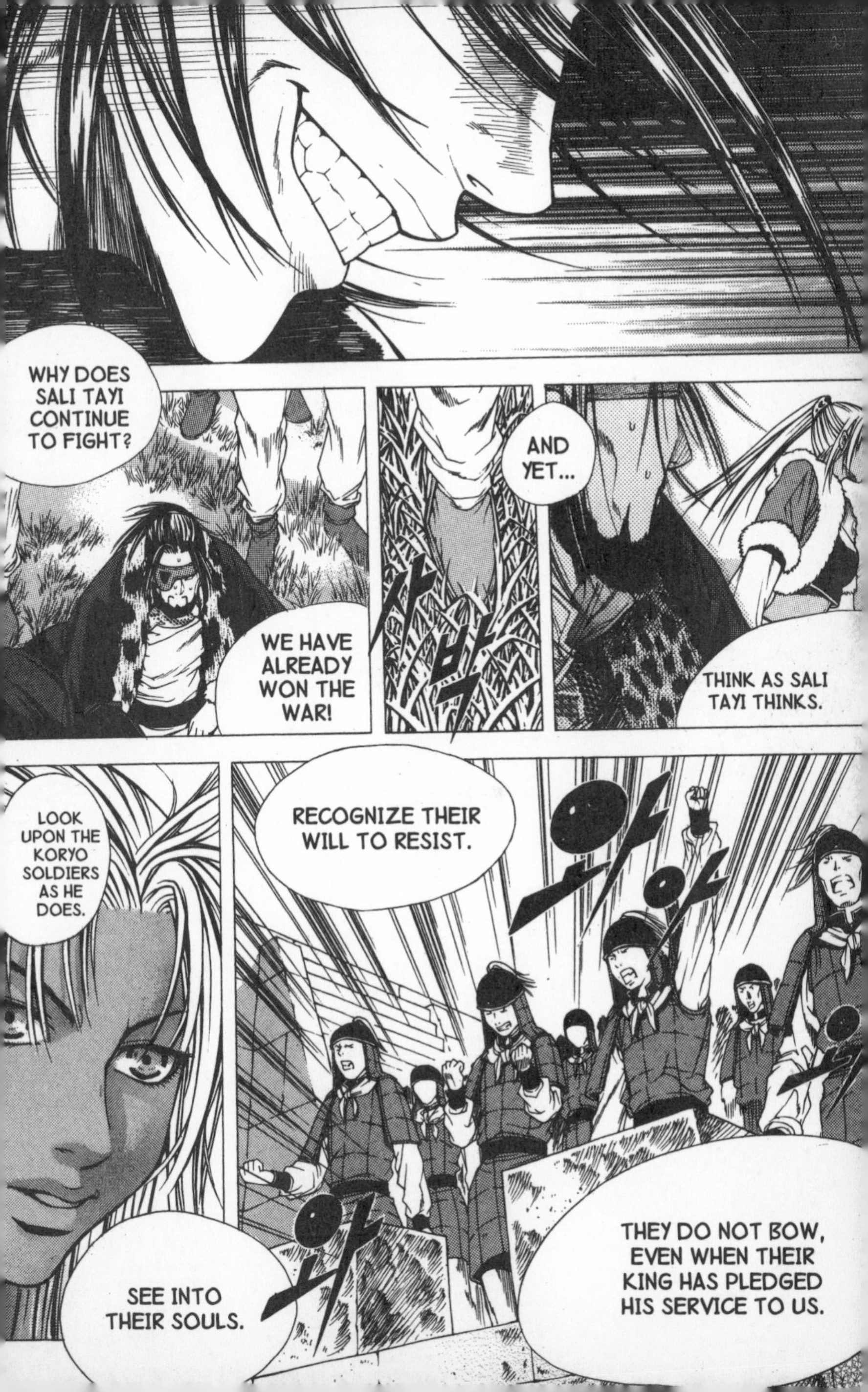
WHY DOES SALI TAYI CONTINUE TO FIGHT?
WE HAVE ALREADY WON THE WAR!
AND YET...
THINK AS SALI TAYI THINKS.
LOOK UPON THE KORYO SOLDIERS AS HE DOES.
RECOGNIZE THEIR WILL TO RESIST.
SEE INTO THEIR SOULS.
THEY DO NOT BOW, EVEN WHEN THEIR KING HAS PLEDGED HIS SERVICE TO US.

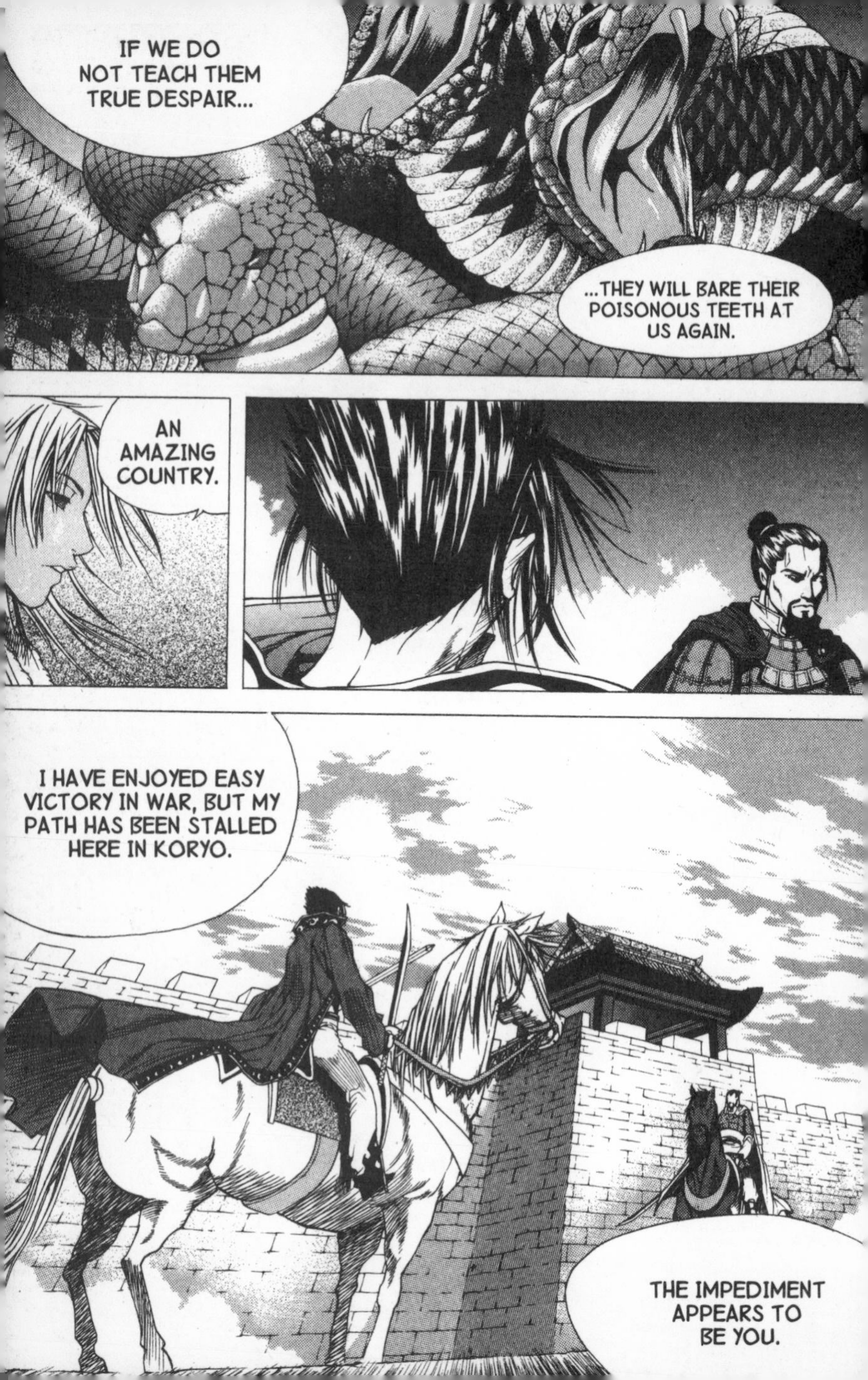
IF WE DO NOT TEACH THEM TRUE DESPAIR...
...THEY WILL BARE THEIR POISONOUS TEETH AT US AGAIN.
AN AMAZING COUNTRY.
I HAVE ENJOYED EASY VICTORY IN WAR, BUT MY PATH HAS BEEN STALLED HERE IN KORYO.
THE IMPEDIMENT APPEARS TO BE YOU.

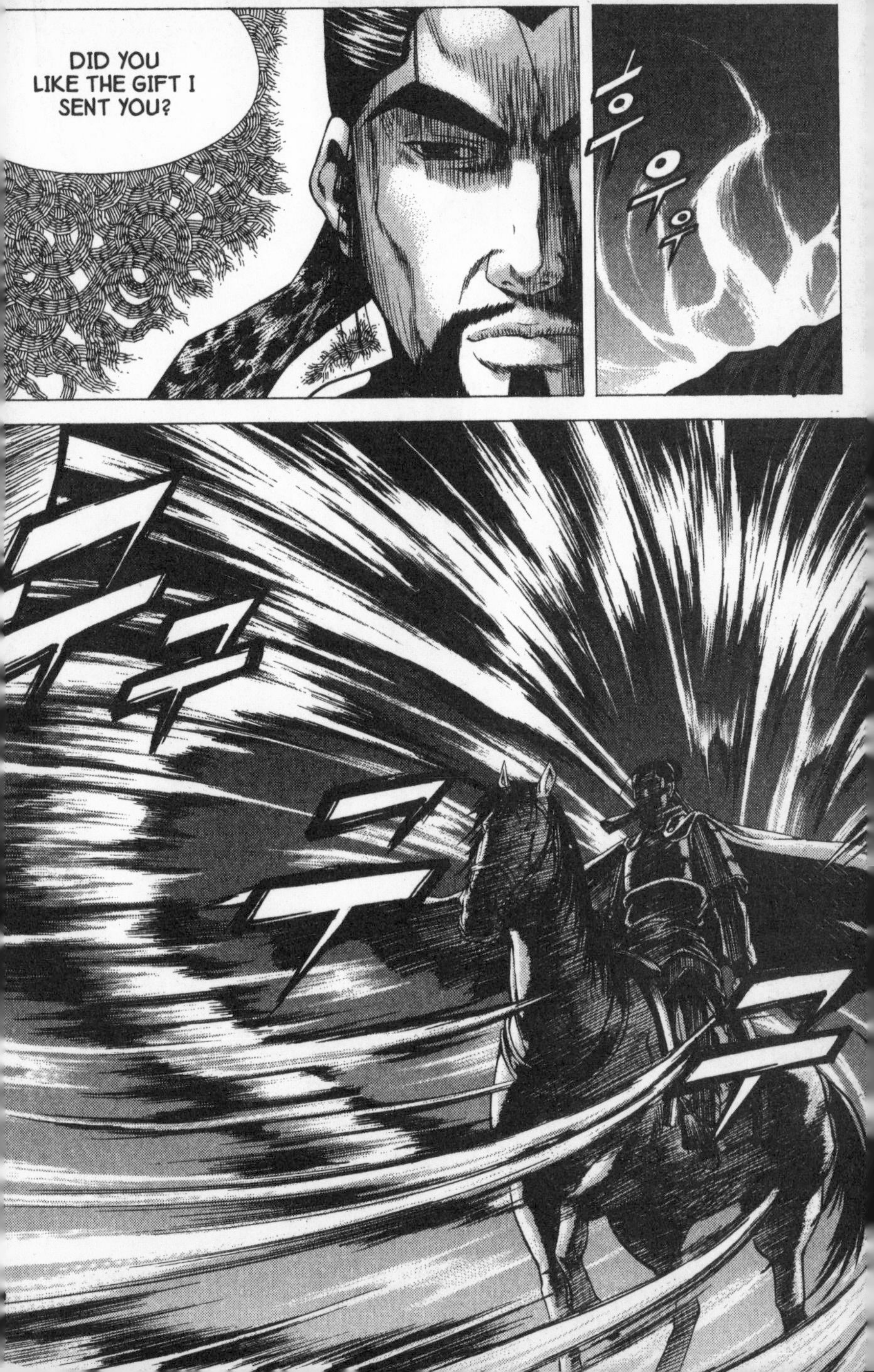
DID YOU LIKE THE GIFT I SENT YOU?

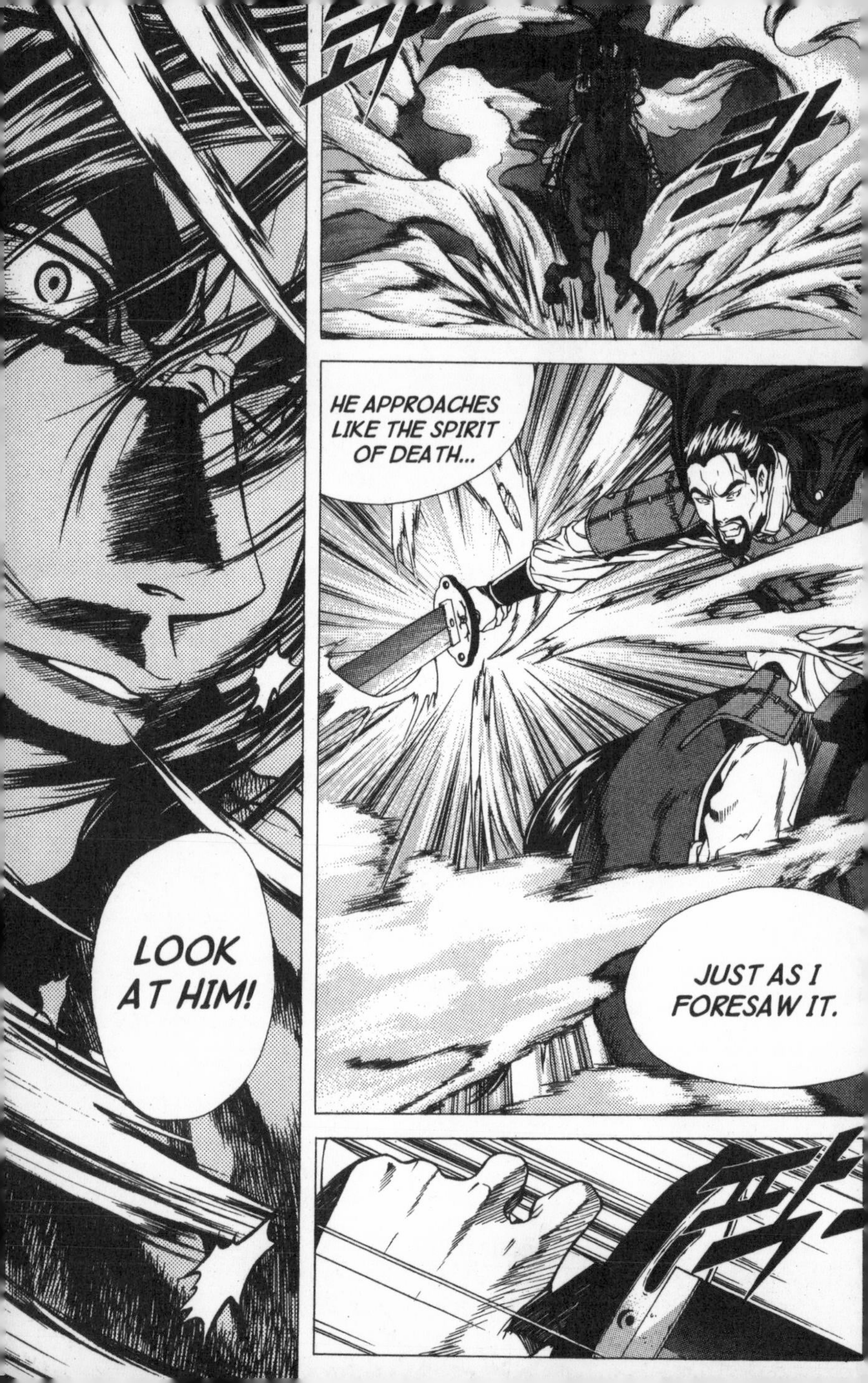
LOOK AT HIM!
HE APPROACHES LIKE THE SPIRIT OF DEATH...
JUST AS I FORESAW IT.

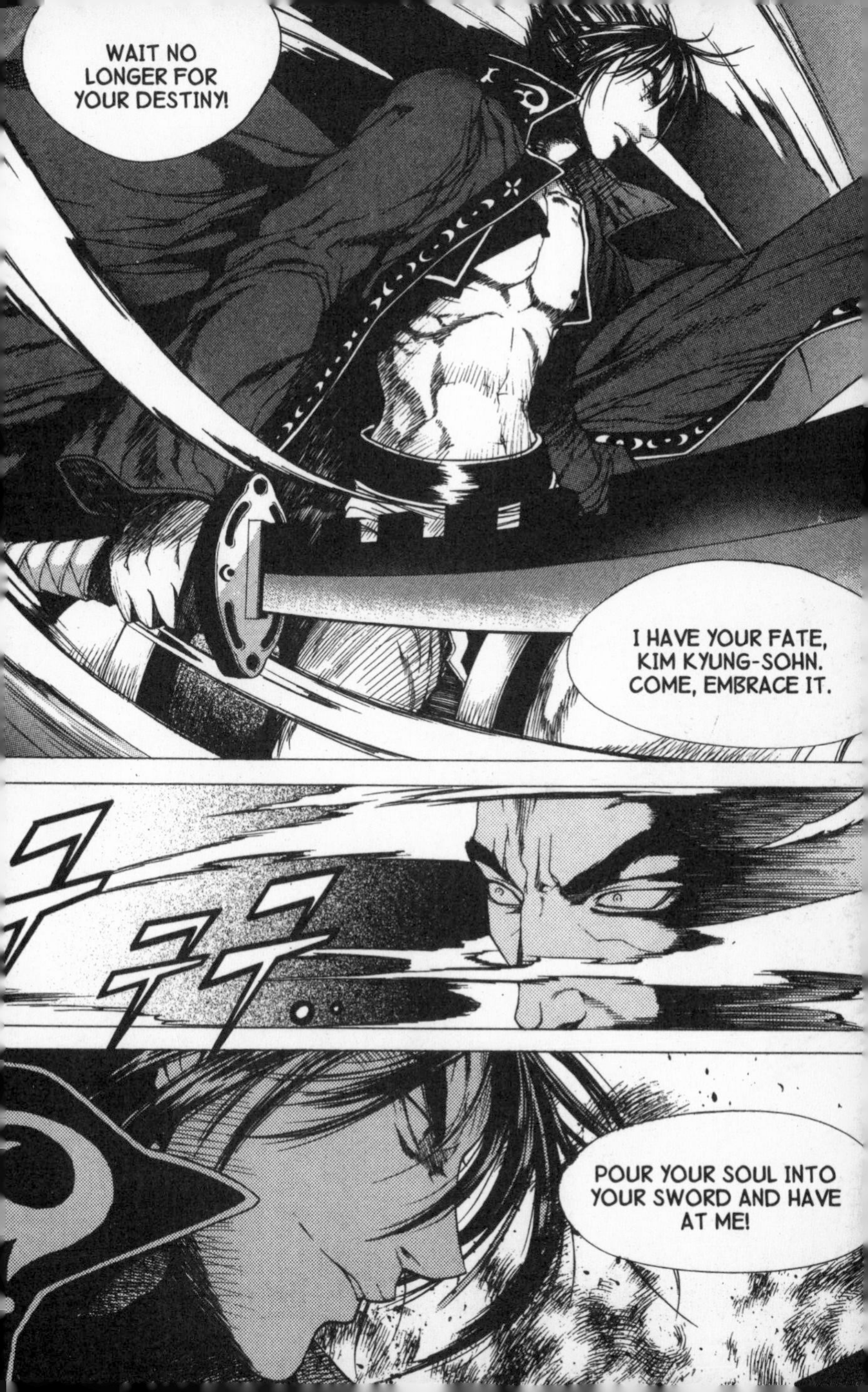
WAIT NO LONGER FOR YOUR DESTINY!
I HAVE YOUR FATE, KIM KYUNG-SOHN. COME, EMBRACE IT.
POUR YOUR SOUL INTO YOUR SWORD AND HAVE AT ME!

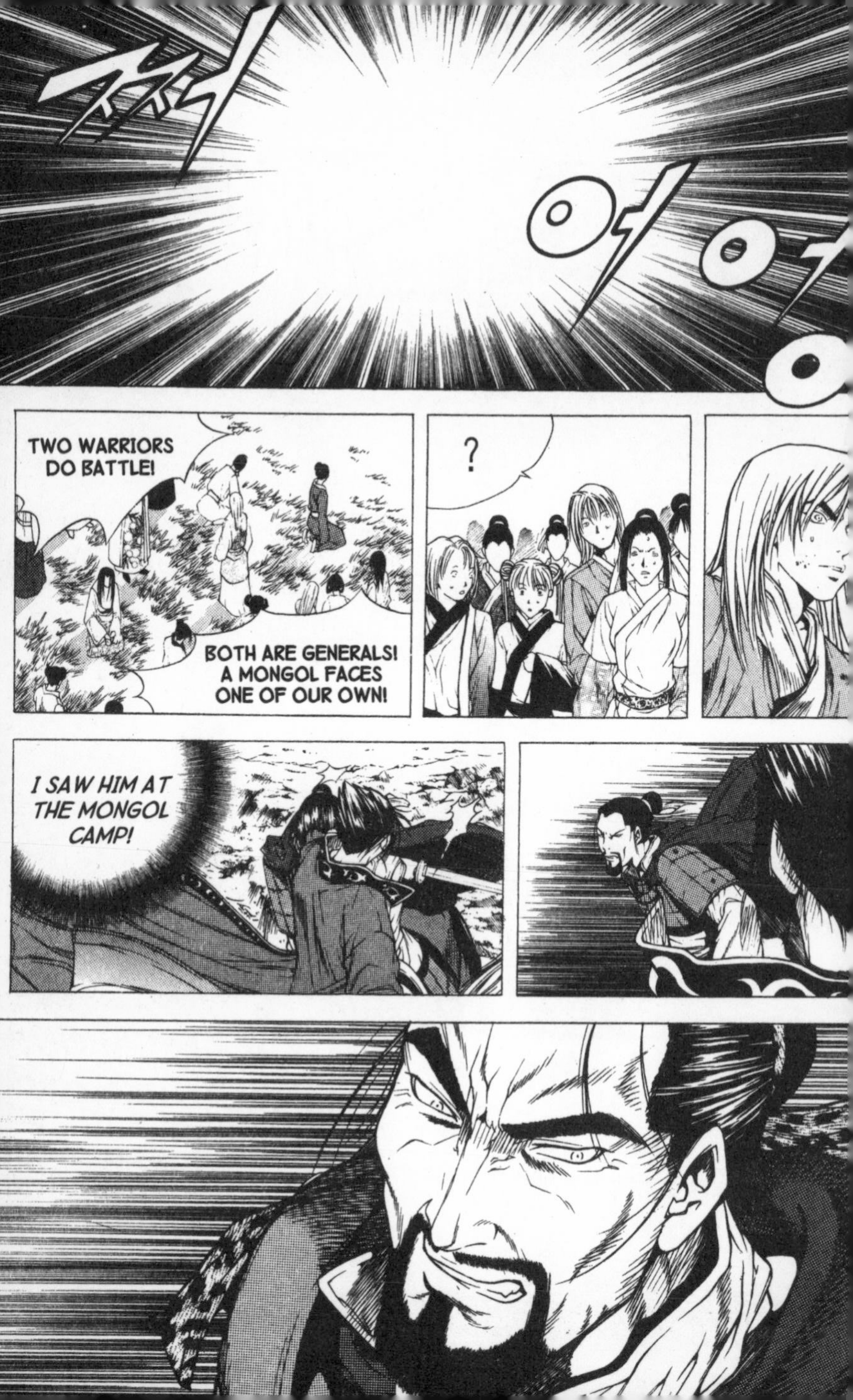
TWO WARRIORS DO BATTLE!
BOTH ARE GENERALS! A MONGOL FACES ONE OF OUR OWN!
?
I SAW HIM AT THE MONGOL CAMP!

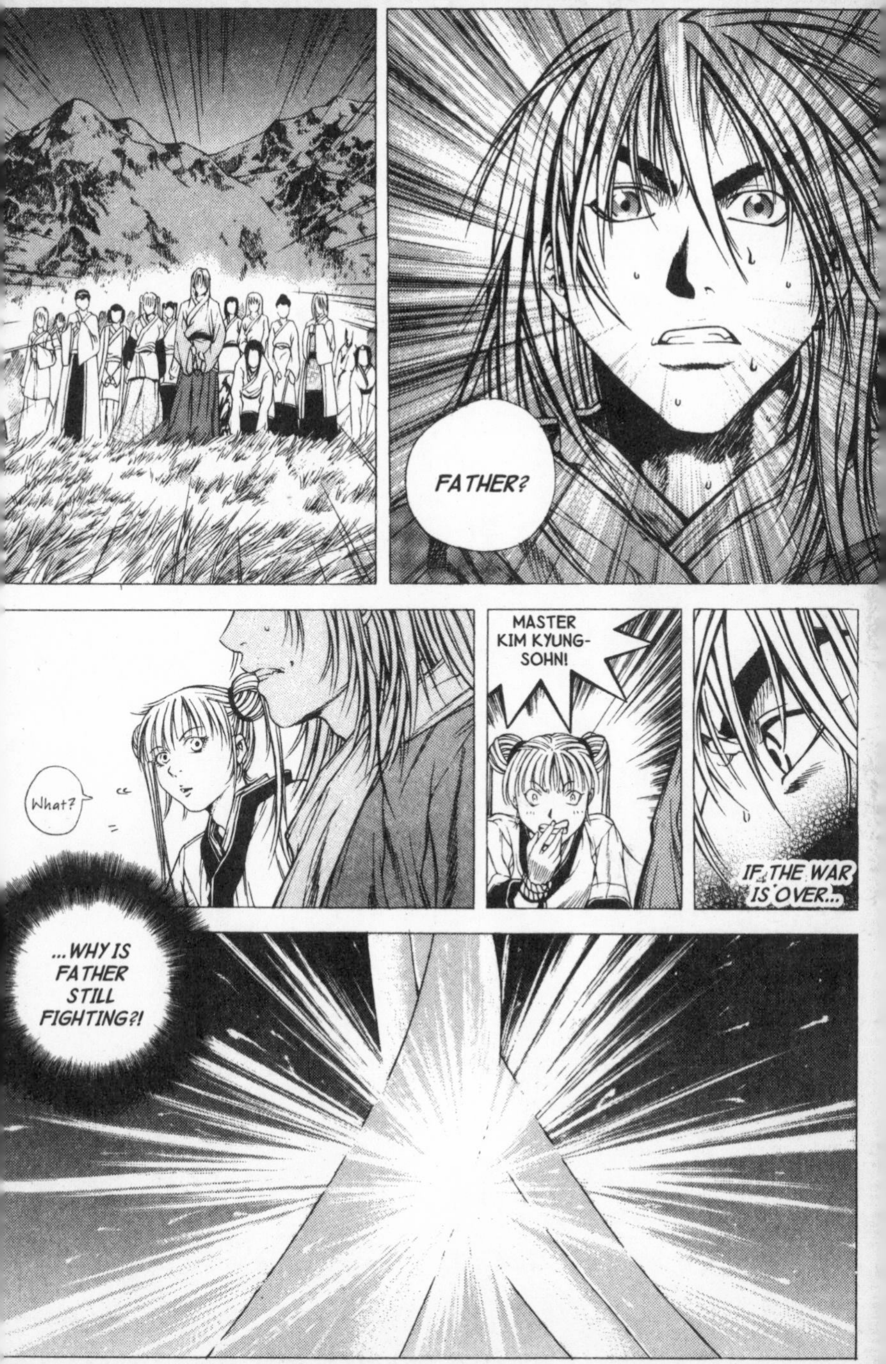
FATHER?
What?
MASTER KIM KYUNG-SOHN!
IF THE WAR IS OVER...
...WHY IS FATHER STILL FIGHTING?!

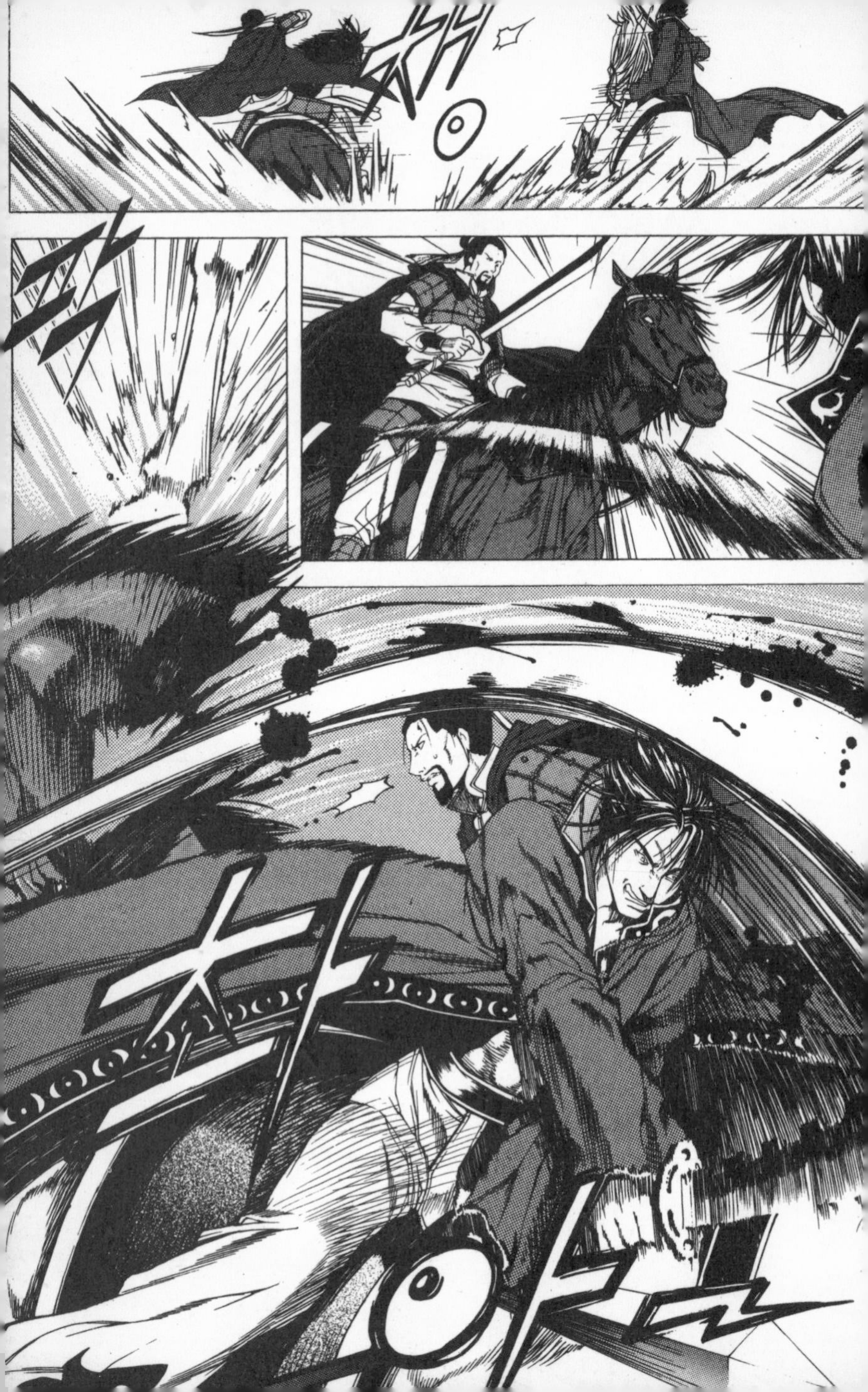

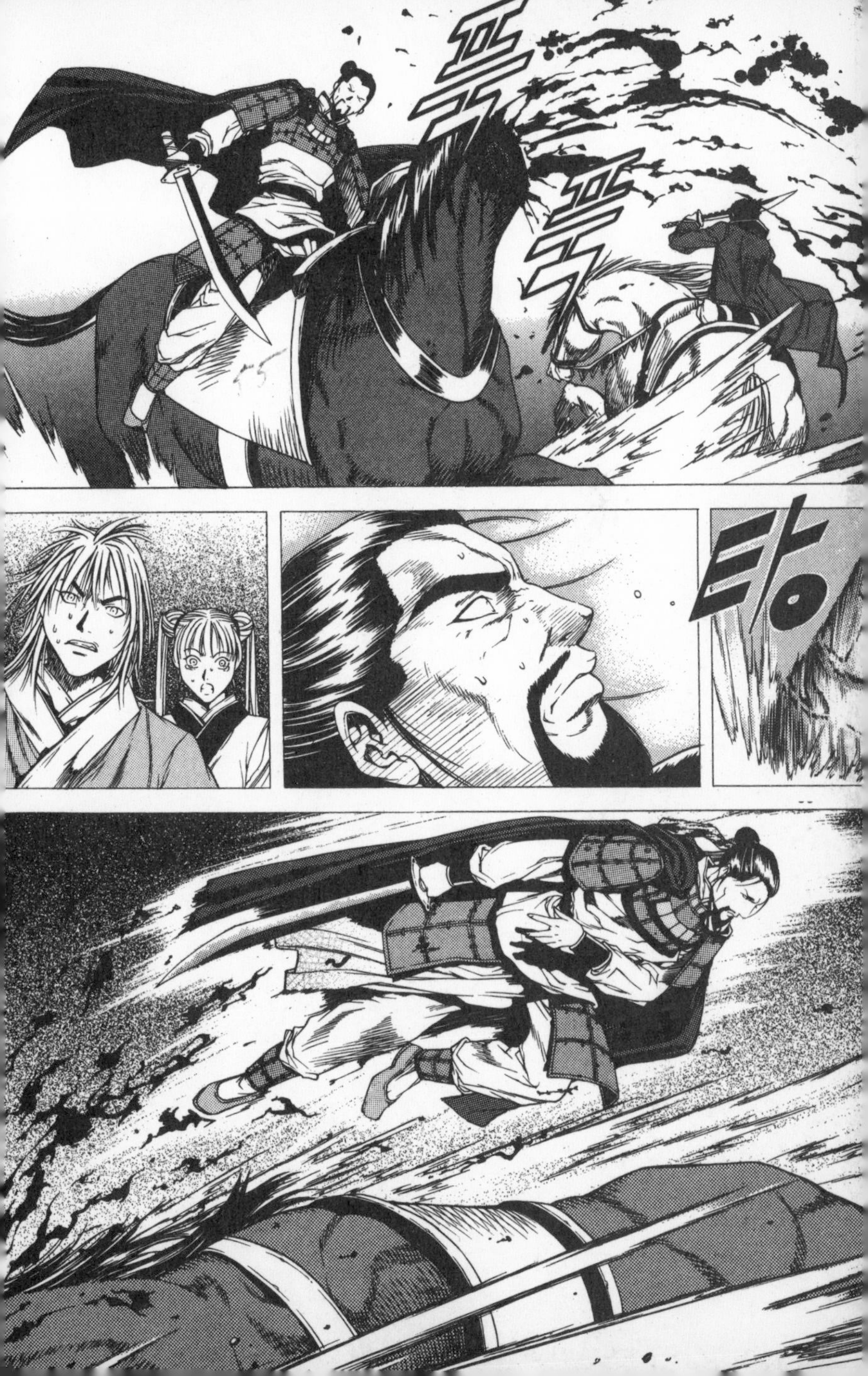
탕

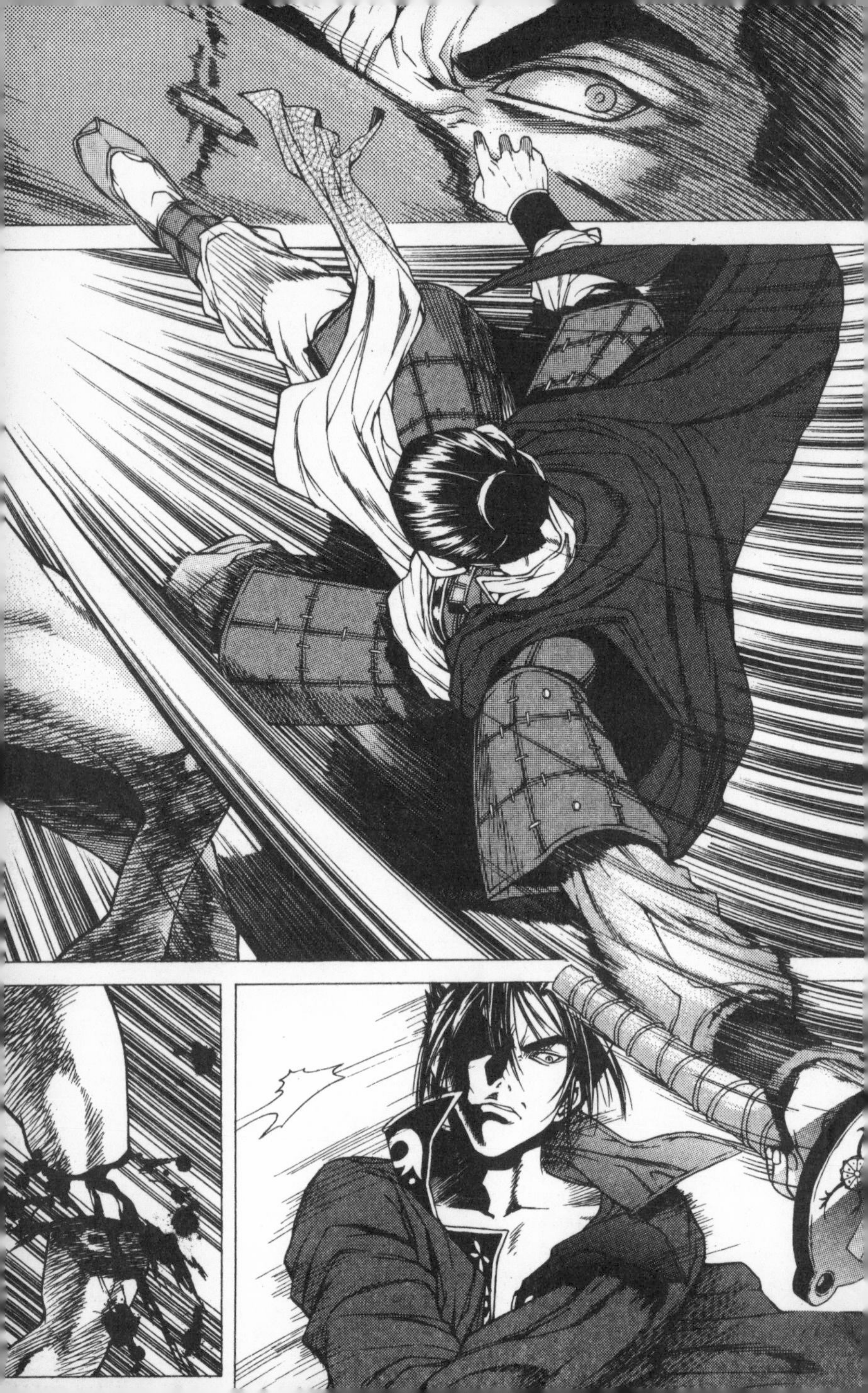

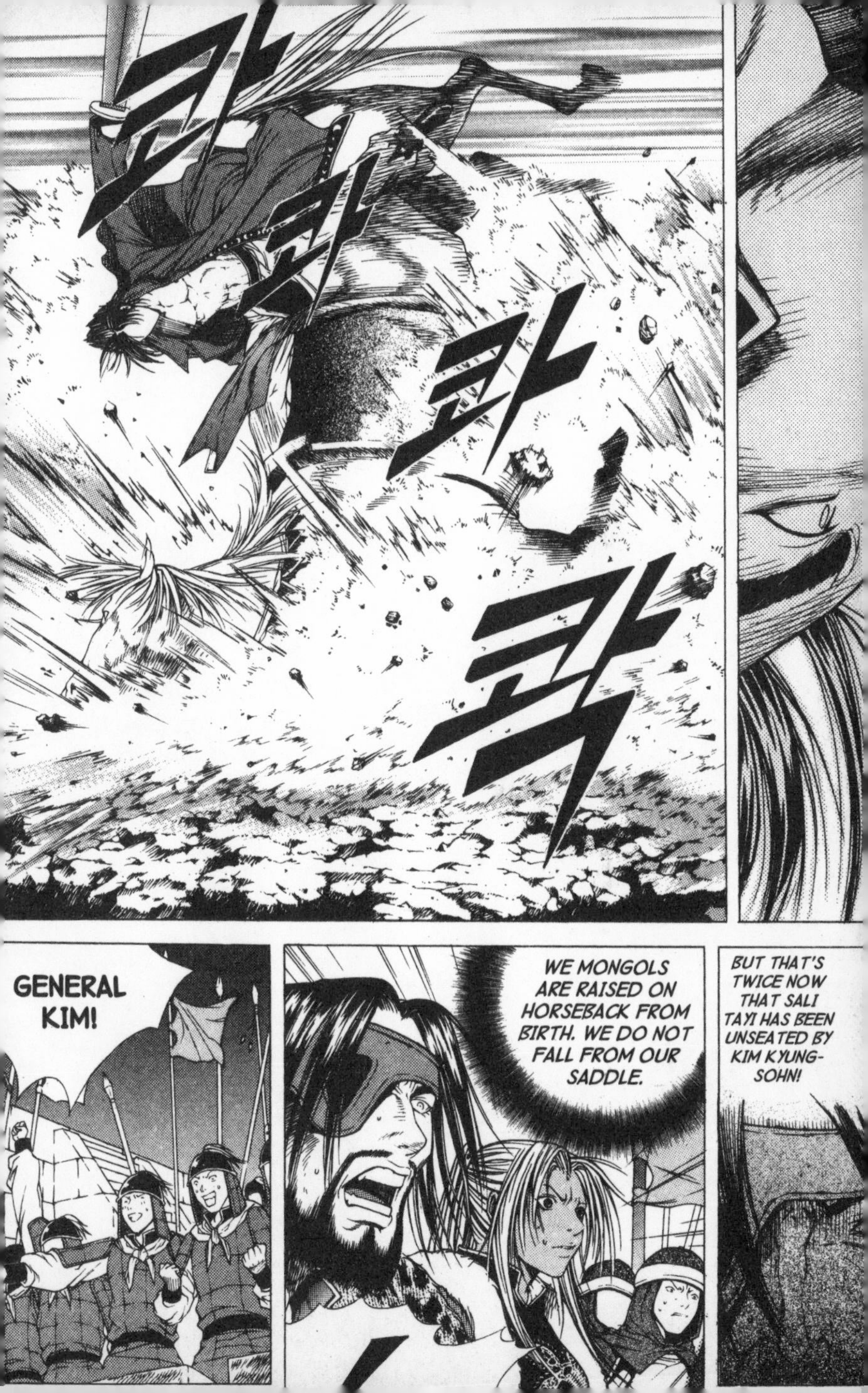
GENERAL KIM!
WE MONGOLS ARE RAISED ON HORSEBACK FROM BIRTH. WE DO NOT FALL FROM OUR SADDLE.
BUT THAT'S TWICE NOW THAT SALI TAYI HAS BEEN UNSEATED BY KIM KYUNG-SOHN!

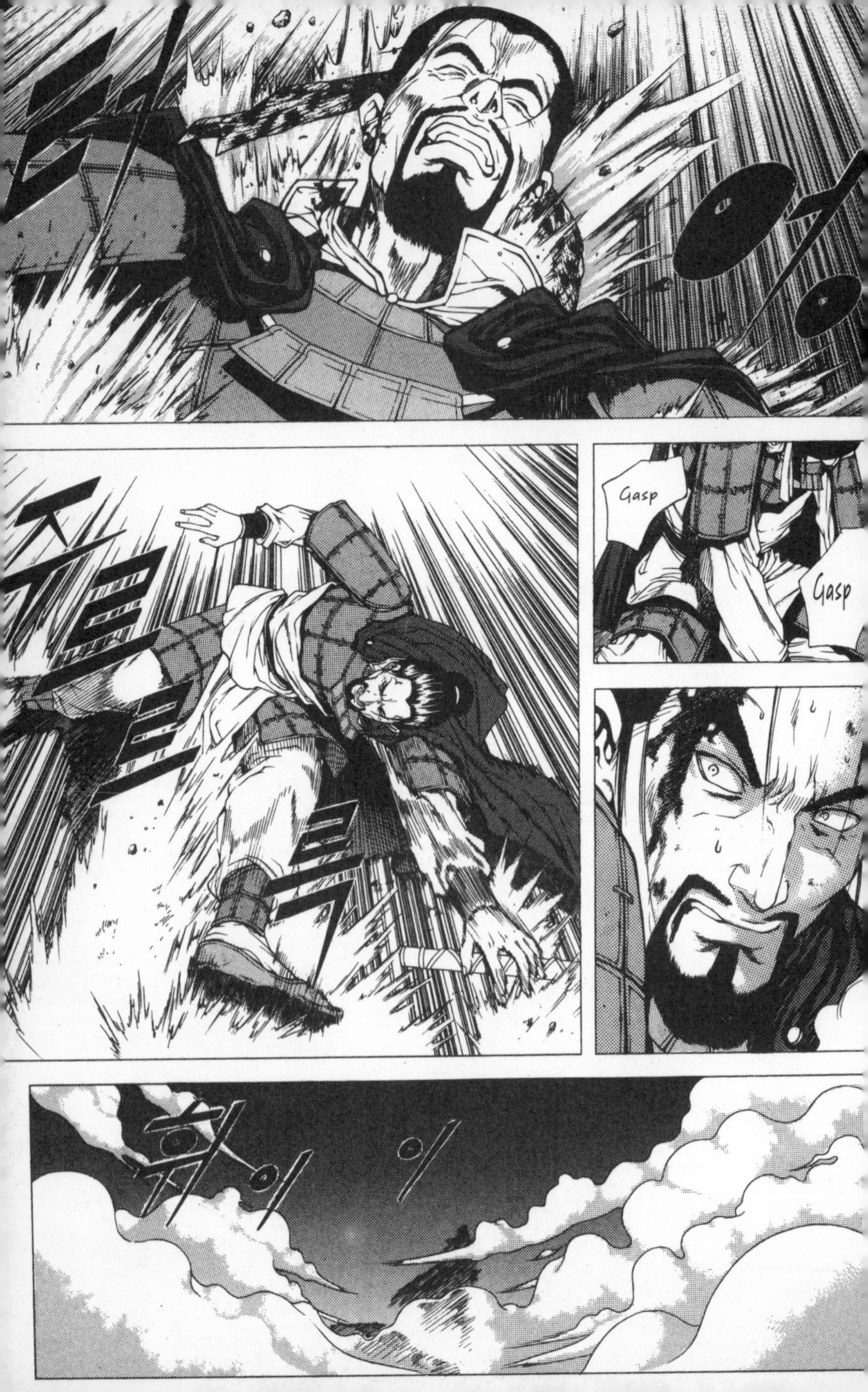
Gasp
Gasp

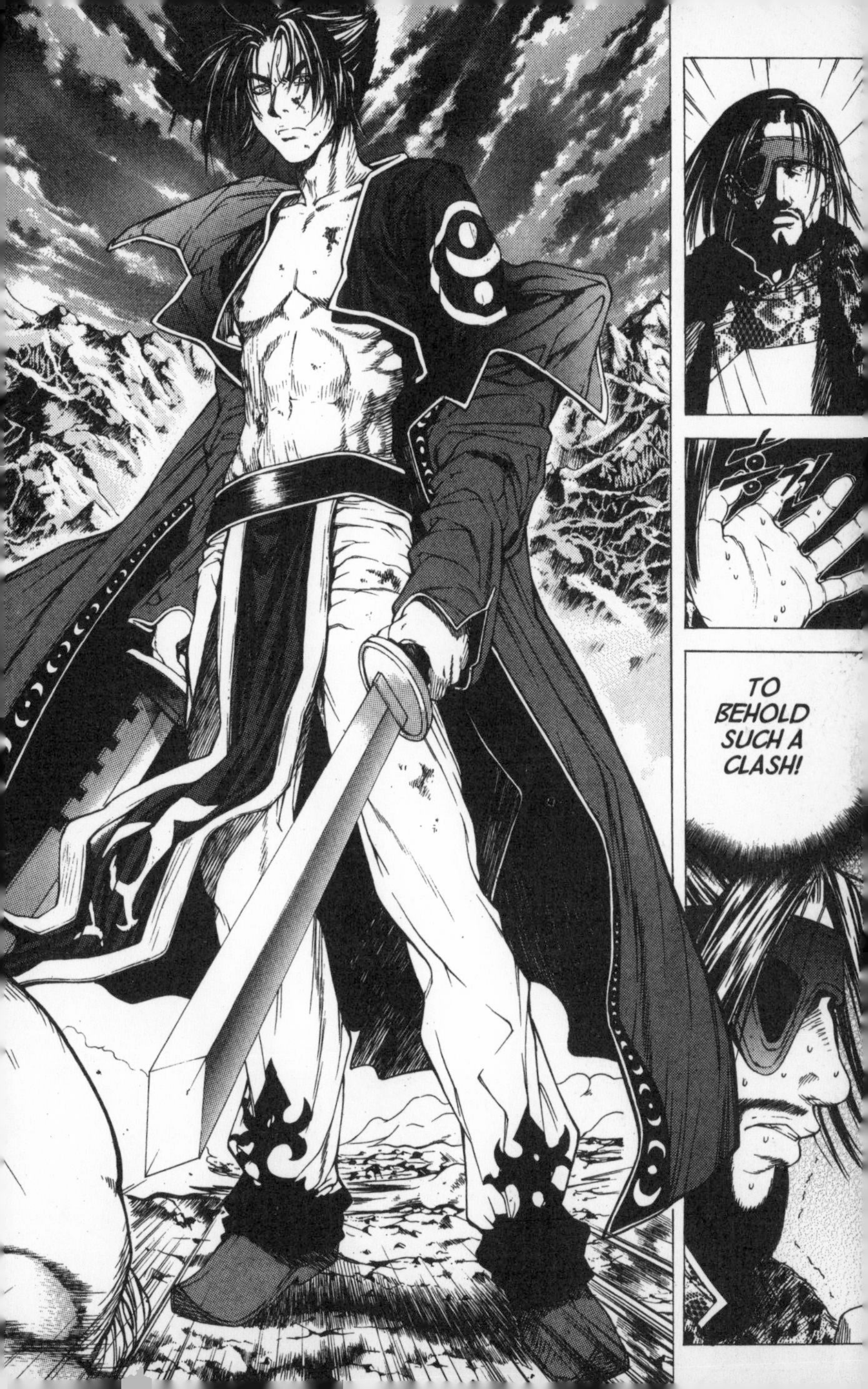
TO BEHOLD SUCH A CLASH!

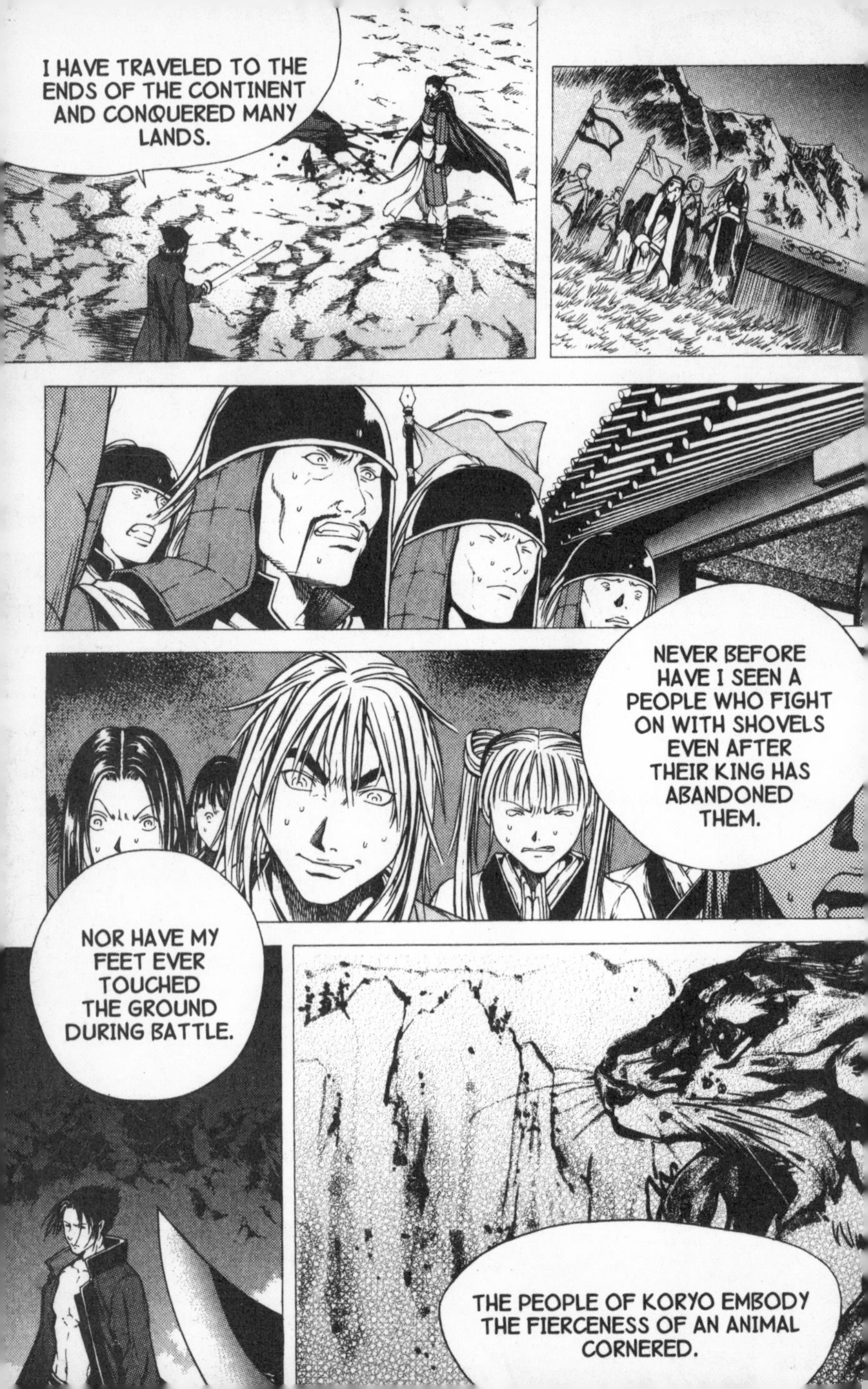
I HAVE TRAVELED TO THE ENDS OF THE CONTINENT AND CONQUERED MANY LANDS.
NEVER BEFORE HAVE I SEEN A PEOPLE WHO FIGHT ON WITH SHOVELS EVEN AFTER THEIR KING HAS ABANDONED THEM.
NOR HAVE MY FEET EVER TOUCHED THE GROUND DURING BATTLE.
THE PEOPLE OF KORYO EMBODY THE FIERCENESS OF AN ANIMAL CORNERED.

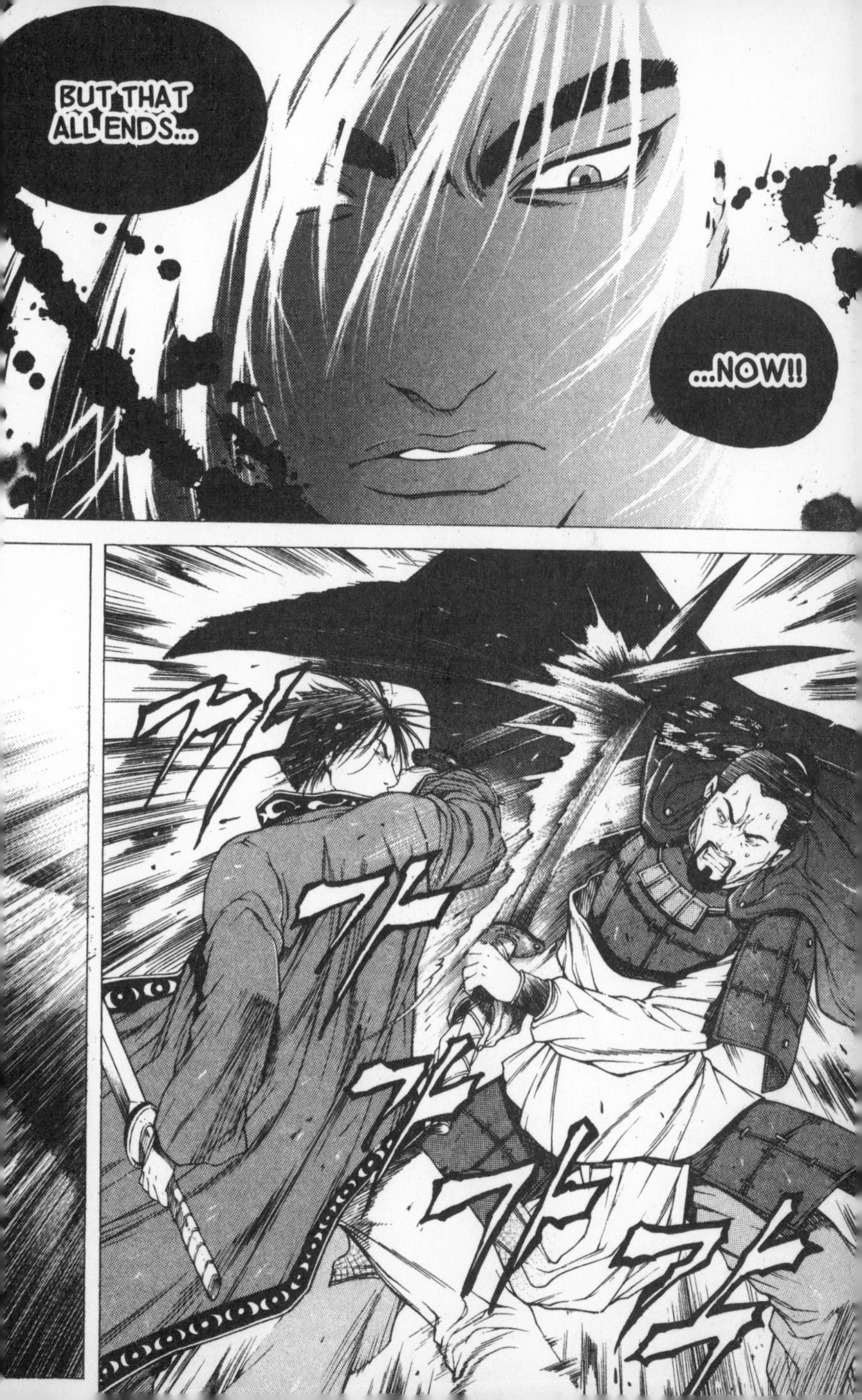
BUT THAT ALL ENDS...
...NOW!!

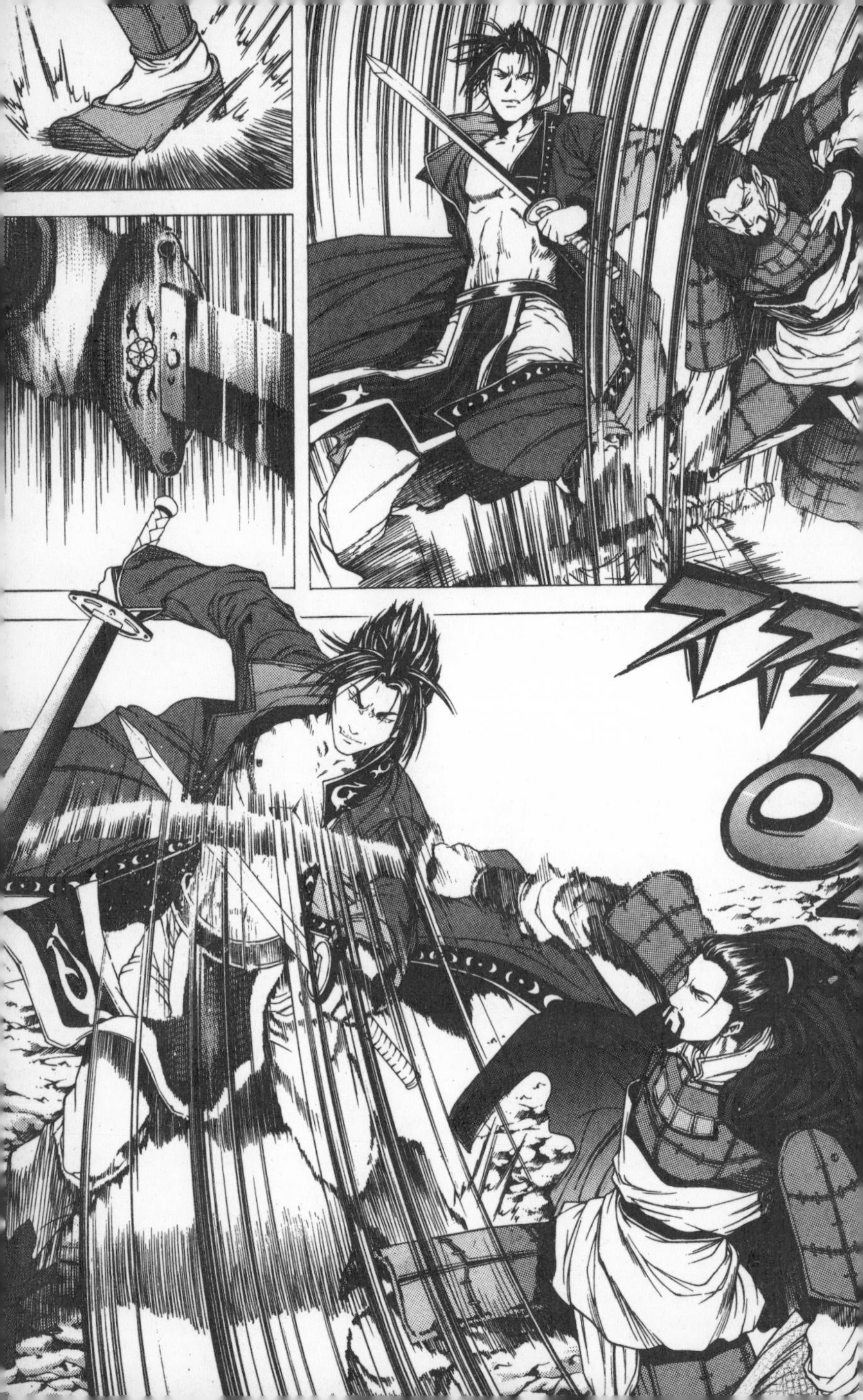

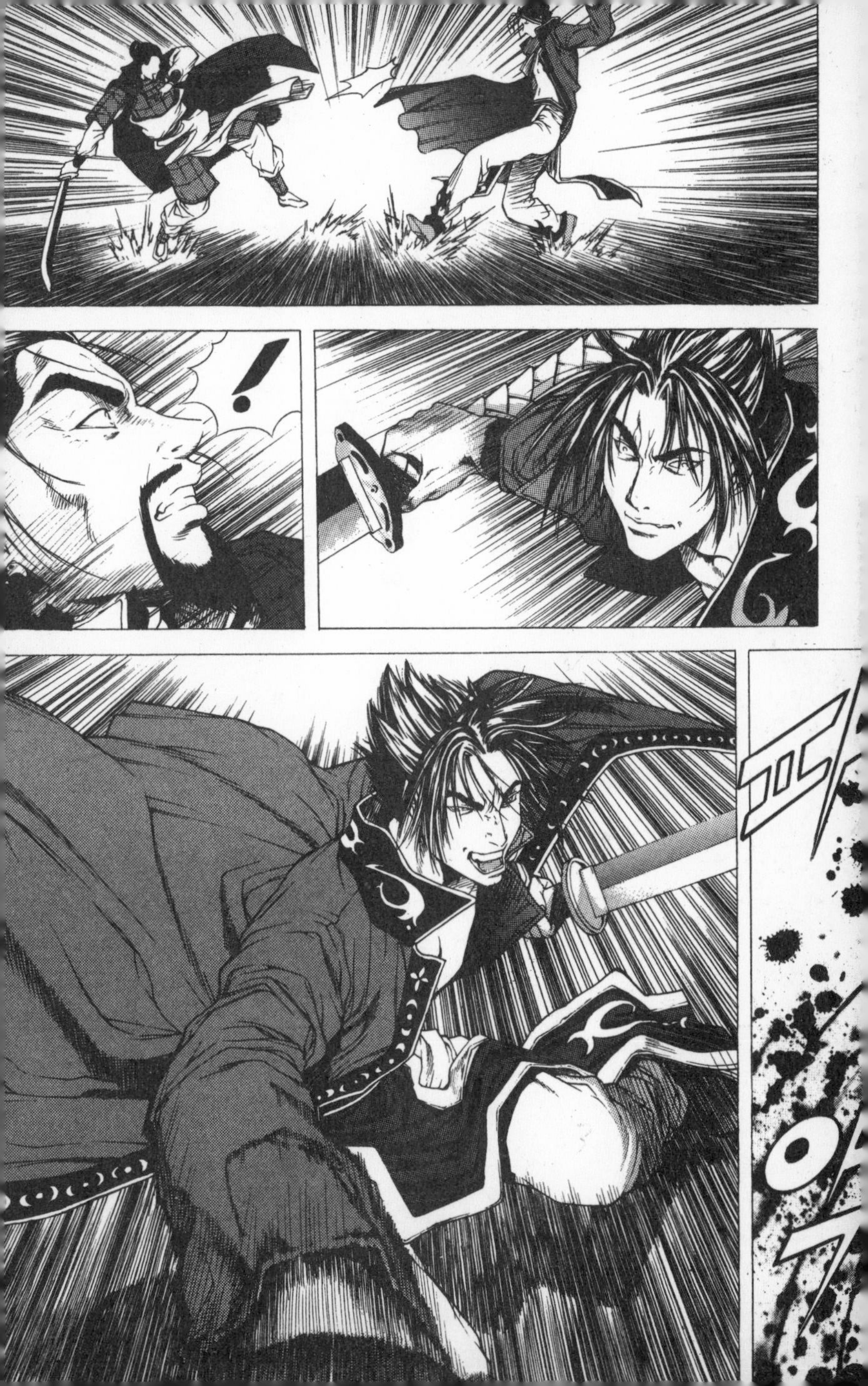
!

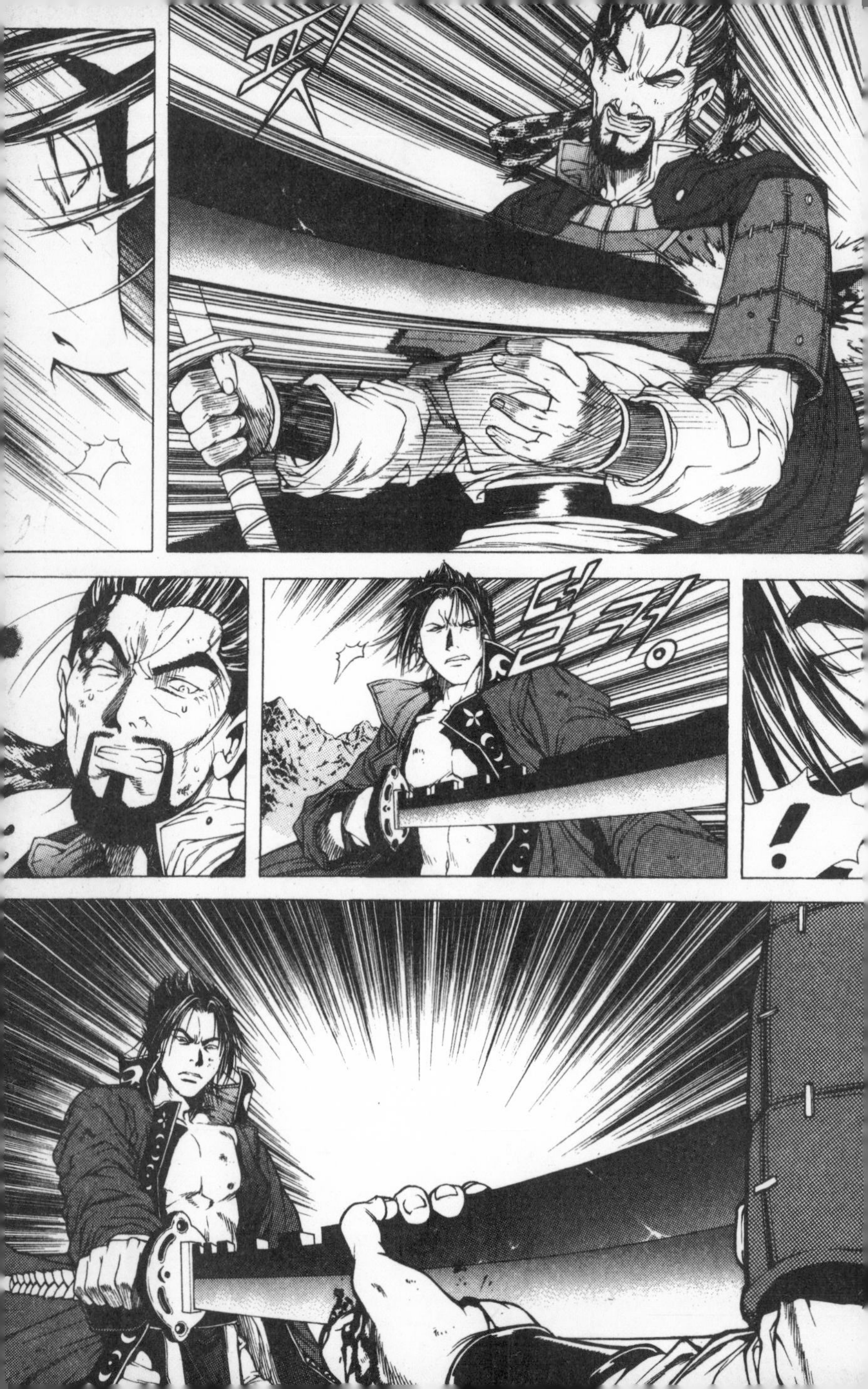
핏
덜컥.
!

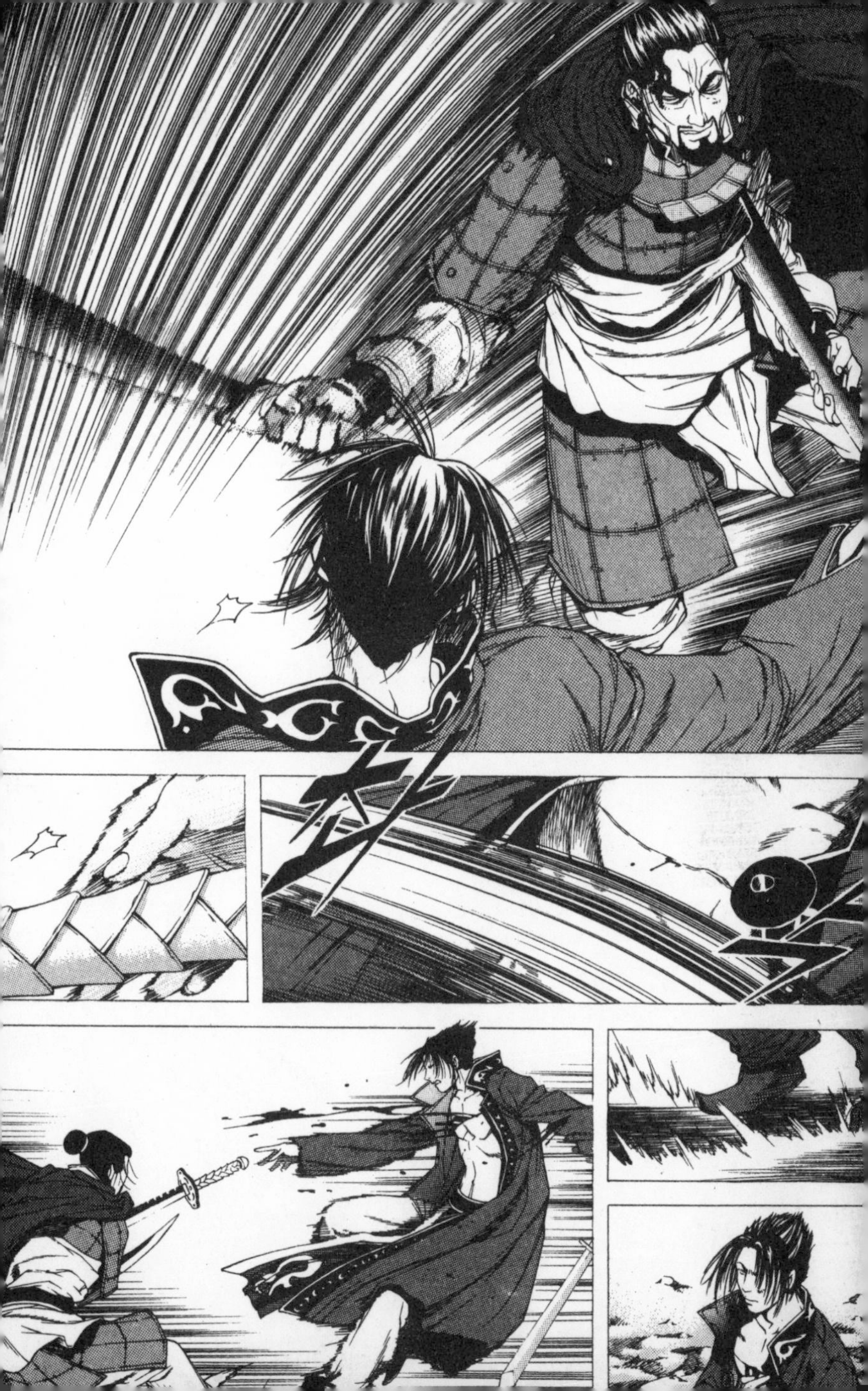

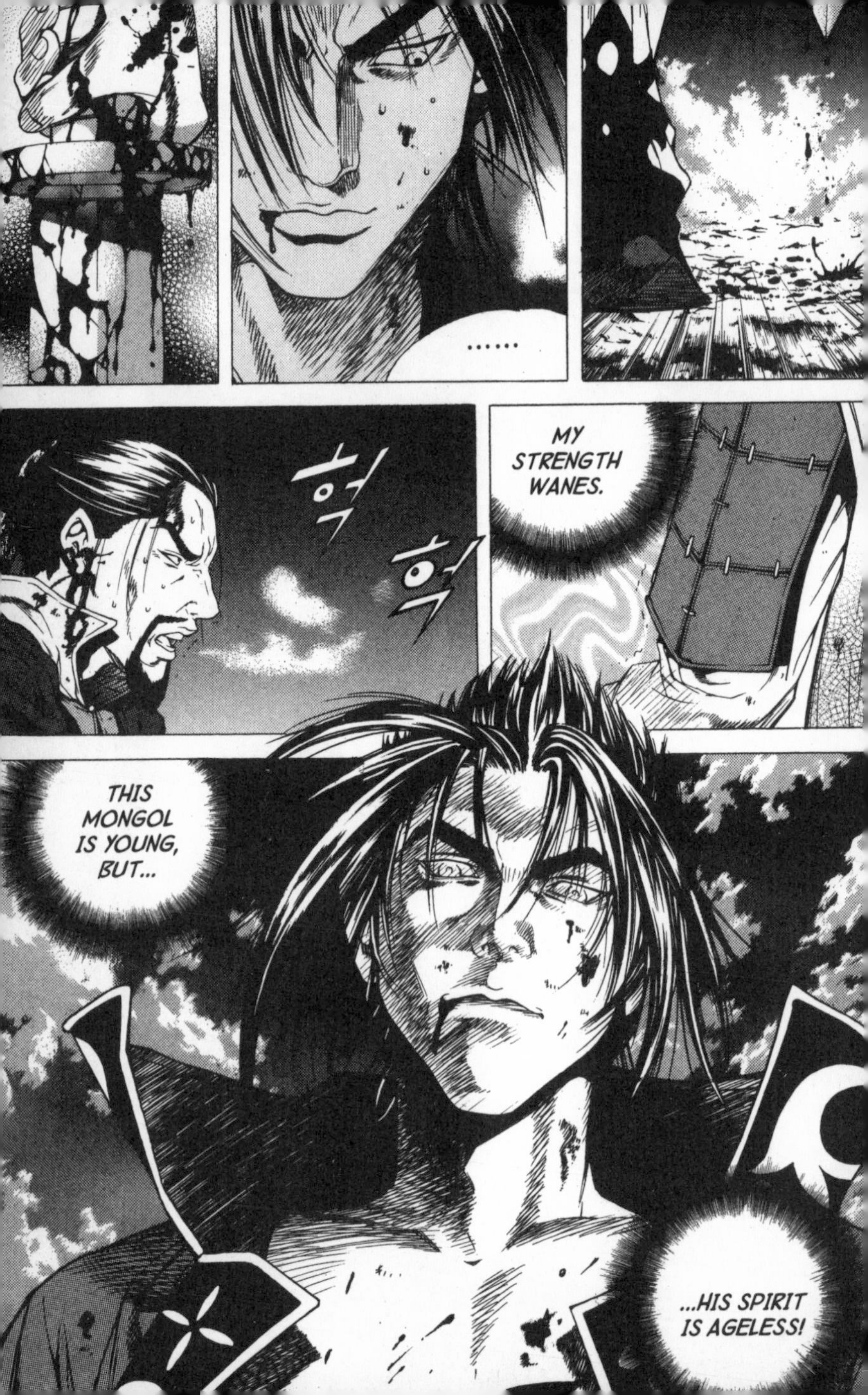
......
헉
헉
MY STRENGTH WANES.
THIS MONGOL IS YOUNG, BUT...
...HIS SPIRIT IS AGELESS!

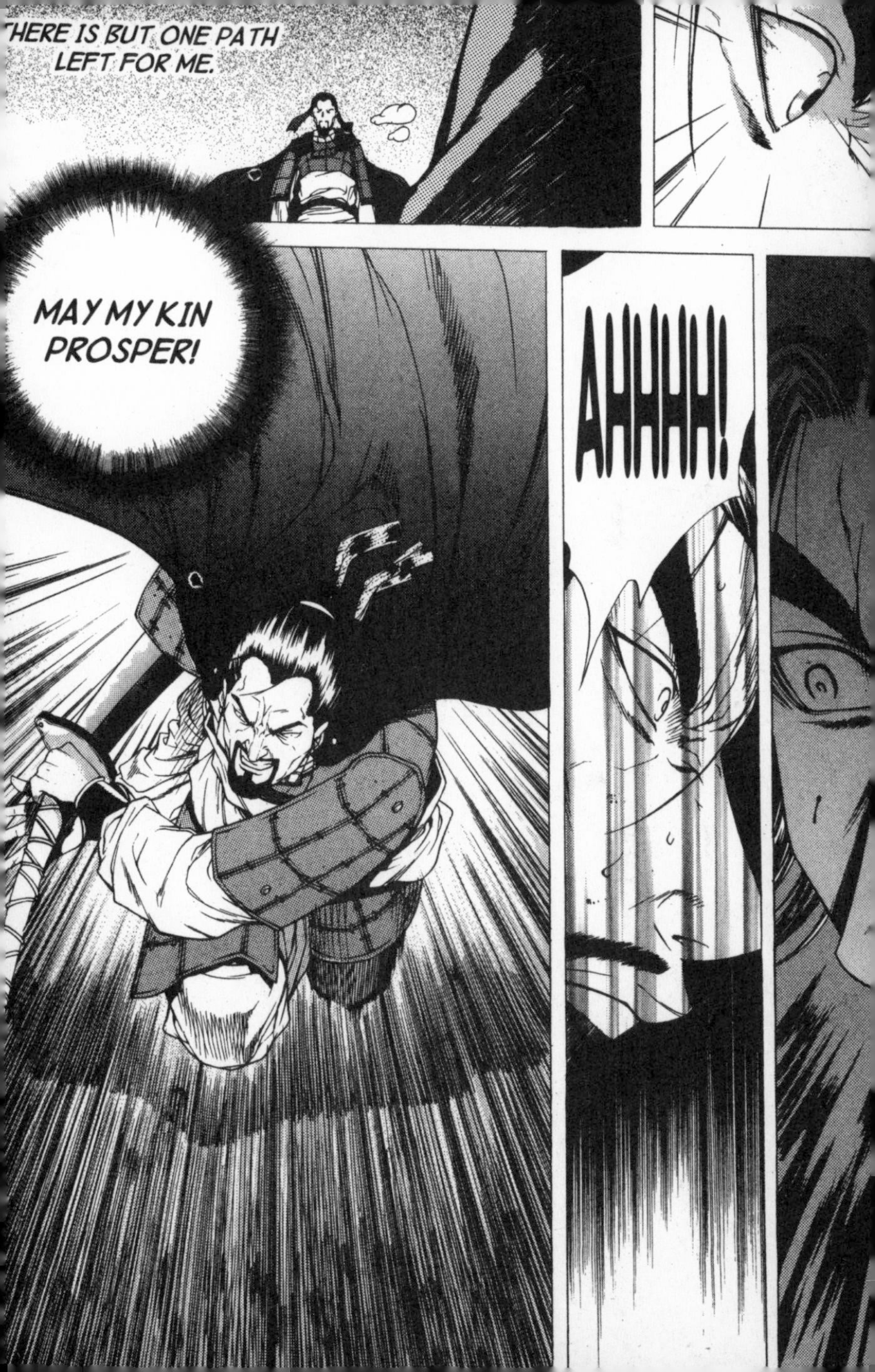
THERE IS BUT ONE PATH LEFT FOR ME.
MAY MY KIN PROSPER!
AHHHH!

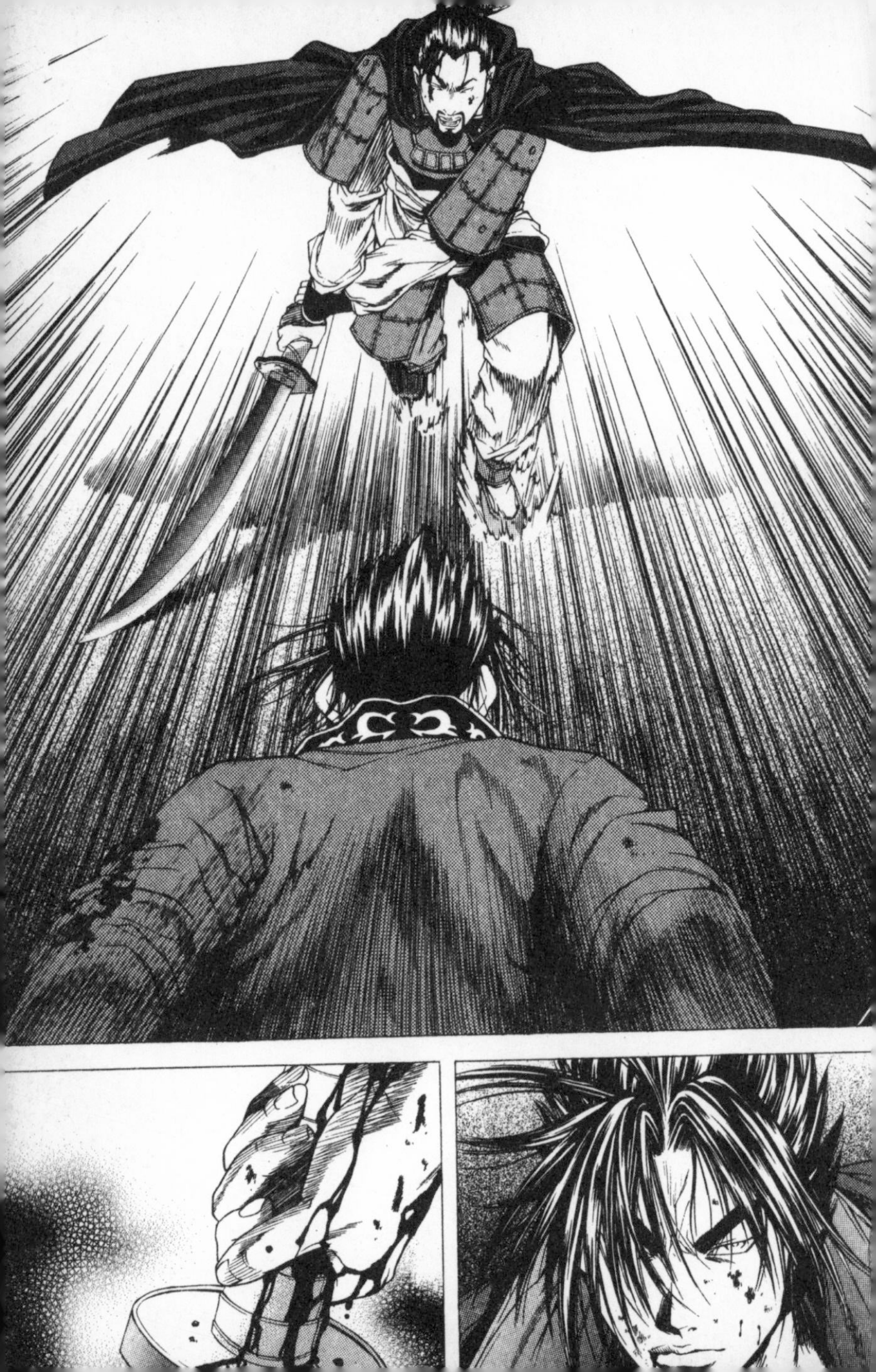

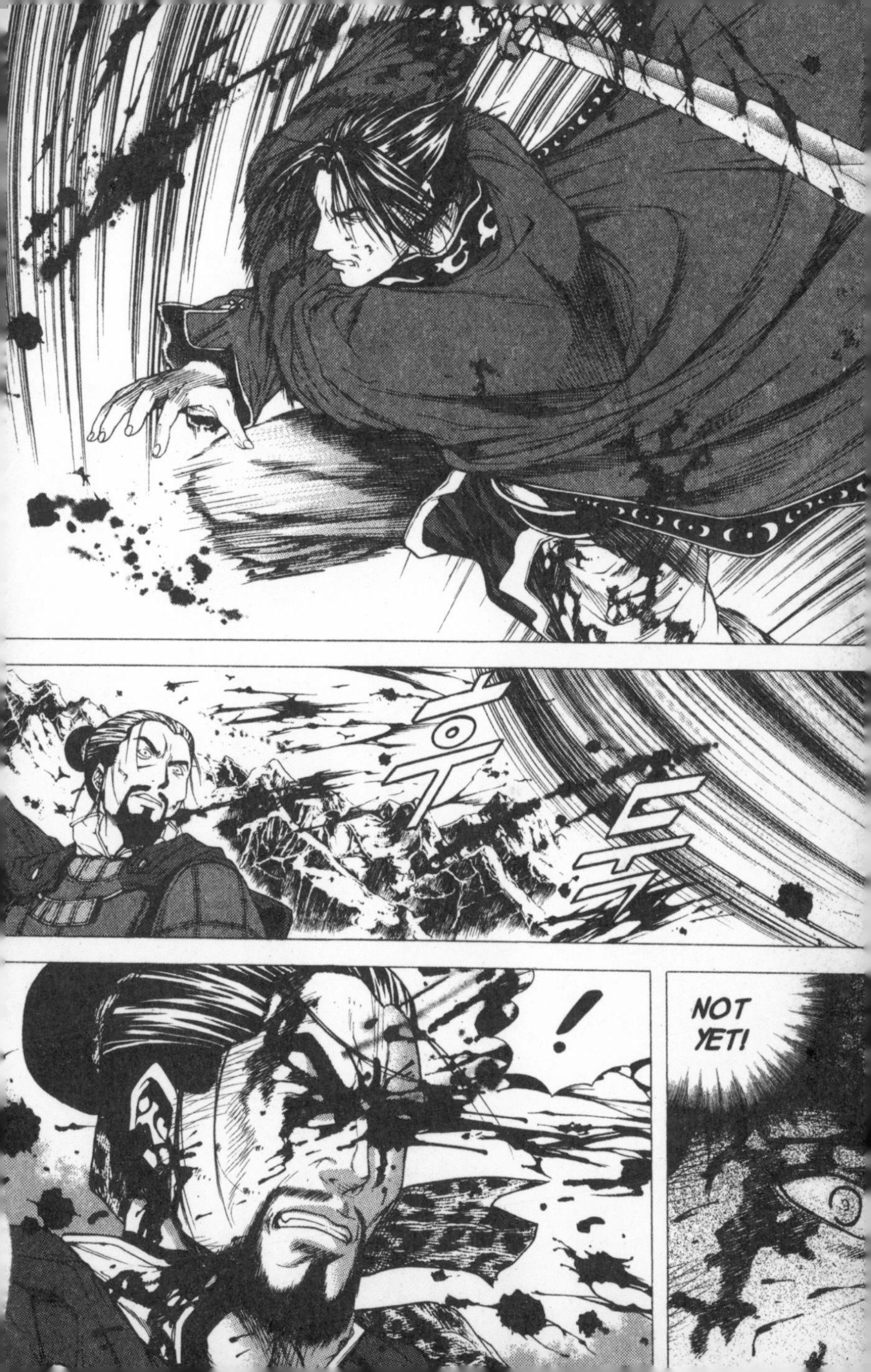
!
NOT YET!

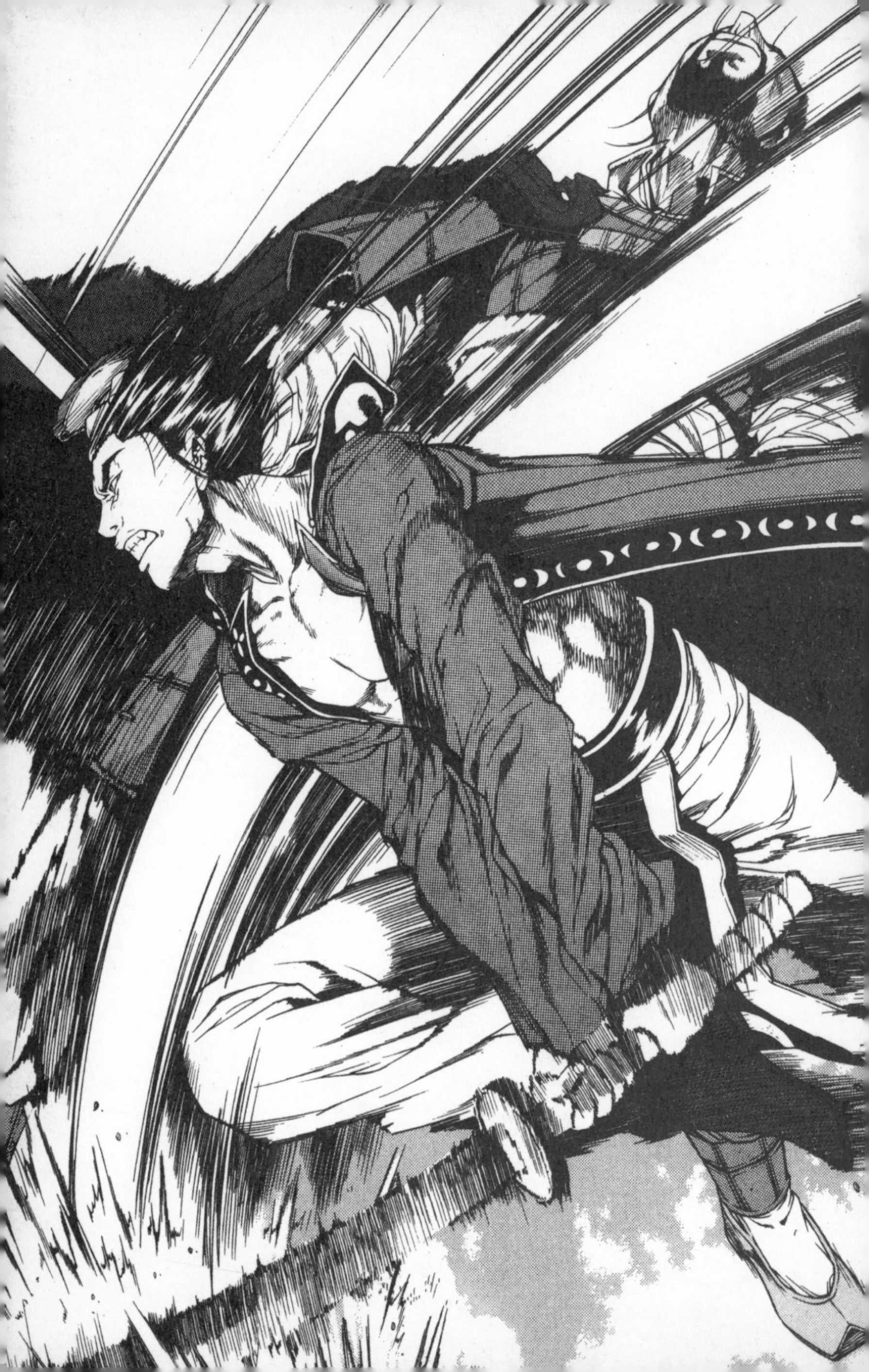

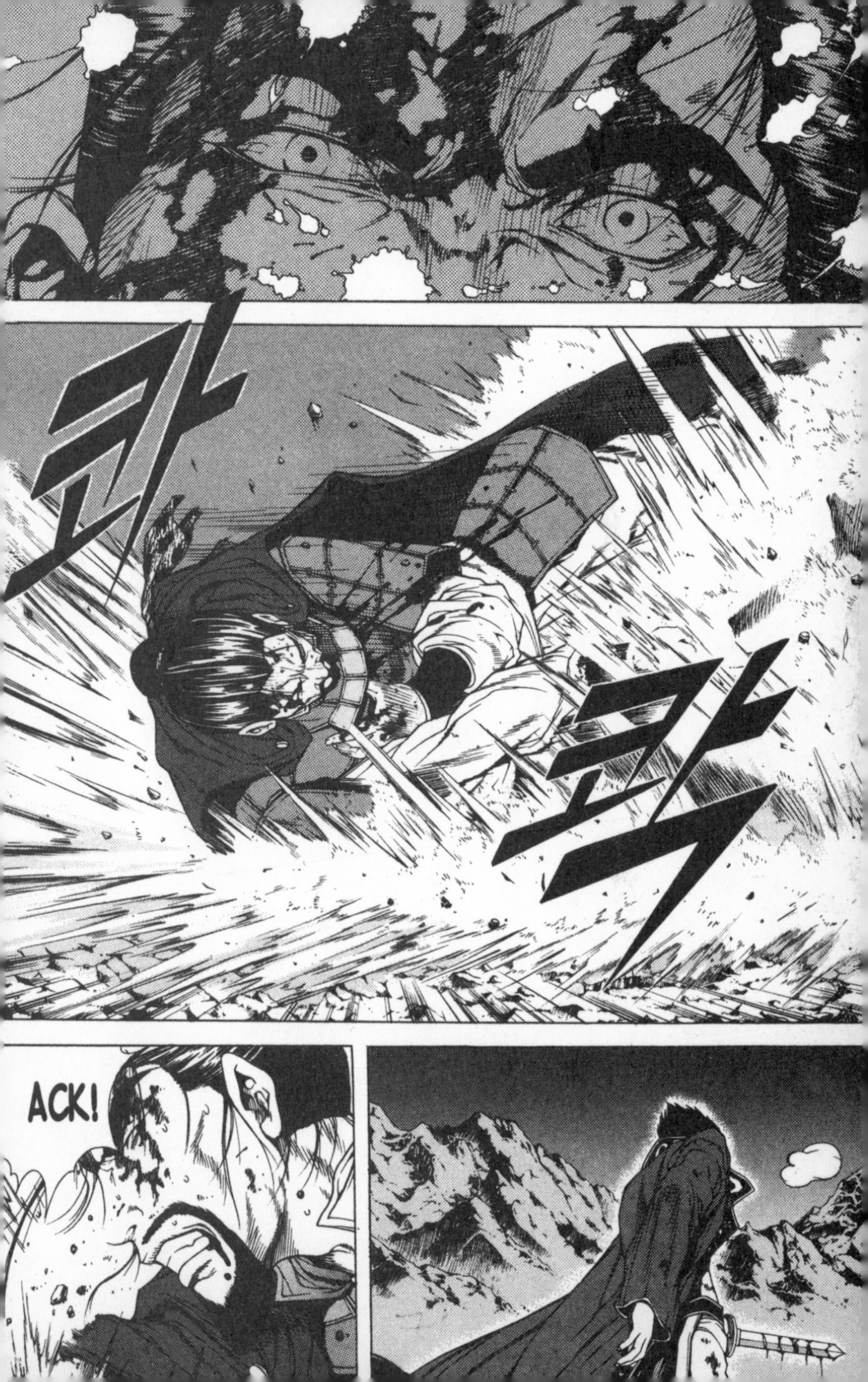
ACK!

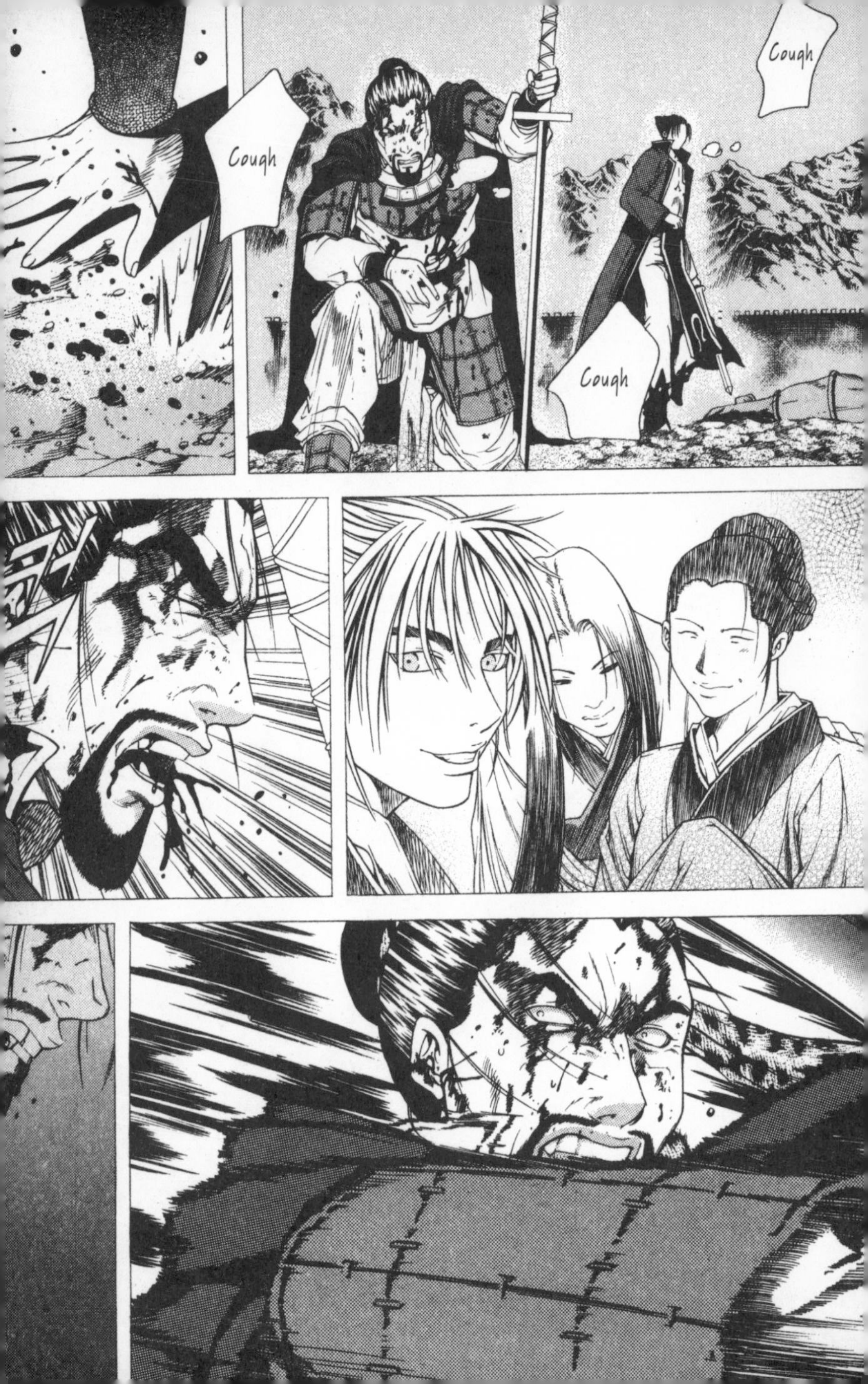

Cough
Cough
Cough

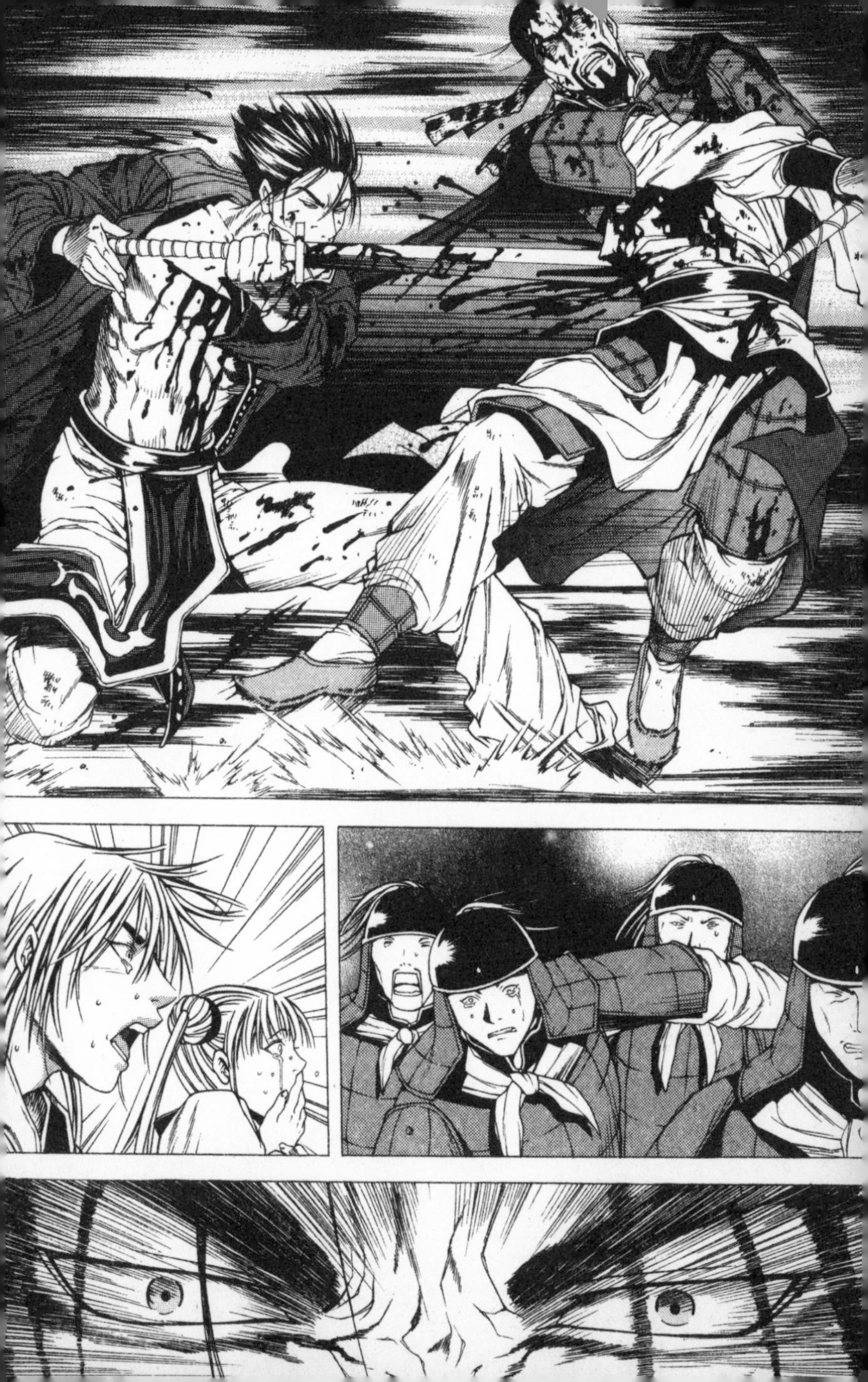

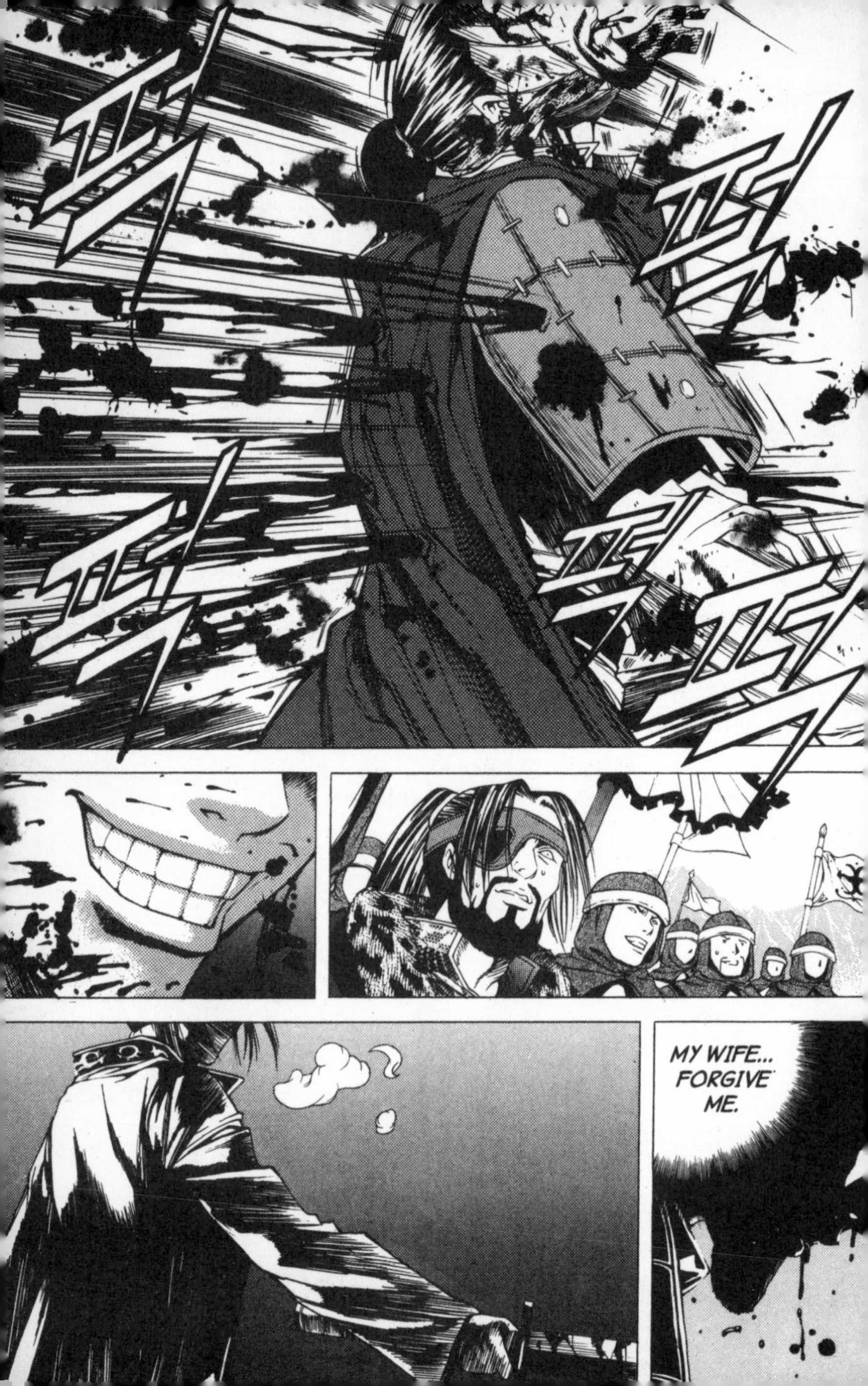
MY WIFE... FORGIVE ME.

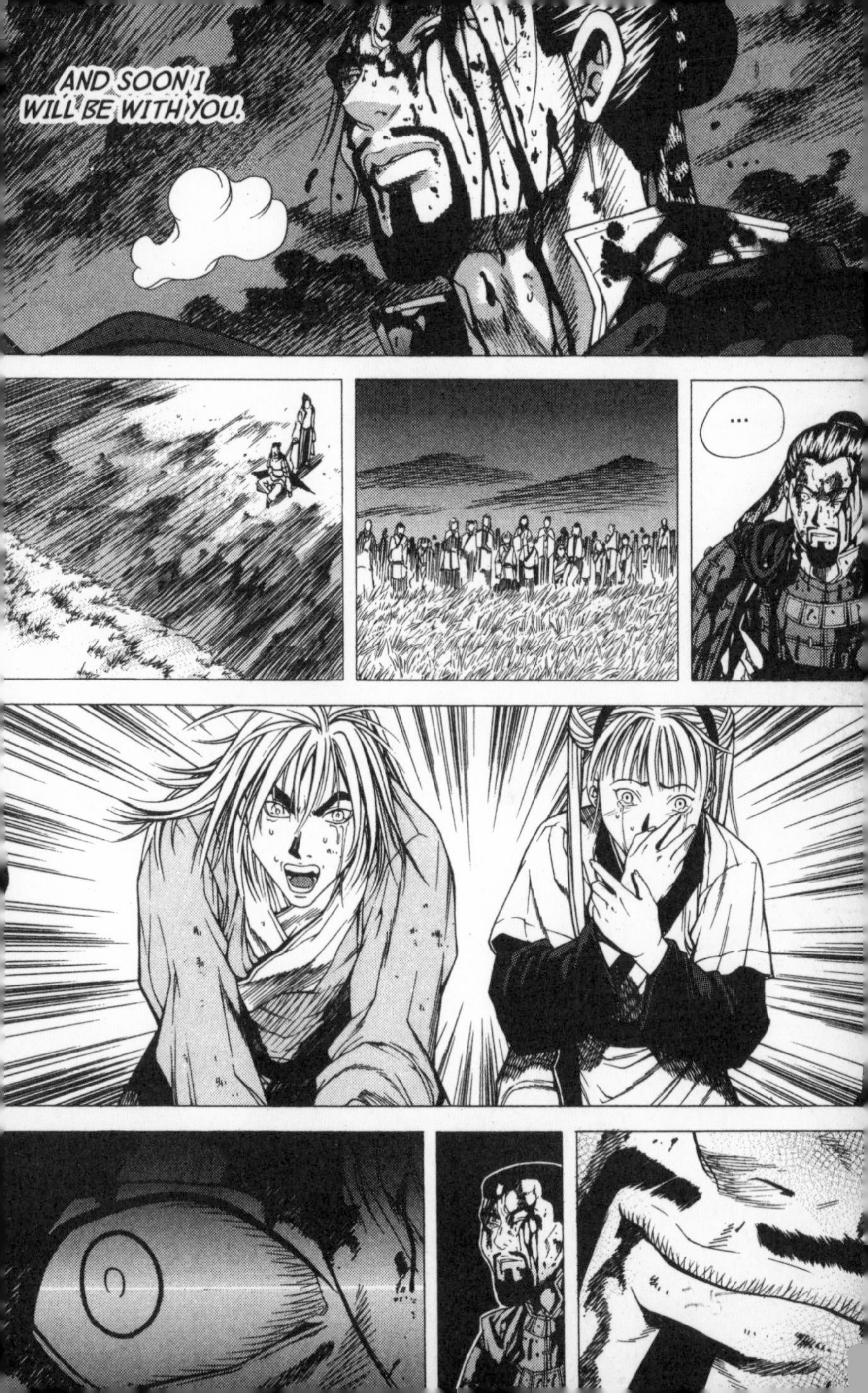
AND SOON I WILL BE WITH YOU.
...

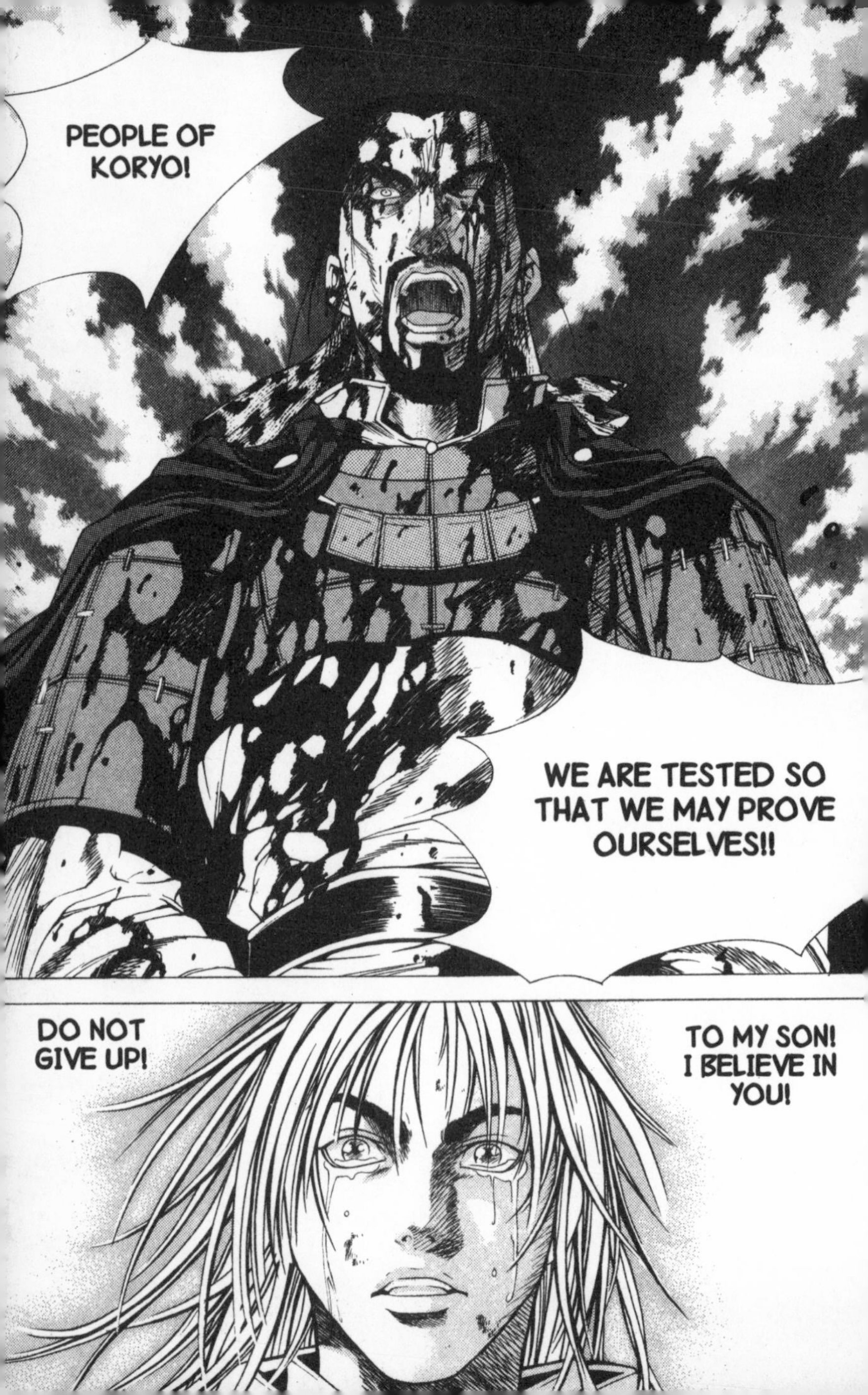
PEOPLE OF KORYO!
WE ARE TESTED SO THAT WE MAY PROVE OURSELVES!!
DO NOT GIVE UP!
TO MY SON! I BELIEVE IN YOU!

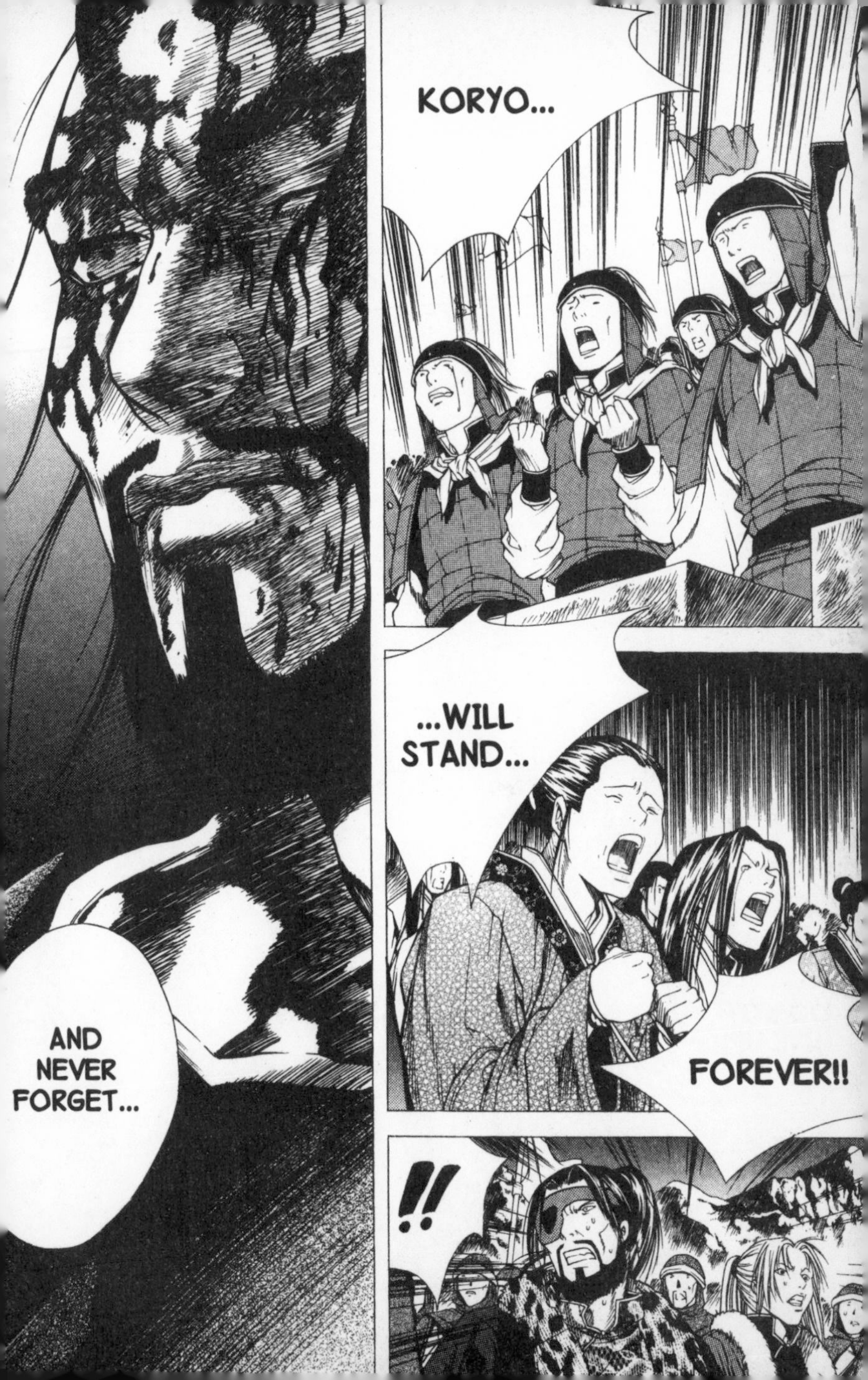
AND NEVER FORGET...
KORYO...
...WILL STAND...
FOREVER!!
!!

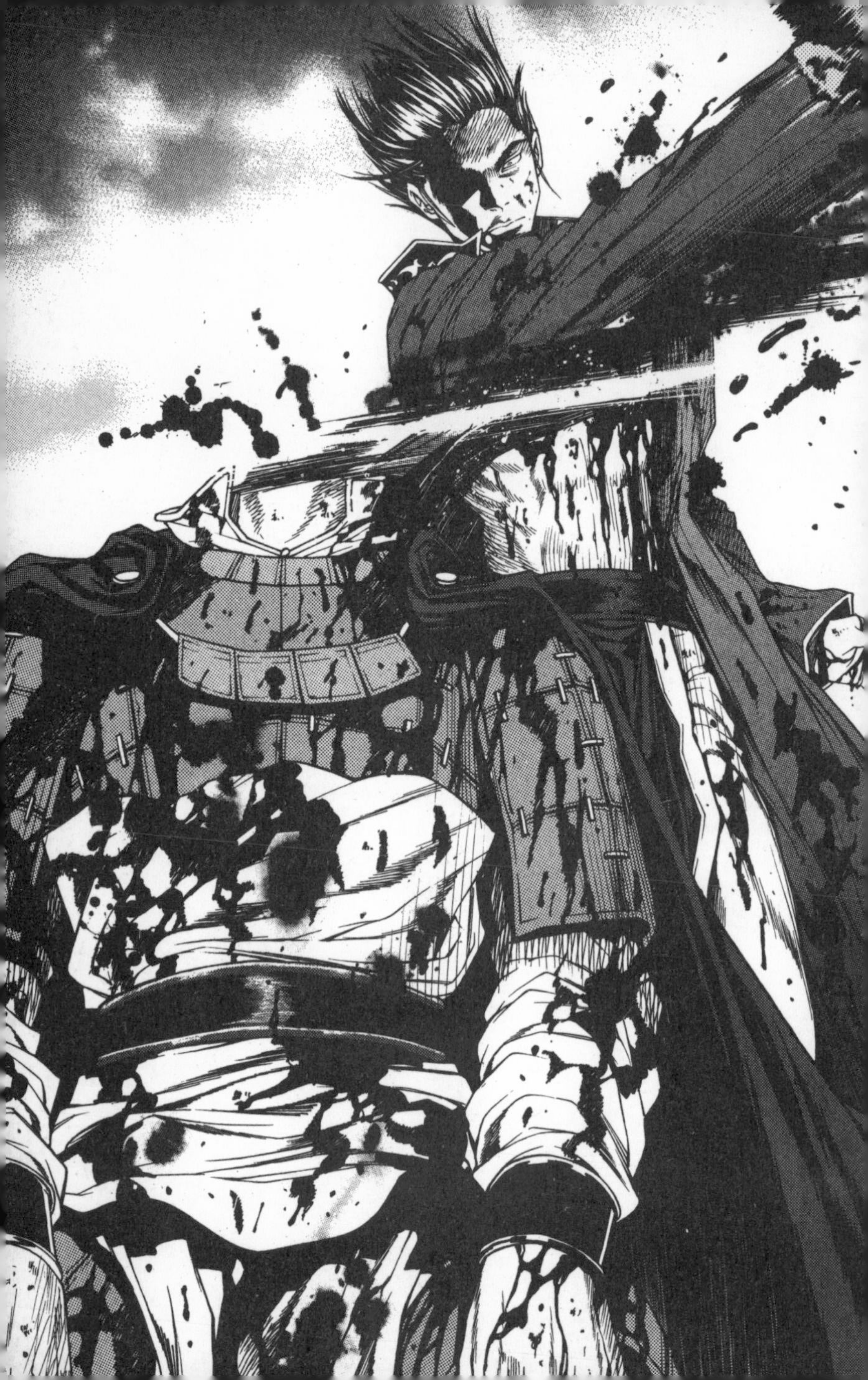

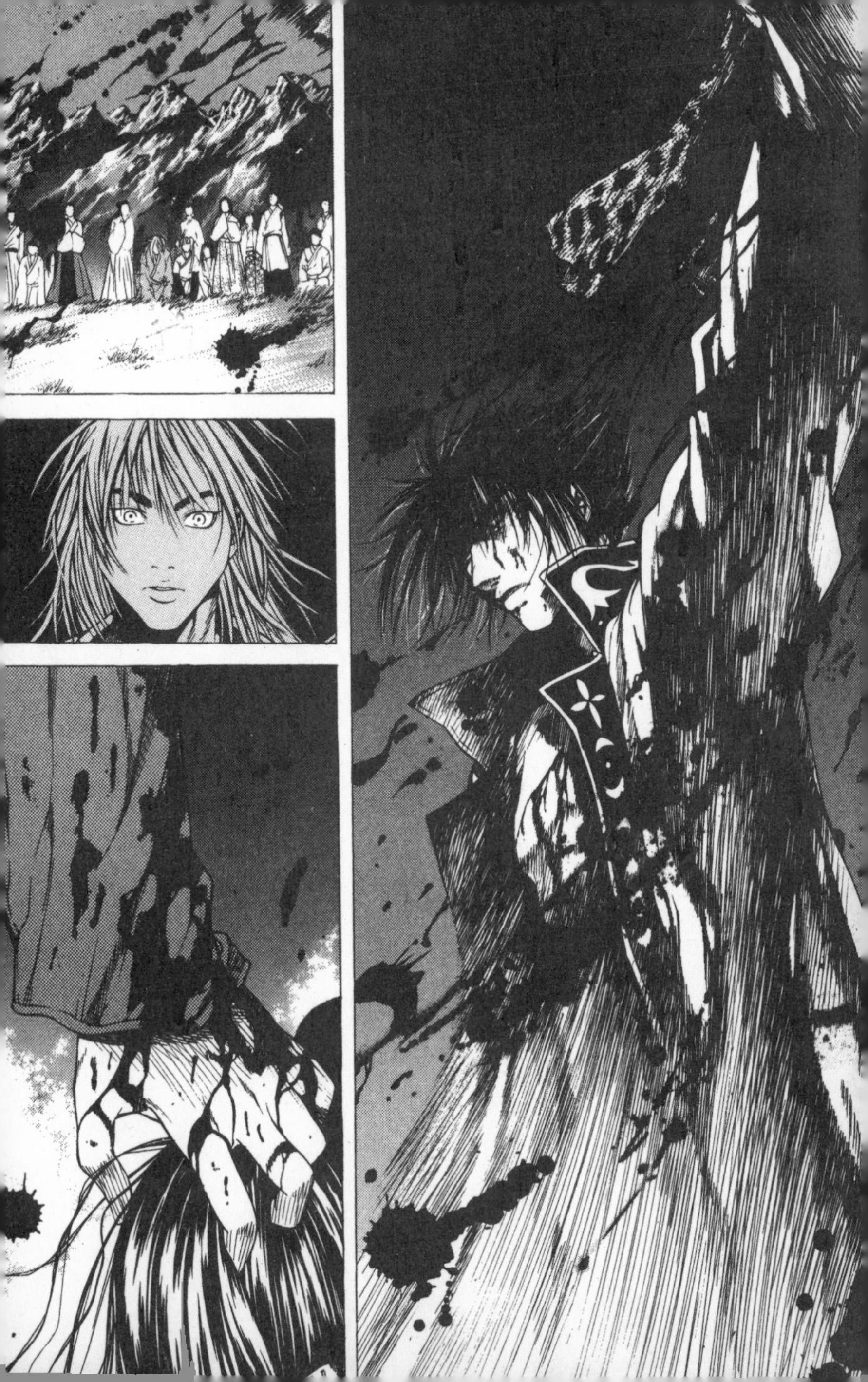

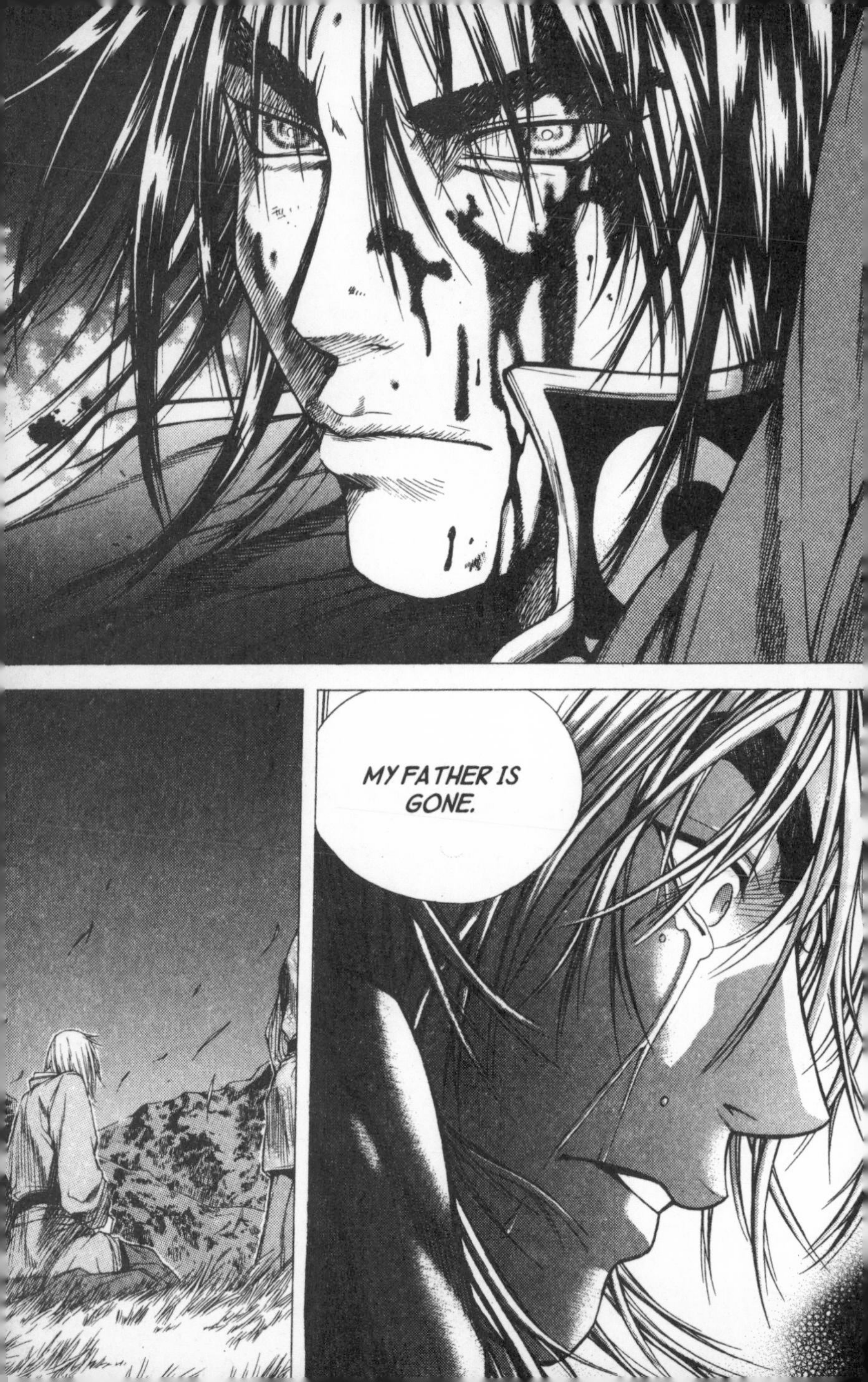
MY FATHER IS GONE.

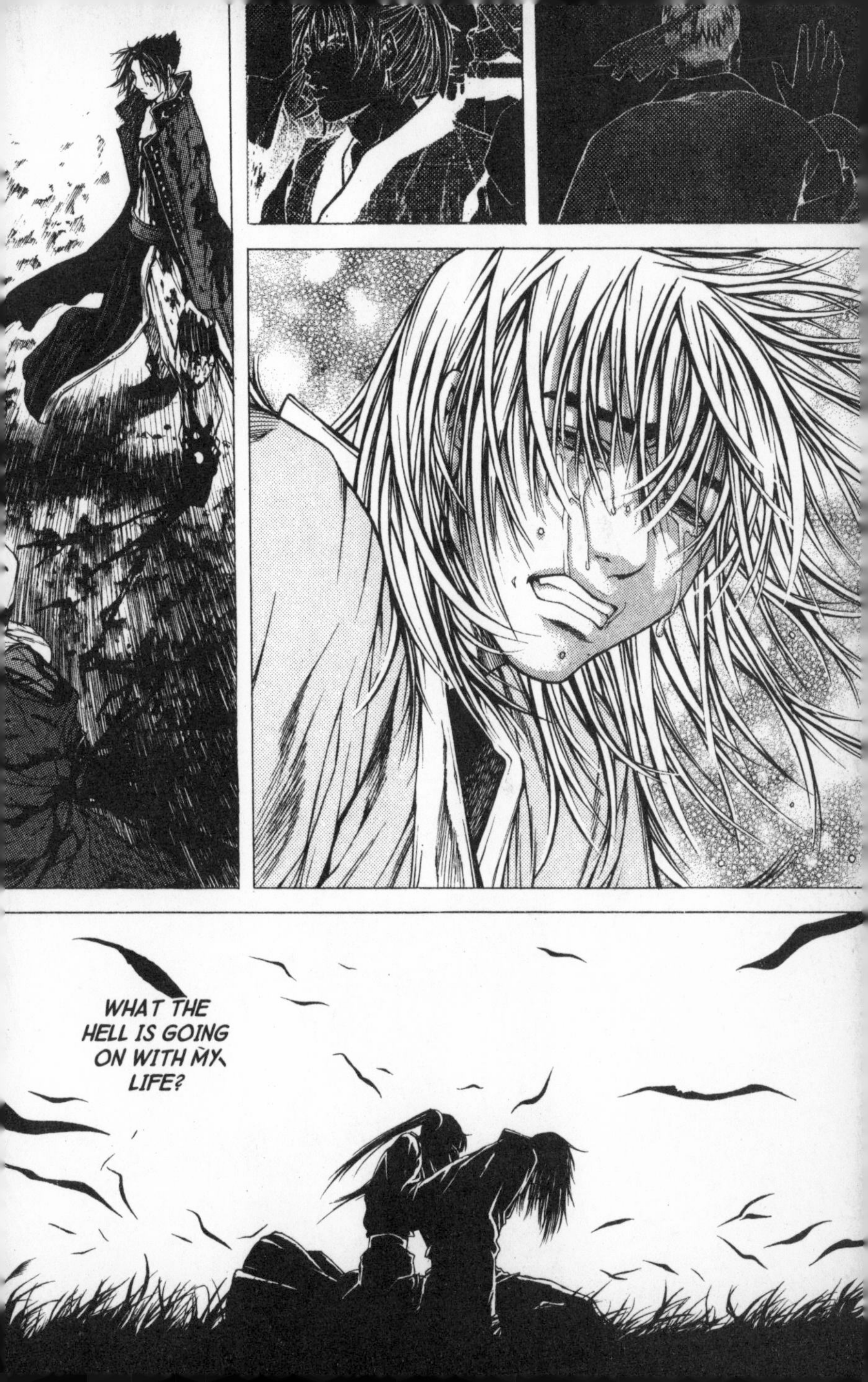
WHAT THE HELL IS GOING ON WITH MY LIFE?

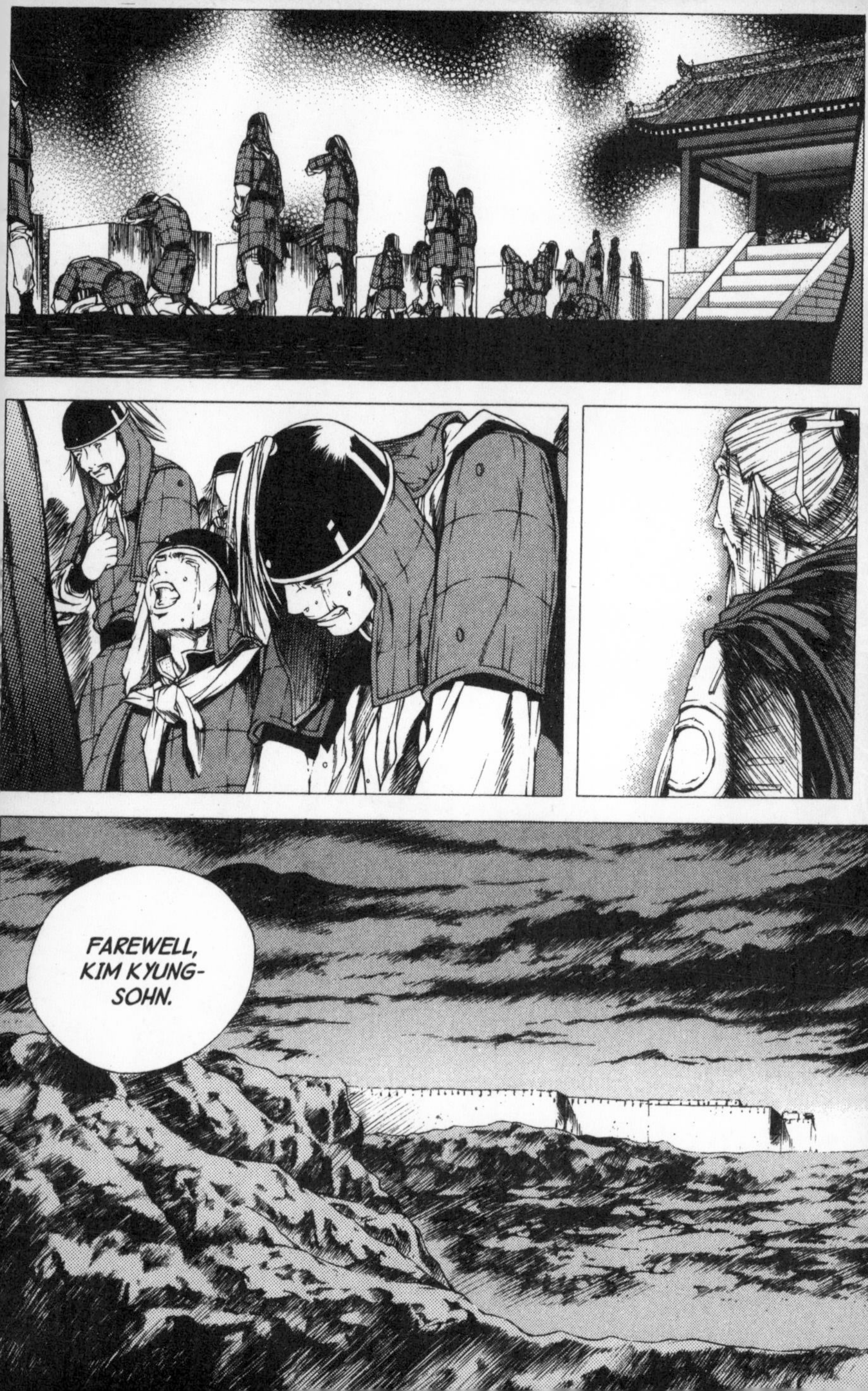
FAREWELL, KIM KYUNG-SOHN.

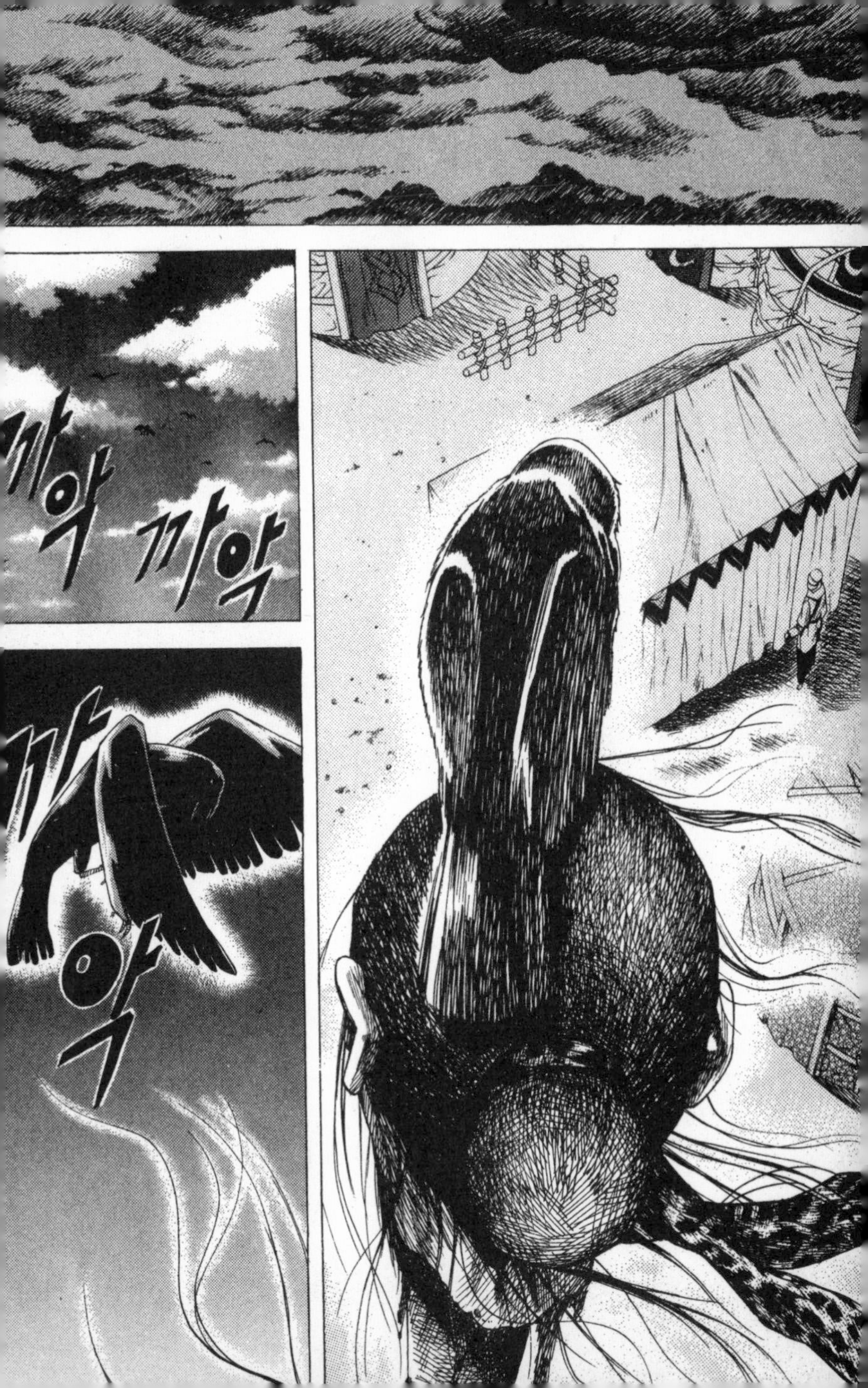
까악 까악
까악

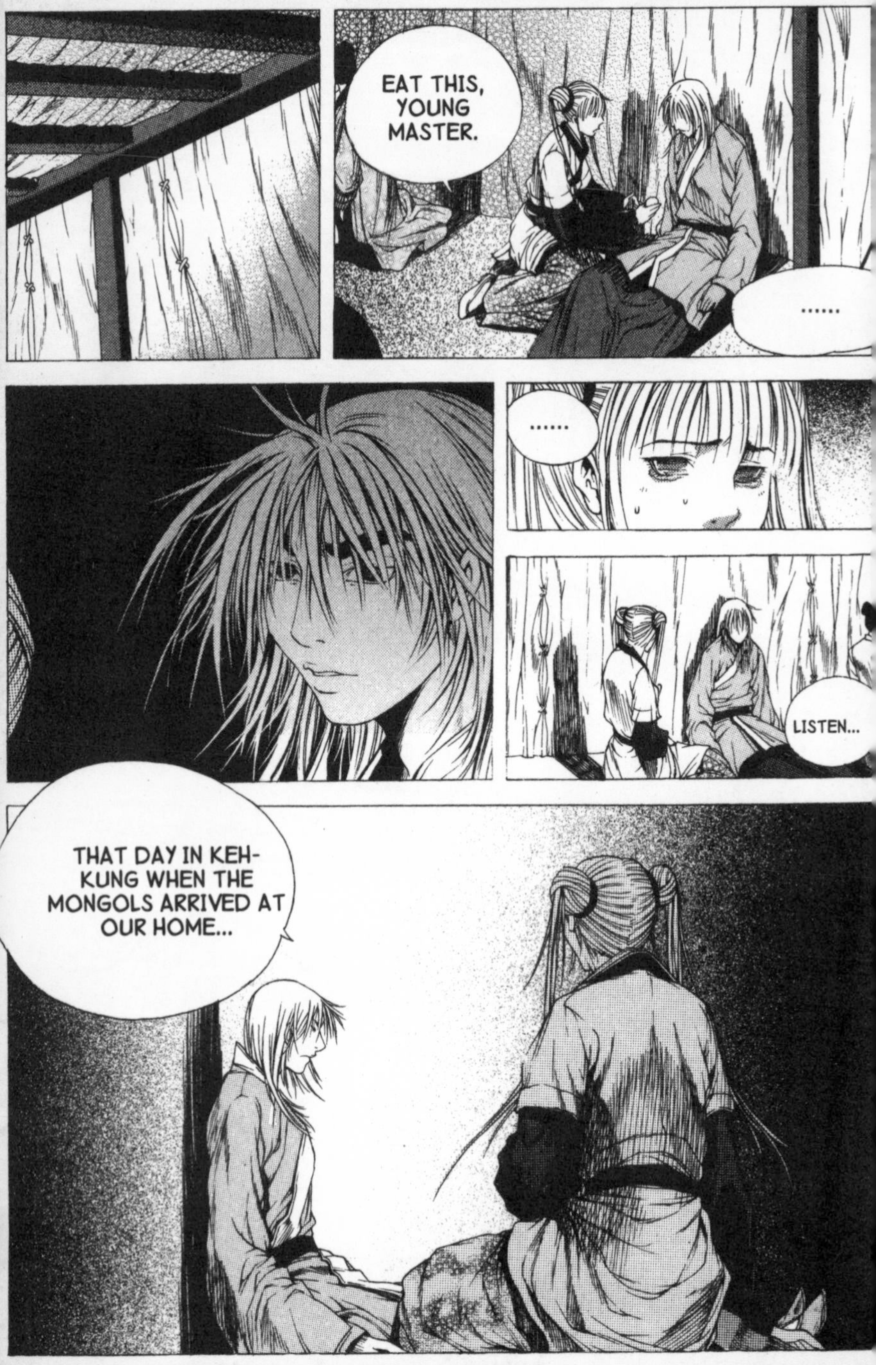
EAT THIS, YOUNG MASTER.
......
......
LISTEN...
THAT DAY IN KEH-KUNG WHEN THE MONGOLS ARRIVED AT OUR HOME...

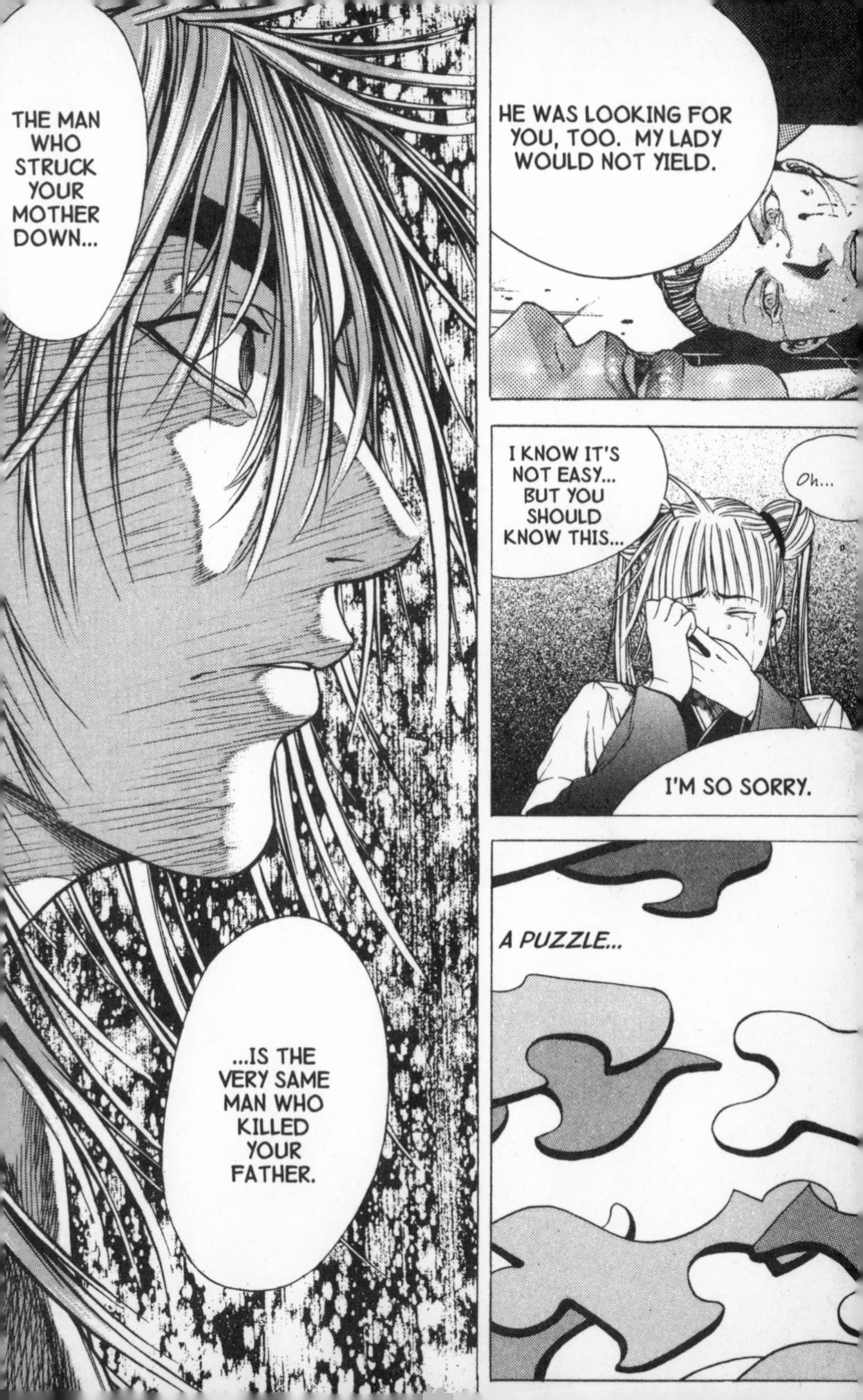
THE MAN WHO STRUCK YOUR MOTHER DOWN...
...IS THE VERY SAME MAN WHO KILLED YOUR FATHER.
HE WAS LOOKING FOR YOU, TOO. MY LADY WOULD NOT YIELD.
I KNOW IT'S NOT EASY... BUT YOU SHOULD KNOW THIS...
Oh...
I'M SO SORRY.
A PUZZLE...

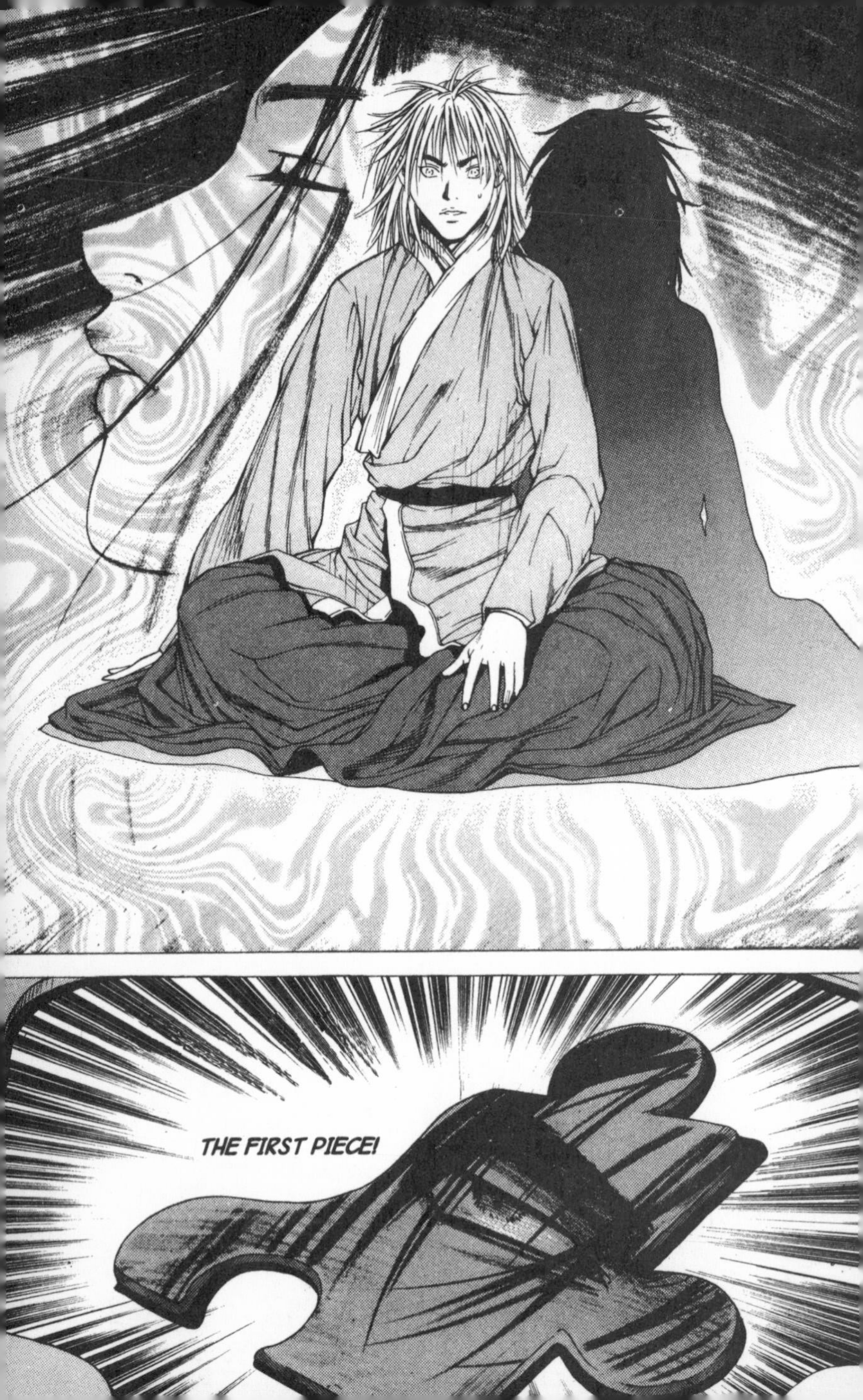
THE FIRST PIECE!

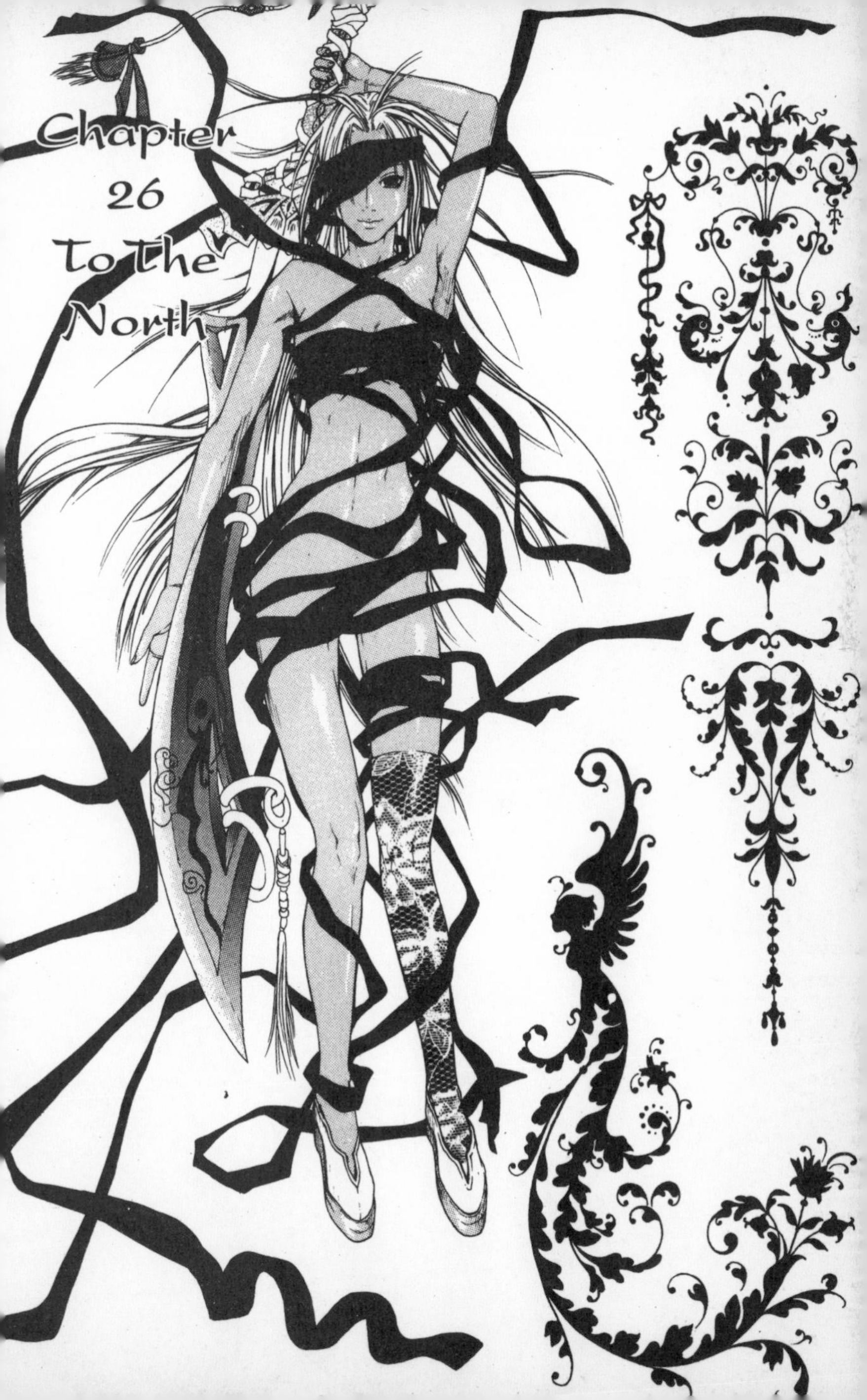
Chapter 26
To the North

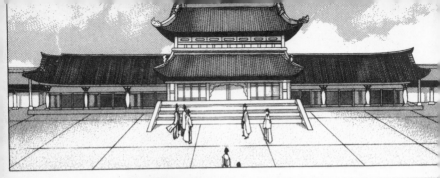

ISN'T THAT HONG DAE-WON AND HIS SON BOCK-WON?

SO IT IS THEY WHO WERE MADE DARUGACHI.

Darugachi - Position instituted by the Mongols to control a conquered area.

LOOK AT THEM FLAUNTING THEIR POWER.

IT IS SAID THAT JO ZHU-CHANG IS SENDING OFF THE MONGOLS.

OH? A TRAITOR SENDS HOME THE INVADERS? WHILE THE BIGGEST TRAITOR SITS ATOP THE ROYAL COURT?

OUR COUNTRY'S SPIRIT IS WEAK...

IF WE PERMIT THIS TREACHERY, MORE WILL LIKELY FOLLOW.

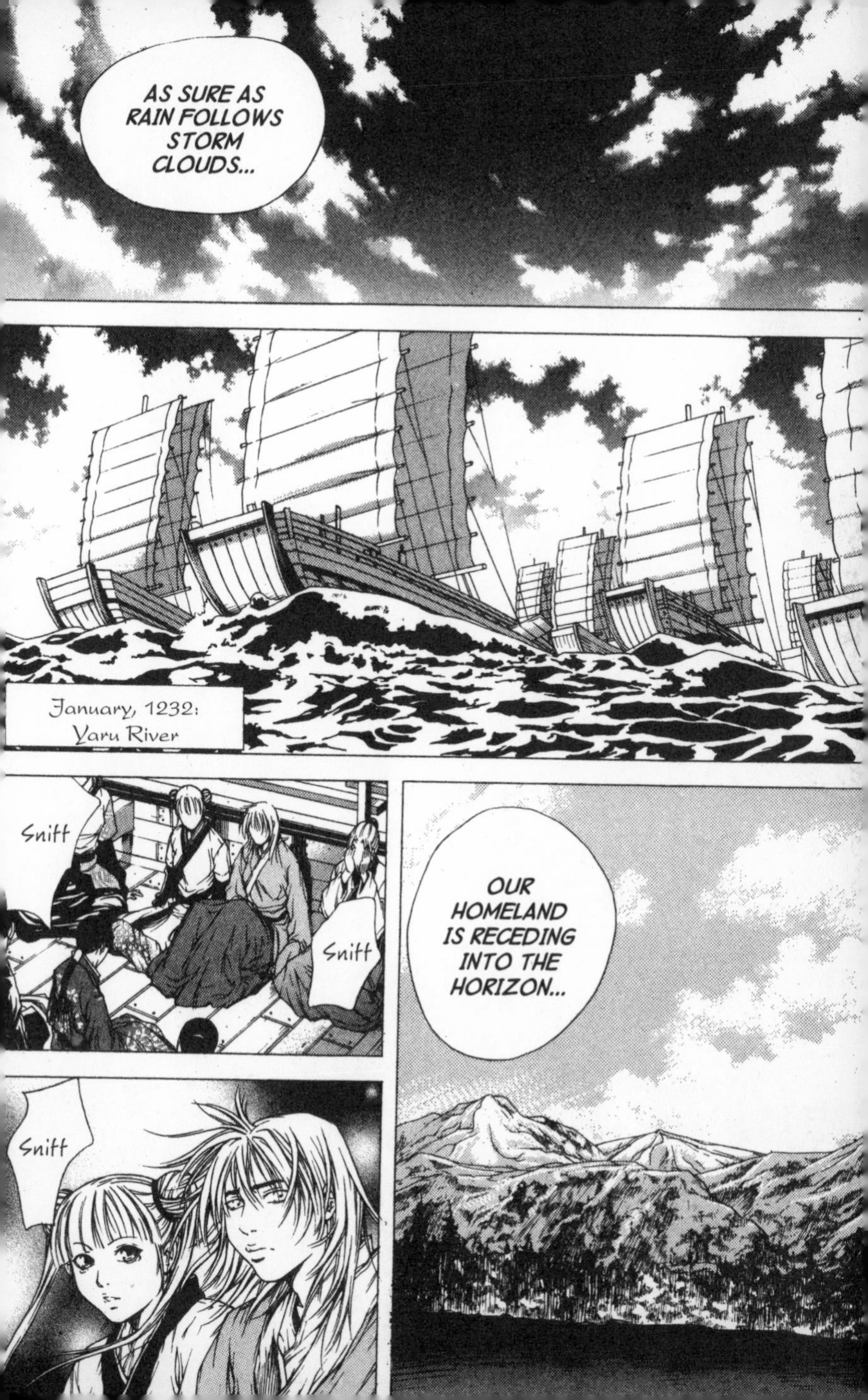
AS SURE AS RAIN FOLLOWS STORM CLOUDS...
January, 1232: Yaru River
Sniff
Sniff
Sniff
OUR HOMELAND IS RECEDING INTO THE HORIZON...

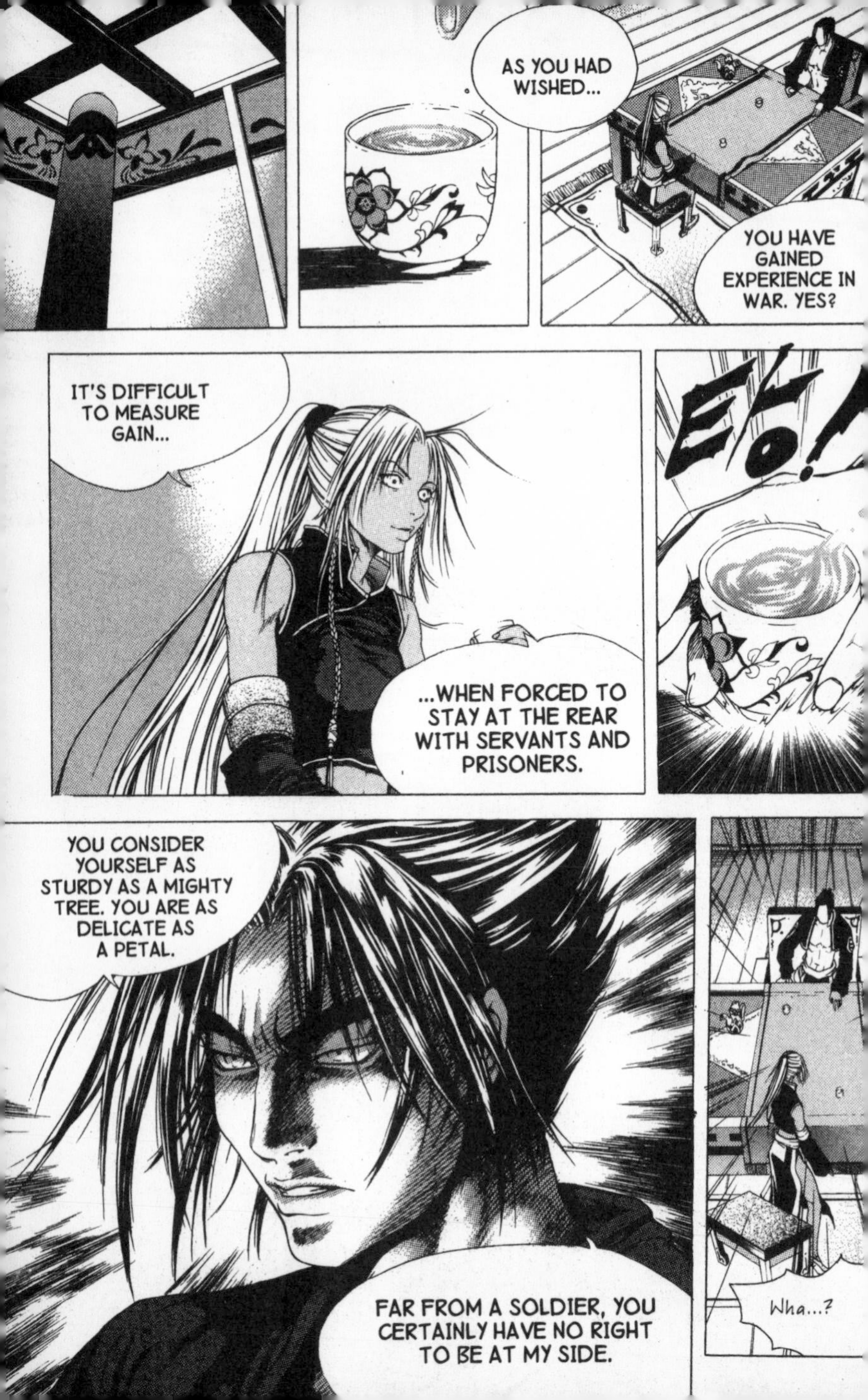
AS YOU HAD WISHED...
YOU HAVE GAINED EXPERIENCE IN WAR. YES?
IT'S DIFFICULT TO MEASURE GAIN...
...WHEN FORCED TO STAY AT THE REAR WITH SERVANTS AND PRISONERS.
EKO!
YOU CONSIDER YOURSELF AS STURDY AS A MIGHTY TREE. YOU ARE AS DELICATE AS A PETAL.
FAR FROM A SOLDIER, YOU CERTAINLY HAVE NO RIGHT TO BE AT MY SIDE.
Wha...?

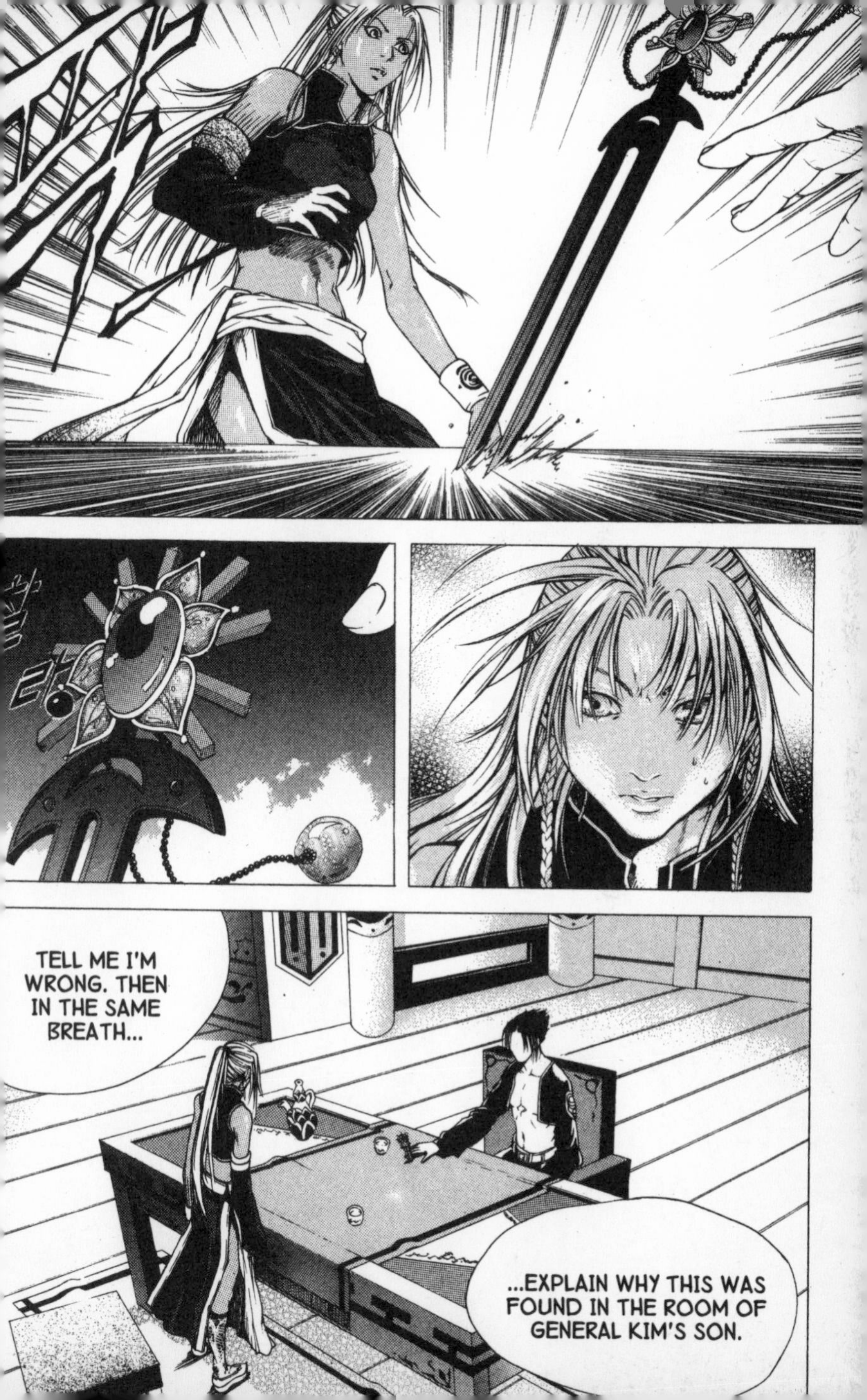
TELL ME I'M WRONG. THEN IN THE SAME BREATH...
...EXPLAIN WHY THIS WAS FOUND IN THE ROOM OF GENERAL KIM'S SON.

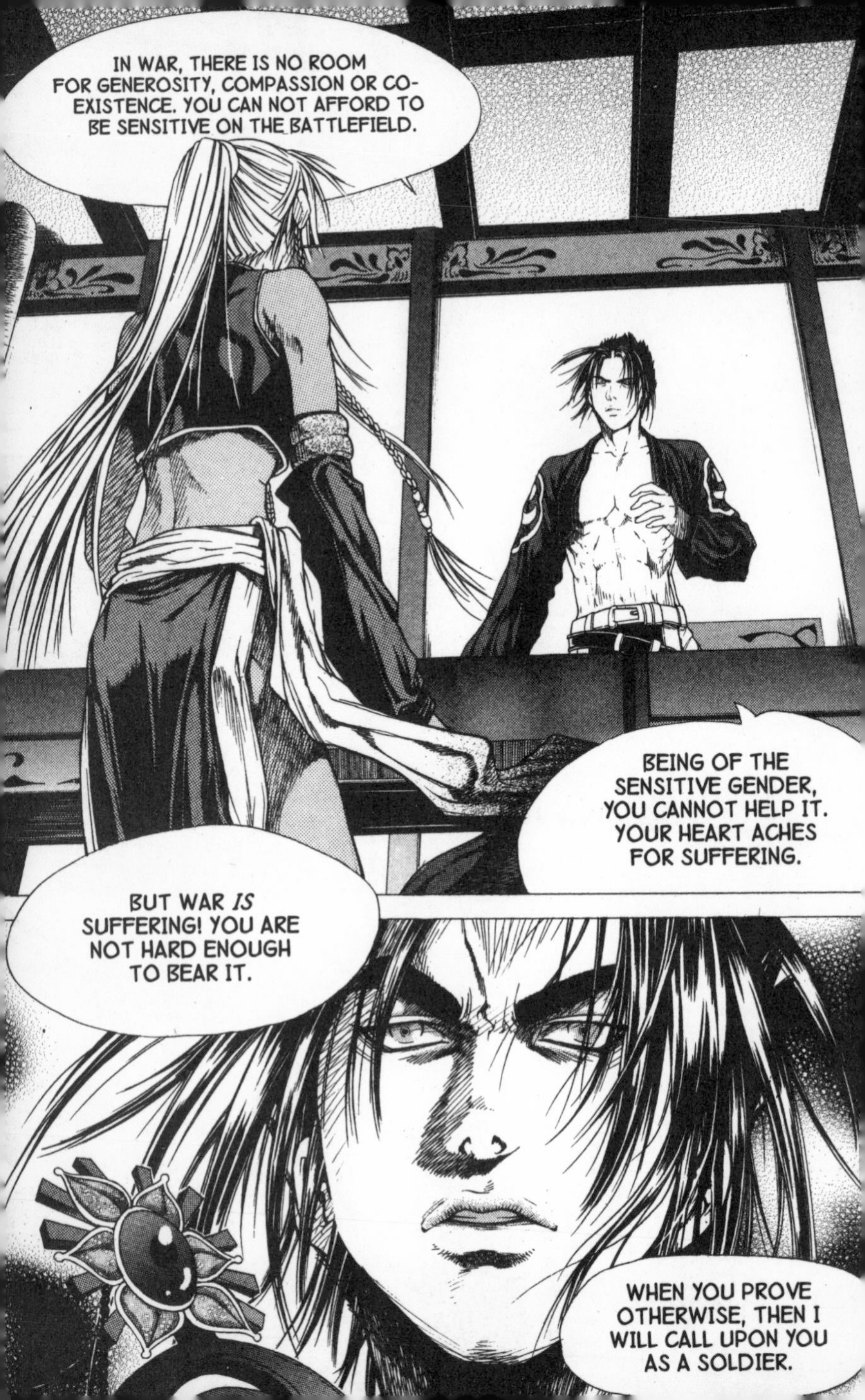
IN WAR, THERE IS NO ROOM FOR GENEROSITY, COMPASSION OR CO-EXISTENCE. YOU CAN NOT AFFORD TO BE SENSITIVE ON THE BATTLEFIELD.
BEING OF THE SENSITIVE GENDER, YOU CANNOT HELP IT. YOUR HEART ACHES FOR SUFFERING.
BUT WAR *IS* SUFFERING! YOU ARE NOT HARD ENOUGH TO BEAR IT.
WHEN YOU PROVE OTHERWISE, THEN I WILL CALL UPON YOU AS A SOLDIER.

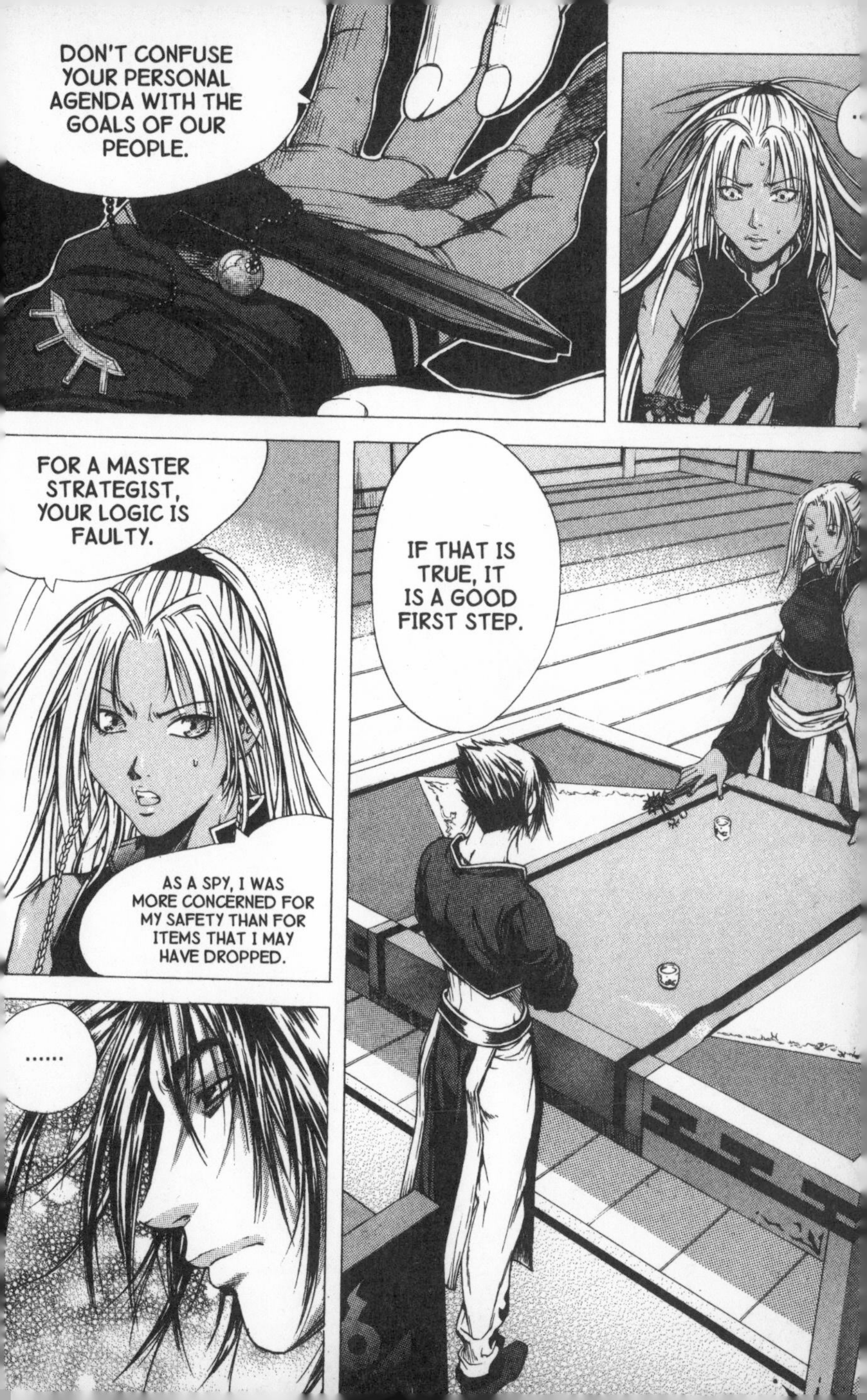
DON'T CONFUSE YOUR PERSONAL AGENDA WITH THE GOALS OF OUR PEOPLE.
..
FOR A MASTER STRATEGIST, YOUR LOGIC IS FAULTY.
AS A SPY, I WAS MORE CONCERNED FOR MY SAFETY THAN FOR ITEMS THAT I MAY HAVE DROPPED.
......
IF THAT IS TRUE, IT IS A GOOD FIRST STEP.

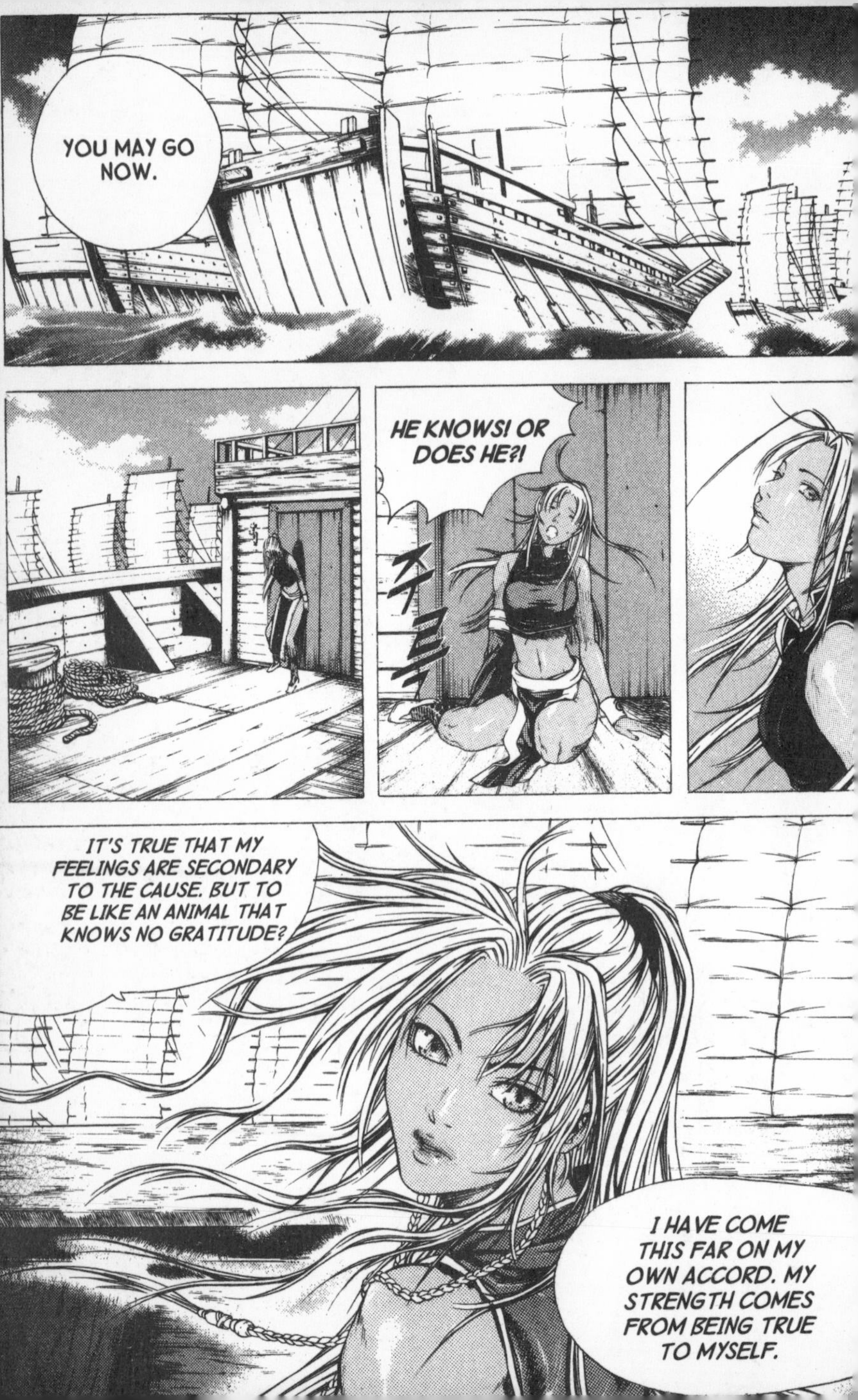
YOU MAY GO NOW.
HE KNOWS! OR DOES HE?!
IT'S TRUE THAT MY FEELINGS ARE SECONDARY TO THE CAUSE. BUT TO BE LIKE AN ANIMAL THAT KNOWS NO GRATITUDE?
I HAVE COME THIS FAR ON MY OWN ACCORD. MY STRENGTH COMES FROM BEING TRUE TO MYSELF.

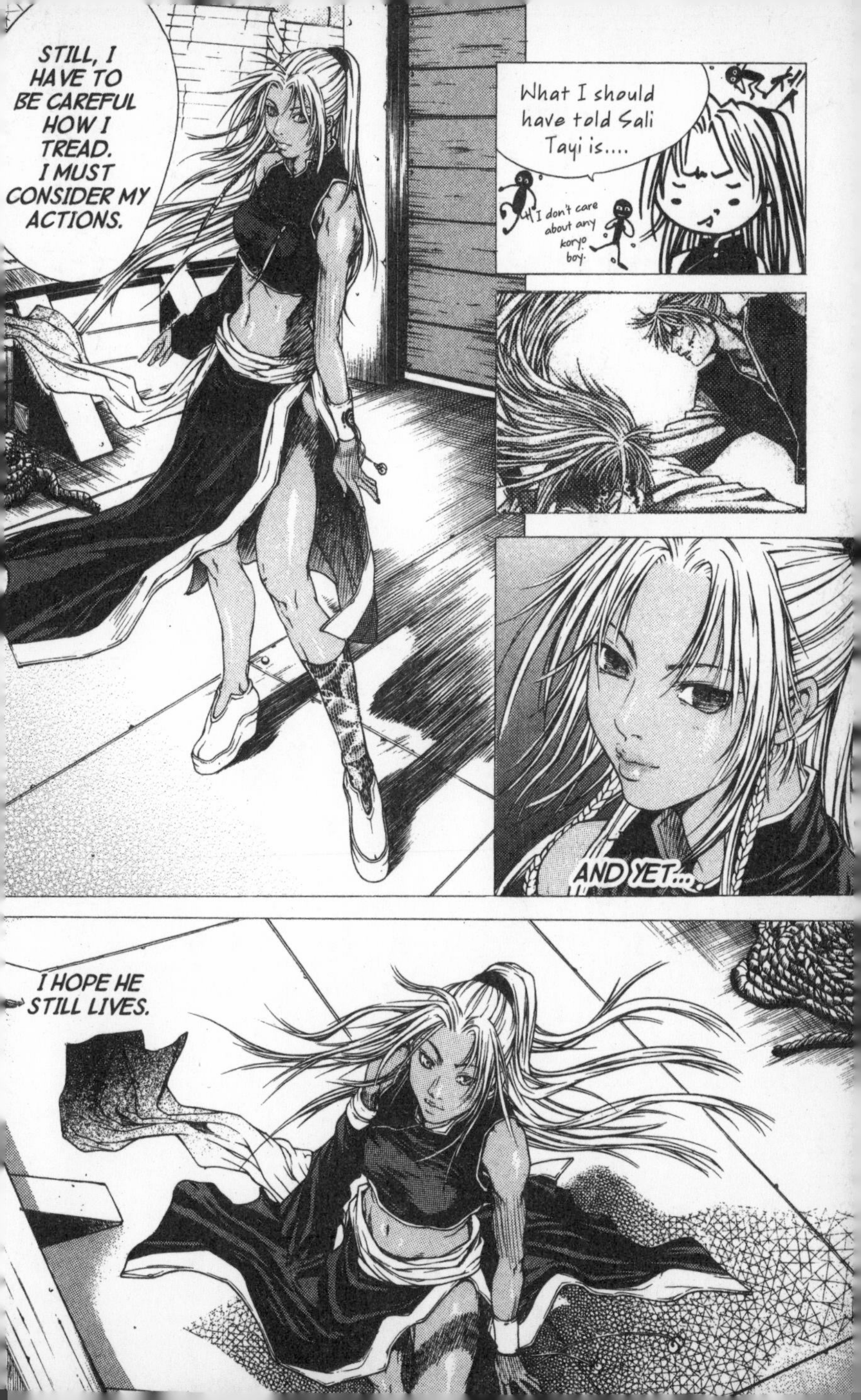

STILL, I HAVE TO BE CAREFUL HOW I TREAD. I MUST CONSIDER MY ACTIONS.
What I should have told Sali Tayi is....
I don't care about any koryo boy.
AND YET...
I HOPE HE STILL LIVES.

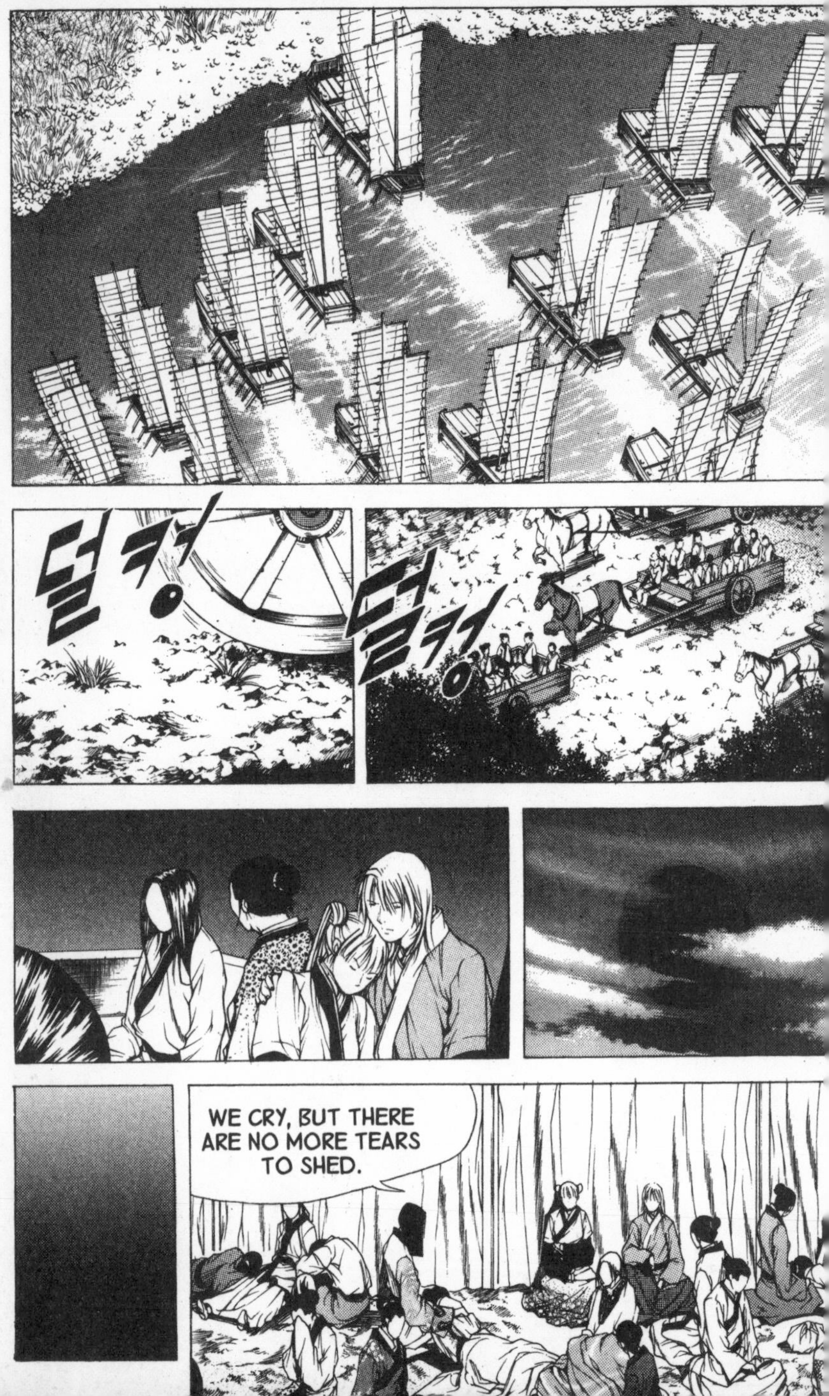
덜컹!
덜컹!
WE CRY, BUT THERE ARE NO MORE TEARS TO SHED.

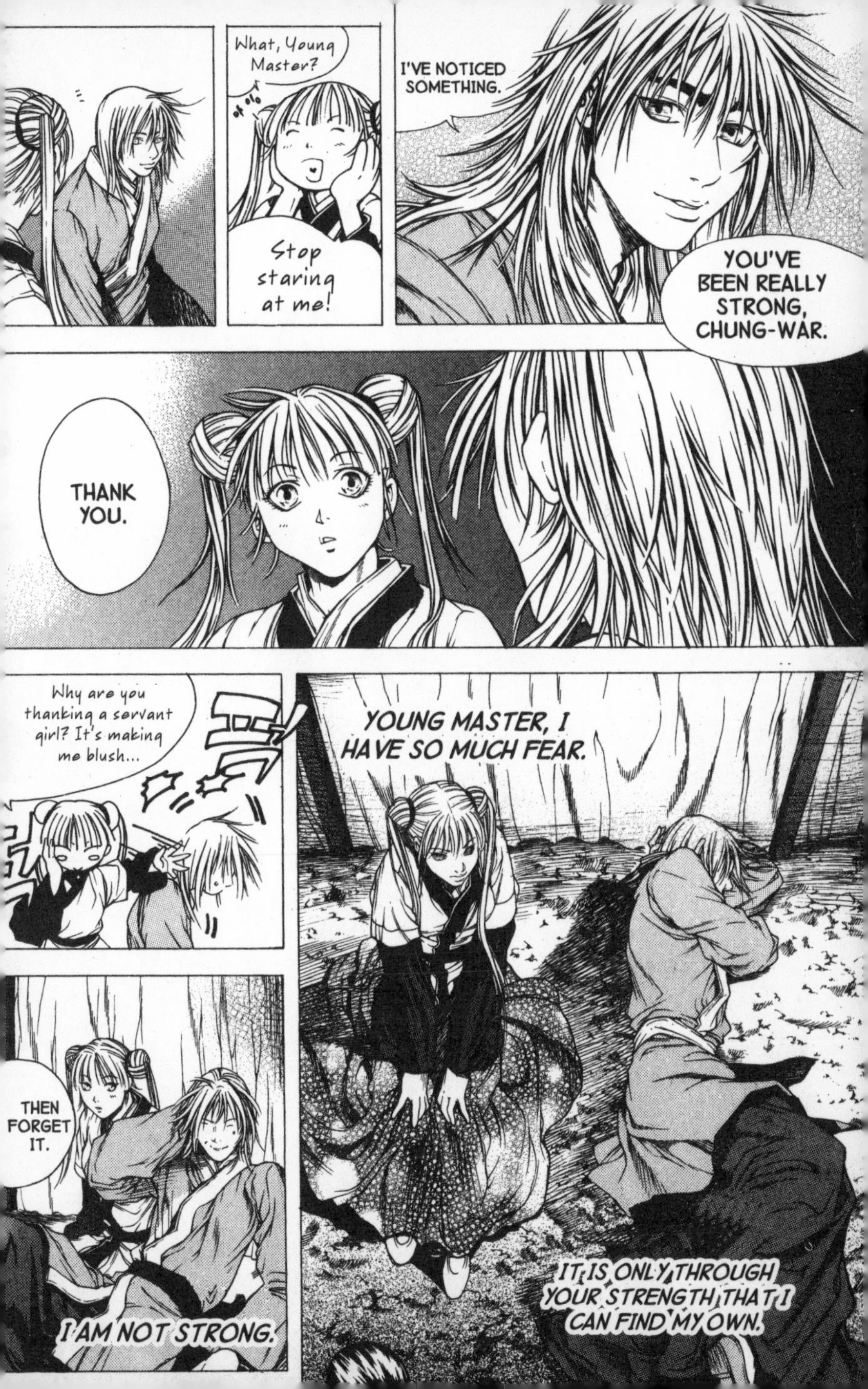
What, Young Master?
Stop staring at me!
I'VE NOTICED SOMETHING.
YOU'VE BEEN REALLY STRONG, CHUNG-WAR.
THANK YOU.
Why are you thanking a servant girl? It's making me blush...
THEN FORGET IT.
I AM NOT STRONG.
YOUNG MASTER, I HAVE SO MUCH FEAR.
IT IS ONLY THROUGH YOUR STRENGTH THAT I CAN FIND MY OWN.

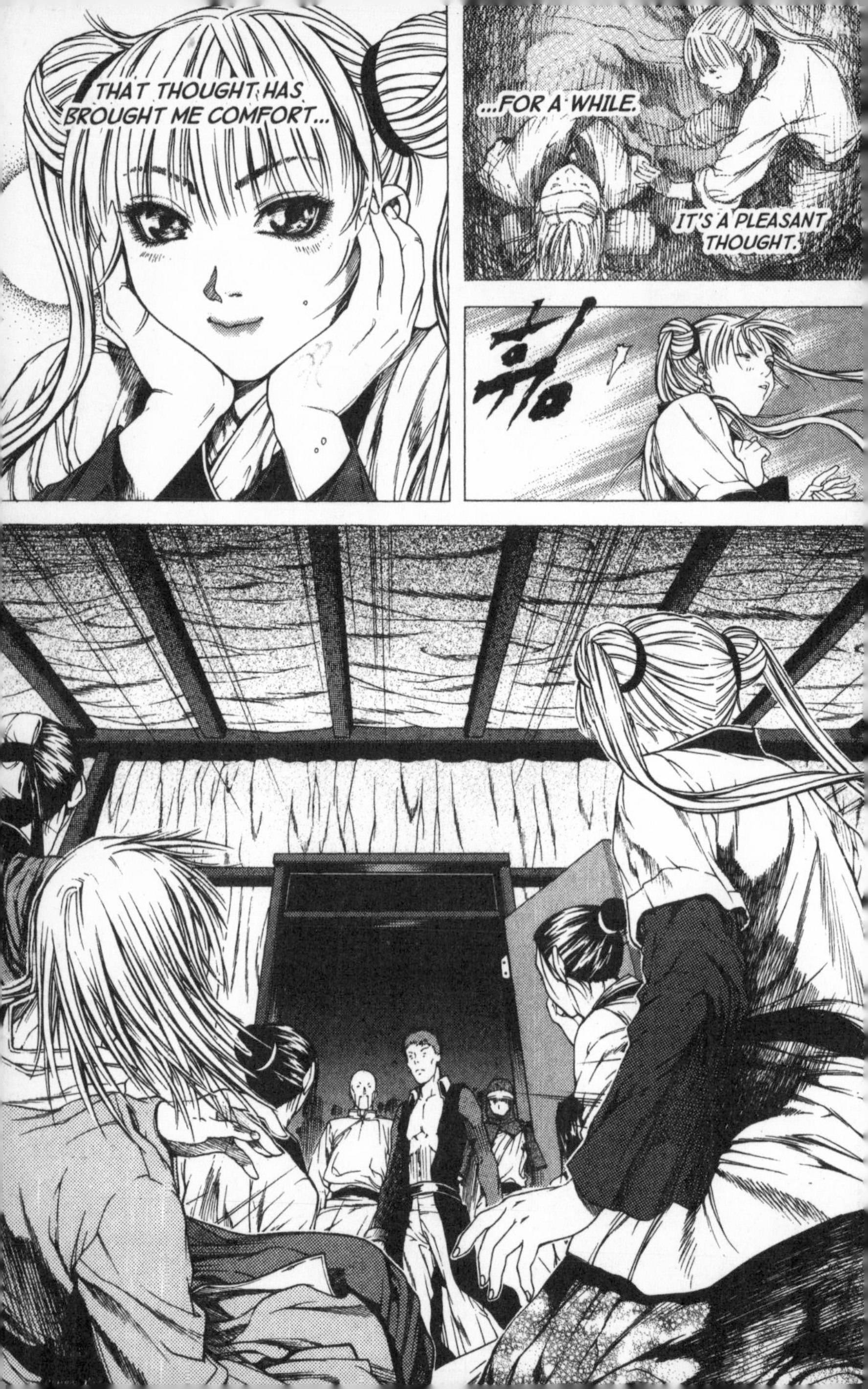
THAT THOUGHT HAS BROUGHT ME COMFORT...
...FOR A WHILE.
IT'S A PLEASANT THOUGHT.

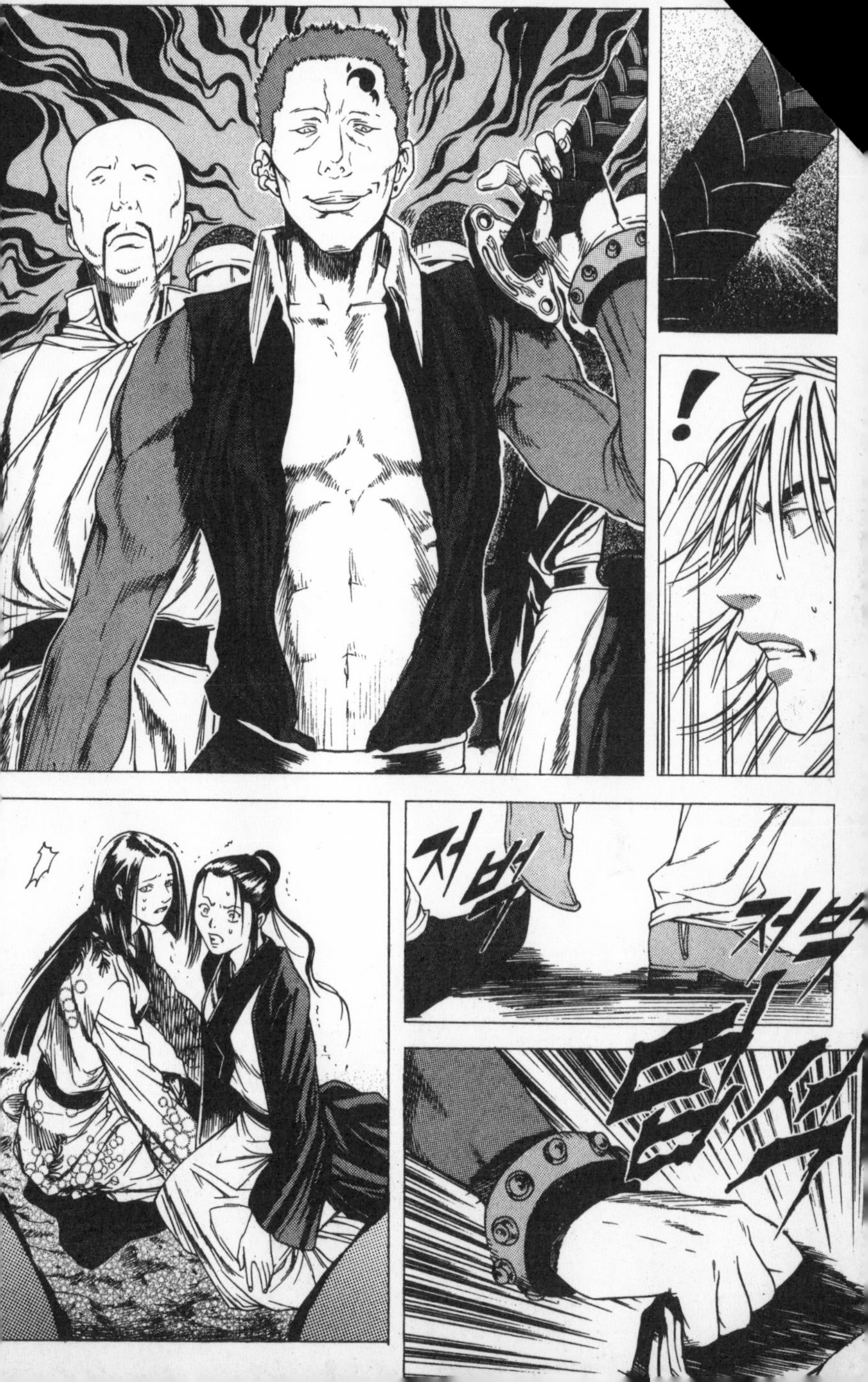
!
저벅
저벅

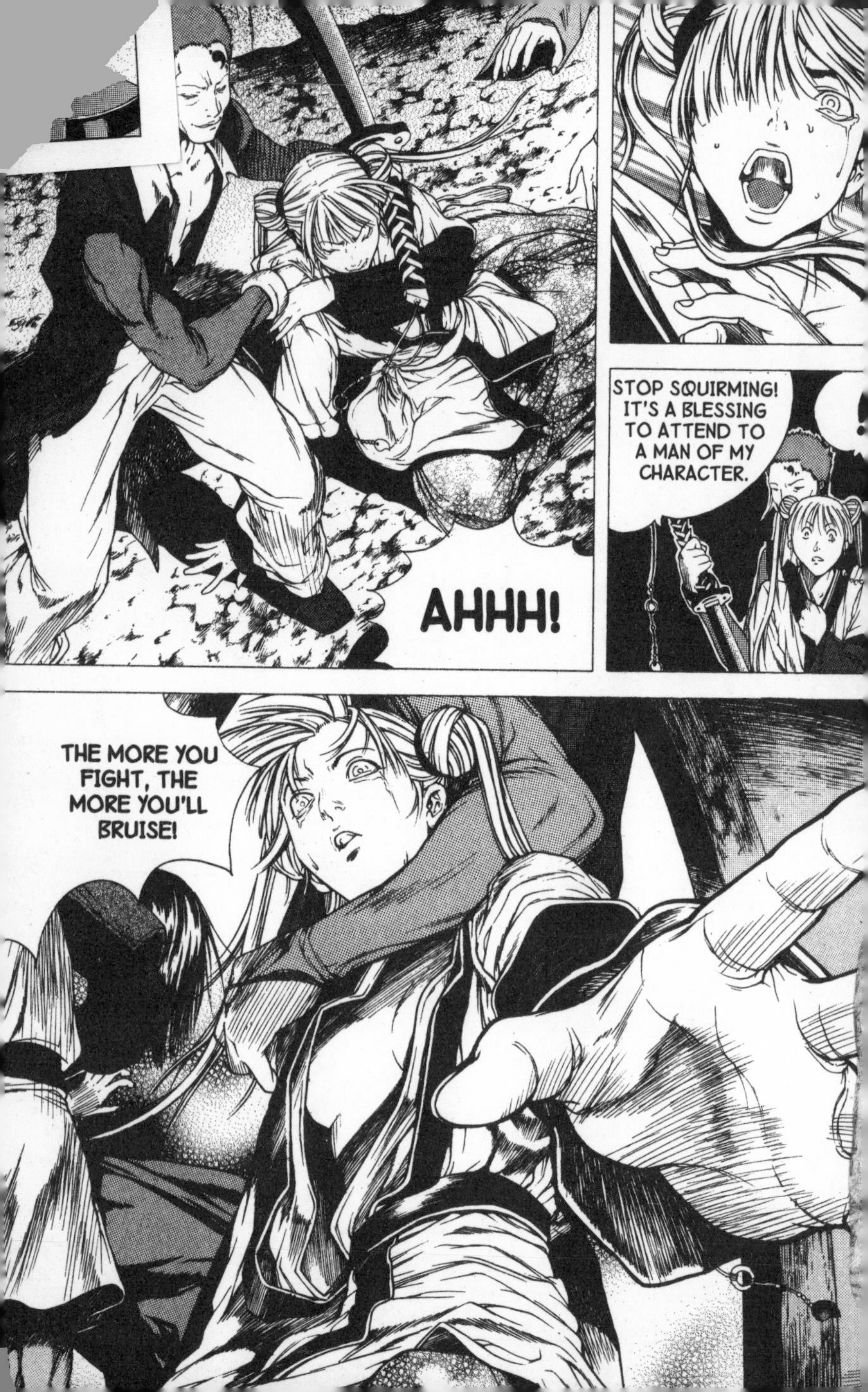
AHHH!
STOP SQUIRMING! IT'S A BLESSING TO ATTEND TO A MAN OF MY CHARACTER.
THE MORE YOU FIGHT, THE MORE YOU'LL BRUISE!

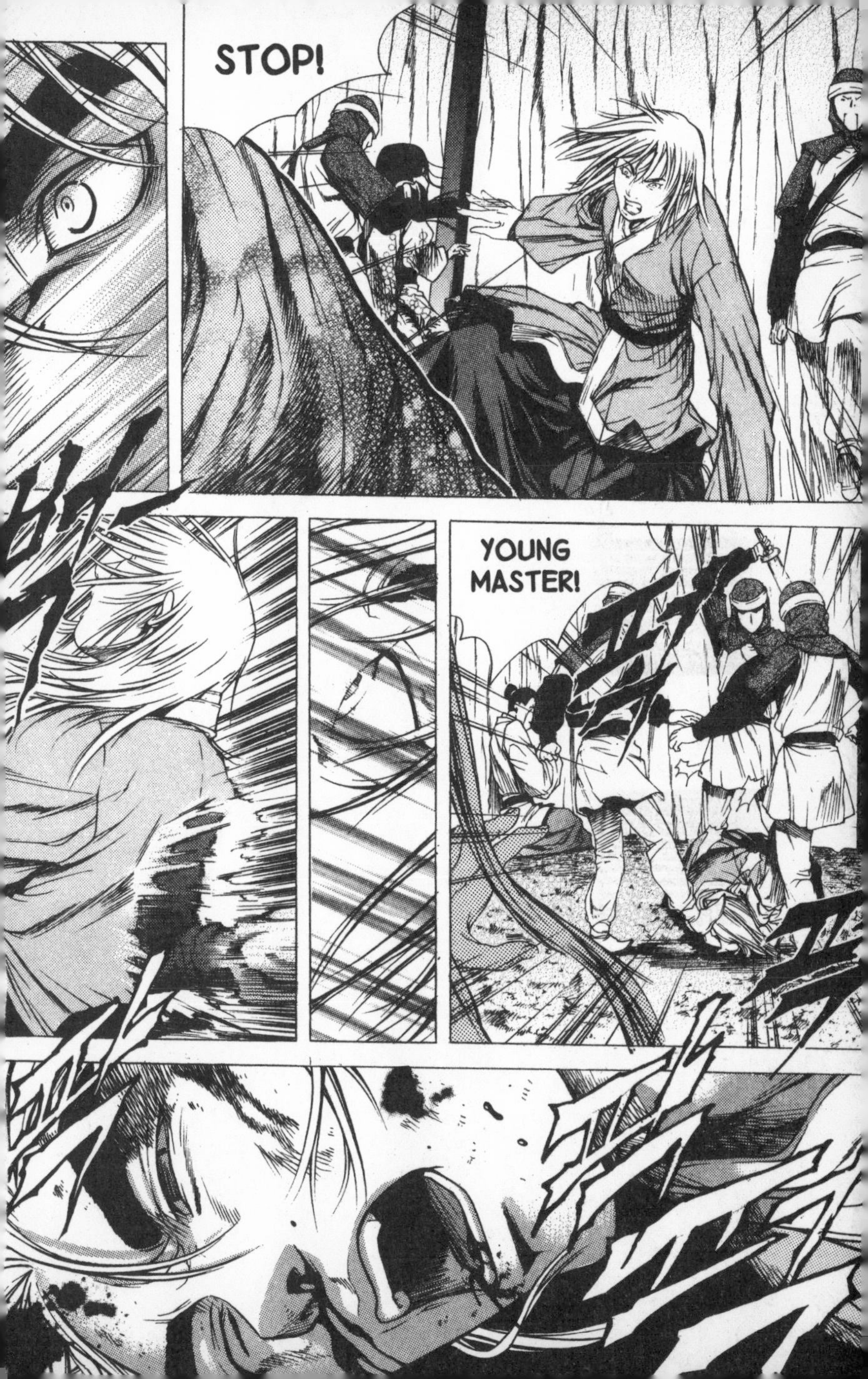
STOP!
YOUNG MASTER!

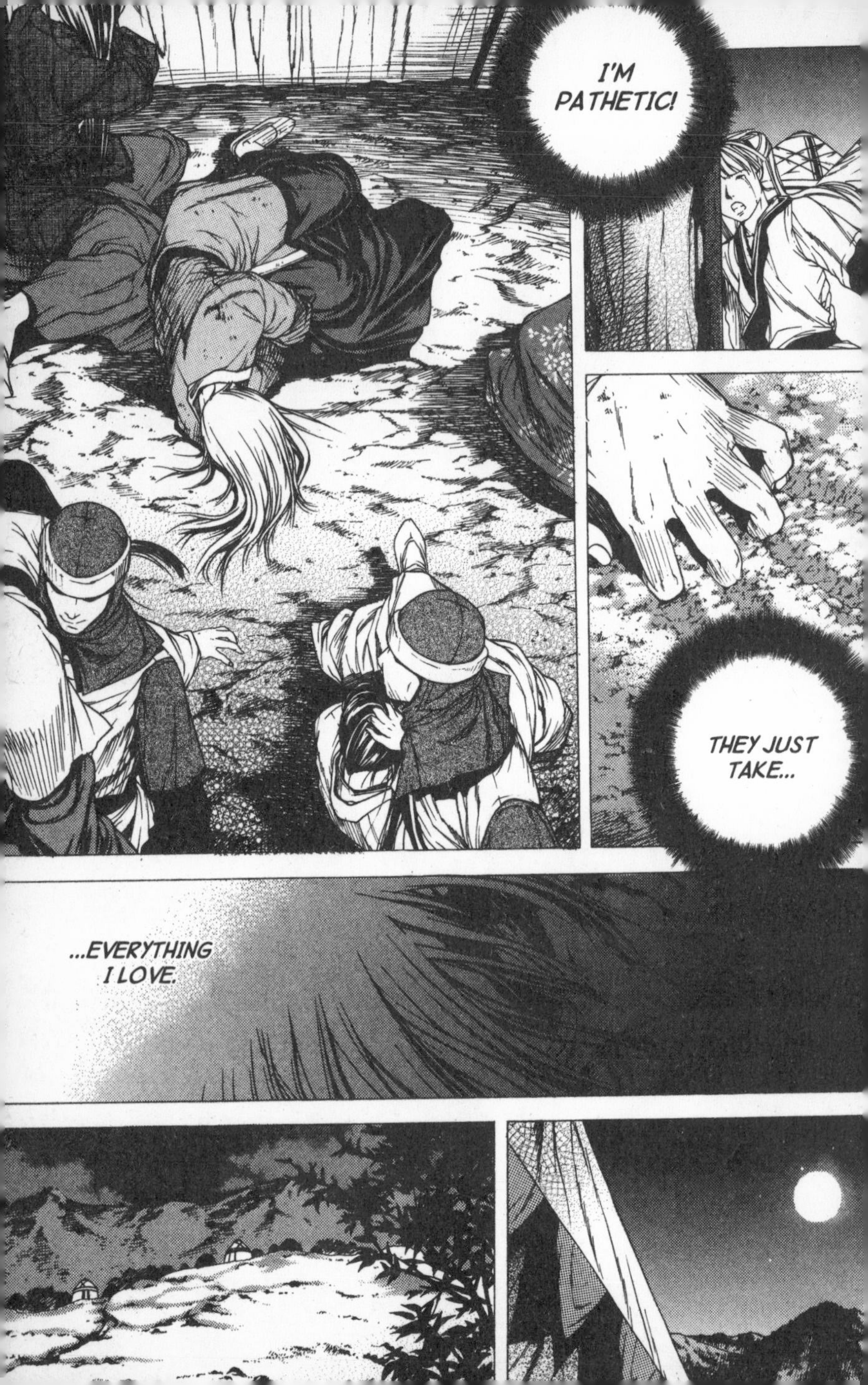
I'M PATHETIC!
THEY JUST TAKE...
...EVERYTHING I LOVE.

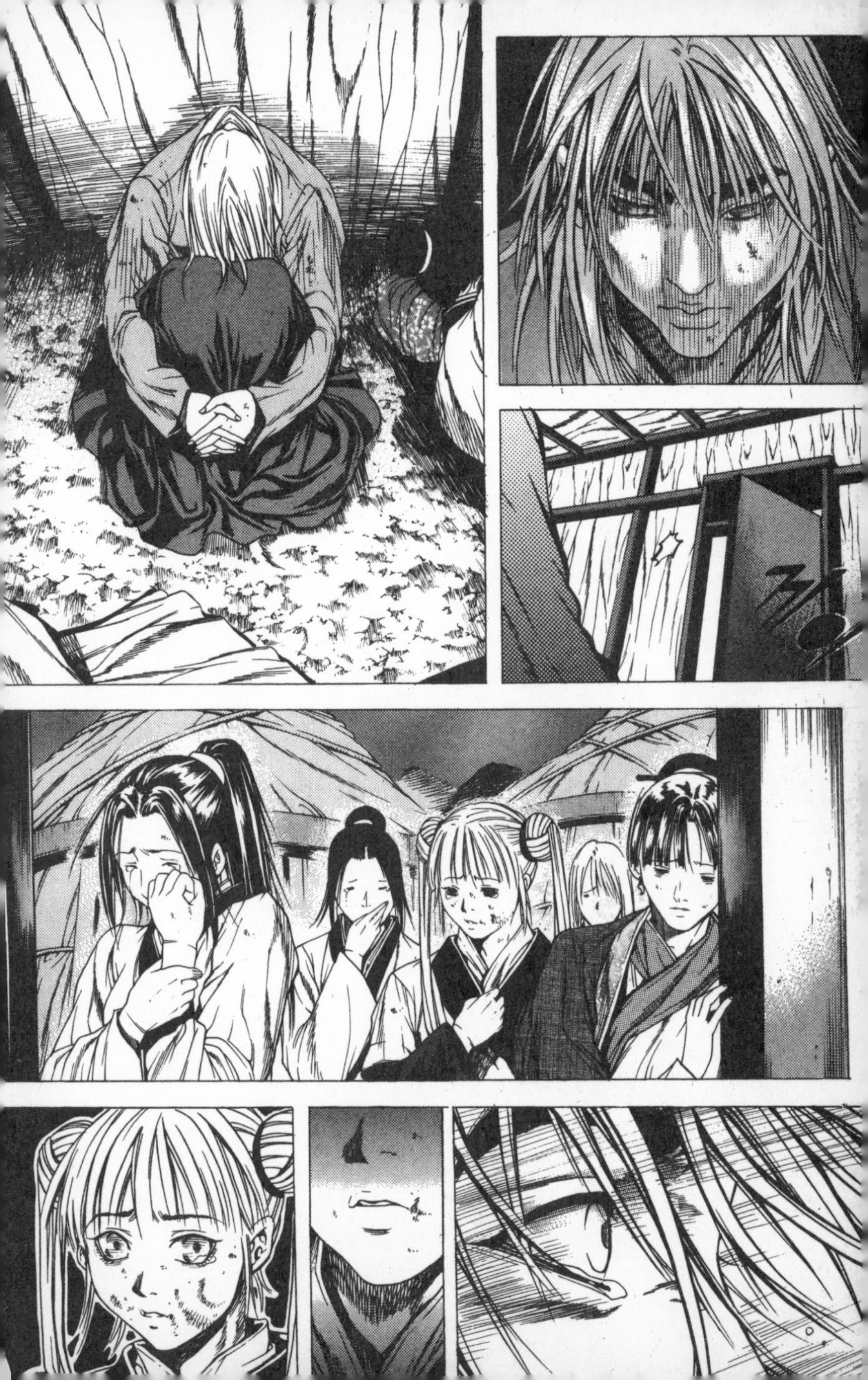

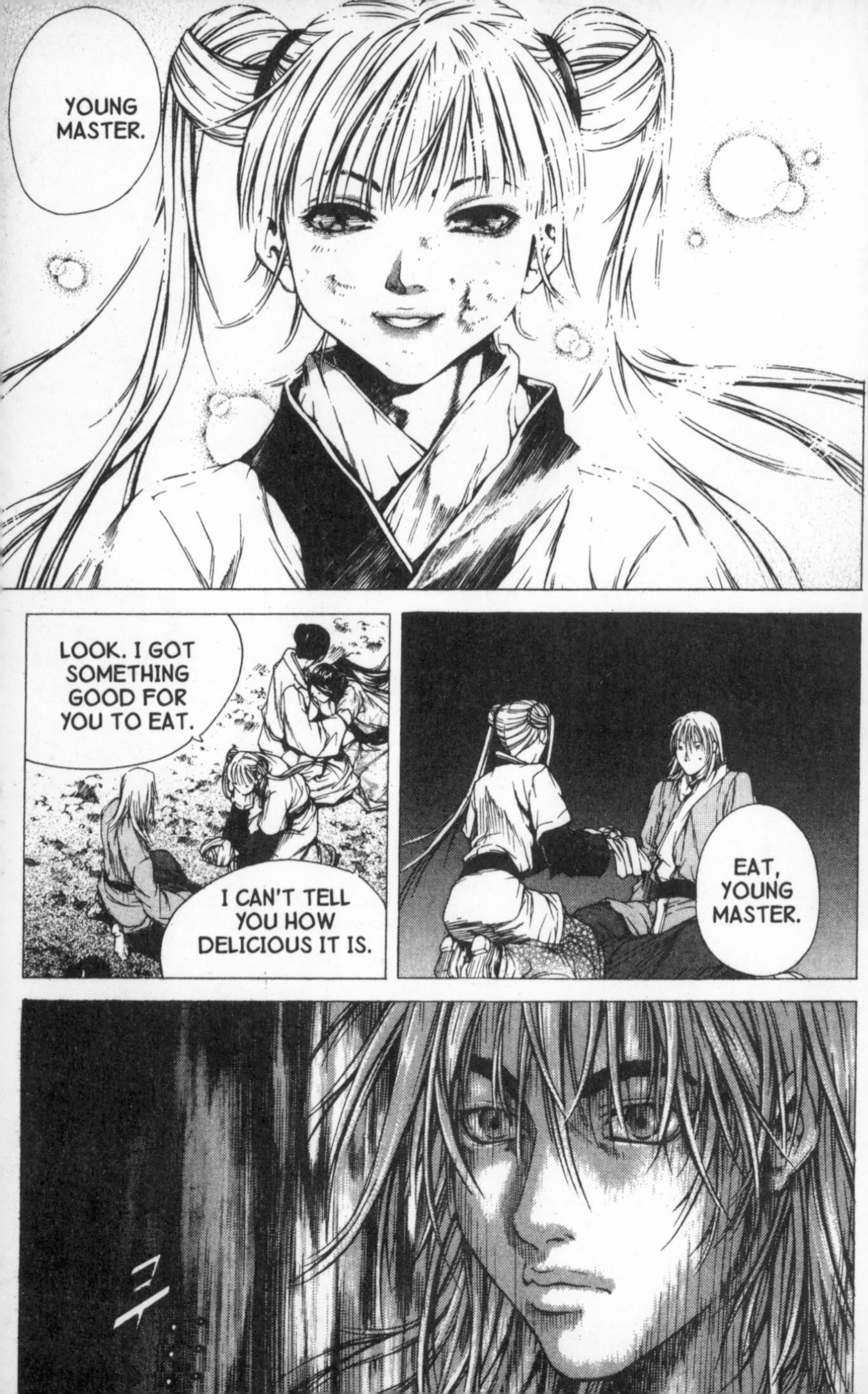
YOUNG MASTER.
LOOK. I GOT SOMETHING GOOD FOR YOU TO EAT.
I CAN'T TELL YOU HOW DELICIOUS IT IS.
EAT, YOUNG MASTER.

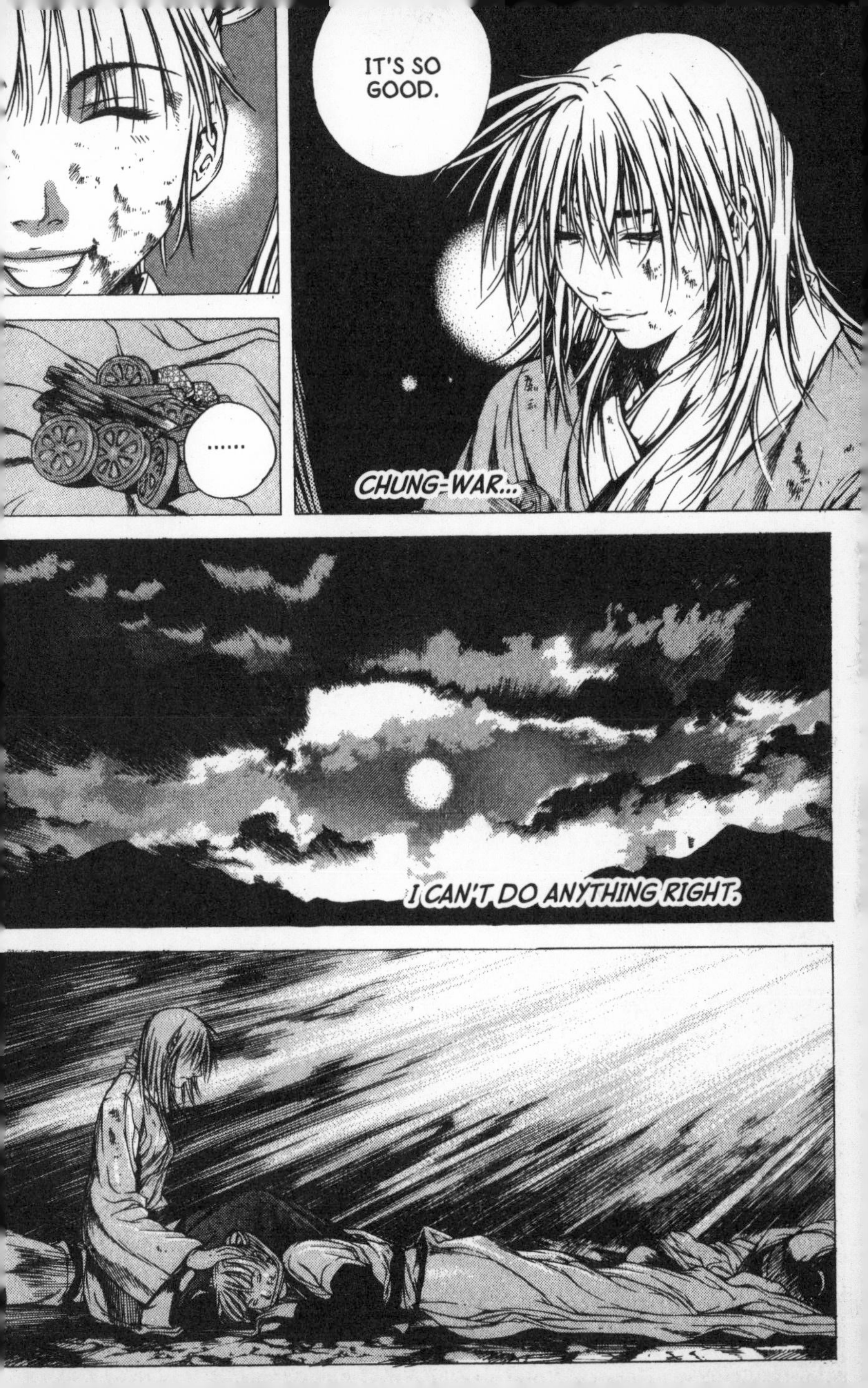
IT'S SO GOOD.
......
CHUNG-WAR...
I CAN'T DO ANYTHING RIGHT.

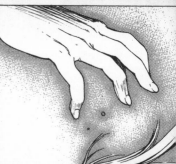

I'LL GET STRONG!

SO THEY CAN'T TAKE ANYTHING ELSE AWAY...

SO I WON'T HURT LIKE THIS...

I WILL BECOME POWERFUL!!

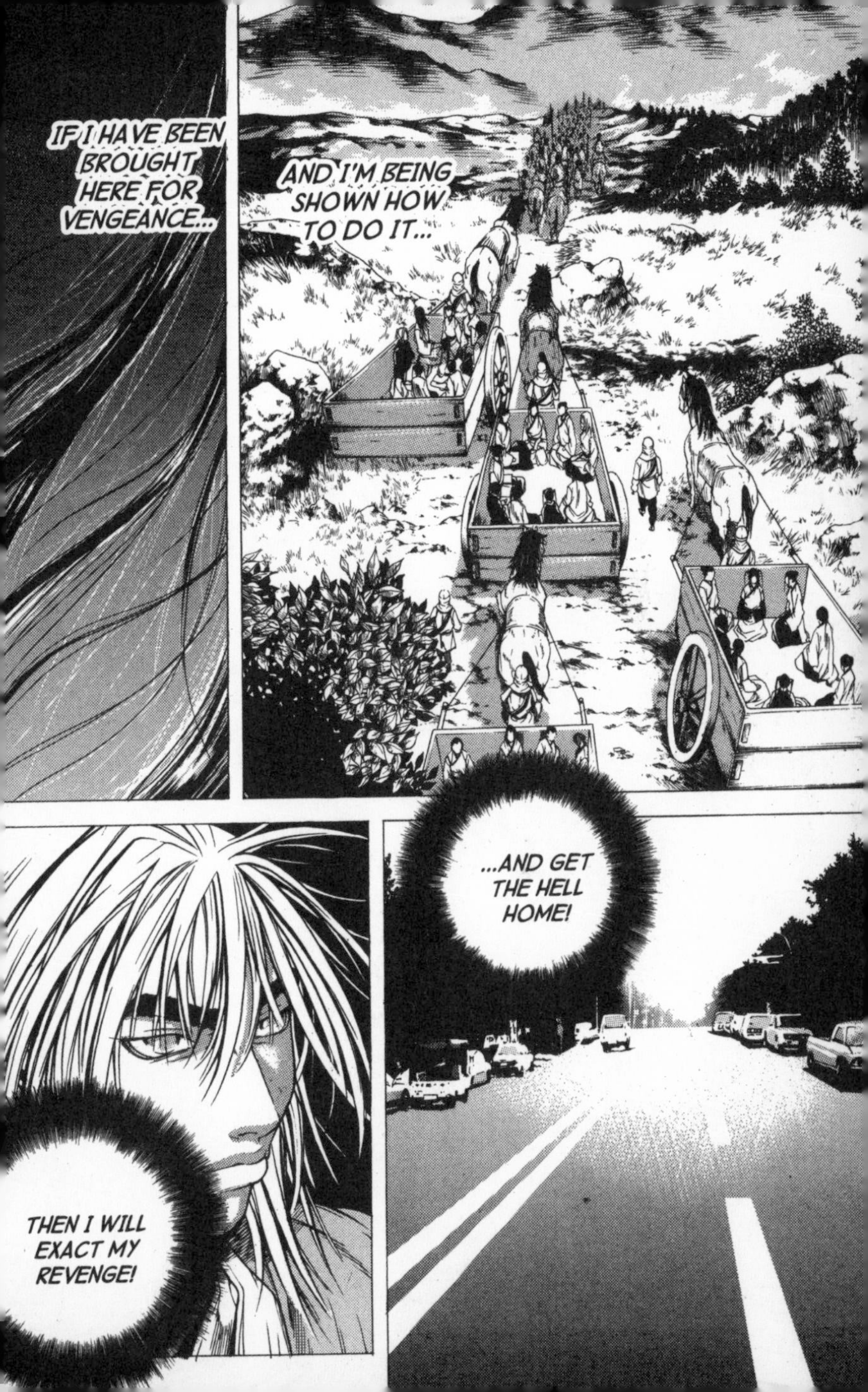
IF I HAVE BEEN BROUGHT HERE FOR VENGEANCE...
AND I'M BEING SHOWN HOW TO DO IT...
THEN I WILL EXACT MY REVENGE!
...AND GET THE HELL HOME!

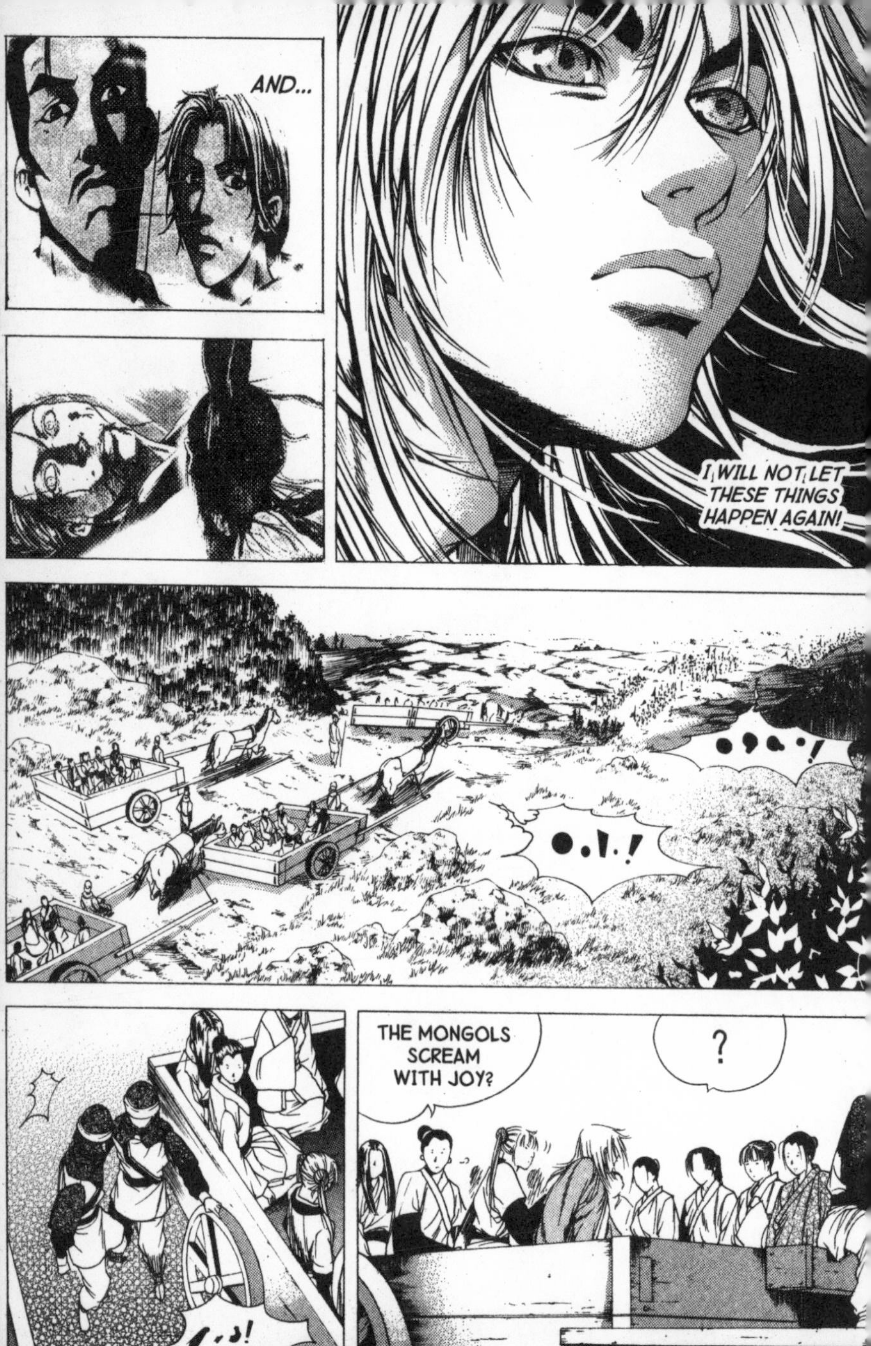
AND...
I WILL NOT LET THESE THINGS HAPPEN AGAIN!
THE MONGOLS SCREAM WITH JOY?
?

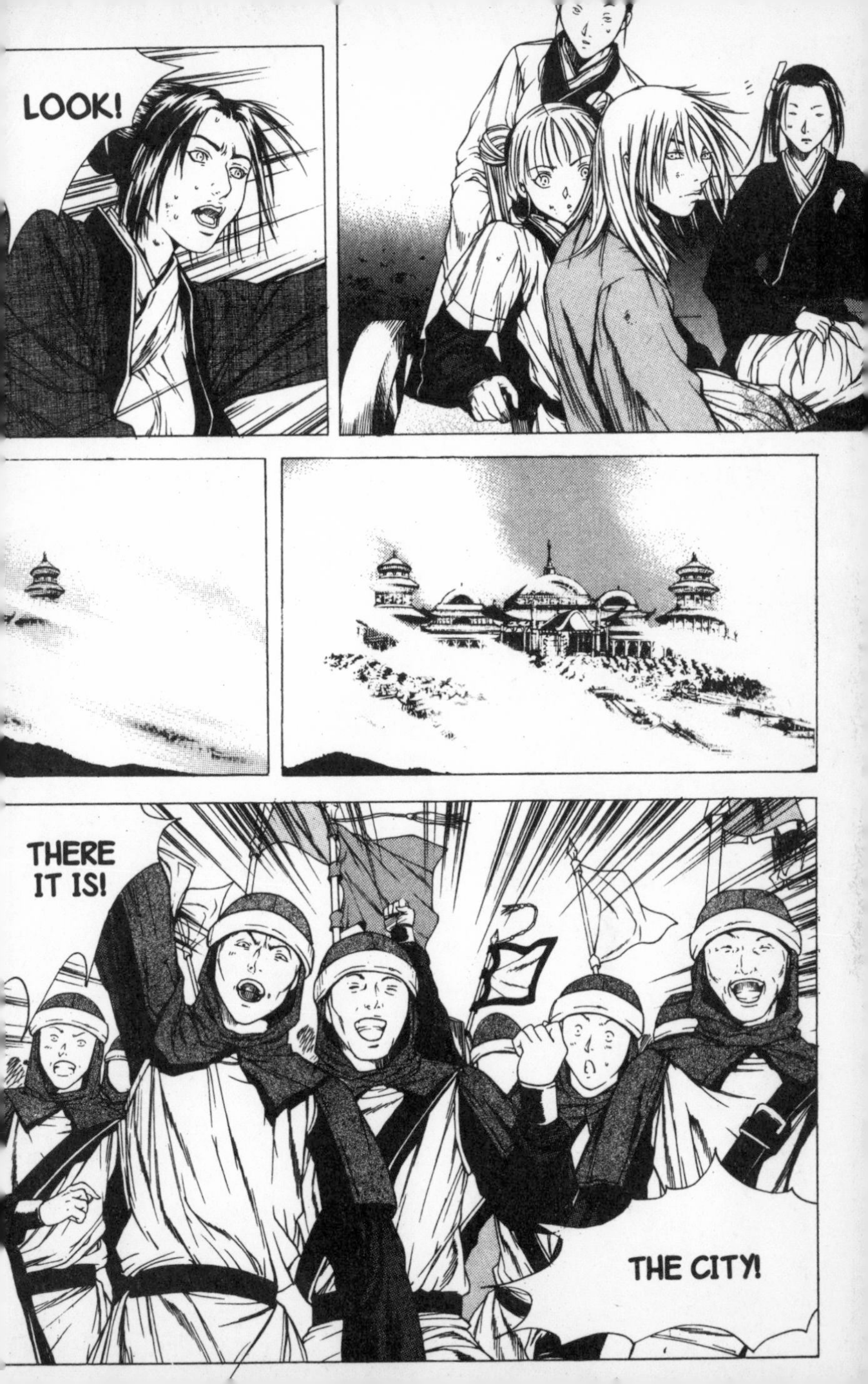
LOOK!
THERE IT IS!
THE CITY!

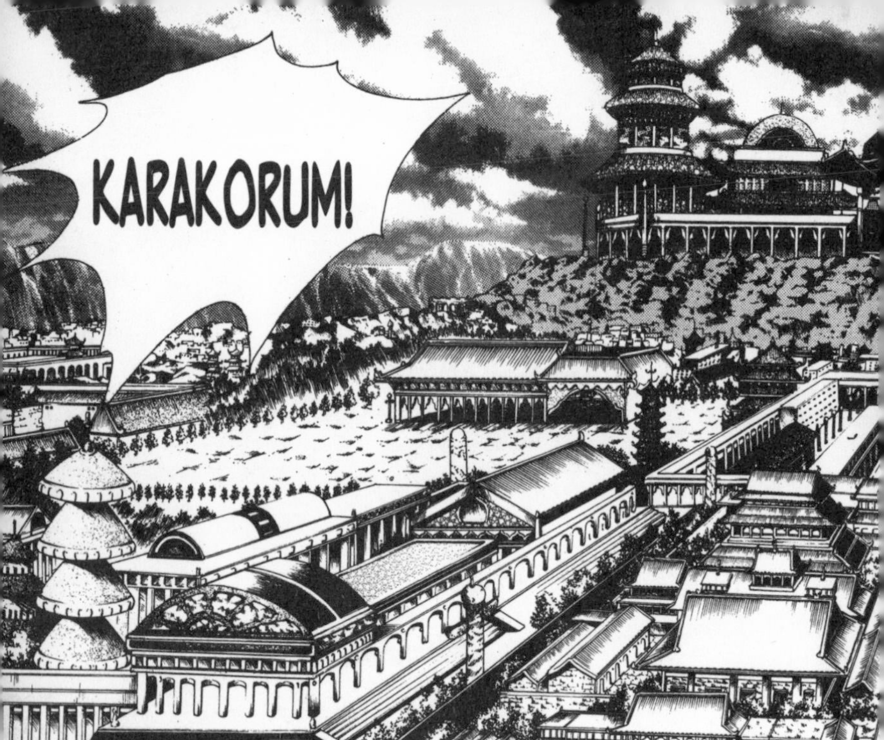
KARAKORUM!

Karakorum – Capital of the Mongol Nation situated above the Oru River.

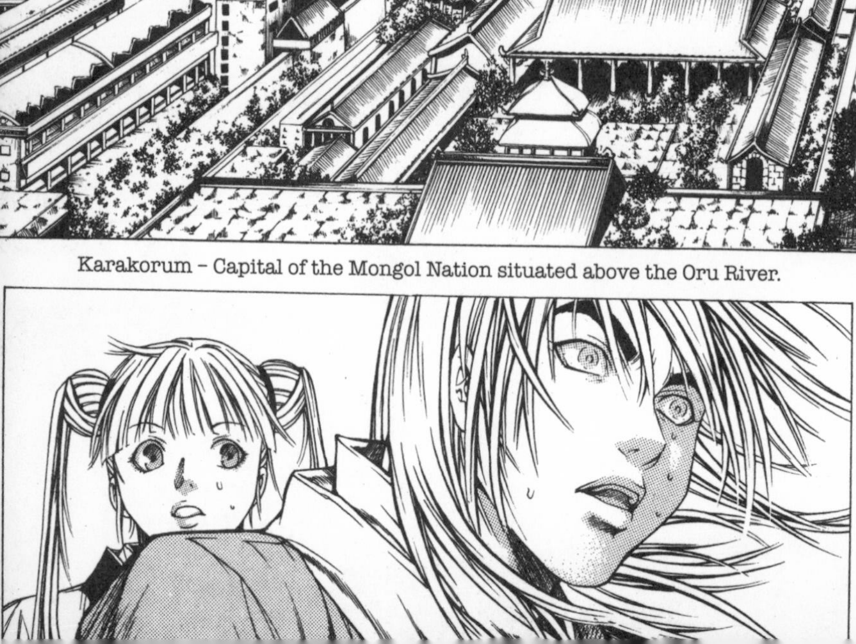

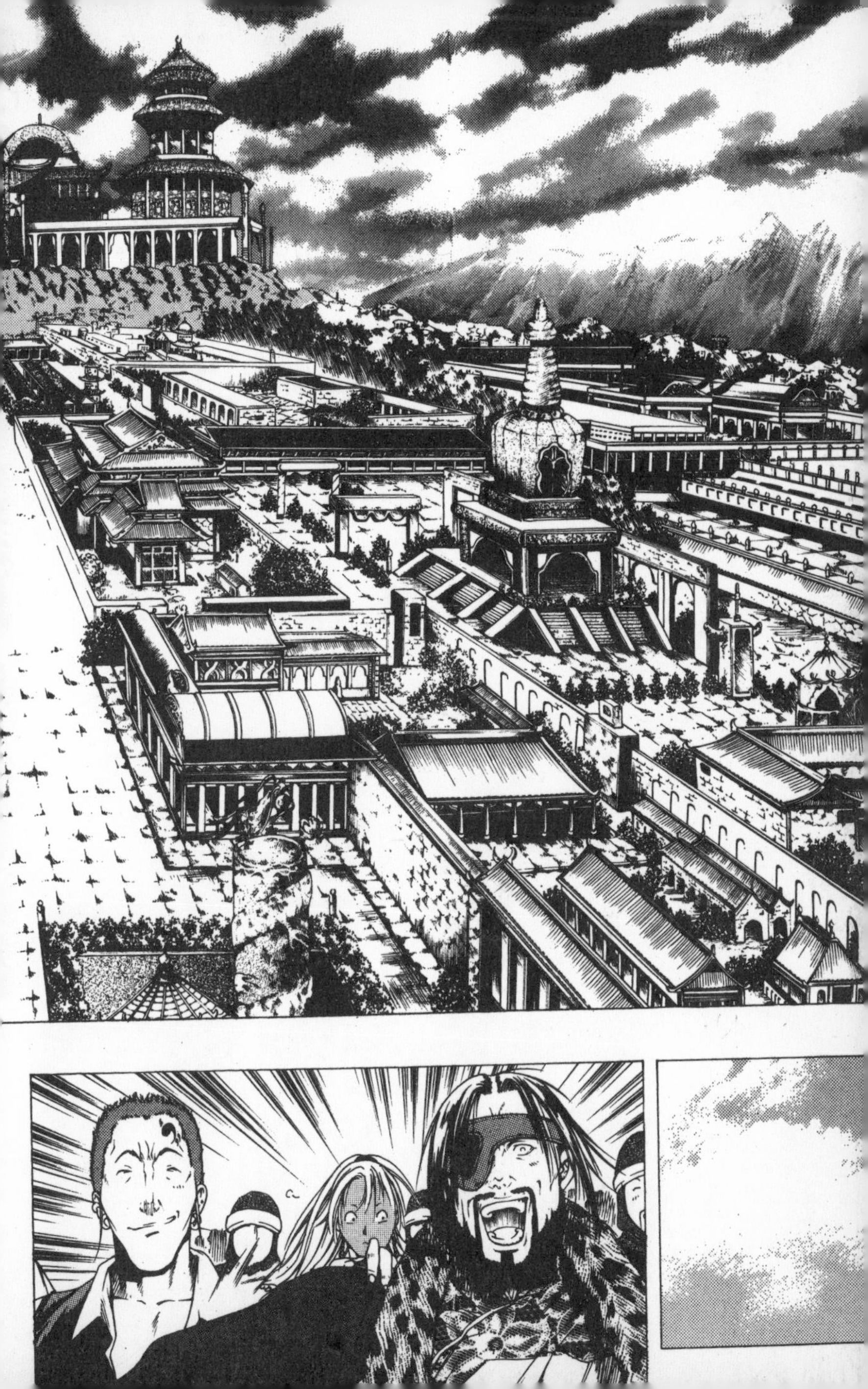

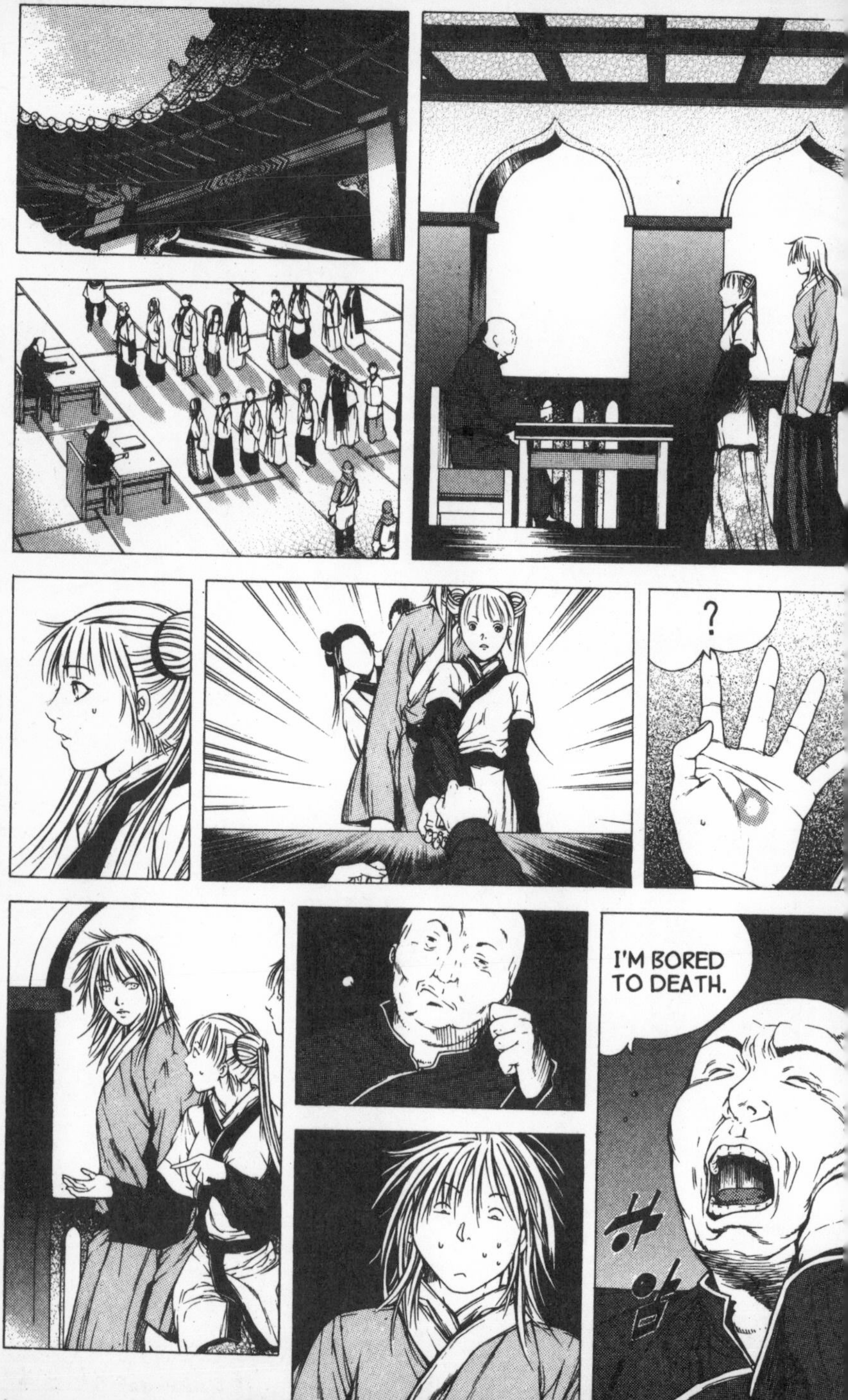
?
I'M BORED TO DEATH.

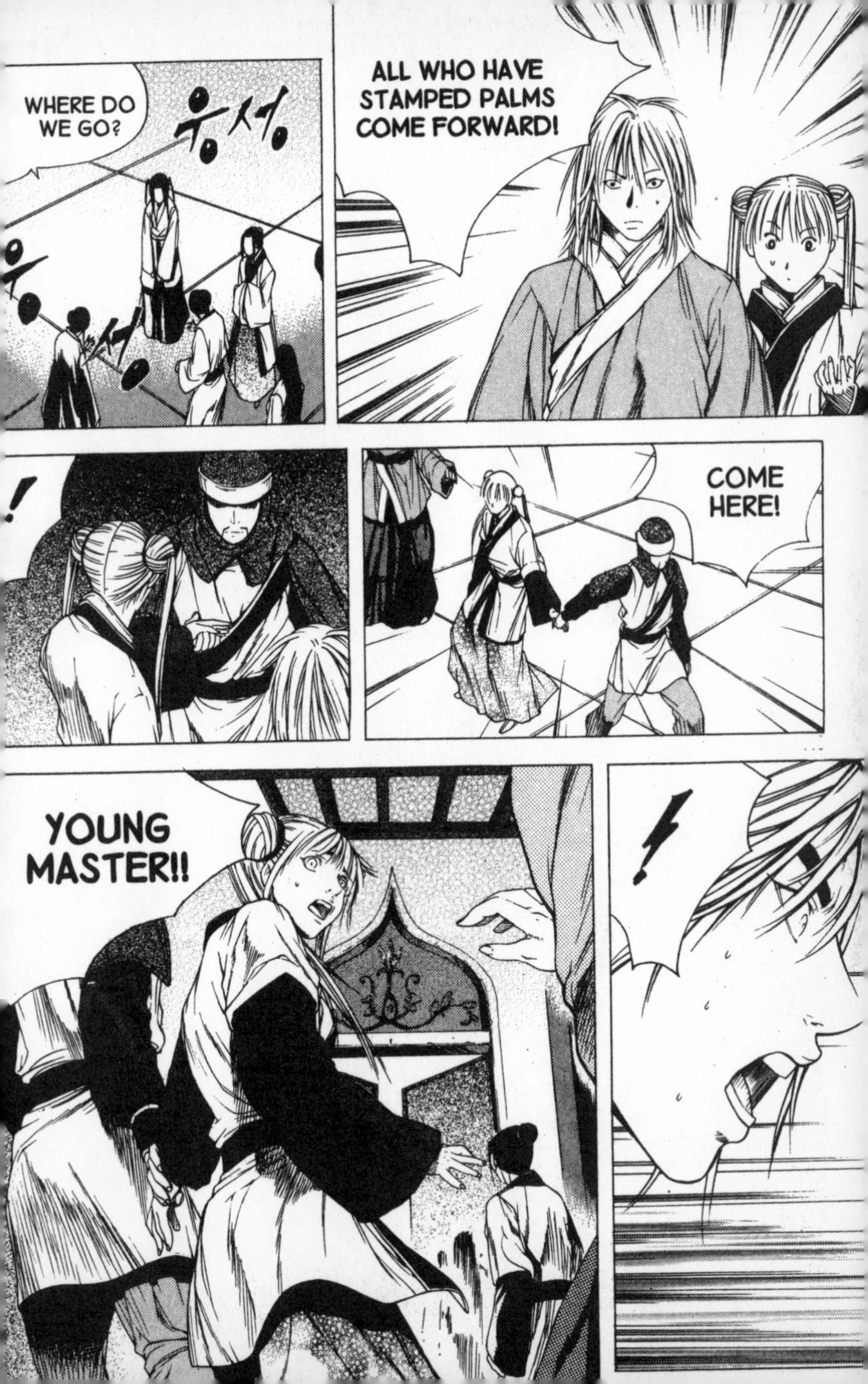
WHERE DO WE GO?
웅성
웅성
ALL WHO HAVE STAMPED PALMS COME FORWARD!
!
COME HERE!
YOUNG MASTER!!
!

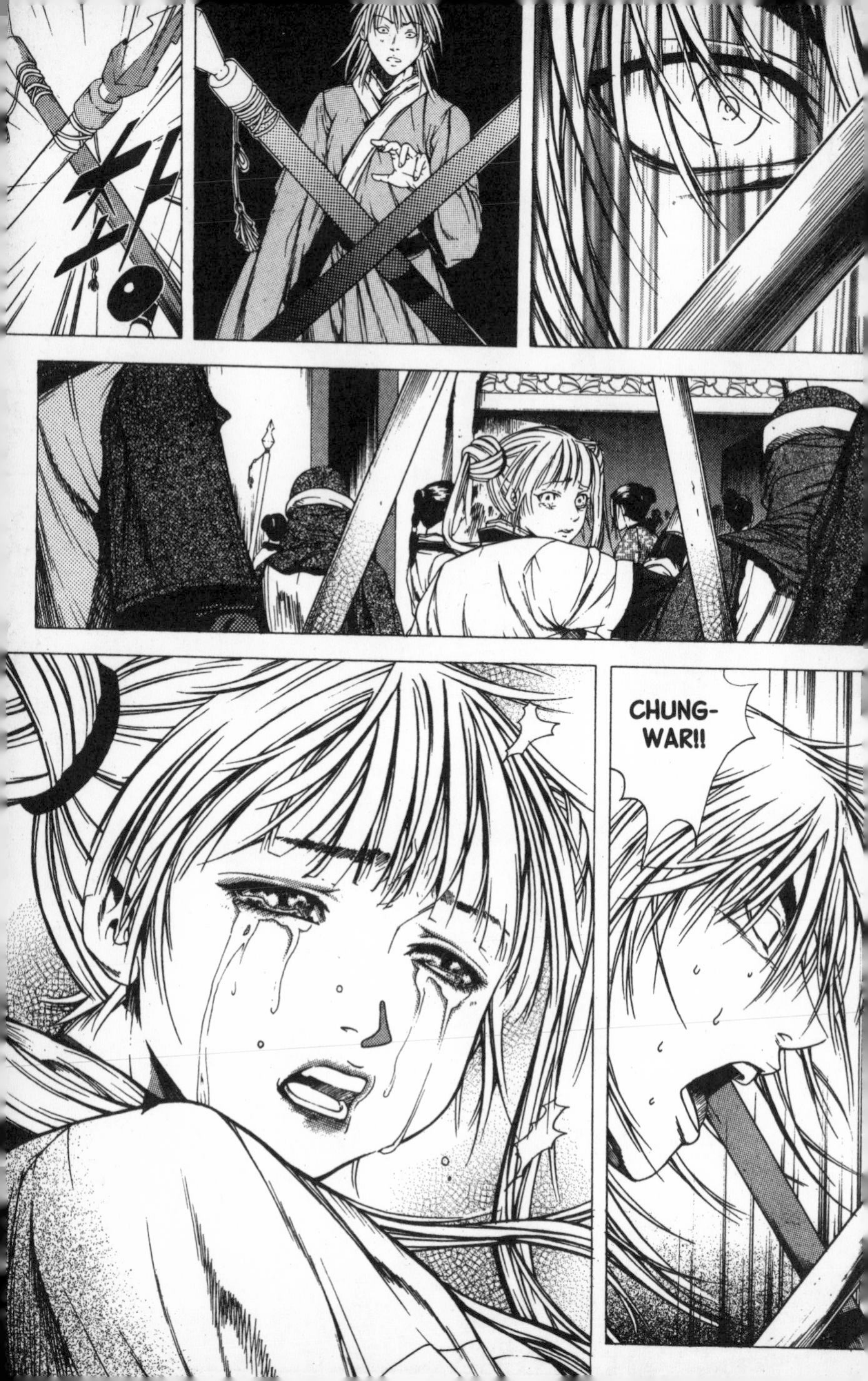
CHUNG-WAR!!

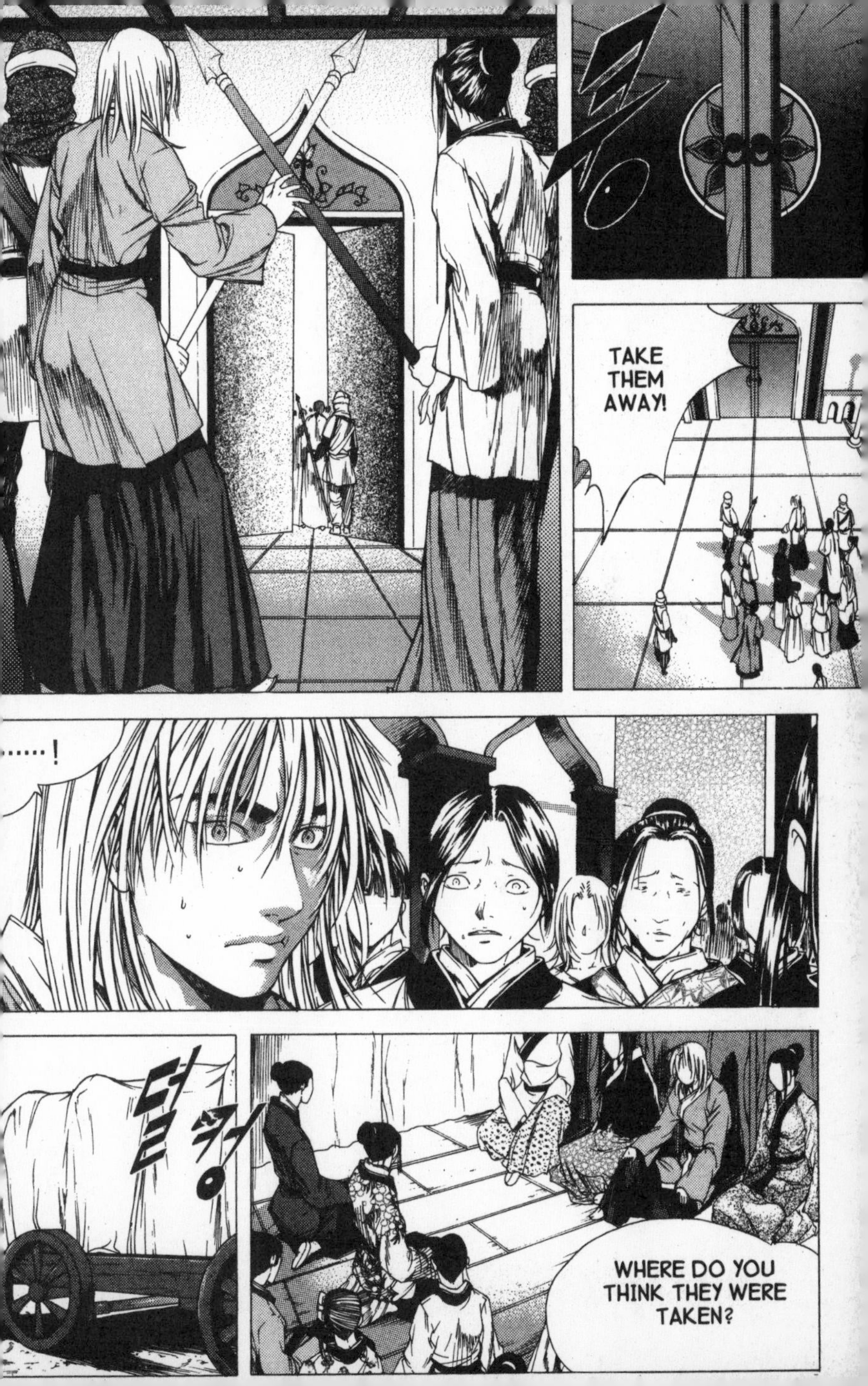
TAKE THEM AWAY!
......!
WHERE DO YOU THINK THEY WERE TAKEN?

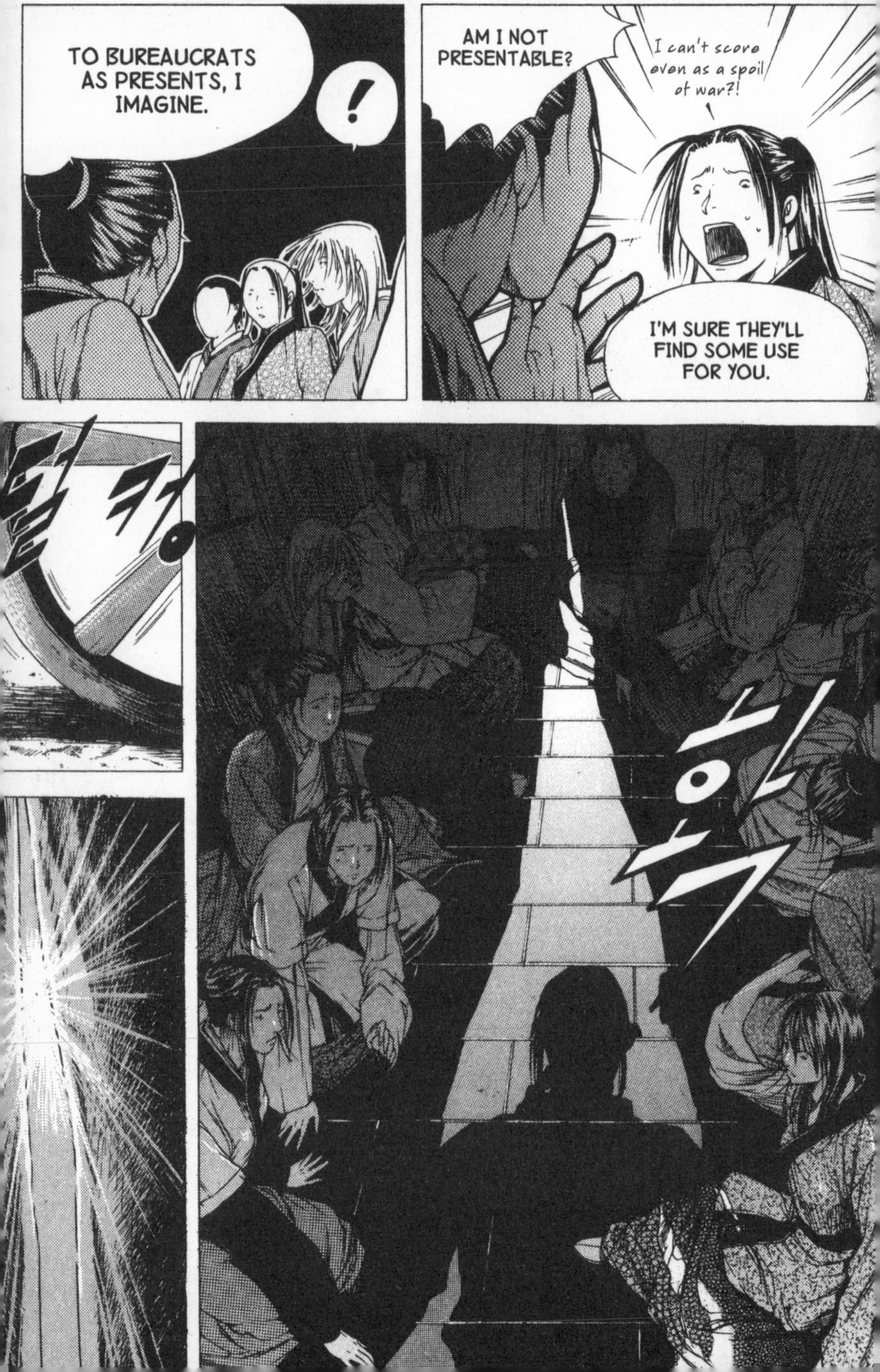
TO BUREAUCRATS AS PRESENTS, I IMAGINE.
!
AM I NOT PRESENTABLE?
I can't score even as a spoil of war?!
I'M SURE THEY'LL FIND SOME USE FOR YOU.

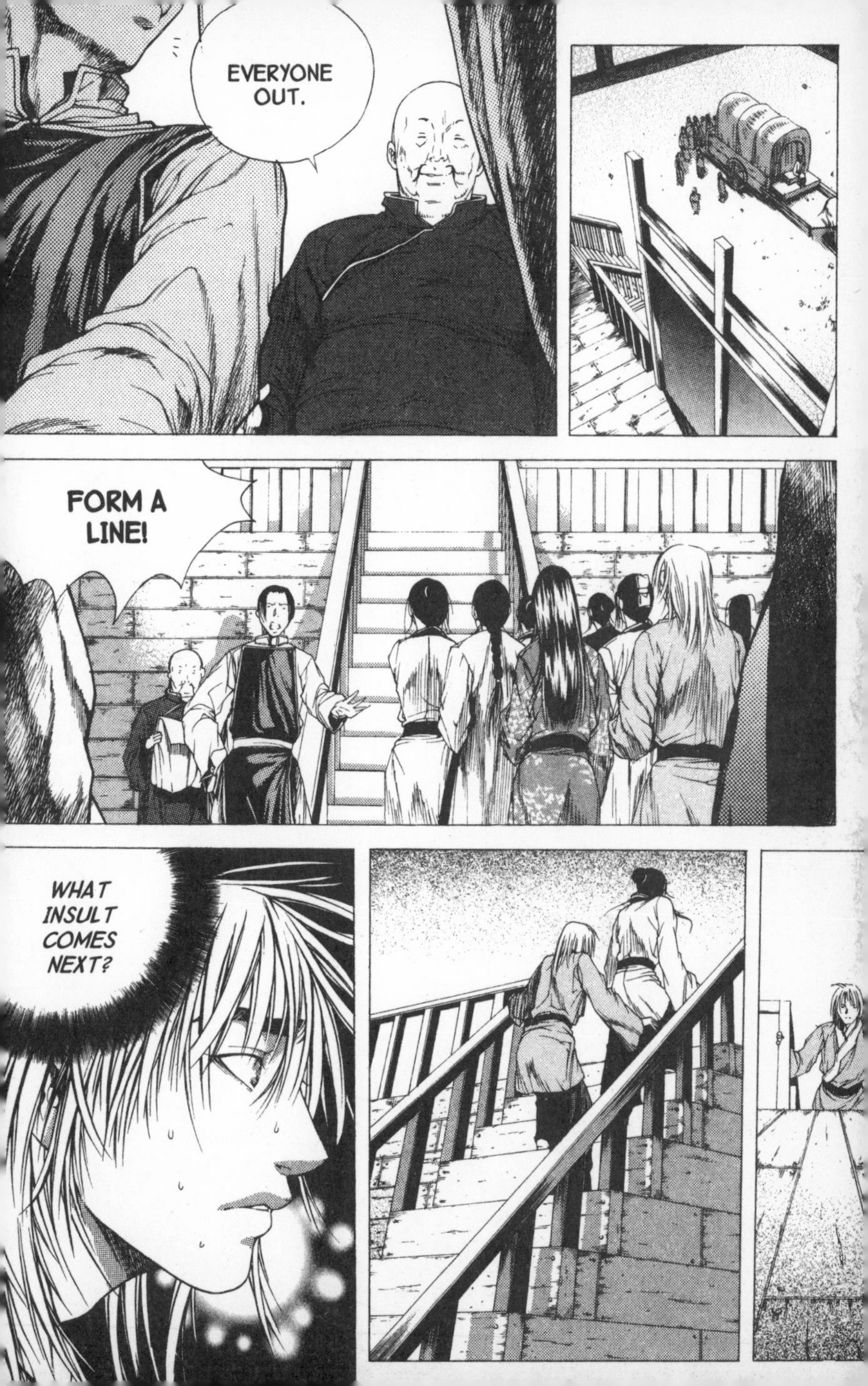
EVERYONE OUT.
FORM A LINE!
WHAT INSULT COMES NEXT?

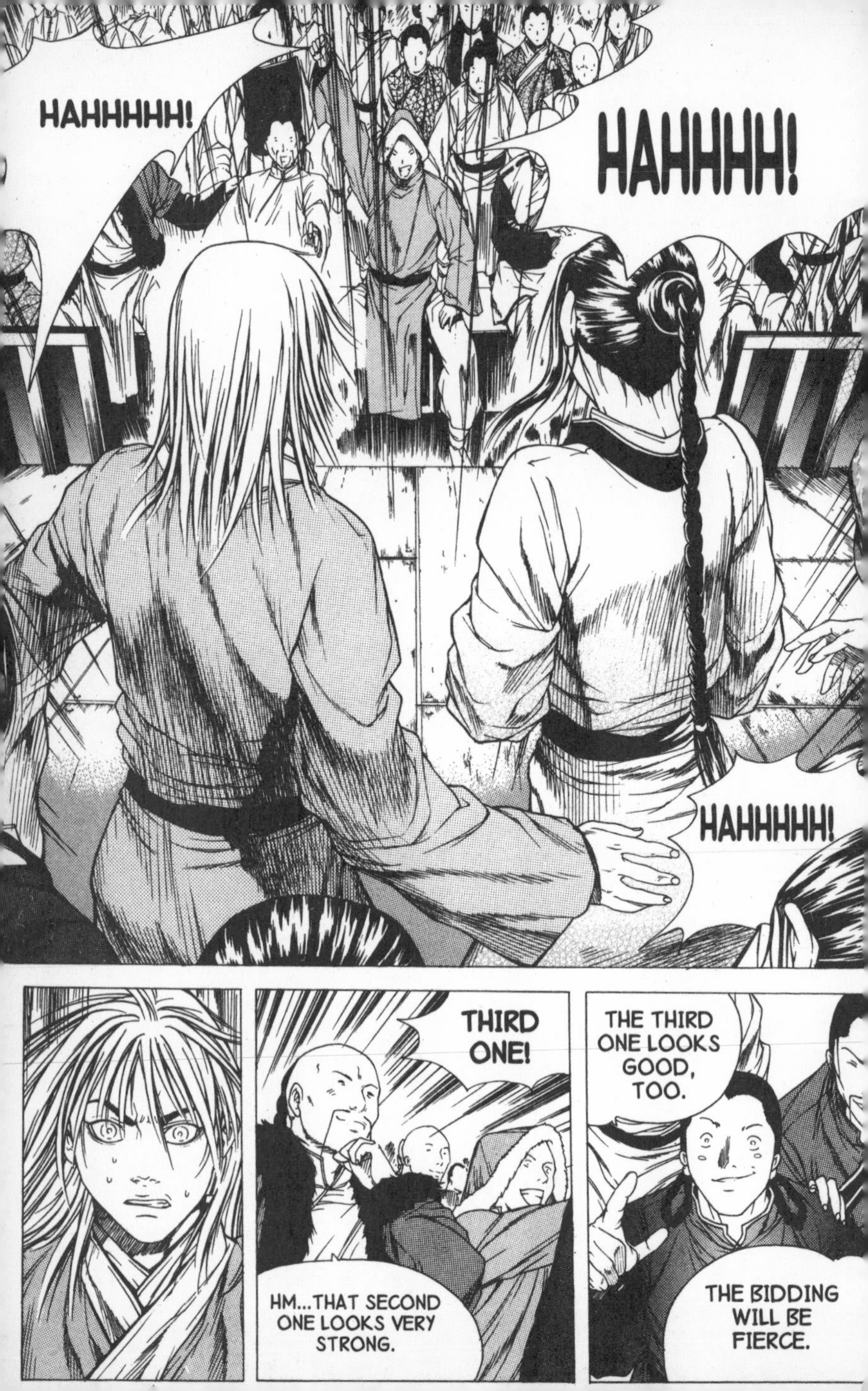
HAHHHHH!
HAHHHHH!
HAHHHHH!
THIRD ONE!
HM...THAT SECOND ONE LOOKS VERY STRONG.
THE THIRD ONE LOOKS GOOD, TOO.
THE BIDDING WILL BE FIERCE.

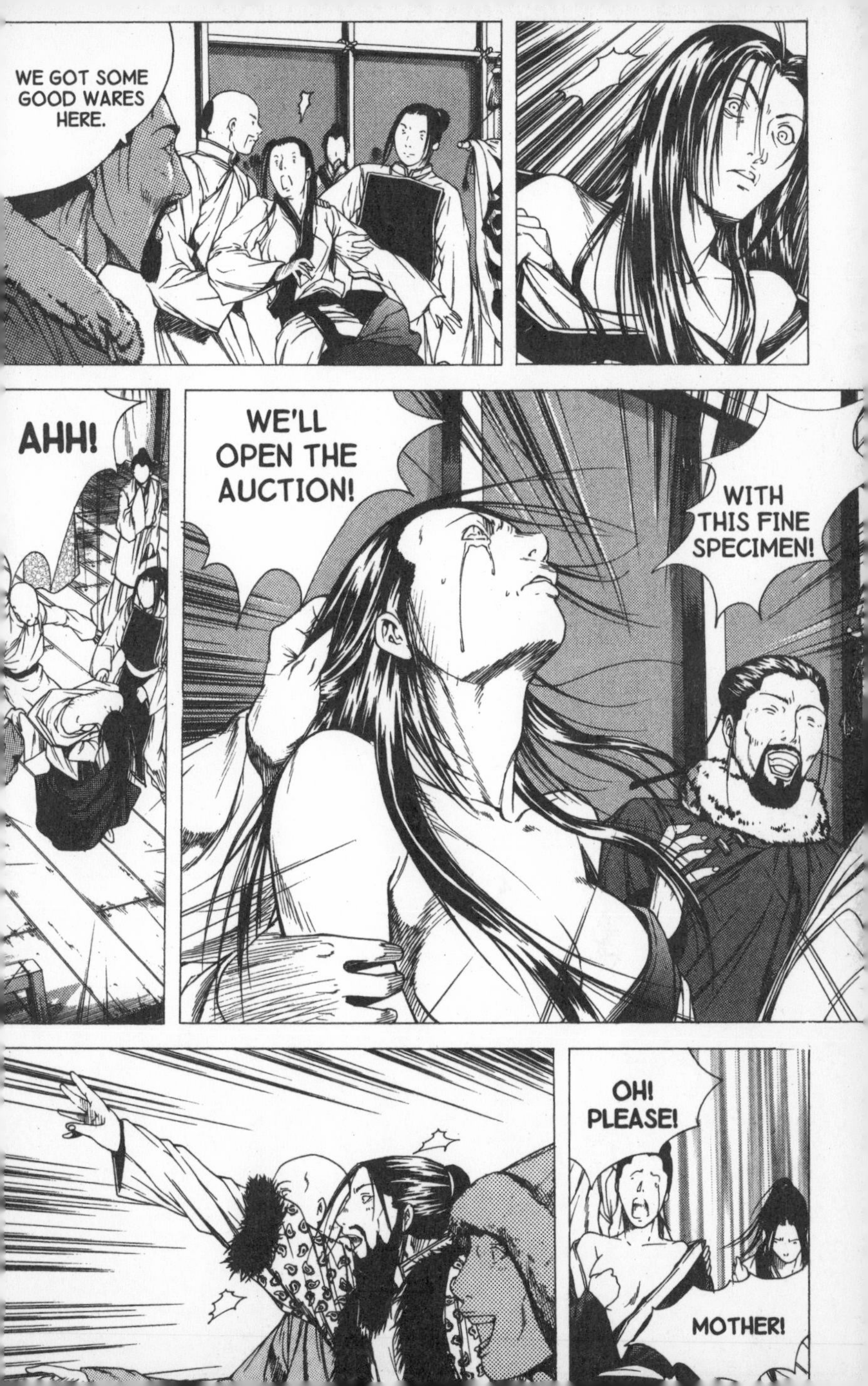
WE GOT SOME GOOD WARES HERE.
AHH!
WE'LL OPEN THE AUCTION!
WITH THIS FINE SPECIMEN!
OH! PLEASE!
MOTHER!

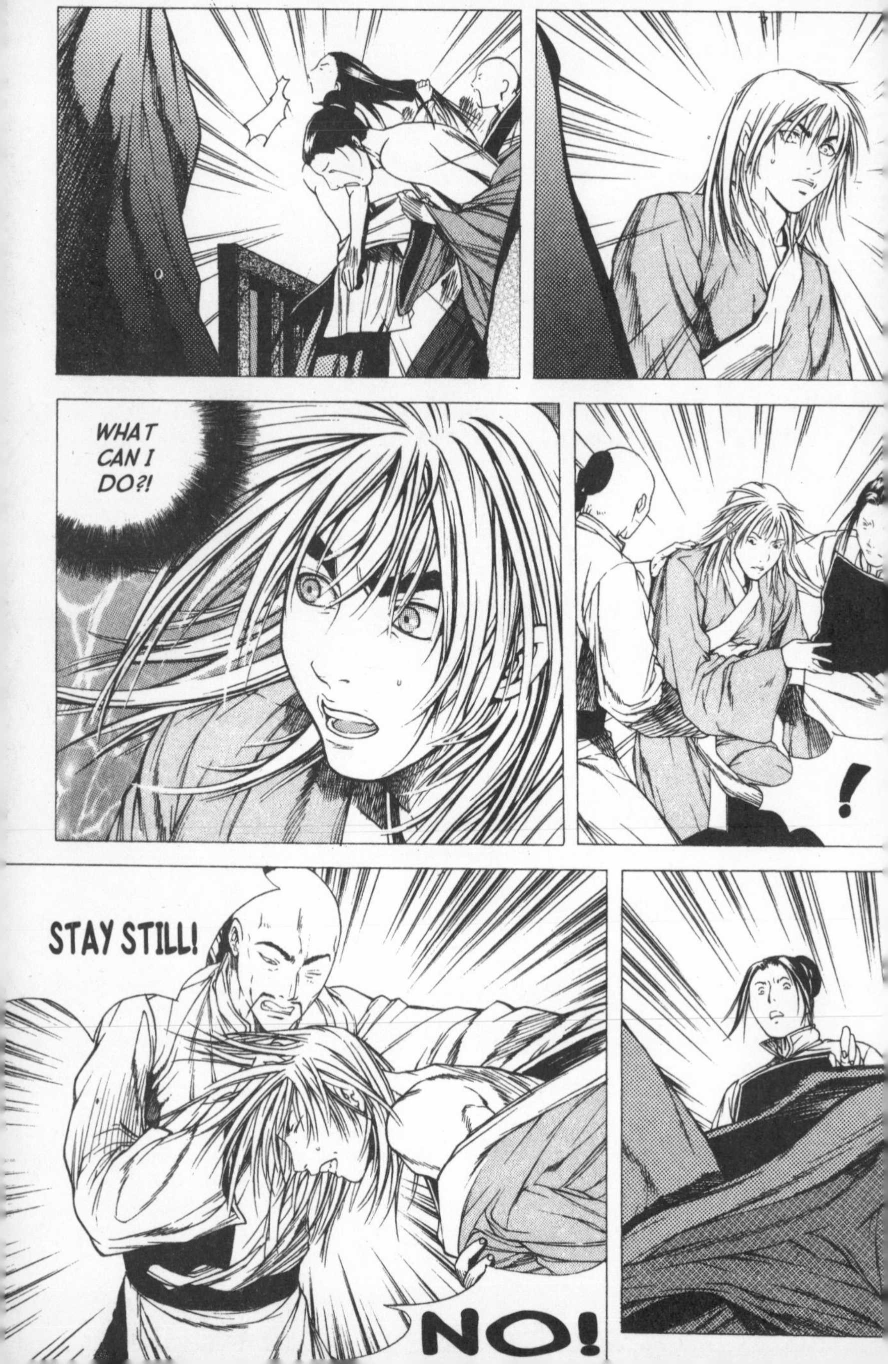
WHAT CAN I DO?!
!
STAY STILL!
NO!

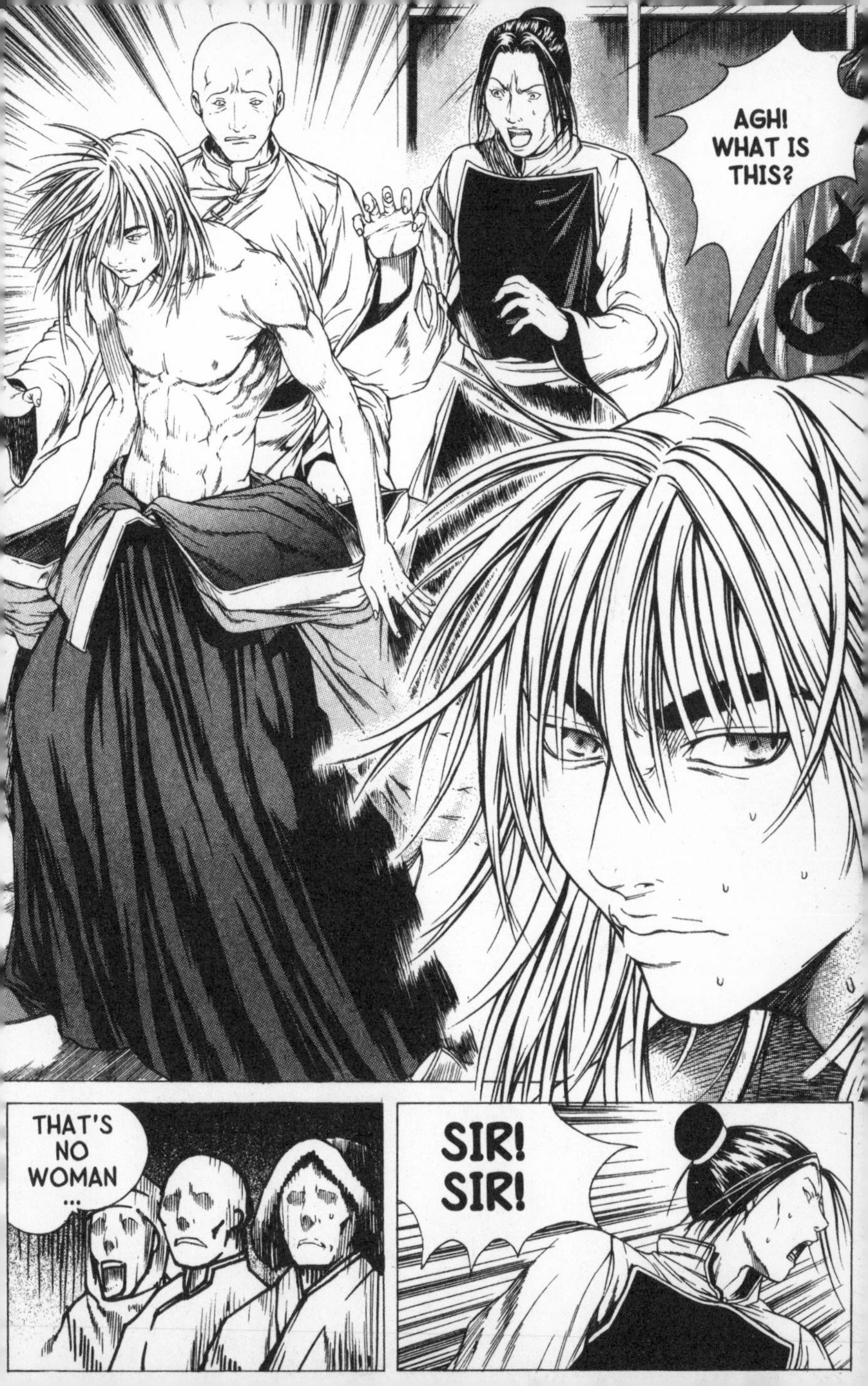
AGH! WHAT IS THIS?
THAT'S NO WOMAN ...
SIR! SIR!

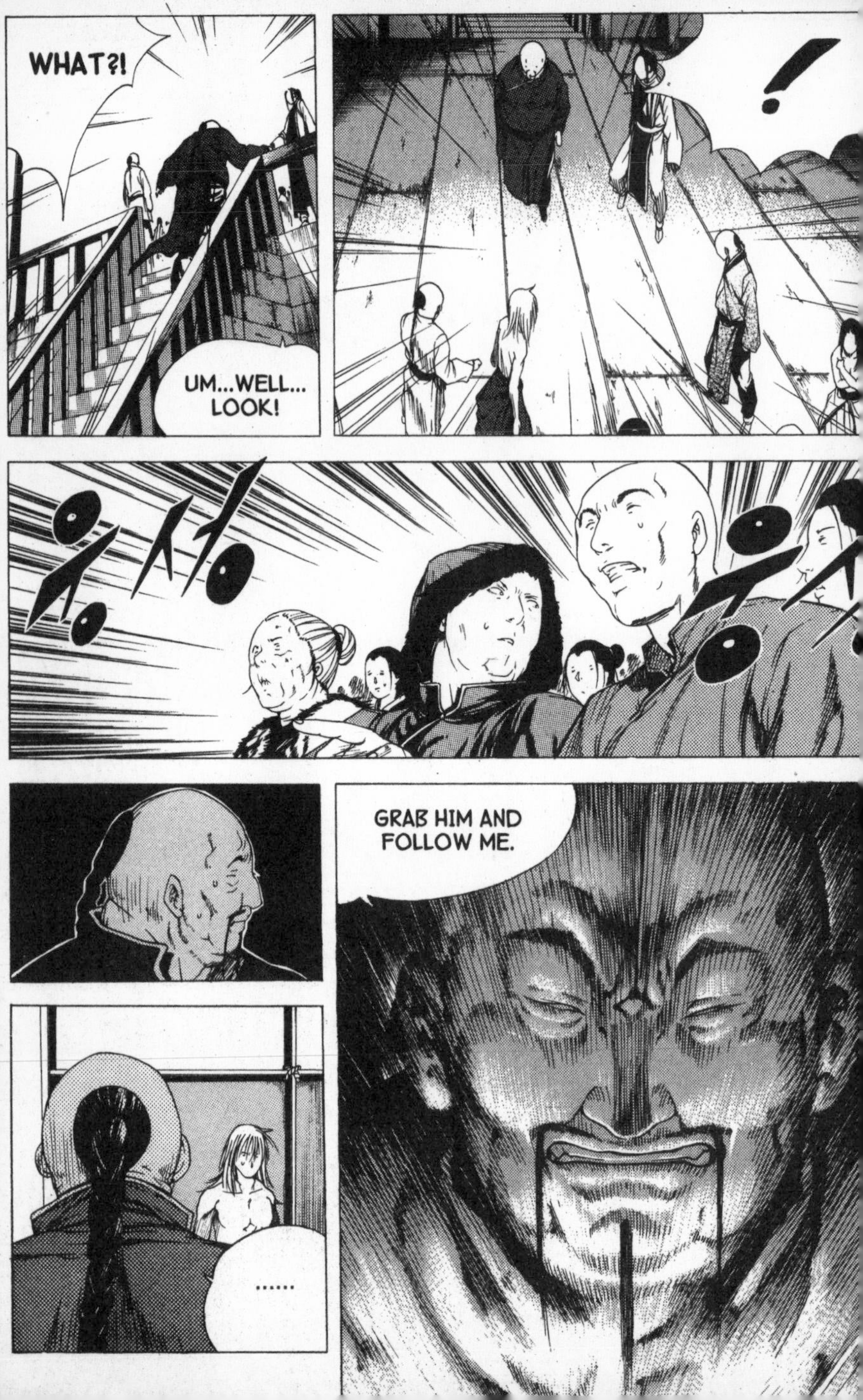
WHAT?!
UM...WELL... LOOK!
!
GRAB HIM AND FOLLOW ME.
......

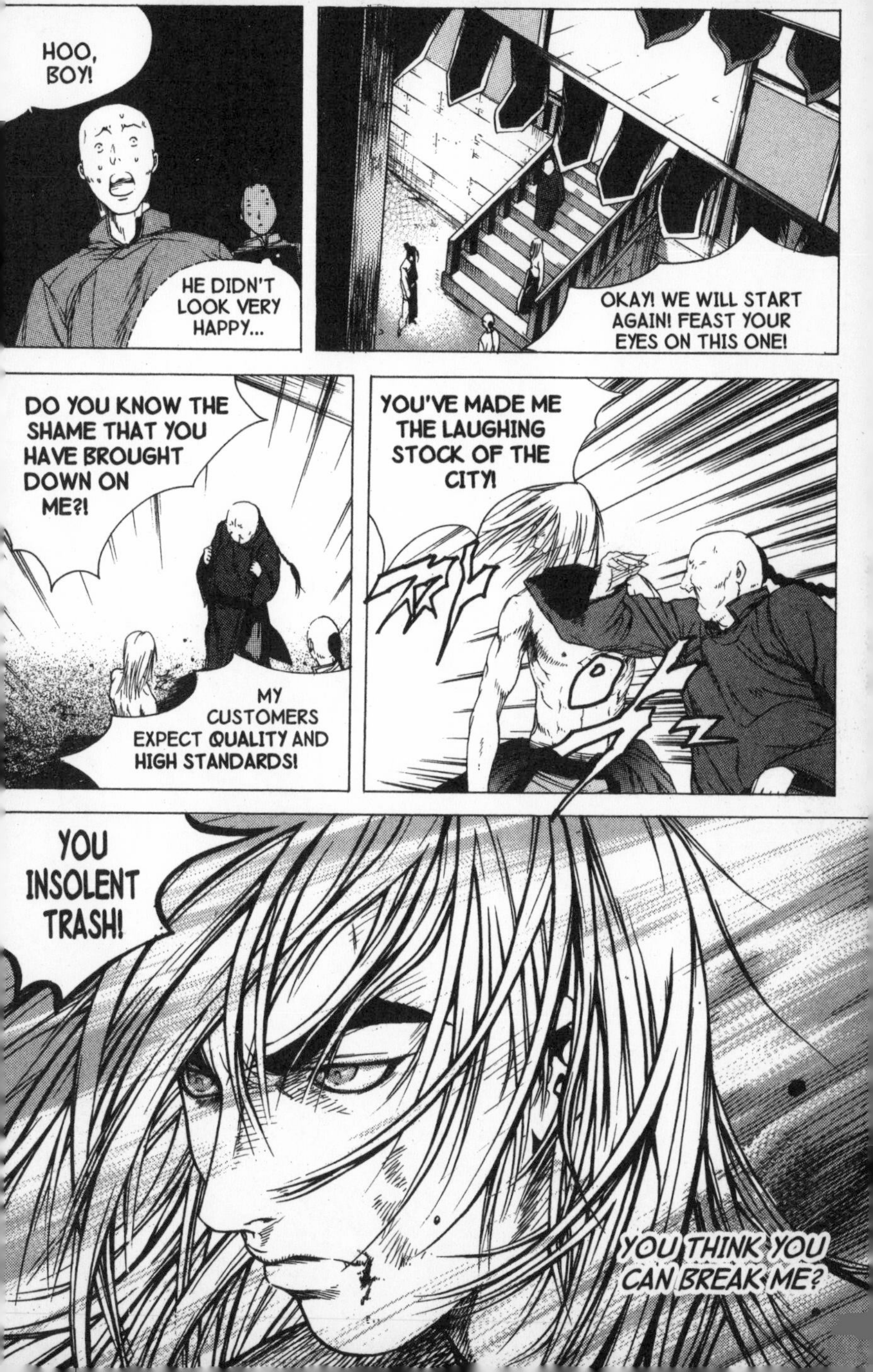
HOO, BOY!
HE DIDN'T LOOK VERY HAPPY...
OKAY! WE WILL START AGAIN! FEAST YOUR EYES ON THIS ONE!
DO YOU KNOW THE SHAME THAT YOU HAVE BROUGHT DOWN ON ME?!
MY CUSTOMERS EXPECT QUALITY AND HIGH STANDARDS!
YOU'VE MADE ME THE LAUGHING STOCK OF THE CITY!
YOU INSOLENT TRASH!
YOU THINK YOU CAN BREAK ME?

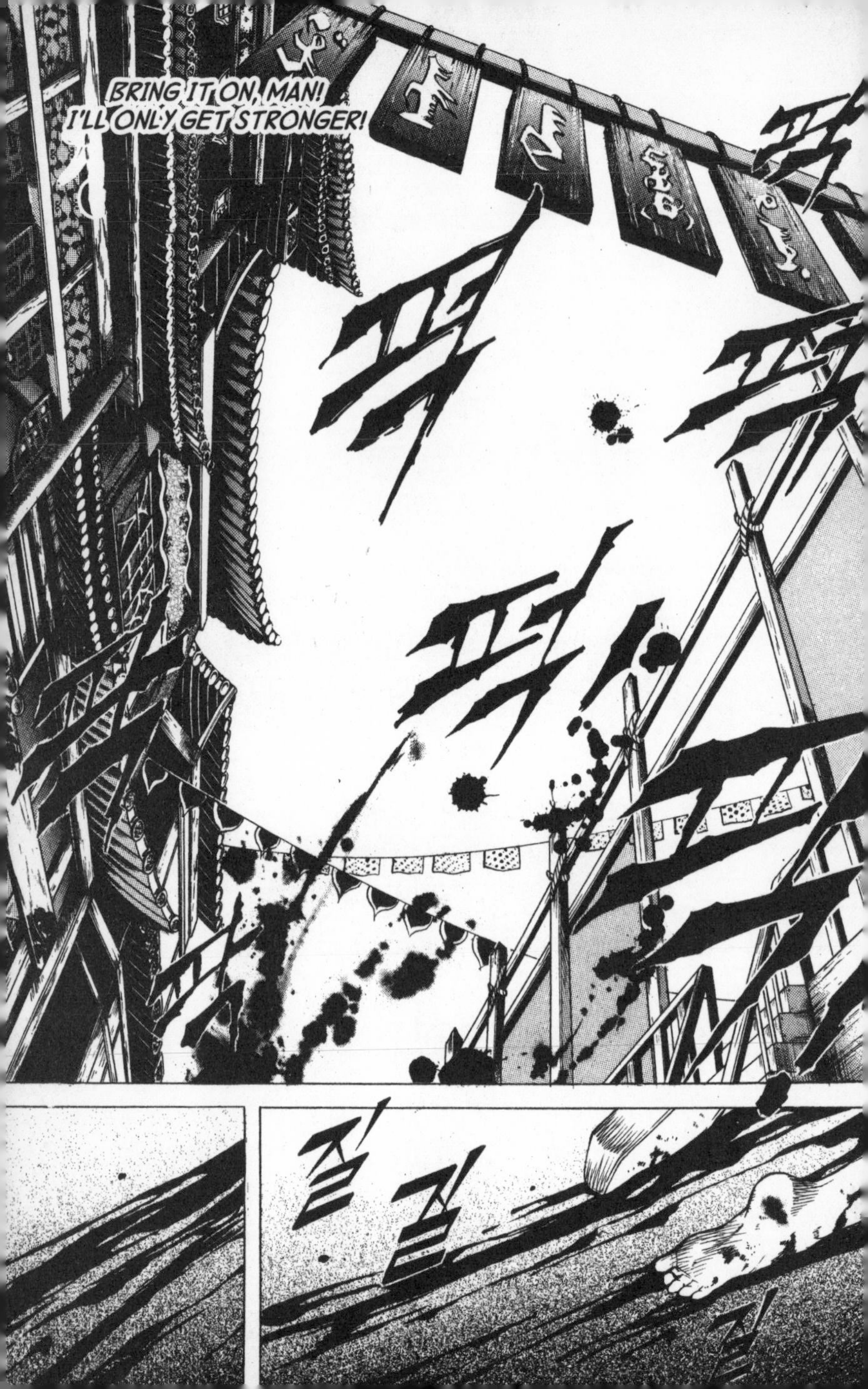
BRING IT ON, MAN!
I'LL ONLY GET STRONGER!
팍
팍
팍
팍
질
질

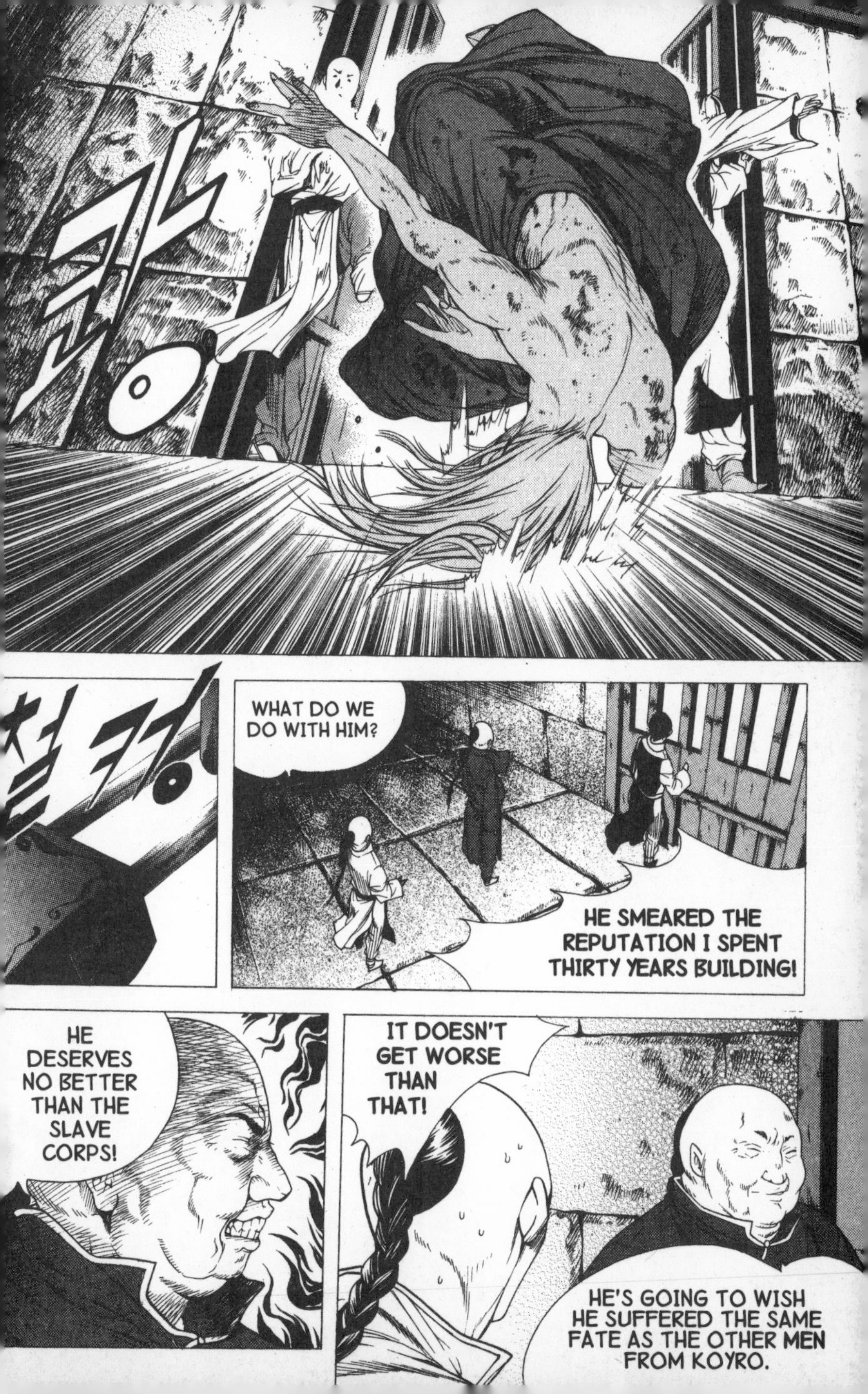
WHAT DO WE DO WITH HIM?
HE SMEARED THE REPUTATION I SPENT THIRTY YEARS BUILDING!
HE DESERVES NO BETTER THAN THE SLAVE CORPS!
IT DOESN'T GET WORSE THAN THAT!
HE'S GOING TO WISH HE SUFFERED THE SAME FATE AS THE OTHER MEN FROM KOYRO.

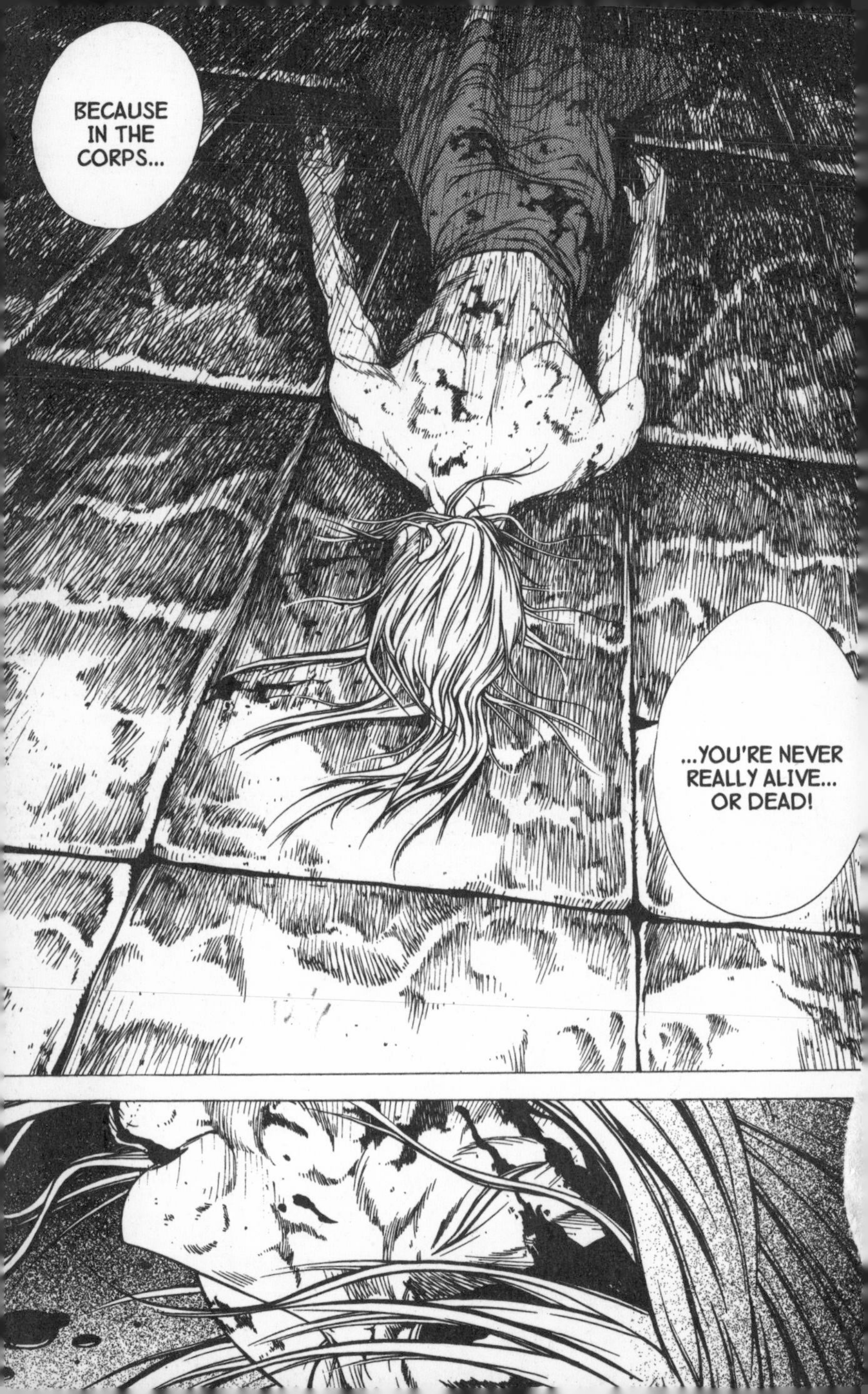
BECAUSE IN THE CORPS...
...YOU'RE NEVER REALLY ALIVE... OR DEAD!

Chapter 27
A Distant
Memory

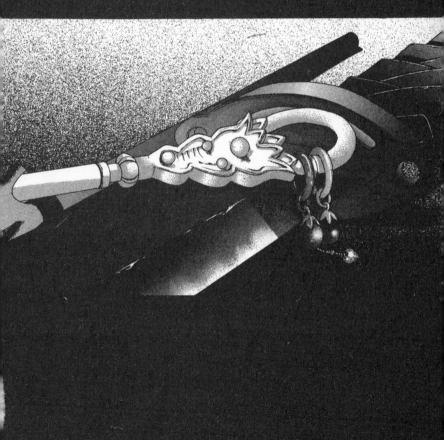

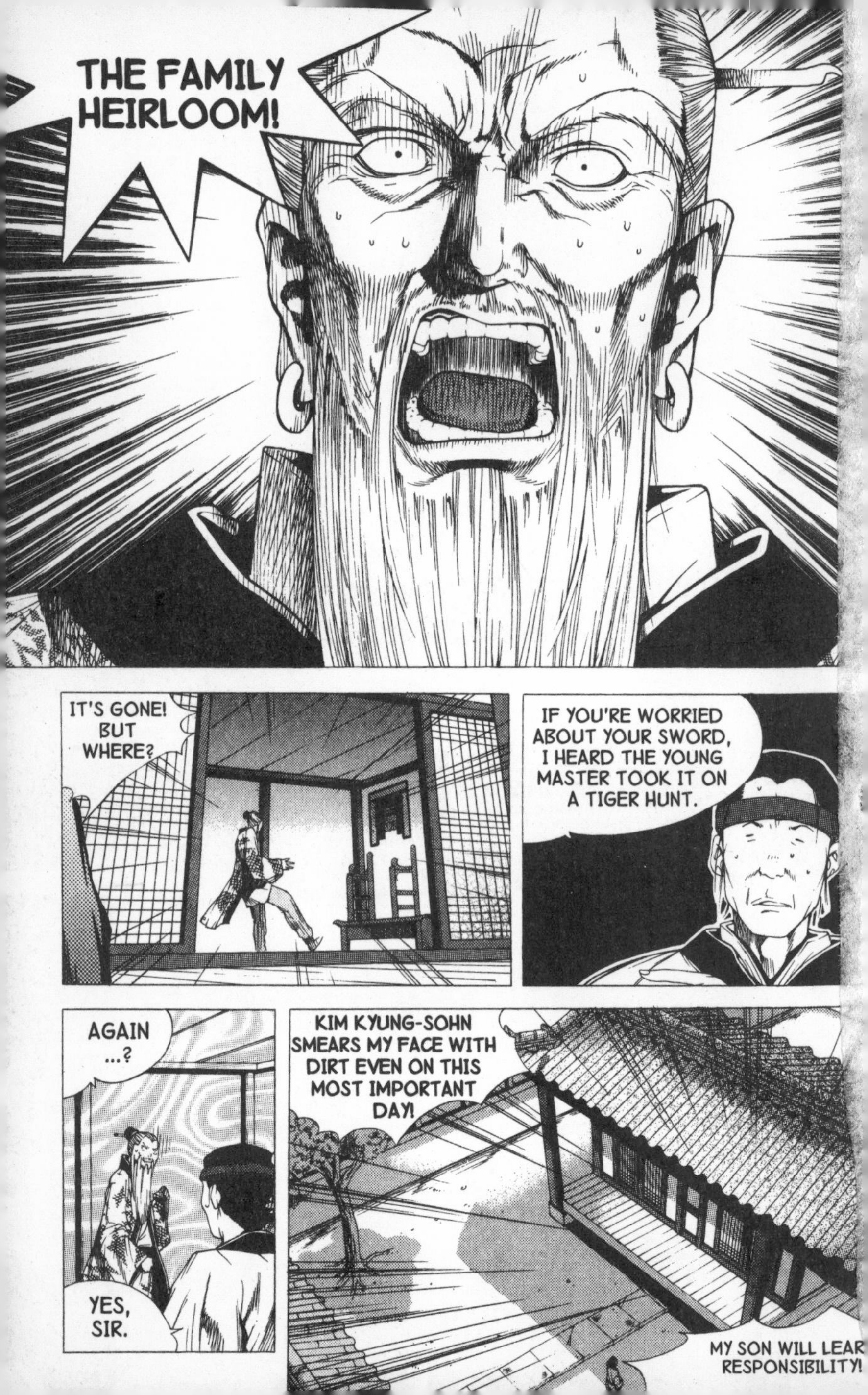
THE FAMILY HEIRLOOM!
IT'S GONE! BUT WHERE?
IF YOU'RE WORRIED ABOUT YOUR SWORD, I HEARD THE YOUNG MASTER TOOK IT ON A TIGER HUNT.
AGAIN ...?
YES, SIR.
KIM KYUNG-SOHN SMEARS MY FACE WITH DIRT EVEN ON THIS MOST IMPORTANT DAY!
MY SON WILL LEAR
RESPONSIBILITY!

IT'S JUST OVER THE NEXT HILL, MISS.

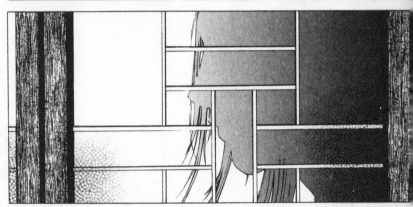

OH...

STOP CRYING! THIS IS A HAPPY DAY!

OUR POOR LADY...

HOW DREADFUL, TO BE SOLD TO A FAMILY OF WARRIORS... THAT IS NO LIFE FOR A NOBLE WOMAN.

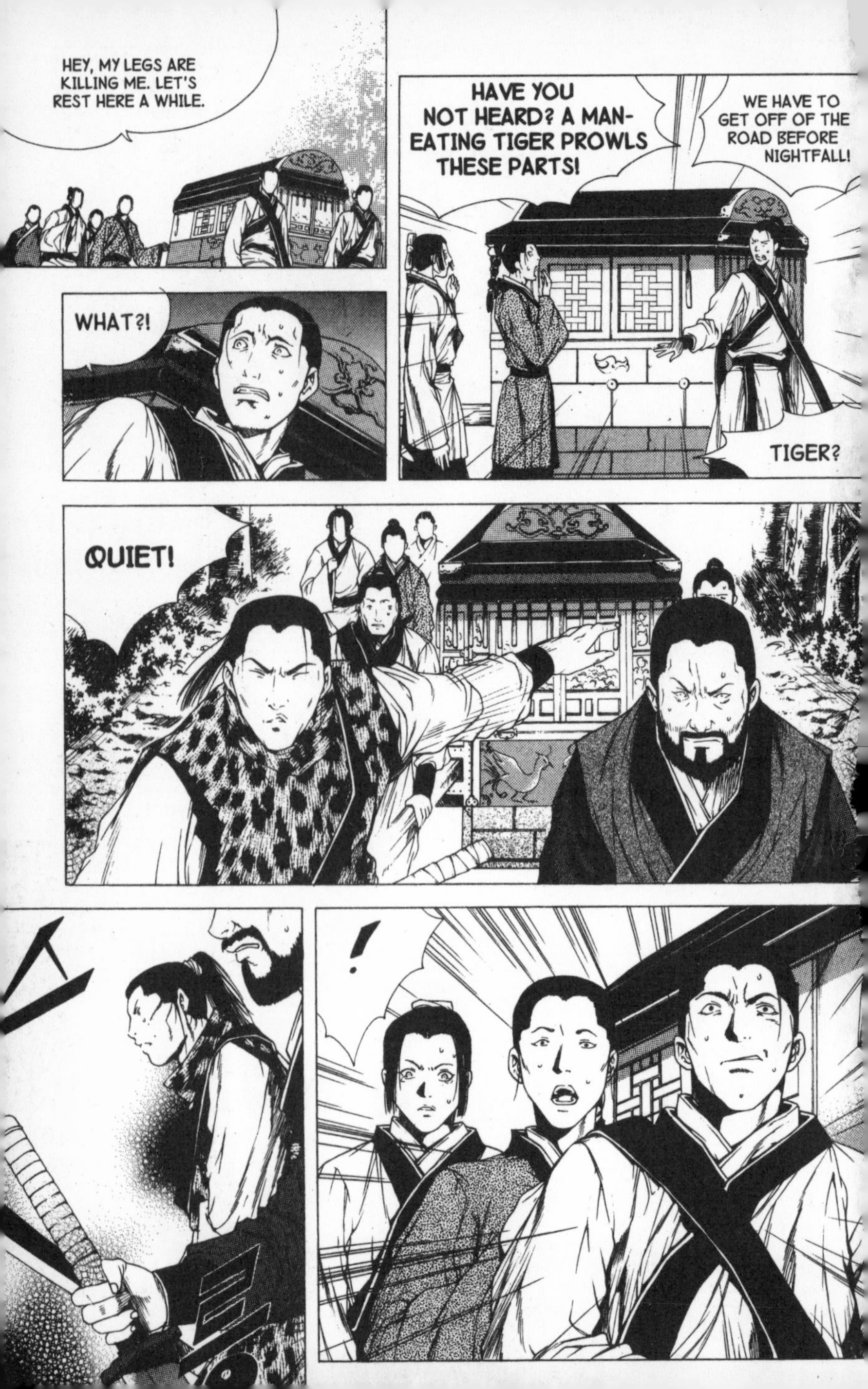
HEY, MY LEGS ARE KILLING ME. LET'S REST HERE A WHILE.
HAVE YOU NOT HEARD? A MAN-EATING TIGER PROWLS THESE PARTS!
WE HAVE TO GET OFF OF THE ROAD BEFORE NIGHTFALL!
WHAT?!
TIGER?
QUIET!
!

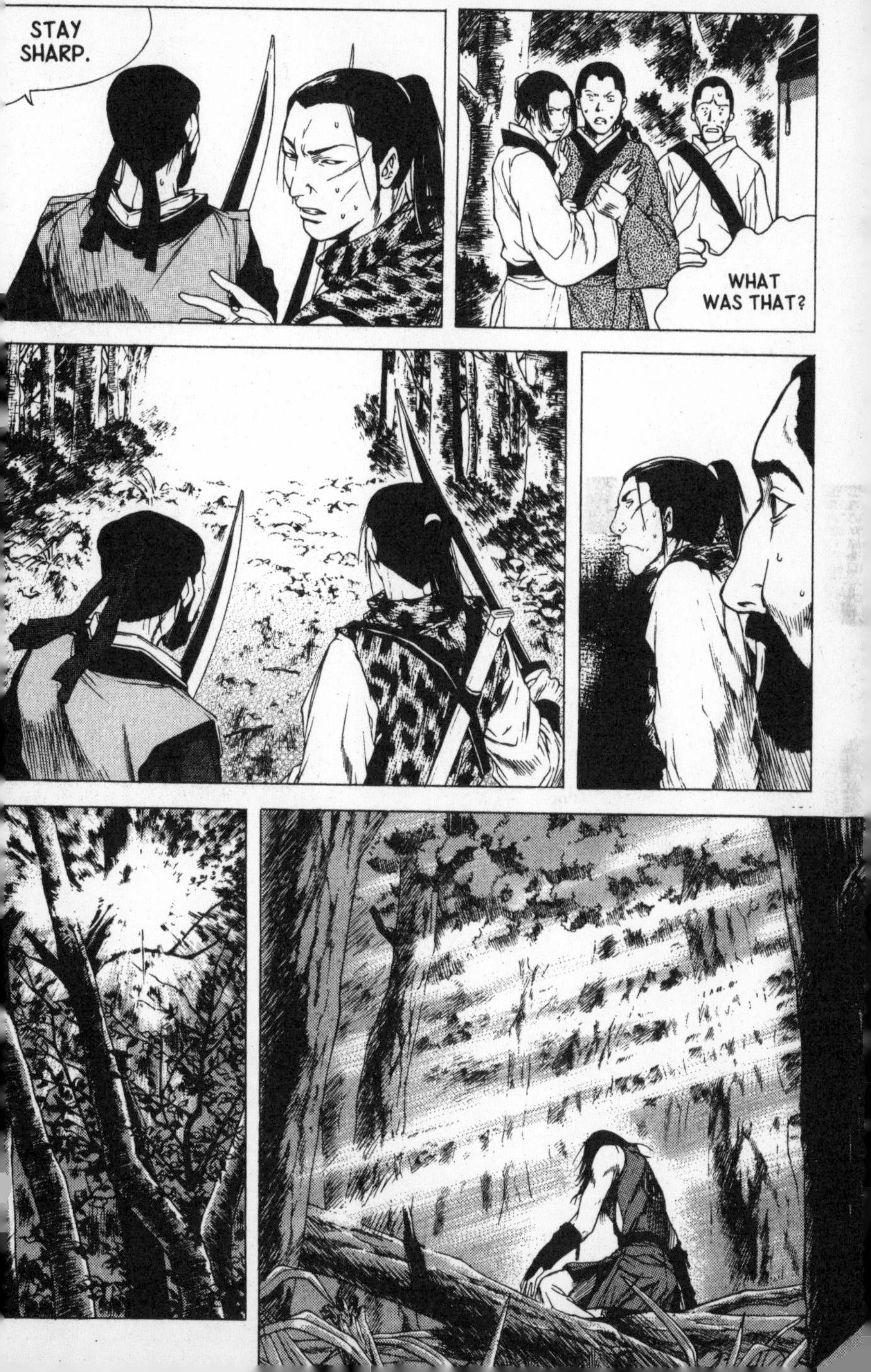
STAY SHARP.
WHAT WAS THAT?

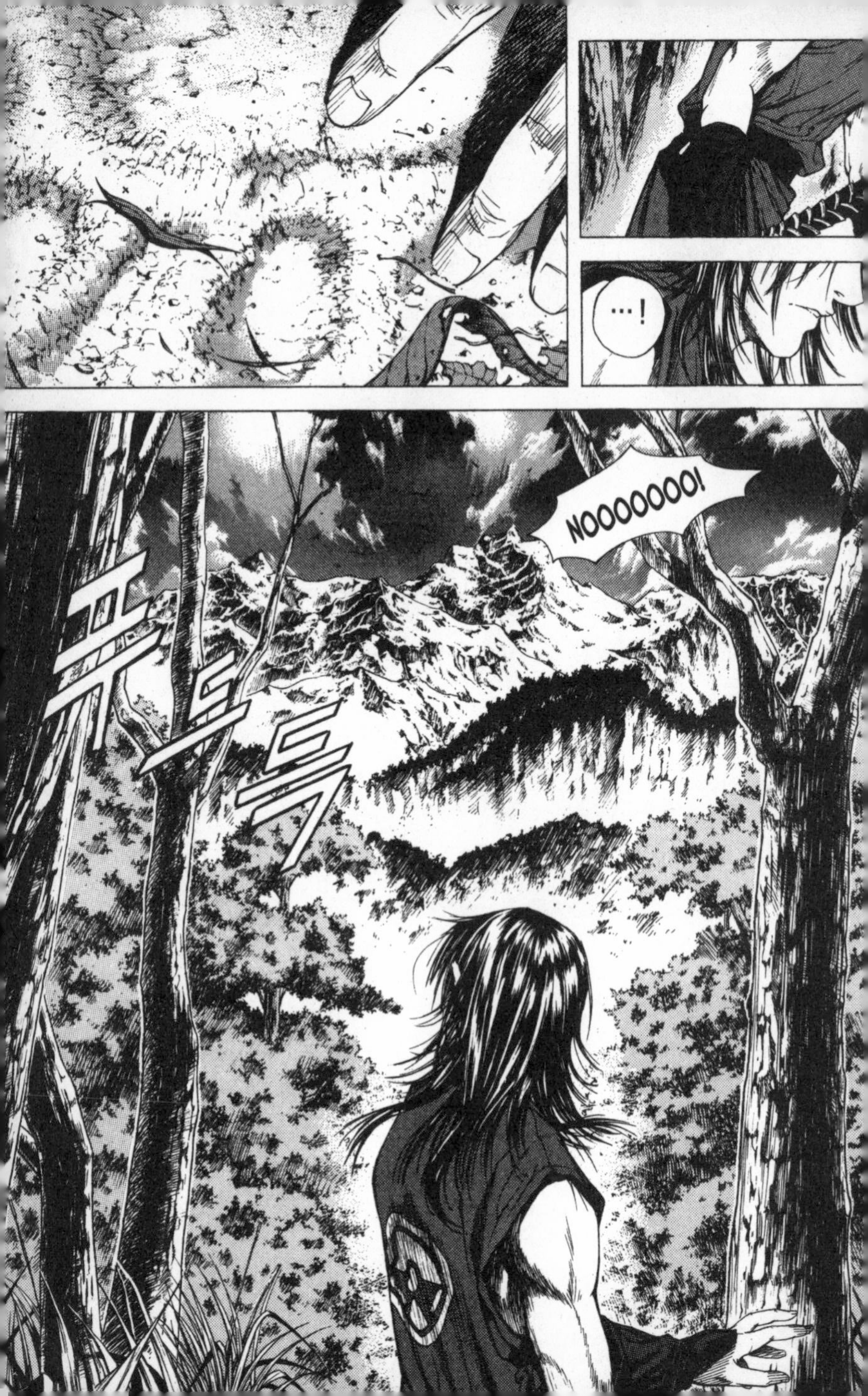

...!
NOOOOOOO!

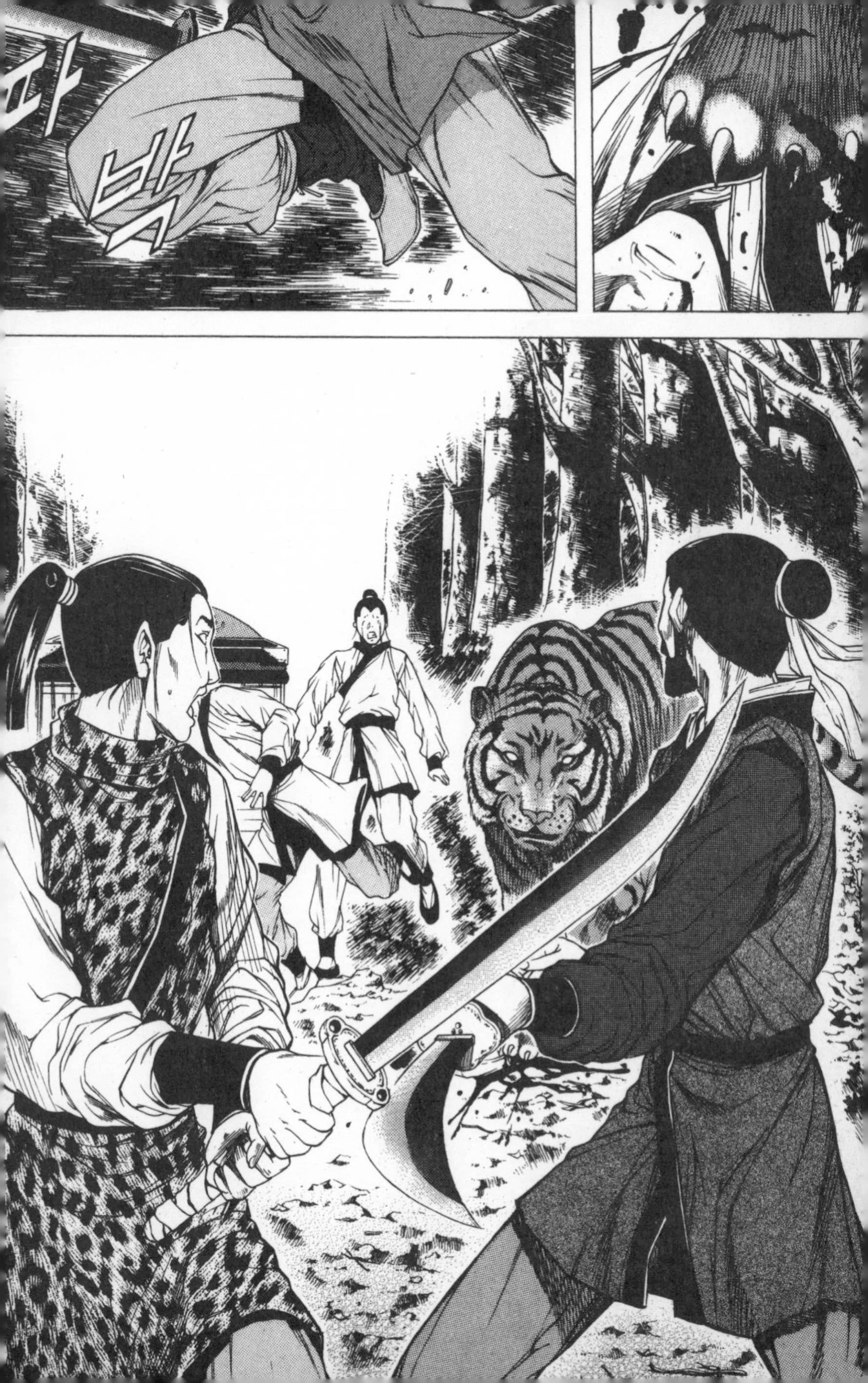
파밧

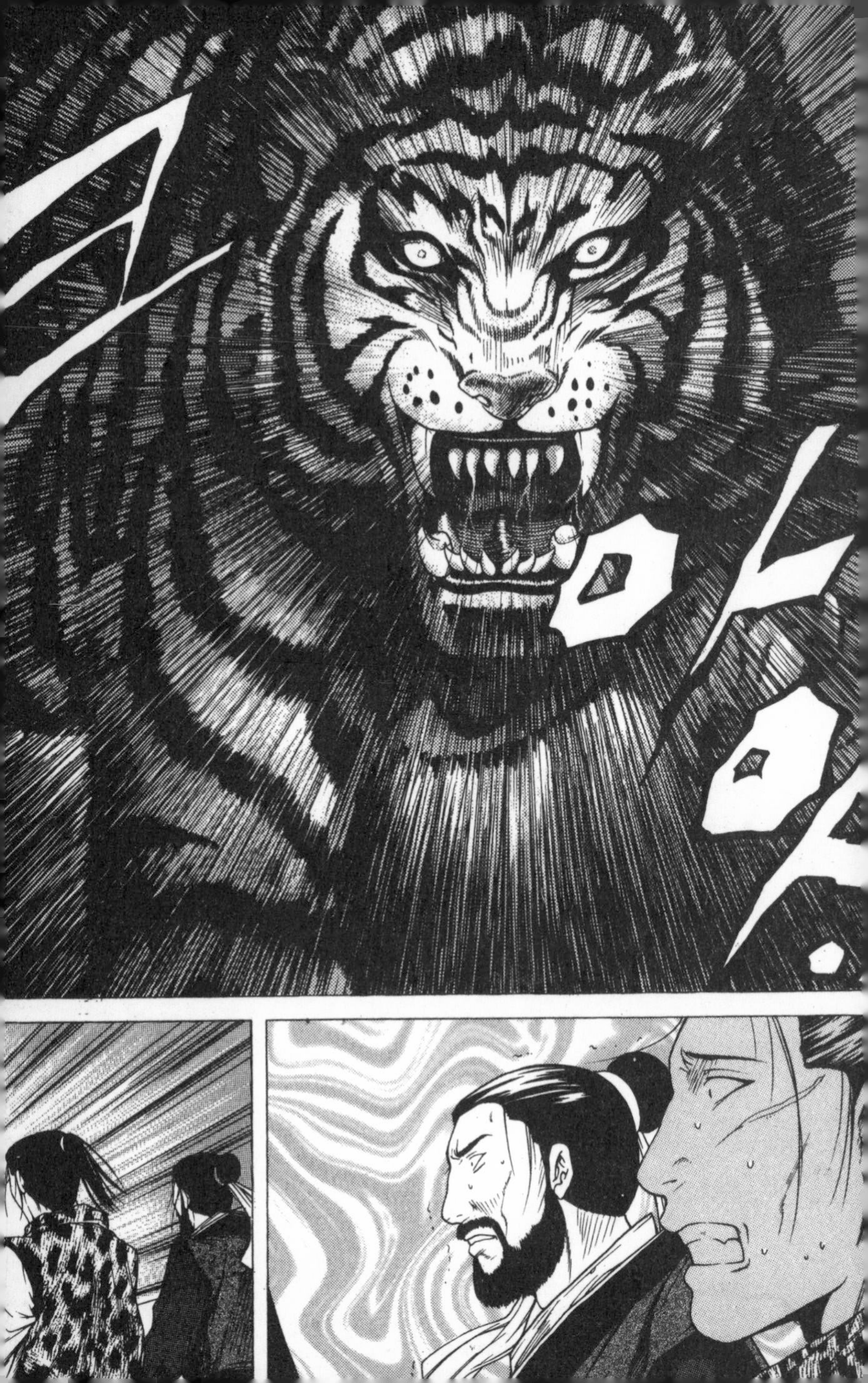

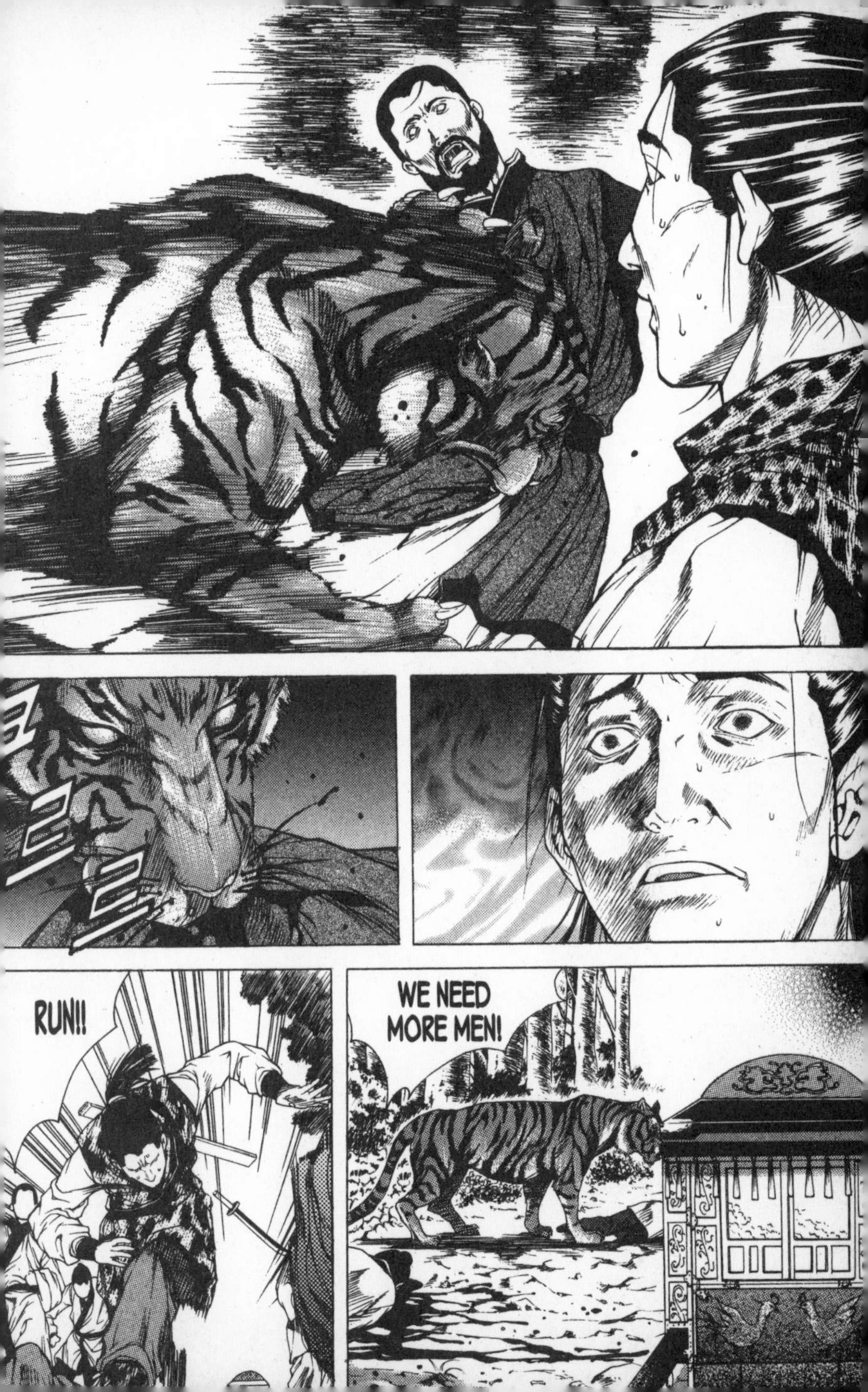
RUN!!
WE NEED MORE MEN!

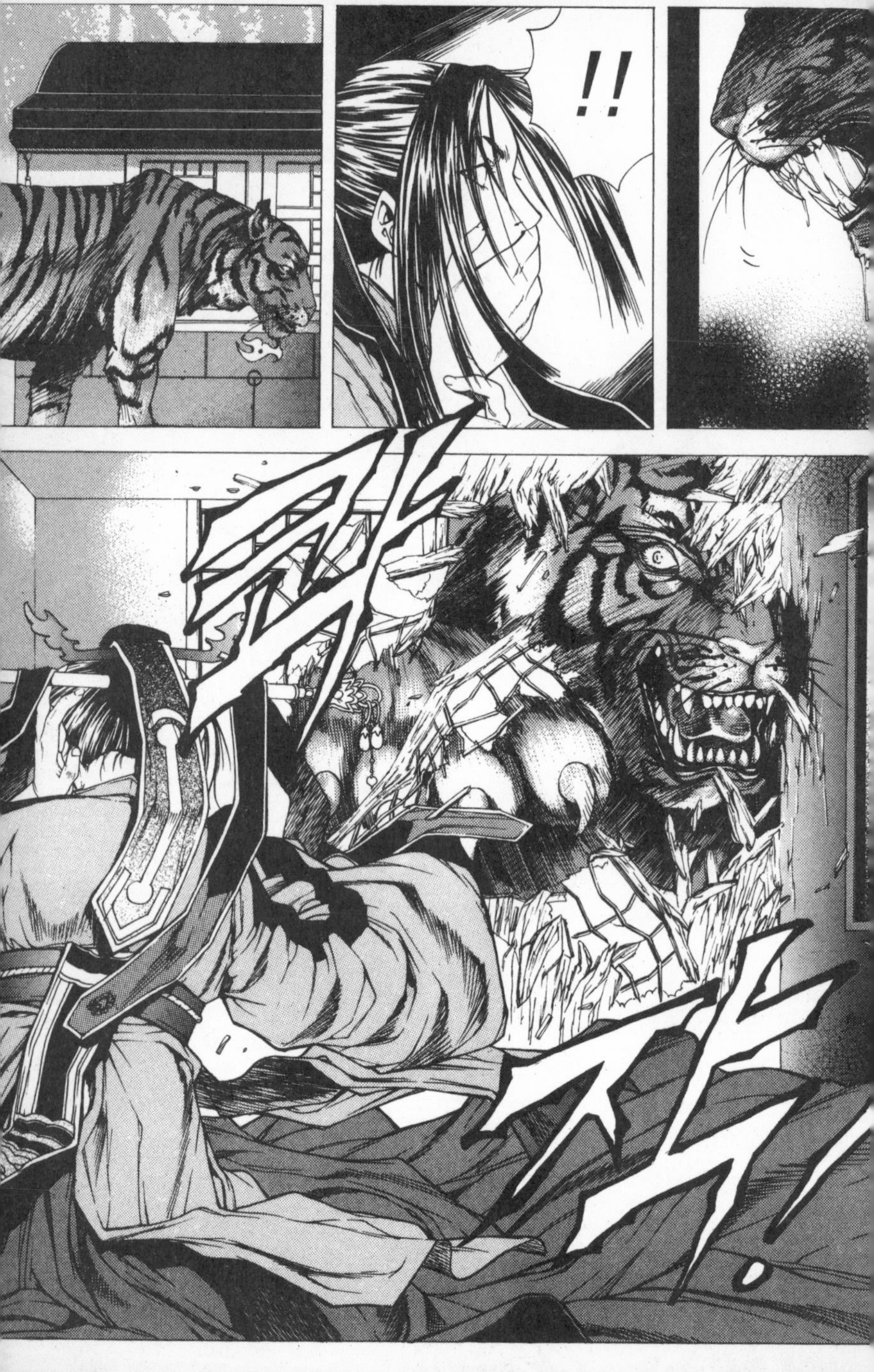
!!

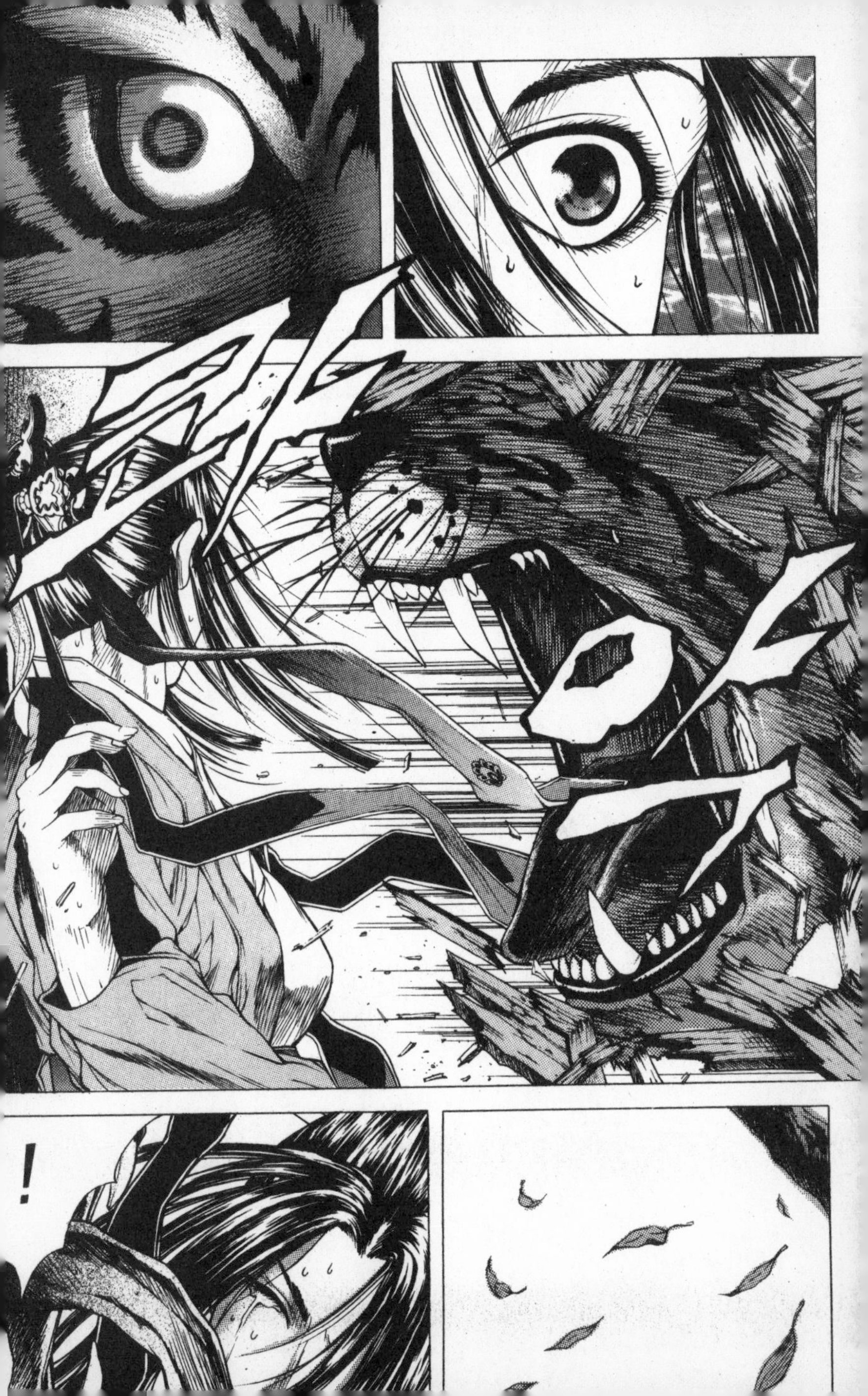
!

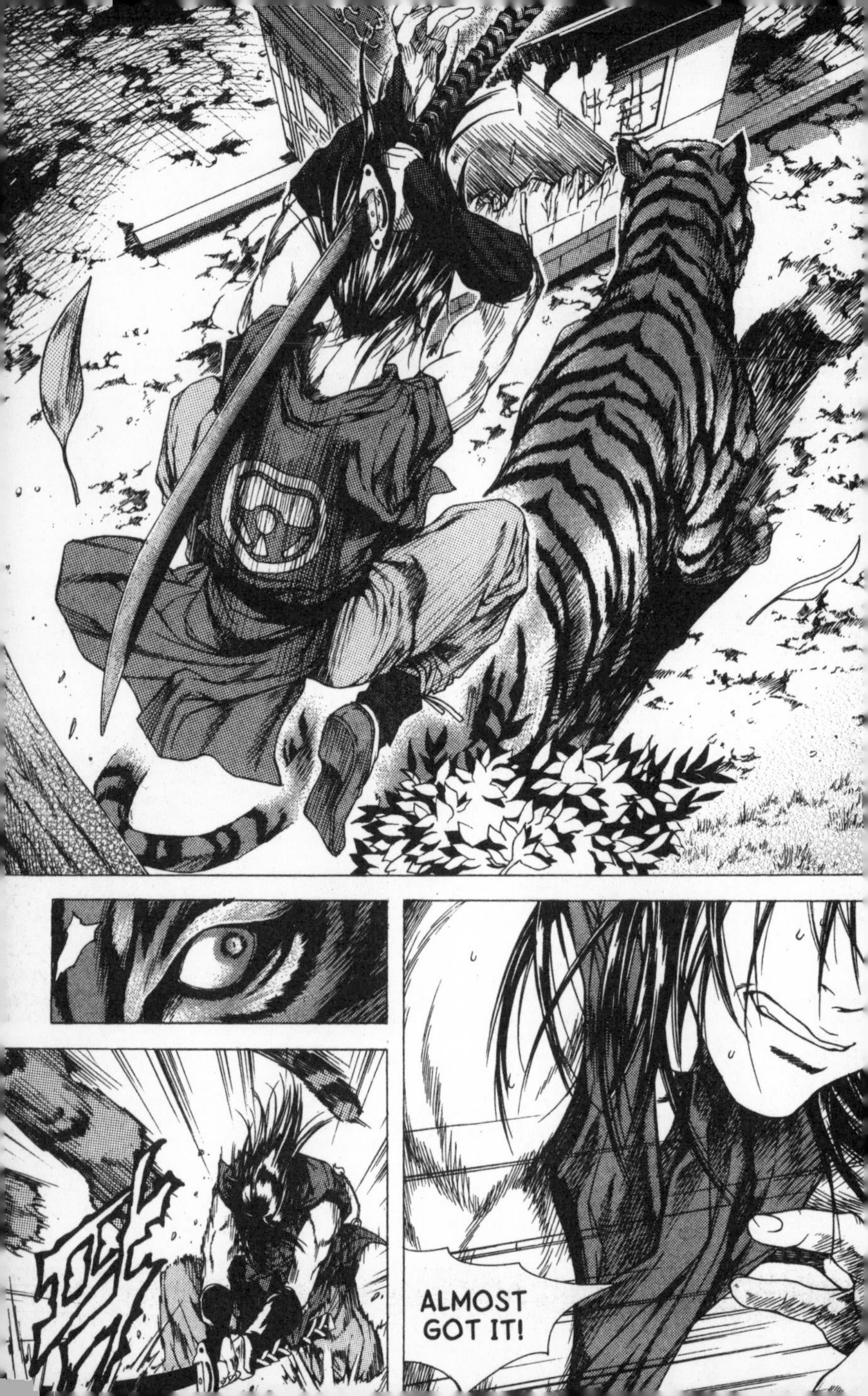
ALMOST GOT IT!

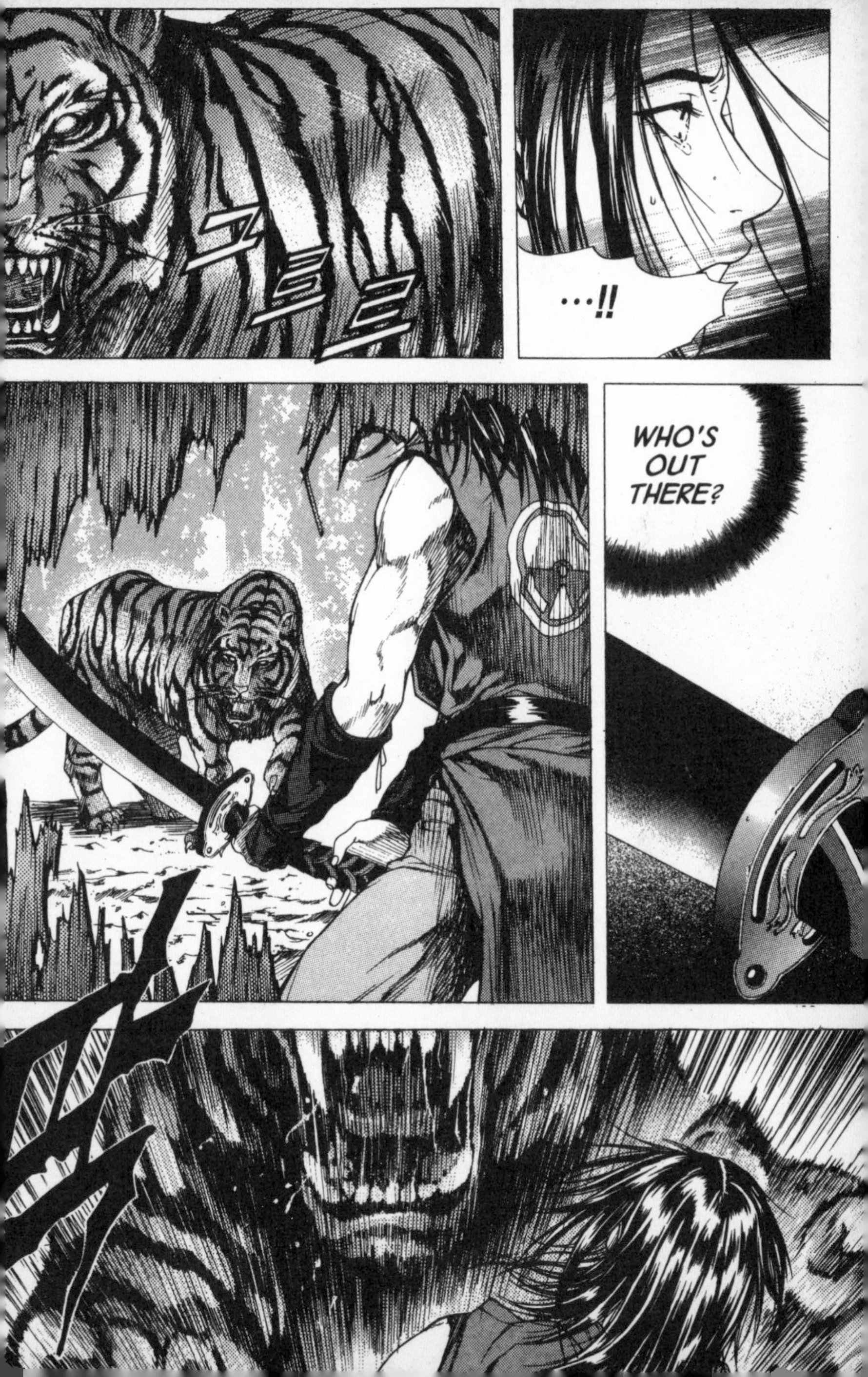
그르르
...!!
WHO'S OUT THERE?

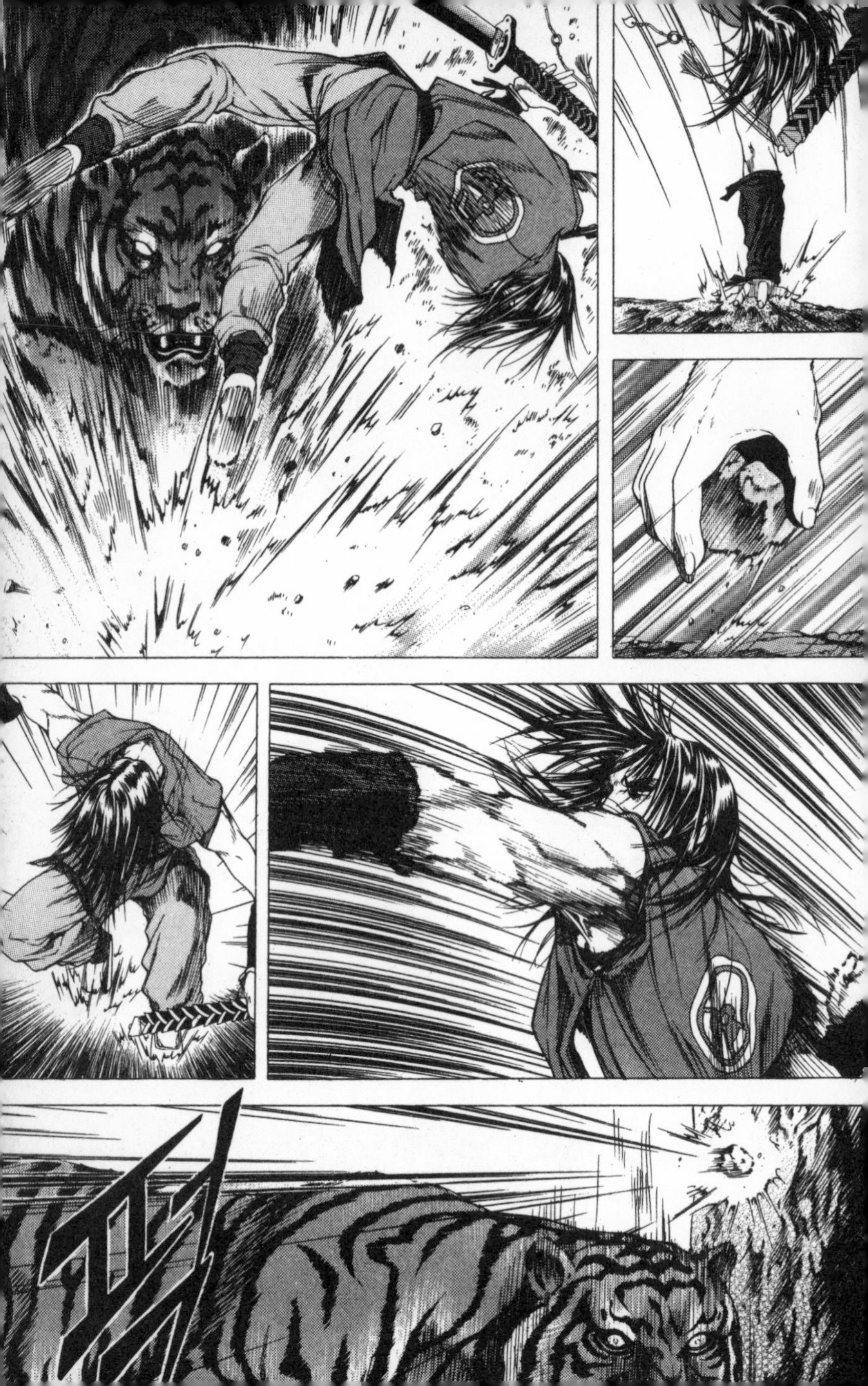

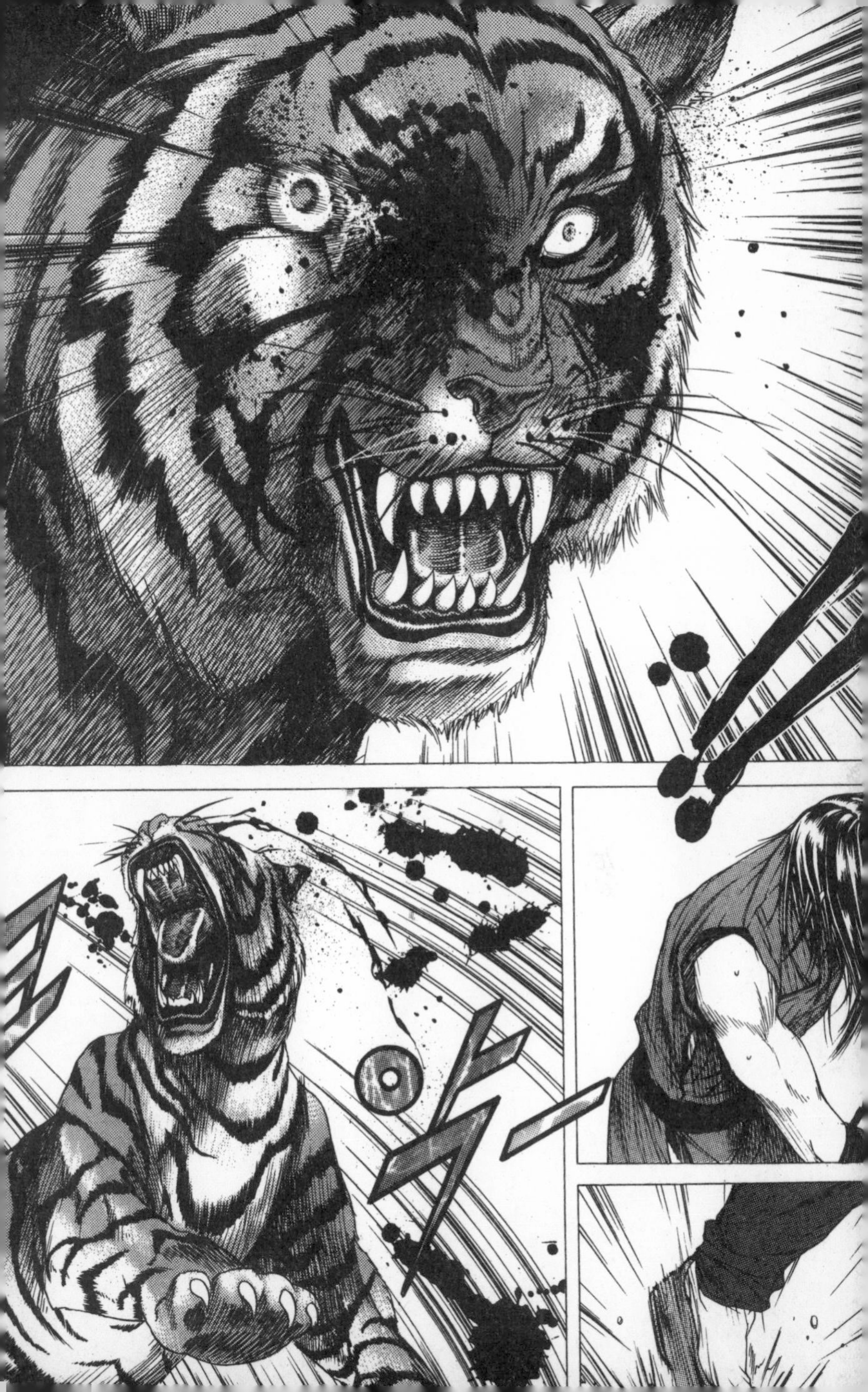

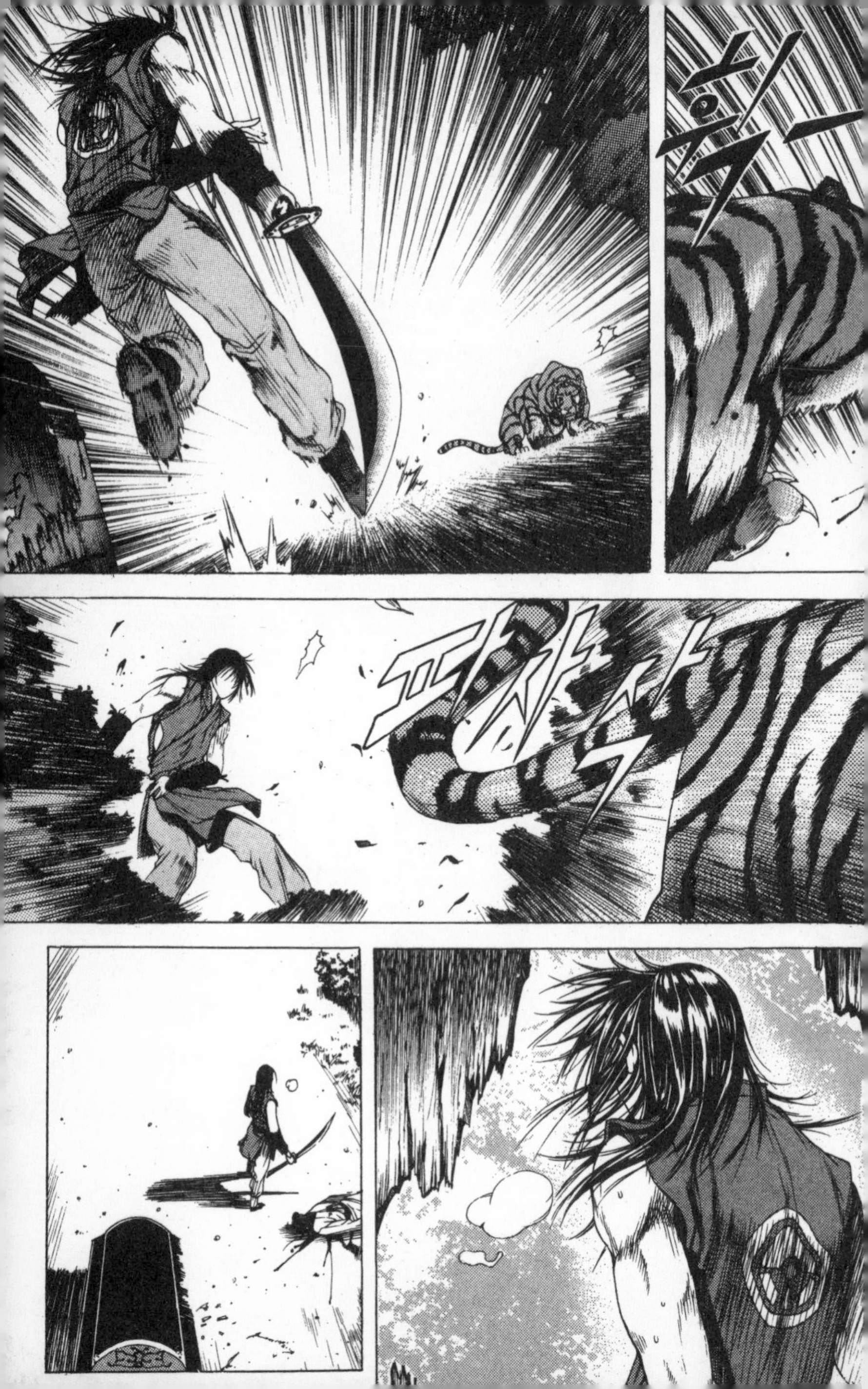

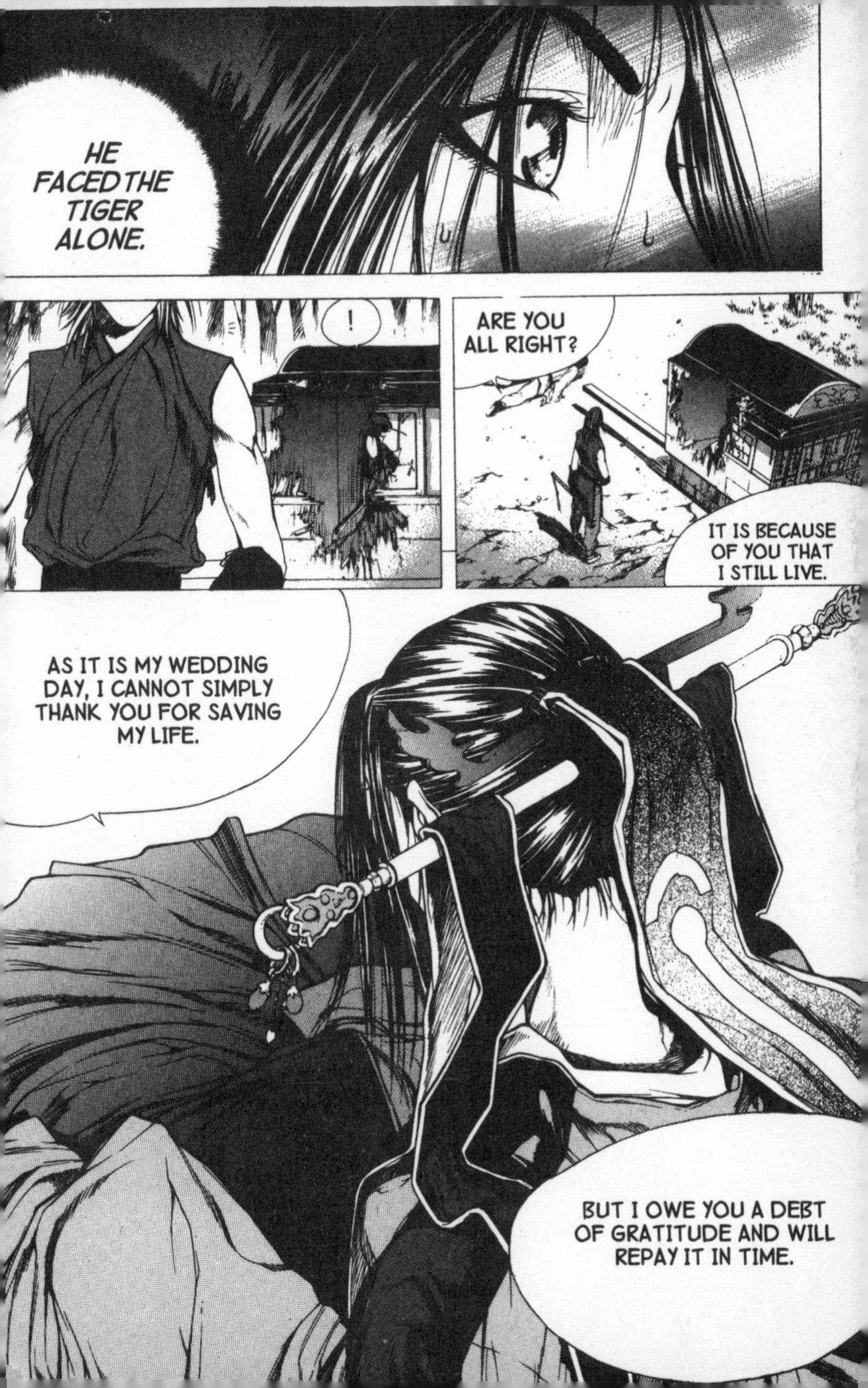
HE FACED THE TIGER ALONE.
!
ARE YOU ALL RIGHT?
IT IS BECAUSE OF YOU THAT I STILL LIVE.
AS IT IS MY WEDDING DAY, I CANNOT SIMPLY THANK YOU FOR SAVING MY LIFE.
BUT I OWE YOU A DEBT OF GRATITUDE AND WILL REPAY IT IN TIME.

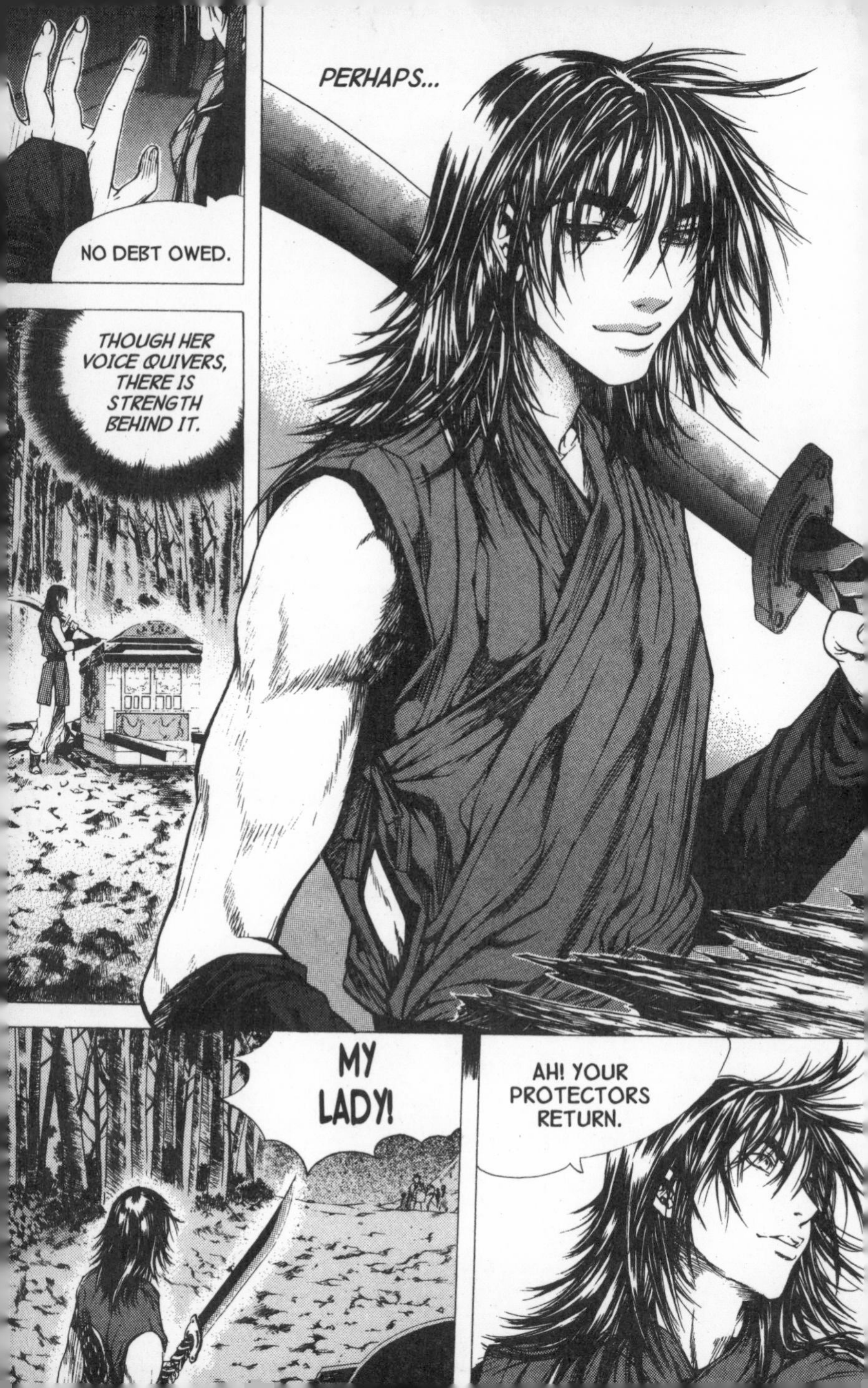
NO DEBT OWED.
PERHAPS...
THOUGH HER VOICE QUIVERS, THERE IS STRENGTH BEHIND IT.
MY LADY!
AH! YOUR PROTECTORS RETURN.

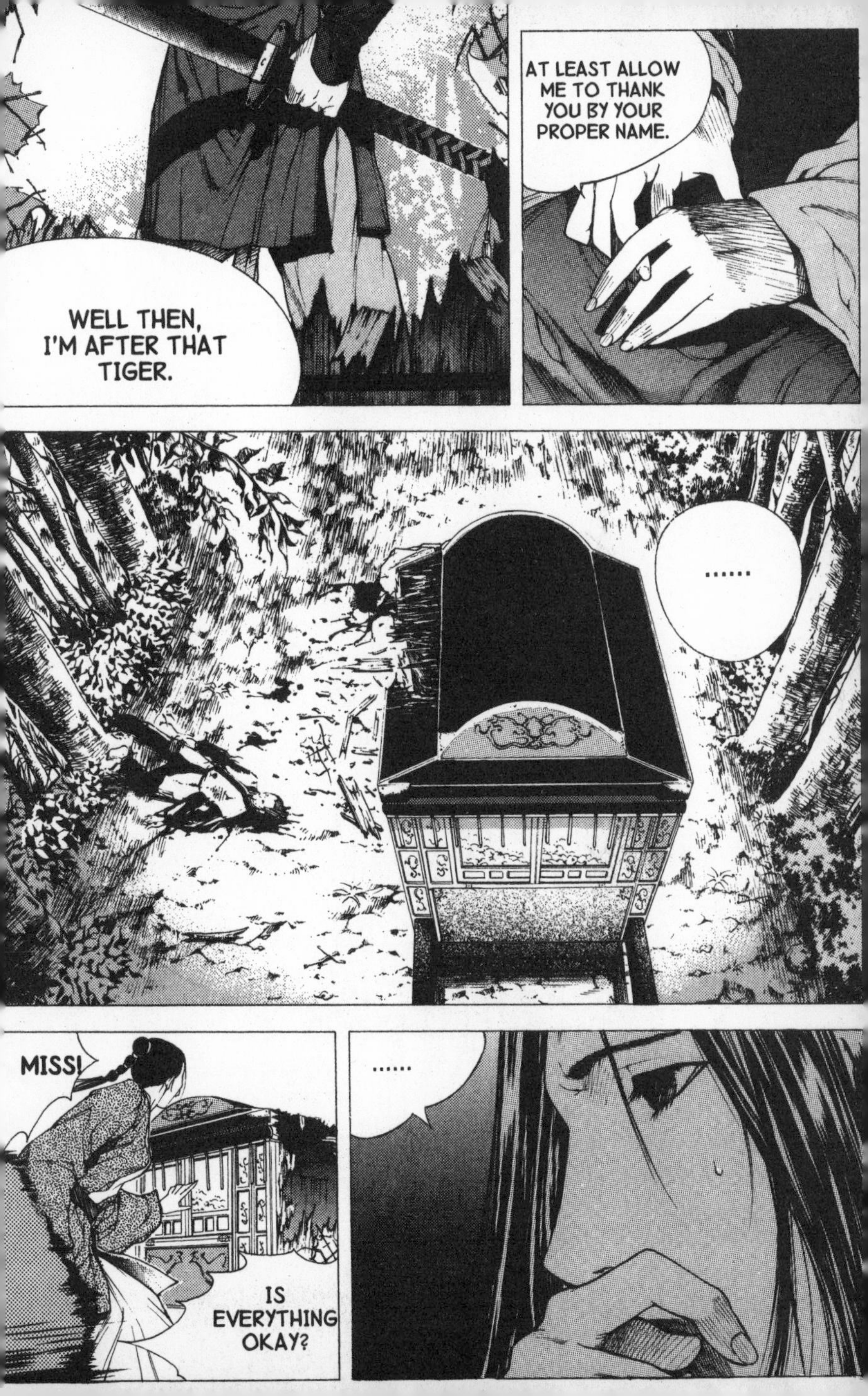
WELL THEN, I'M AFTER THAT TIGER.
AT LEAST ALLOW ME TO THANK YOU BY YOUR PROPER NAME.
......
MISS!
IS EVERYTHING OKAY?
......

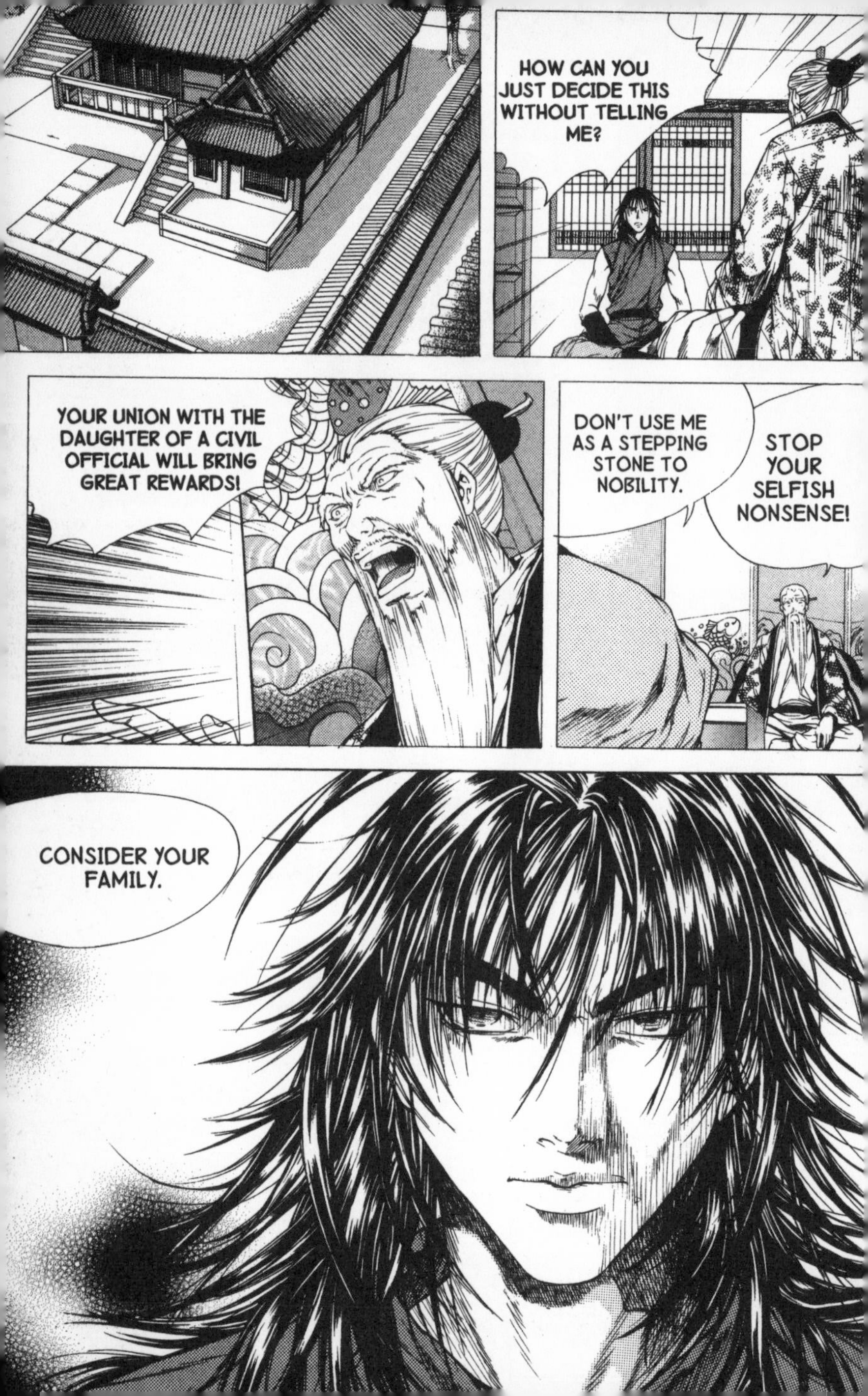
HOW CAN YOU JUST DECIDE THIS WITHOUT TELLING ME?
YOUR UNION WITH THE DAUGHTER OF A CIVIL OFFICIAL WILL BRING GREAT REWARDS!
DON'T USE ME AS A STEPPING STONE TO NOBILITY.
STOP YOUR SELFISH NONSENSE!
CONSIDER YOUR FAMILY.

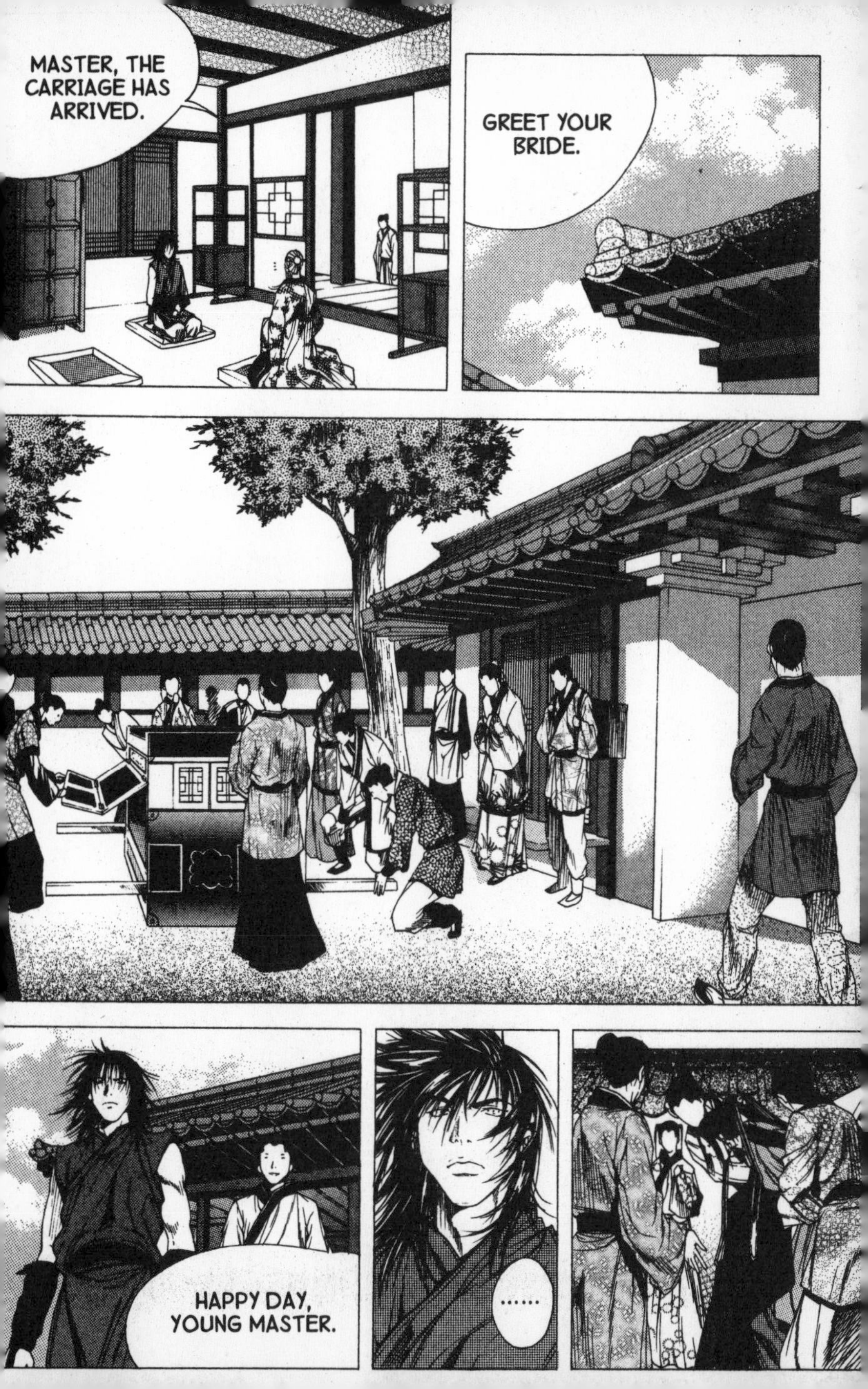
MASTER, THE CARRIAGE HAS ARRIVED.
GREET YOUR BRIDE.
HAPPY DAY, YOUNG MASTER.
......

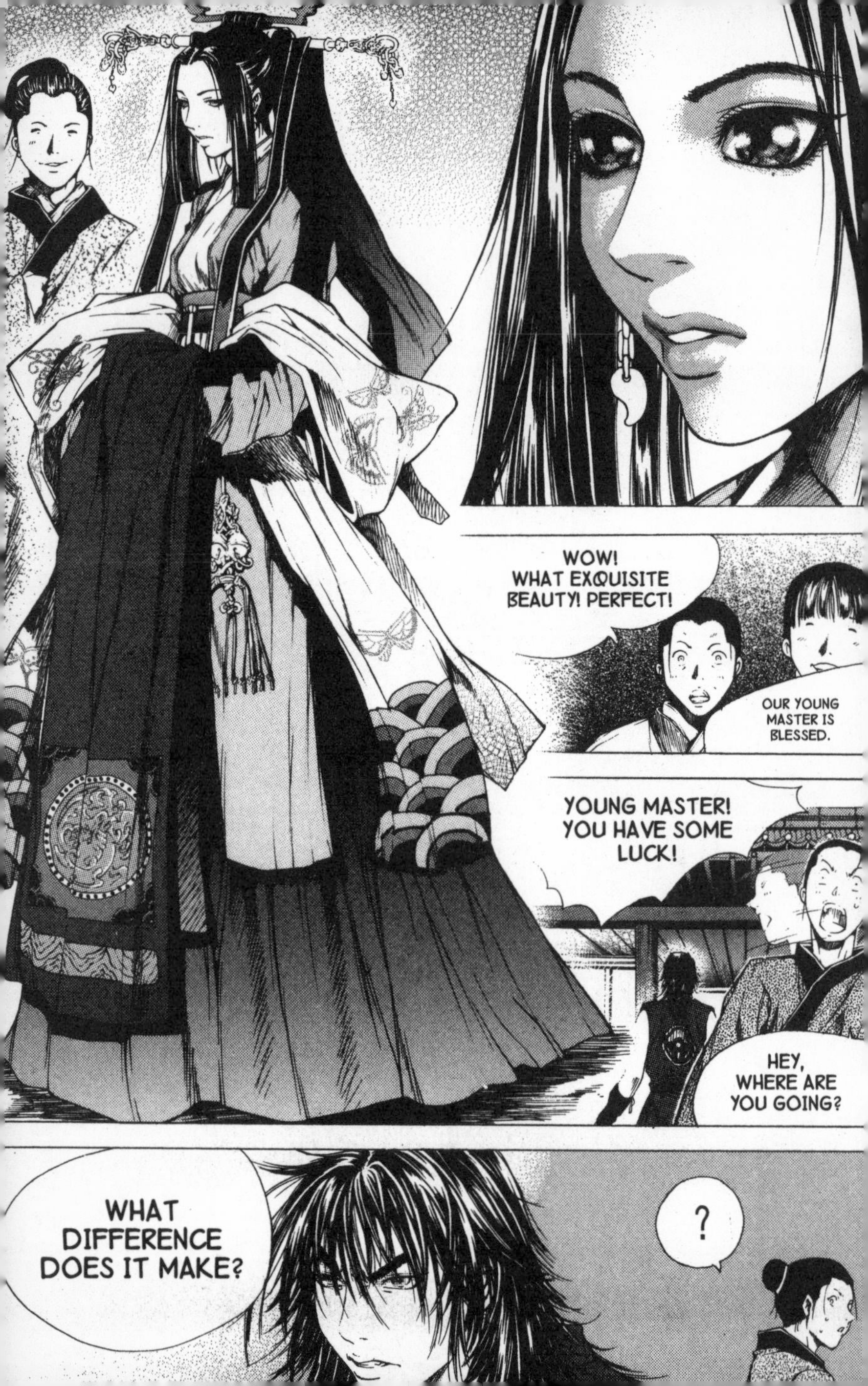
WOW! WHAT EXQUISITE BEAUTY! PERFECT!
OUR YOUNG MASTER IS BLESSED.
YOUNG MASTER! YOU HAVE SOME LUCK!
HEY, WHERE ARE YOU GOING?
WHAT DIFFERENCE DOES IT MAKE?
?

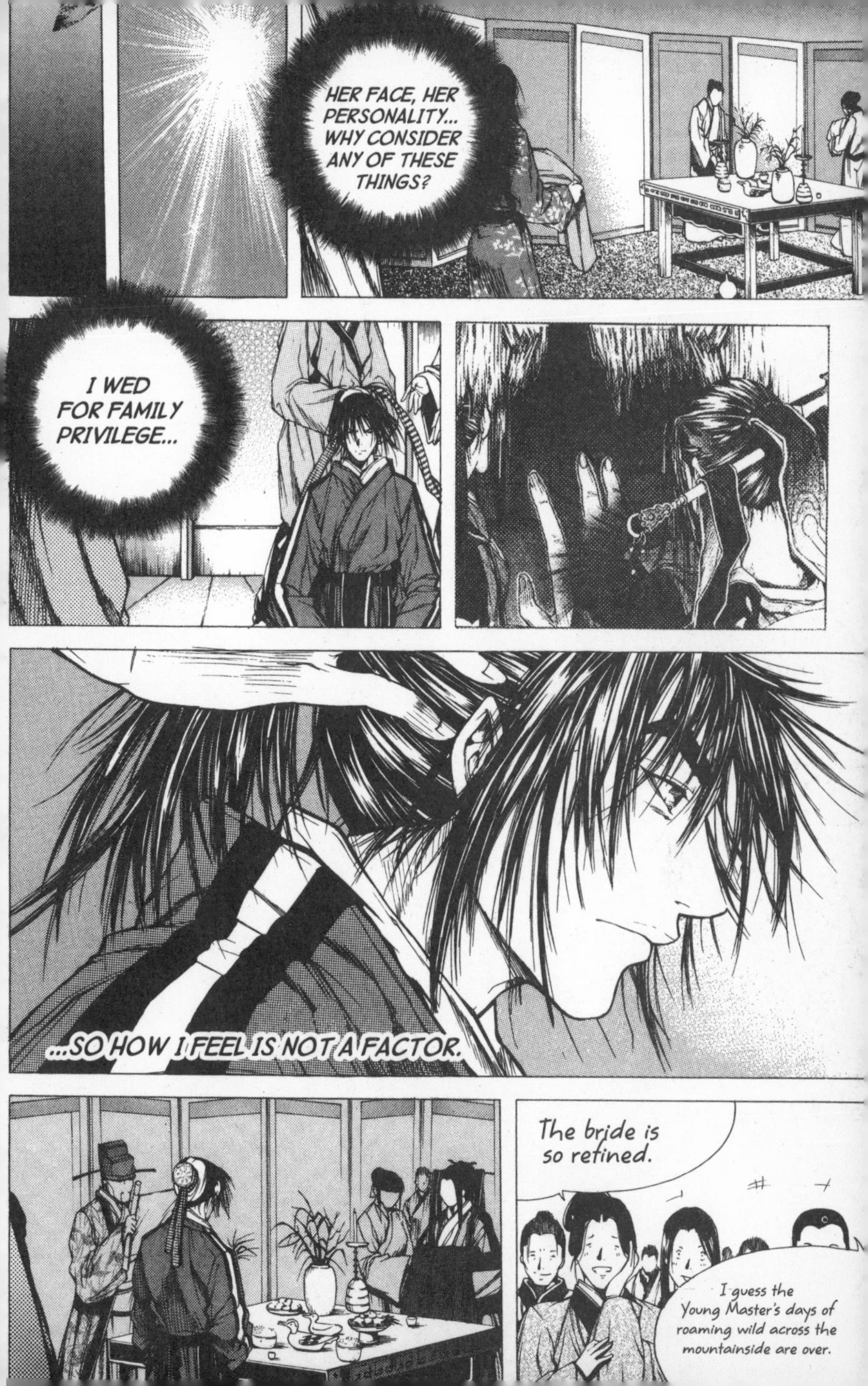
HER FACE, HER PERSONALITY... WHY CONSIDER ANY OF THESE THINGS?
I WED FOR FAMILY PRIVILEGE...
...SO HOW I FEEL IS NOT A FACTOR.
The bride is so refined.
I guess the Young Master's days of roaming wild across the mountainside are over.

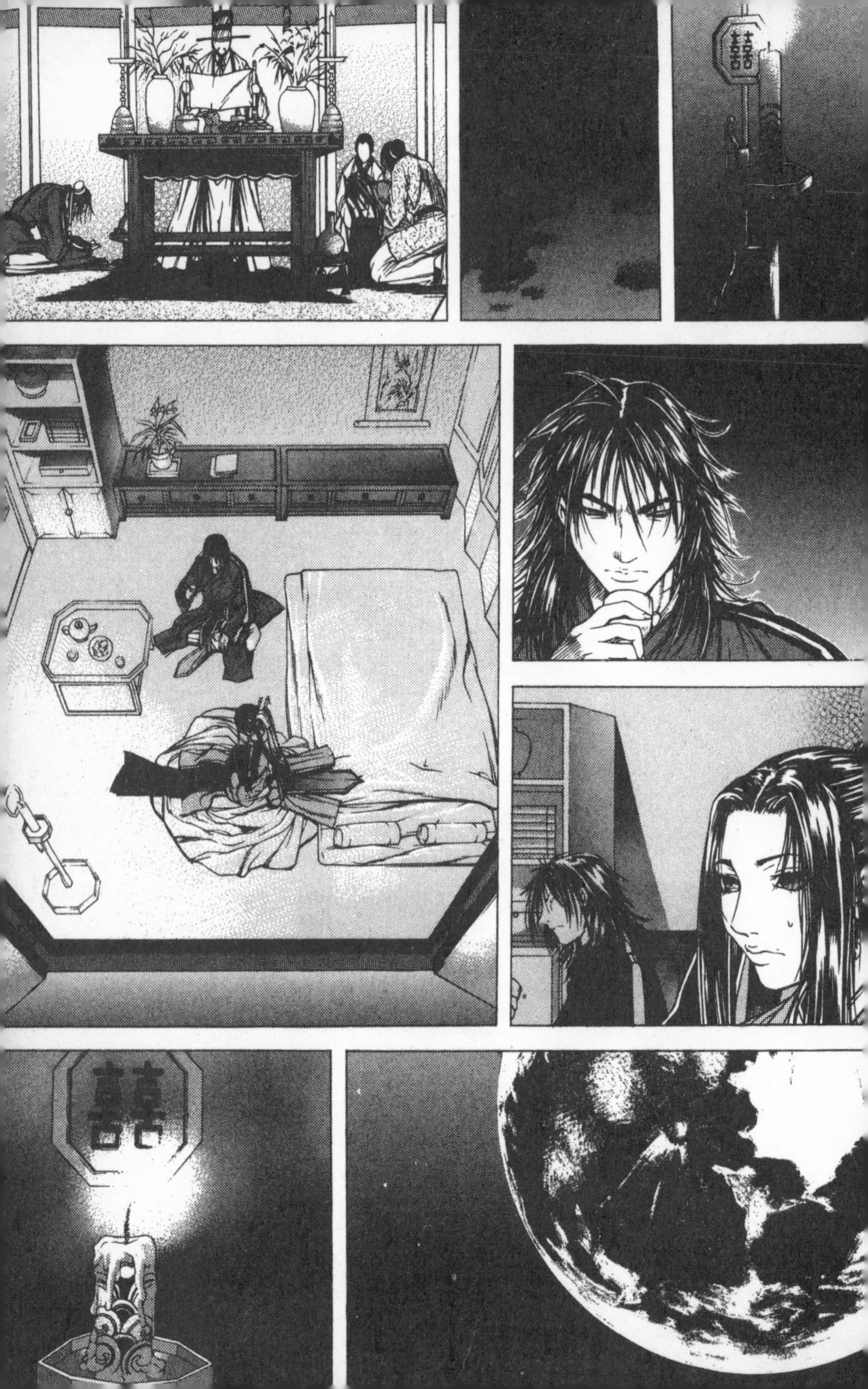
囍
囍

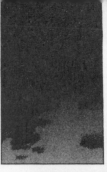

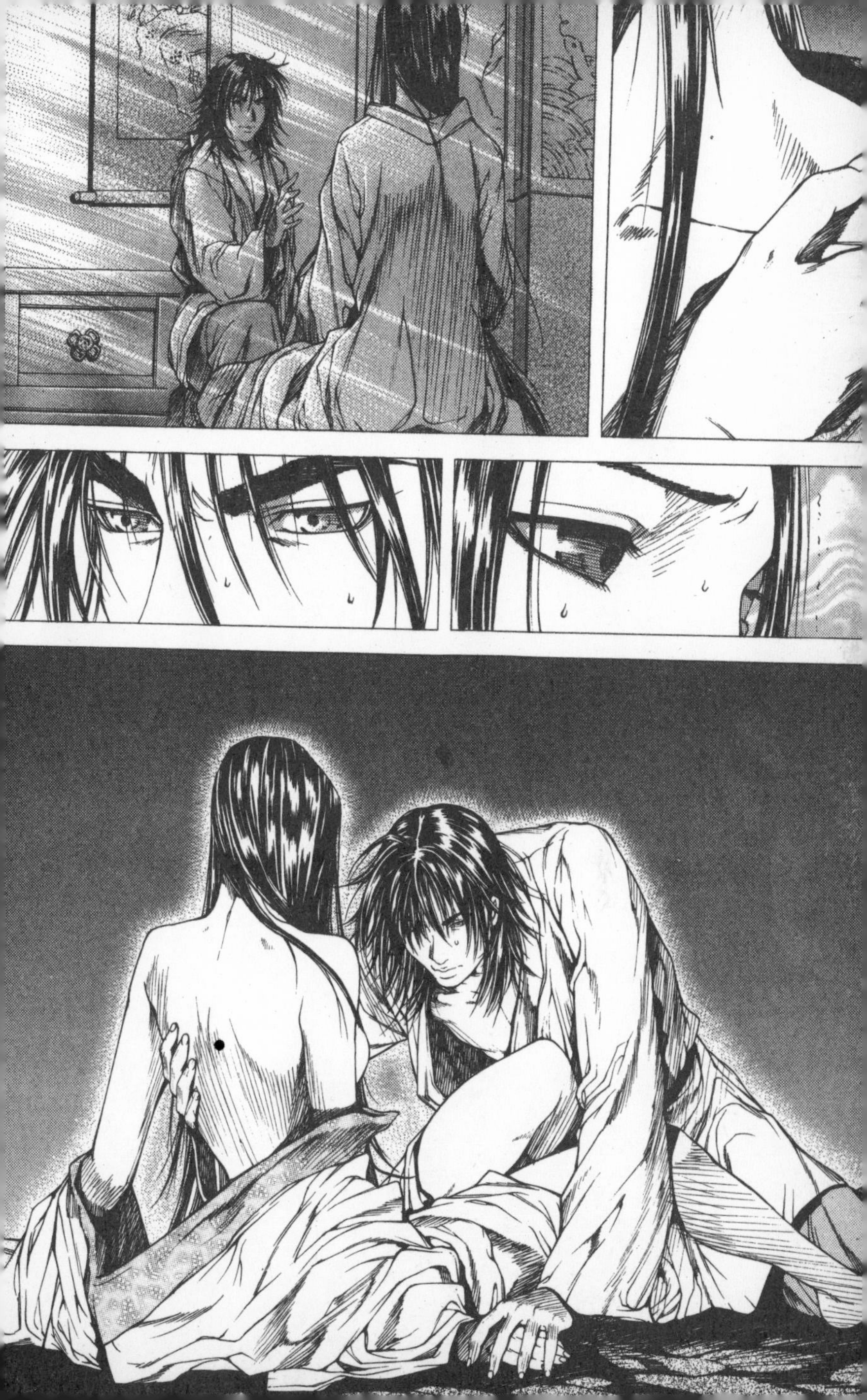

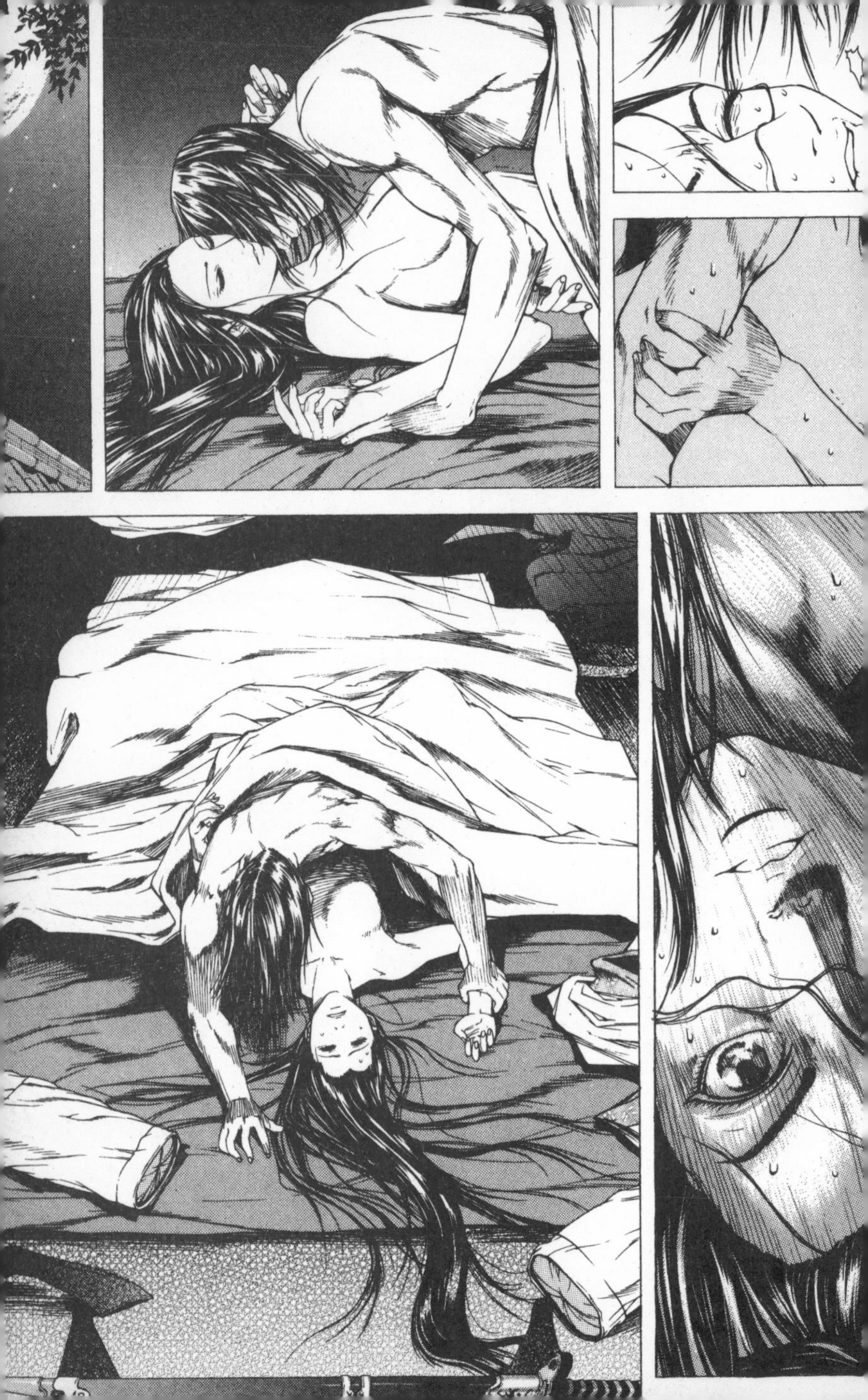

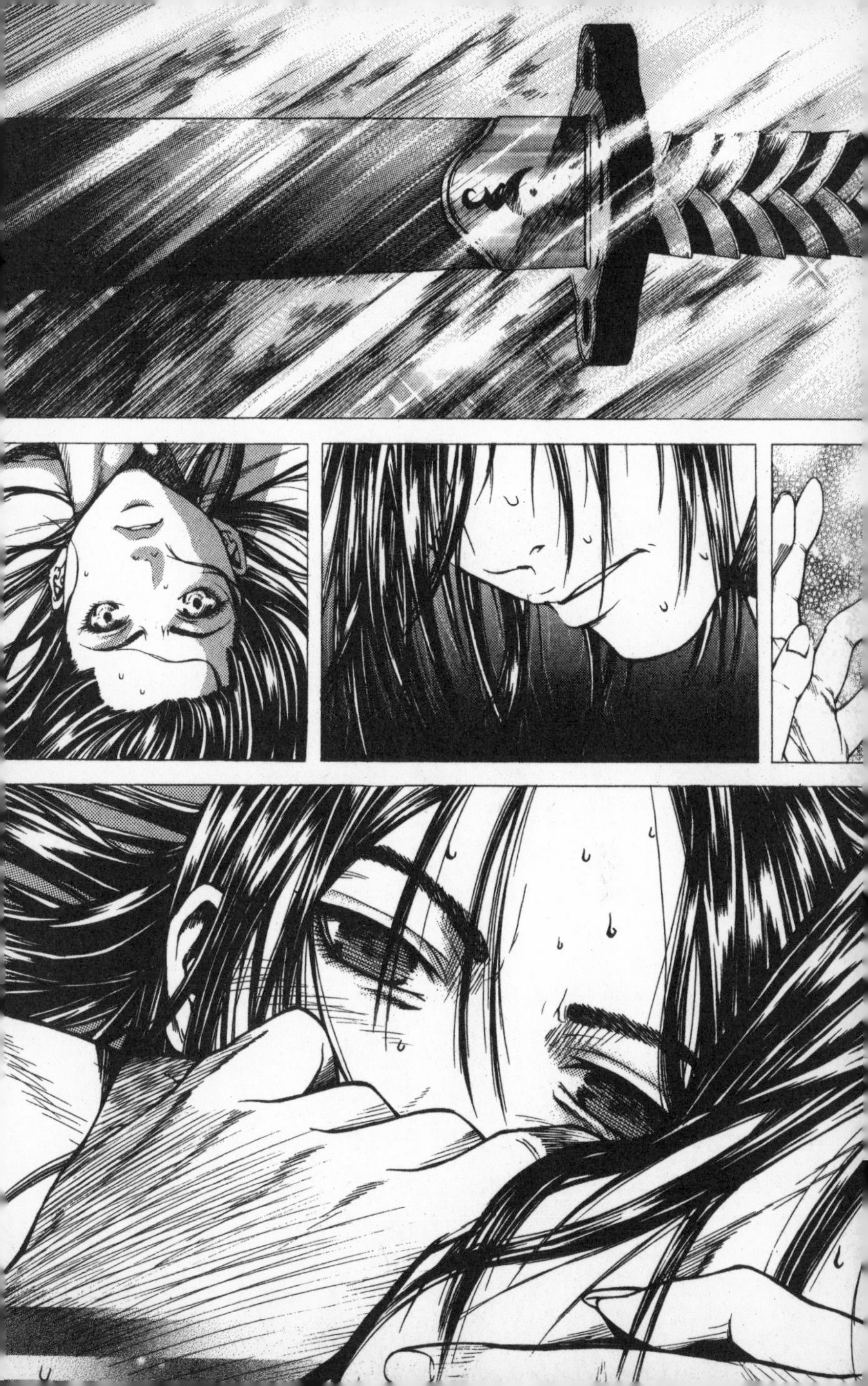

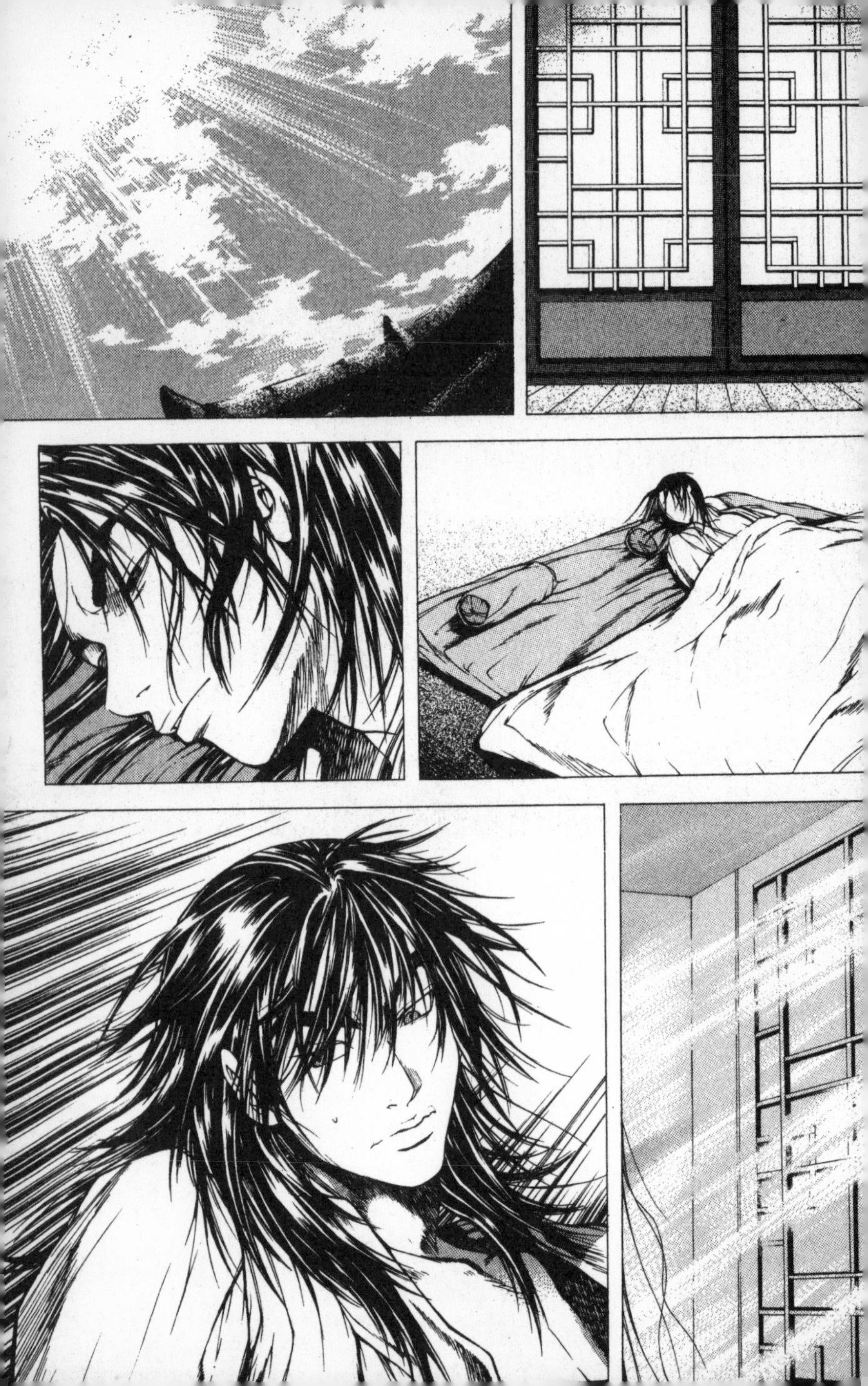

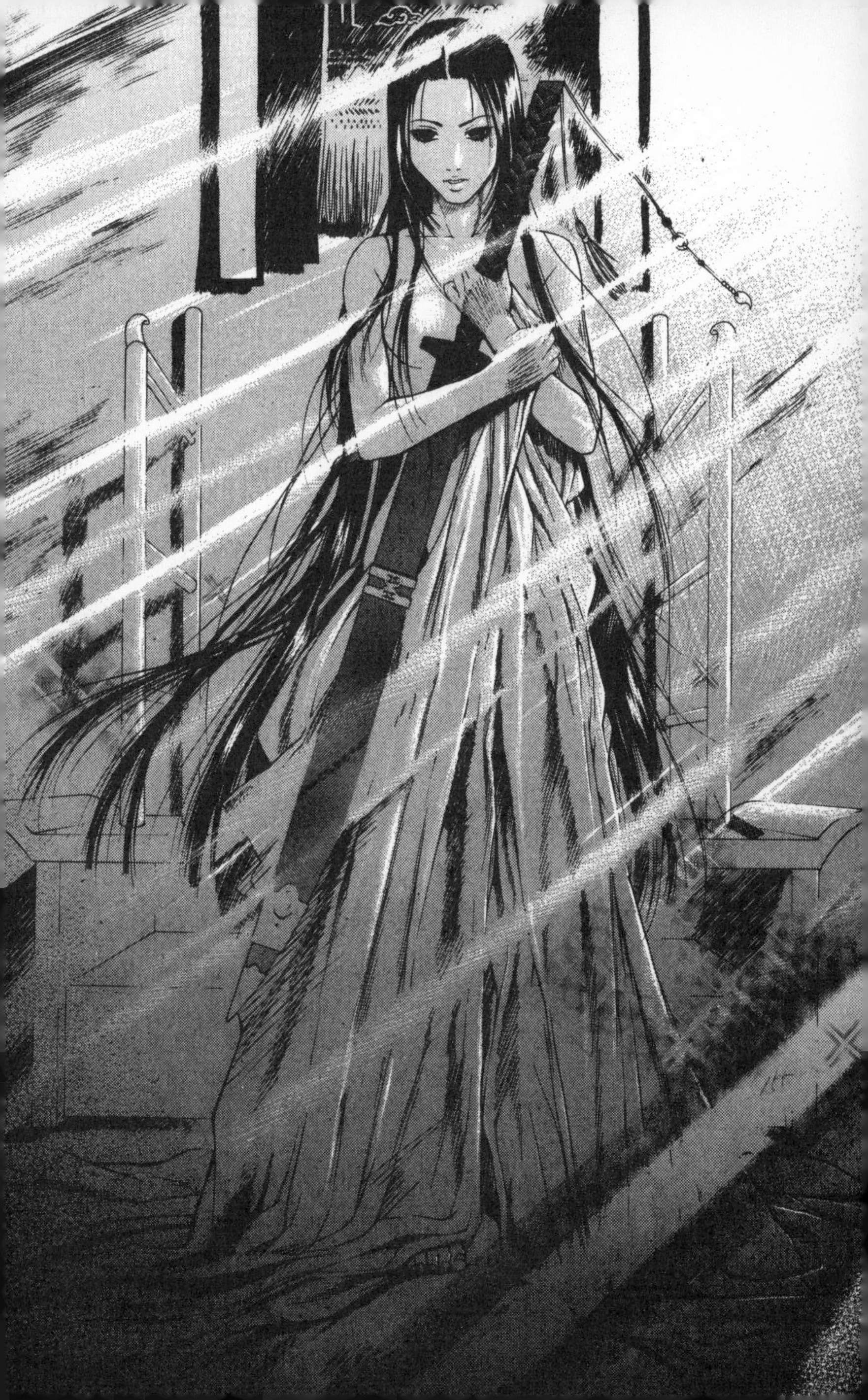

THIS IS THE SWORD.

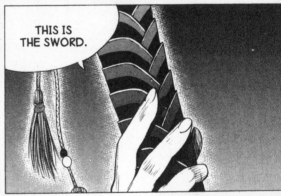

YOU SAVED MY LIFE ON THE ROAD.

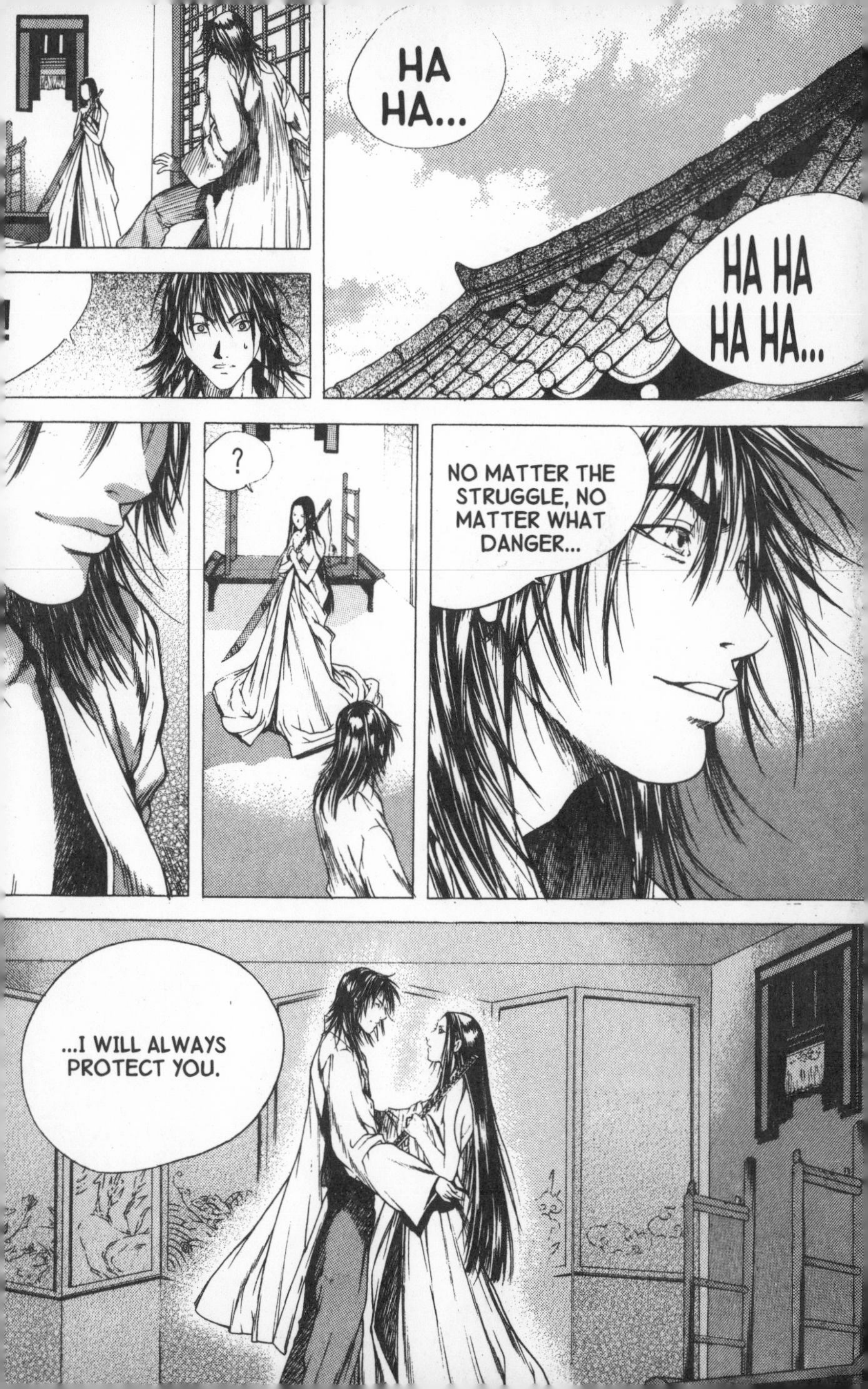
!
HA HA...
HA HA HA HA...
?
NO MATTER THE STRUGGLE, NO MATTER WHAT DANGER...
...I WILL ALWAYS PROTECT YOU.

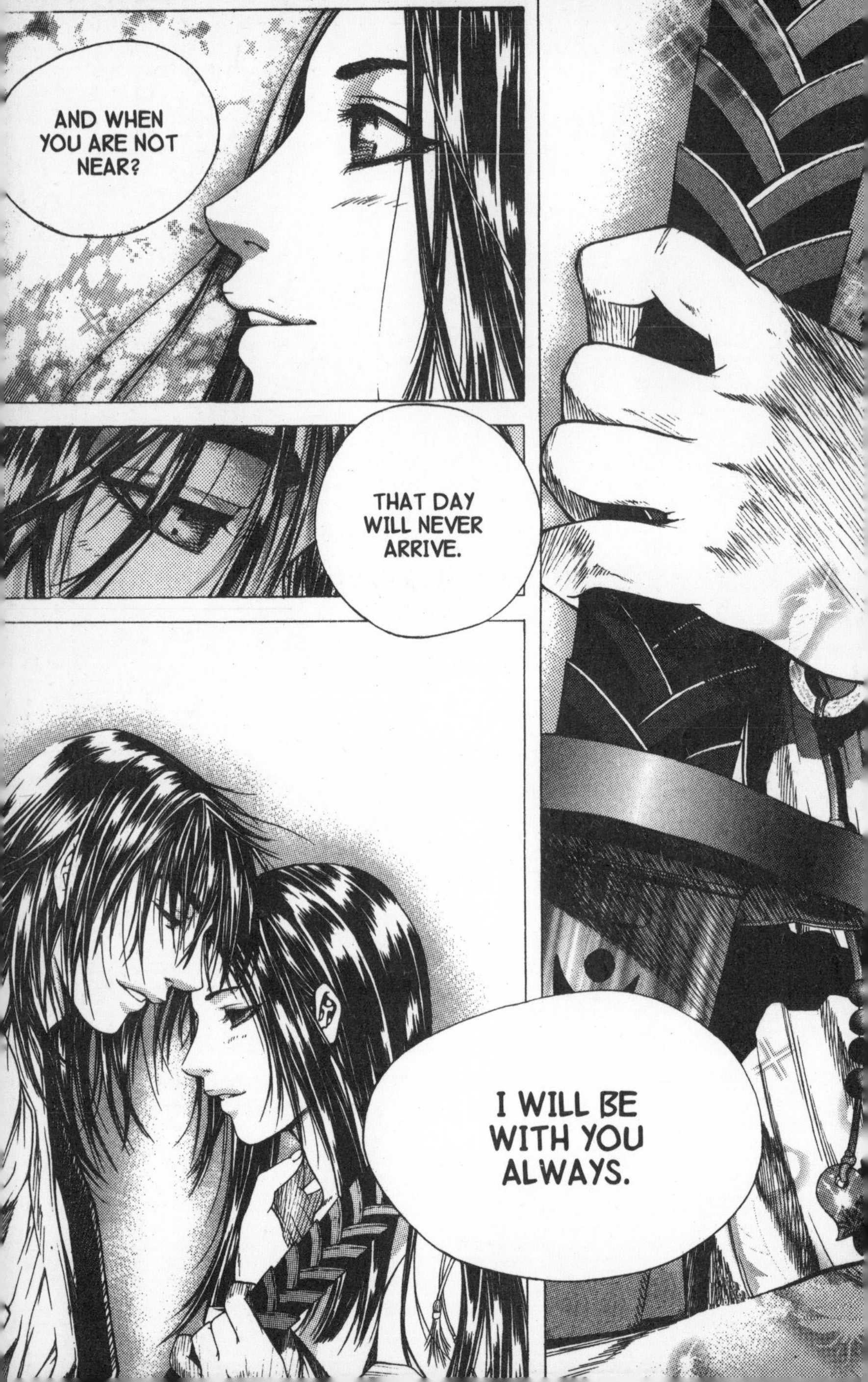
AND WHEN YOU ARE NOT NEAR?
THAT DAY WILL NEVER ARRIVE.
I WILL BE WITH YOU ALWAYS.

MY FAMILY HELPS

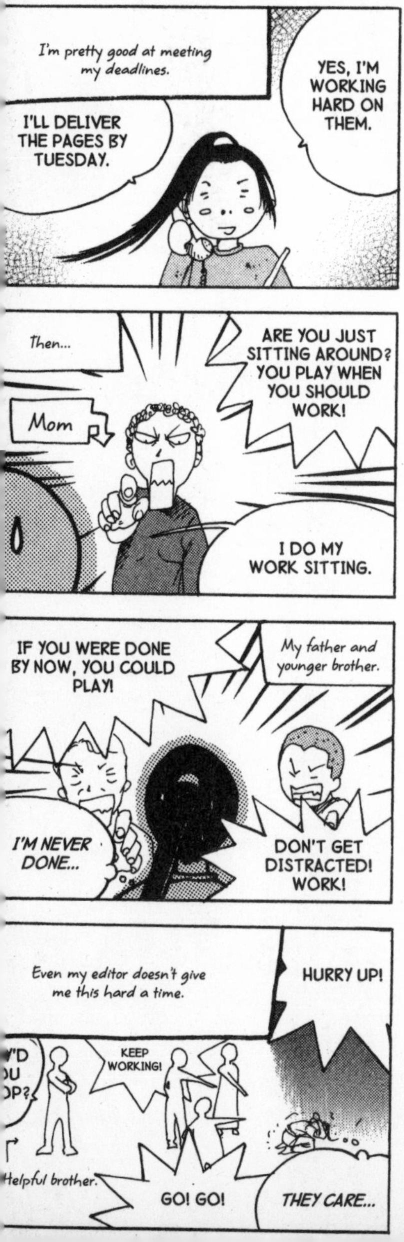

I'm pretty good at meeting my deadlines.
I'LL DELIVER THE PAGES BY TUESDAY.
YES, I'M WORKING HARD ON THEM.
Then...
Mom
ARE YOU JUST SITTING AROUND? YOU PLAY WHEN YOU SHOULD WORK!
I DO MY WORK SITTING.
IF YOU WERE DONE BY NOW, YOU COULD PLAY!
My father and younger brother.
I'M NEVER DONE...
DON'T GET DISTRACTED! WORK!
Even my editor doesn't give me this hard a time.
HURRY UP!
KEEP WORKING!
Helpful brother.
GO! GO!
THEY CARE...

CHILD PRODIGY

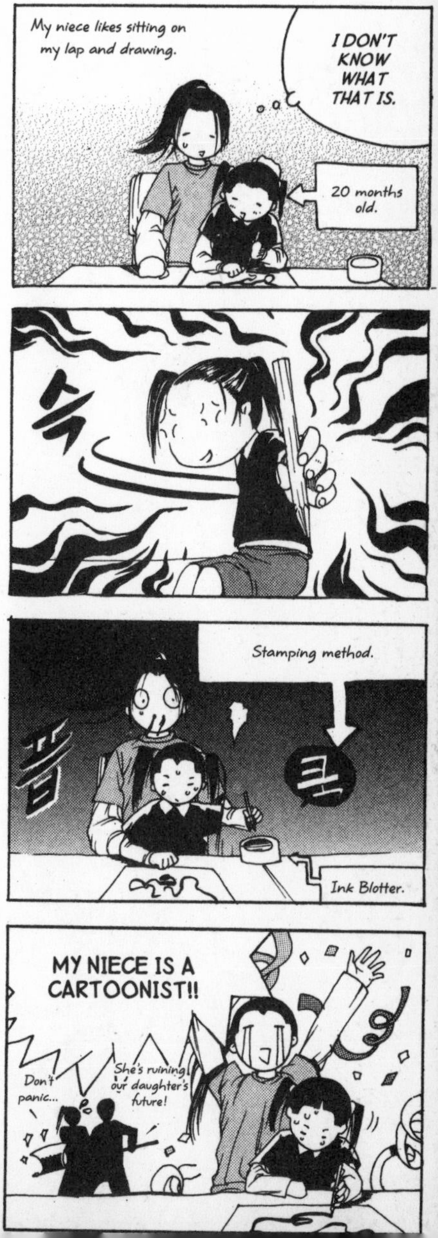

My niece likes sitting on my lap and drawing.
I DON'T KNOW WHAT THAT IS.
20 months old.
Stamping method.
Ink Blotter.
MY NIECE IS A CARTOONIST!!
Don't panic...
She's ruining our daughter's future!

THE HUMAN FORM

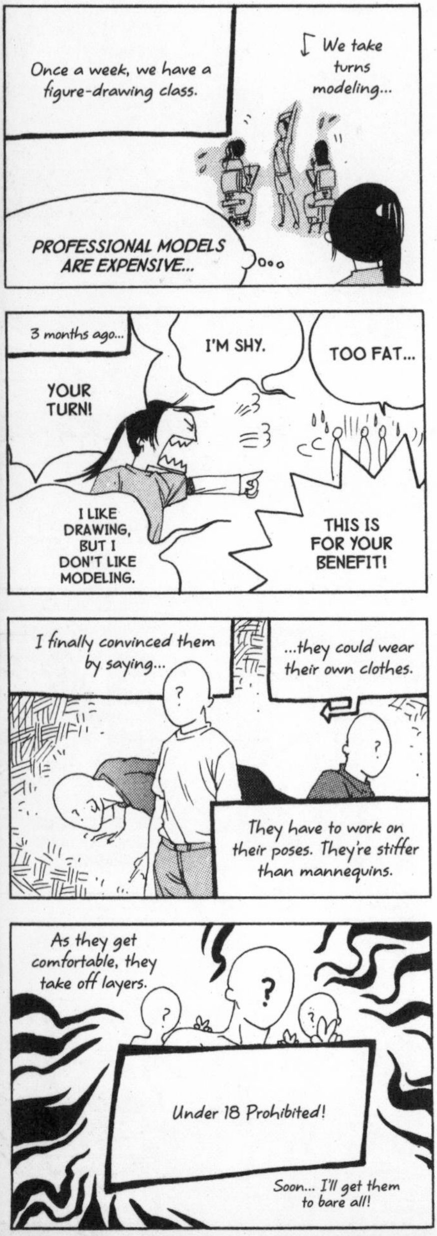
Once a week, we have a figure-drawing class.
We take turns modeling...
PROFESSIONAL MODELS ARE EXPENSIVE...
3 months ago...
YOUR TURN!
I'M SHY.
TOO FAT...
I LIKE DRAWING, BUT I DON'T LIKE MODELING.
THIS IS FOR YOUR BENEFIT!
I finally convinced them by saying...
...they could wear their own clothes.
They have to work on their poses. They're stiffer than mannequins.
As they get comfortable, they take off layers.
Under 18 Prohibited!
Soon... I'll get them to bare all!

TAKING A BREAK

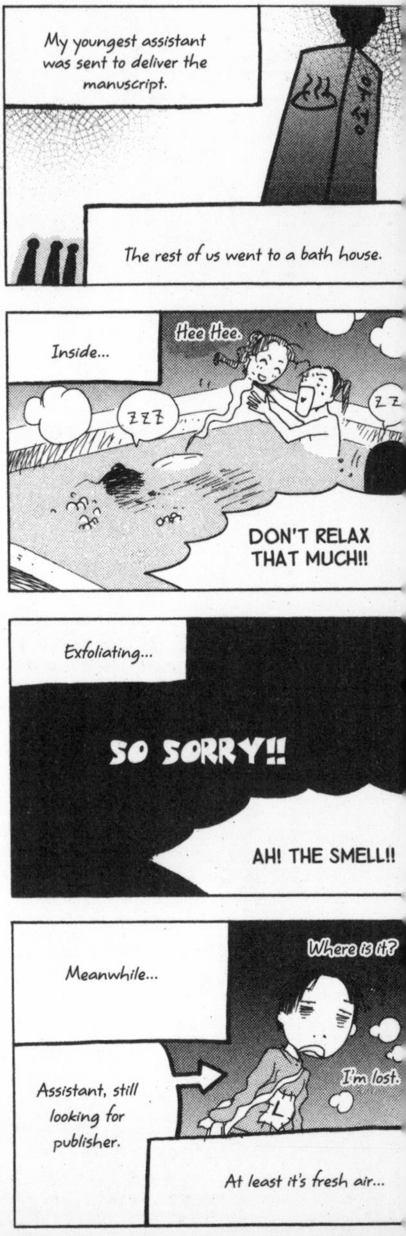
My youngest assistant was sent to deliver the manuscript.
The rest of us went to a bath house.
Inside...
Hee Hee.
ZZZ
ZZ
DON'T RELAX THAT MUCH!!
Exfoliating...
SO SORRY!!
AH! THE SMELL!!
Meanwhile...
Where is it?
Assistant, still looking for publisher.
I'm lost.
At least it's fresh air...

PRIORITIES

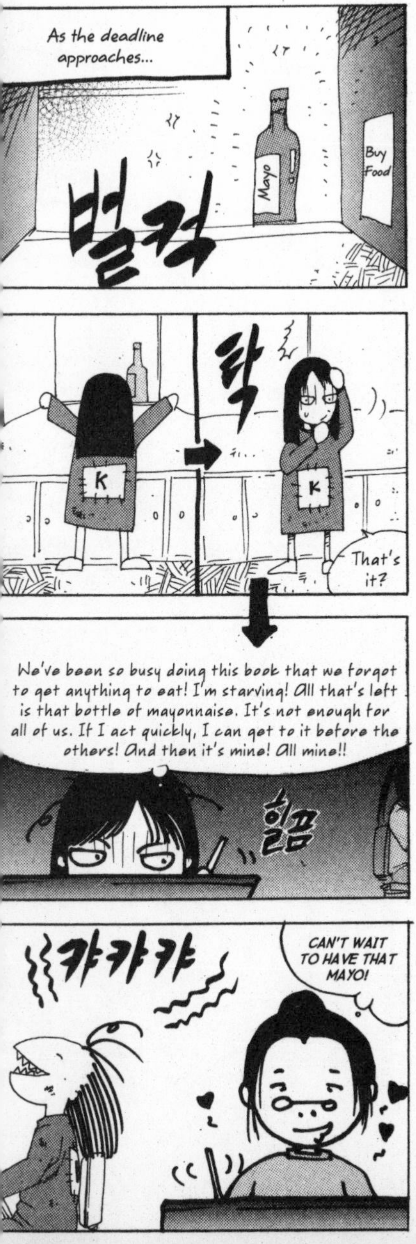
As the deadline approaches...
Mayo
Buy Food
벌컥
탁
That's it?
We've been so busy doing this book that we forgot to get anything to eat! I'm starving! All that's left is that bottle of mayonnaise. It's not enough for all of us. If I act quickly, I can get to it before the others! And then it's mine! All mine!!
힐끔
캬캬캬
CAN'T WAIT TO HAVE THAT MAYO!

PERFECT BOYFRIEND

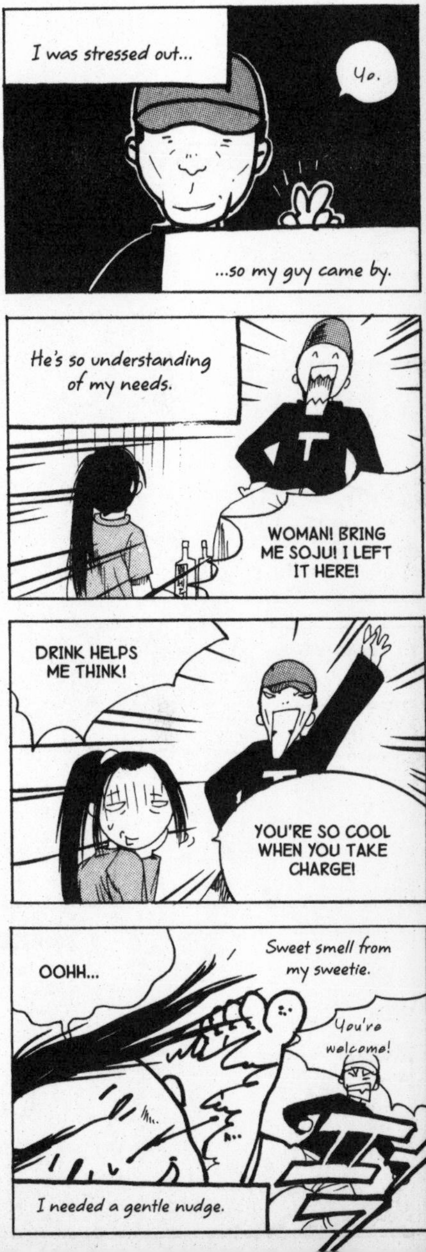
I was stressed out...
Yo.
...so my guy came by.
He's so understanding of my needs.
WOMAN! BRING ME SOJU! I LEFT IT HERE!
DRINK HELPS ME THINK!
YOU'RE SO COOL WHEN YOU TAKE CHARGE!
OOHH...
Sweet smell from my sweetie.
You're welcome!
I needed a gentle nudge.

In the author's sleep, she is a fierce warrior.

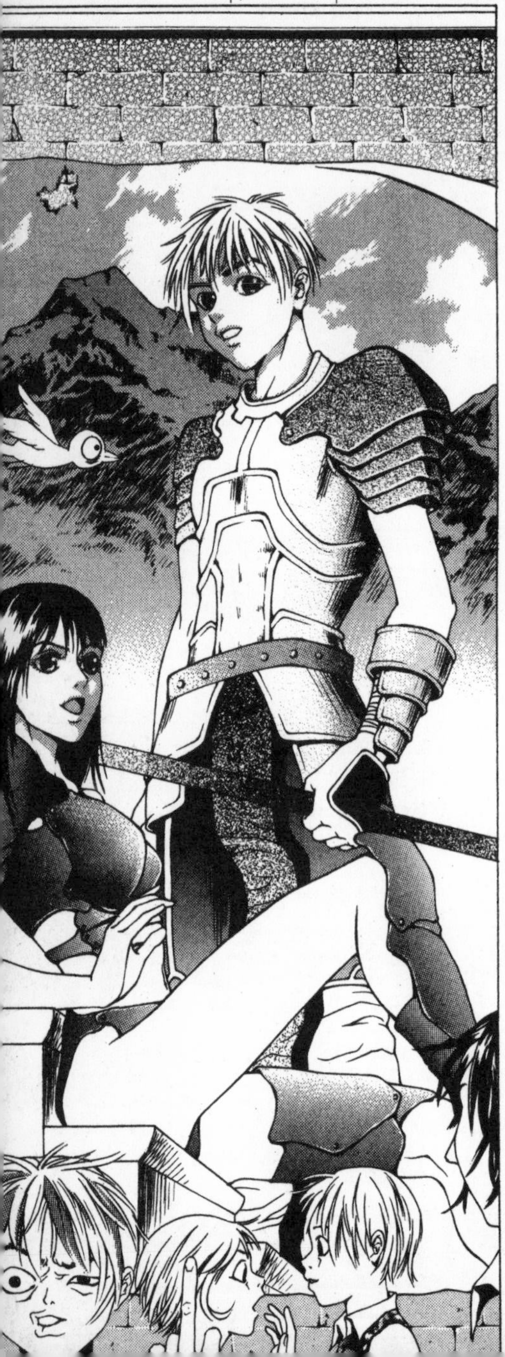

PERCHANCE TO DREAM

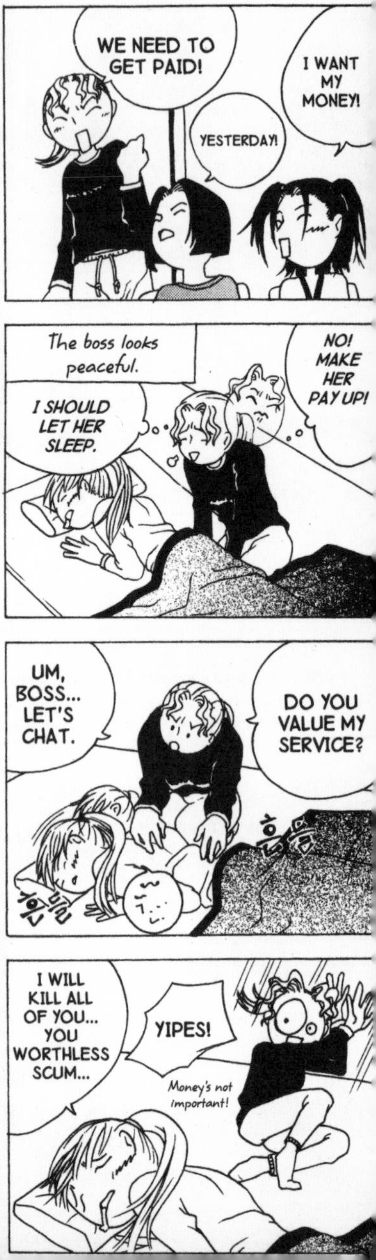
WE NEED TO GET PAID!
YESTERDAY!
I WANT MY MONEY!
The boss looks peaceful.
I SHOULD LET HER SLEEP.
NO! MAKE HER PAY UP!
UM, BOSS... LET'S CHAT.
DO YOU VALUE MY SERVICE?
I WILL KILL ALL OF YOU... YOU WORTHLESS SCUM...
YIPES!
Money's not important!

DOG DAYS

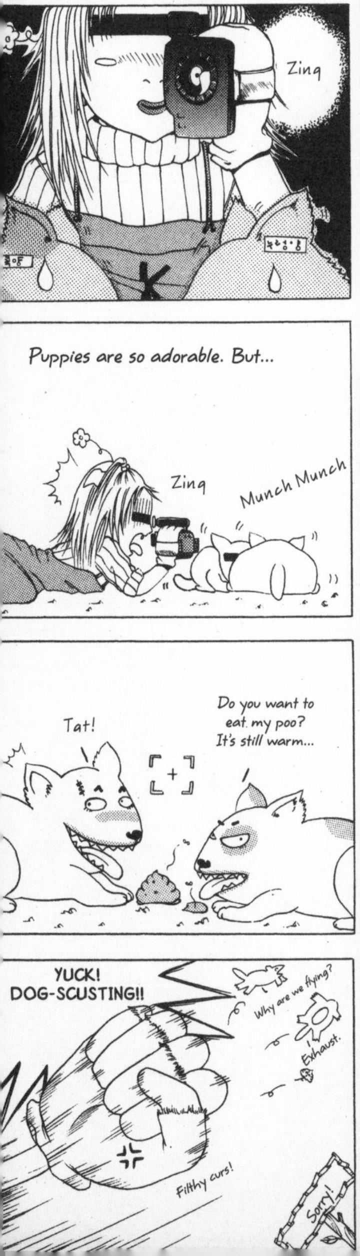

Zing
Puppies are so adorable. But...
Zing
Munch Munch
Tat!
Do you want to eat my poo? It's still warm...
YUCK! DOG-SCUSTING!!
Why are we flying?
Exhaust.
Filthy curs!
Sorry!

Miss K Loves Animals!

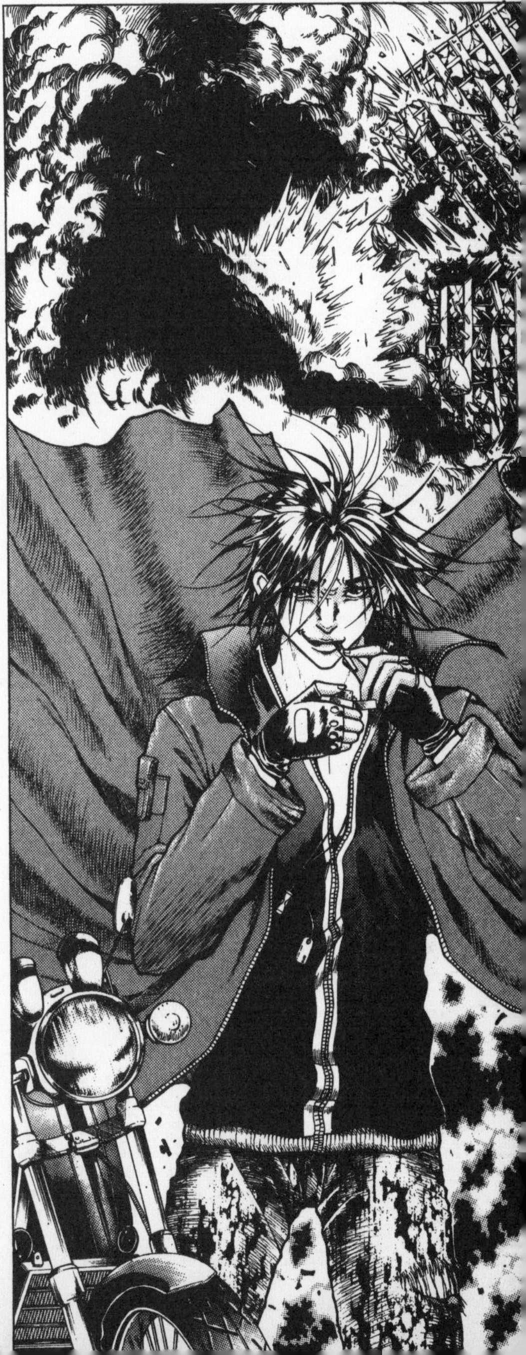

Miss L is the youngest in the studio.

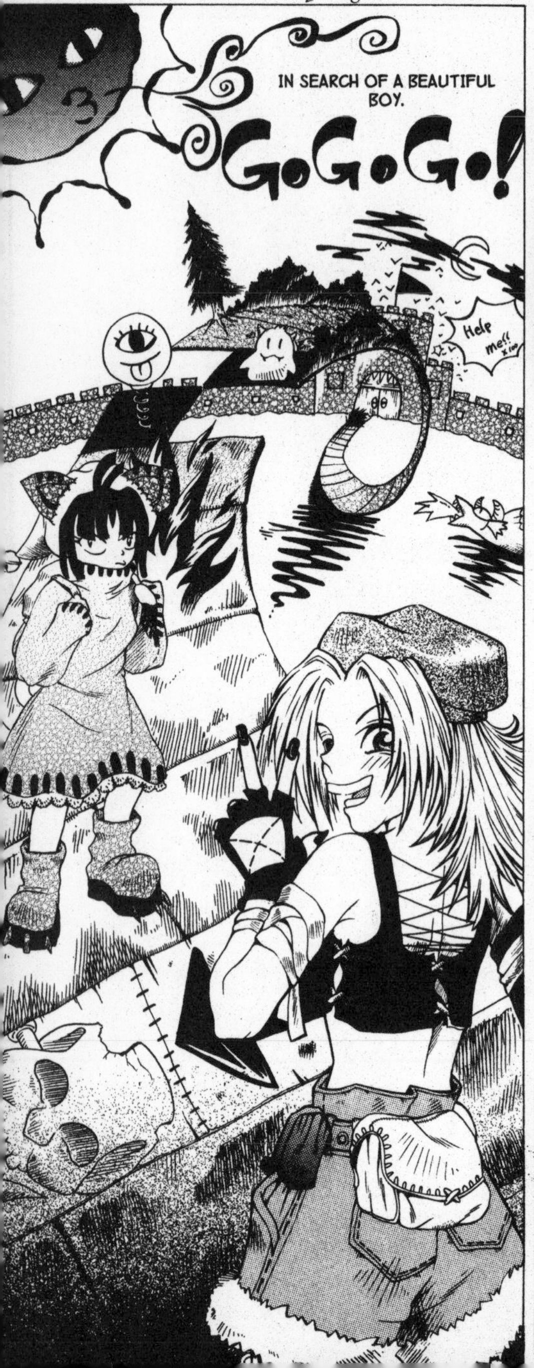
IN SEARCH OF A BEAUTIFUL BOY.
GoGoGo!
Help me!! x100

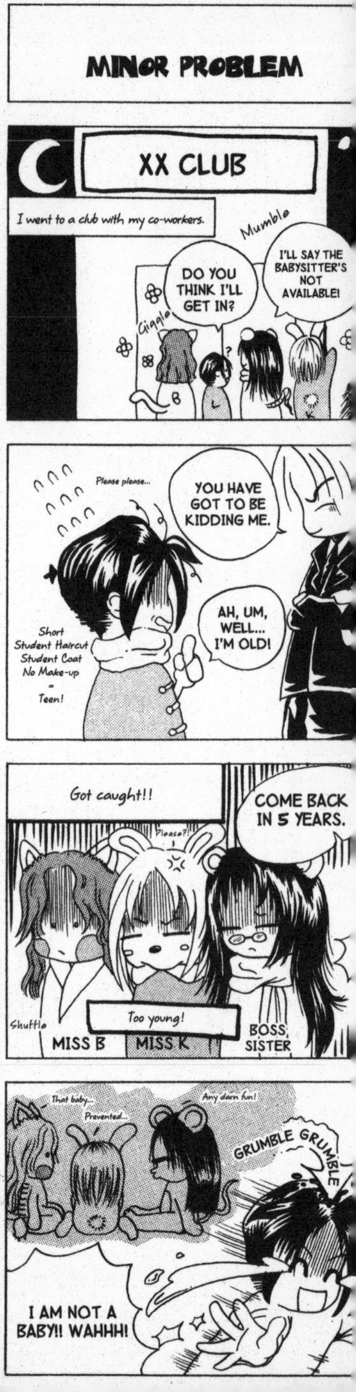
MINOR PROBLEM
XX CLUB
I went to a club with my co-workers.
Mumble
DO YOU THINK I'LL GET IN?
I'LL SAY THE BABYSITTER'S NOT AVAILABLE!
Giggle
Please please...
YOU HAVE GOT TO BE KIDDING ME.
AH, UM, WELL... I'M OLD!
Short Student Haircut Student Coat No Make-up = Teen!
Got caught!!
COME BACK IN 5 YEARS.
Please?!
Shuffle
Too young!
MISS B
MISS K
BOSS, SISTER
That baby...
Prevented...
Any darn fun!
GRUMBLE GRUMBLE
I AM NOT A BABY!! WAHHH!

This is how Threads of Time is made!!

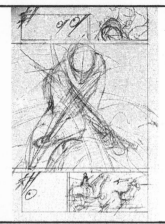

ROUGHS
I GET A ROUGH VERSION OF THE ACTION AND THE DIALOGUE DOWN ON PAPER. NORMALLY I LOOK AT 2-3 DRAFTS AND GO BACK TO THE ORIGINAL AND LOOK AT THE DRAFT ONE MORE TIME. THIS IS THE PART THAT GIVES ME THE MOST GRIEF AND THE PART THAT I MOST WANT TO AVOID.

PENCILS
I THINK THIS TAKES ABOUT 2-3 HOURS. THIS IS THE PART THAT TESTS THE LIMITS OF MY ABILITIES THE MOST. DEPENDING ON THE CONDITION, THE OUTPUT FLUCTUATES A LOT FROM 2 TO 8 PAGES A DAY.

DETAILS
THIS IS WHEN I HAVE TO ENLIVEN THE SKETCH, SO IT TAKES LOT OF CAREFUL WORK. BUT IT IS NOT A JOB IN WHICH YOU BRING SOMETHING FROM NOTHING, SO REGARDLESS OF MY CONDITION, I PRODUCE A SOLID 4-5 PAGES DAY.

FINISH!! (INKING * REVISION * TONE)
THE BACKGROUND IS THE RESULT OF OTHER PEOPLE'S HARD WORK. IT IS WORK THAT REQUIRES SOME SENSE OF COLOR SCHEME. THANKS!! MISS B! MISS L! MISS K!

THE TIME WE POUR INTO ONE PAGE IS 3 HOURS FOR SKETCHING, 3 HOURS FOR THE TOUCH-UP, AND 3 HOURS FOR THE BACKGROUND, ADDING UP TO A TOTAL OF 9 HOURS. AND CONDI TAKES FOREVER. WE POURED A LOT OF LOVE AND EFFORT INTO THIS BOOK. WE HOPE THAT YOU ENJOY IT. WAS IT FUN?

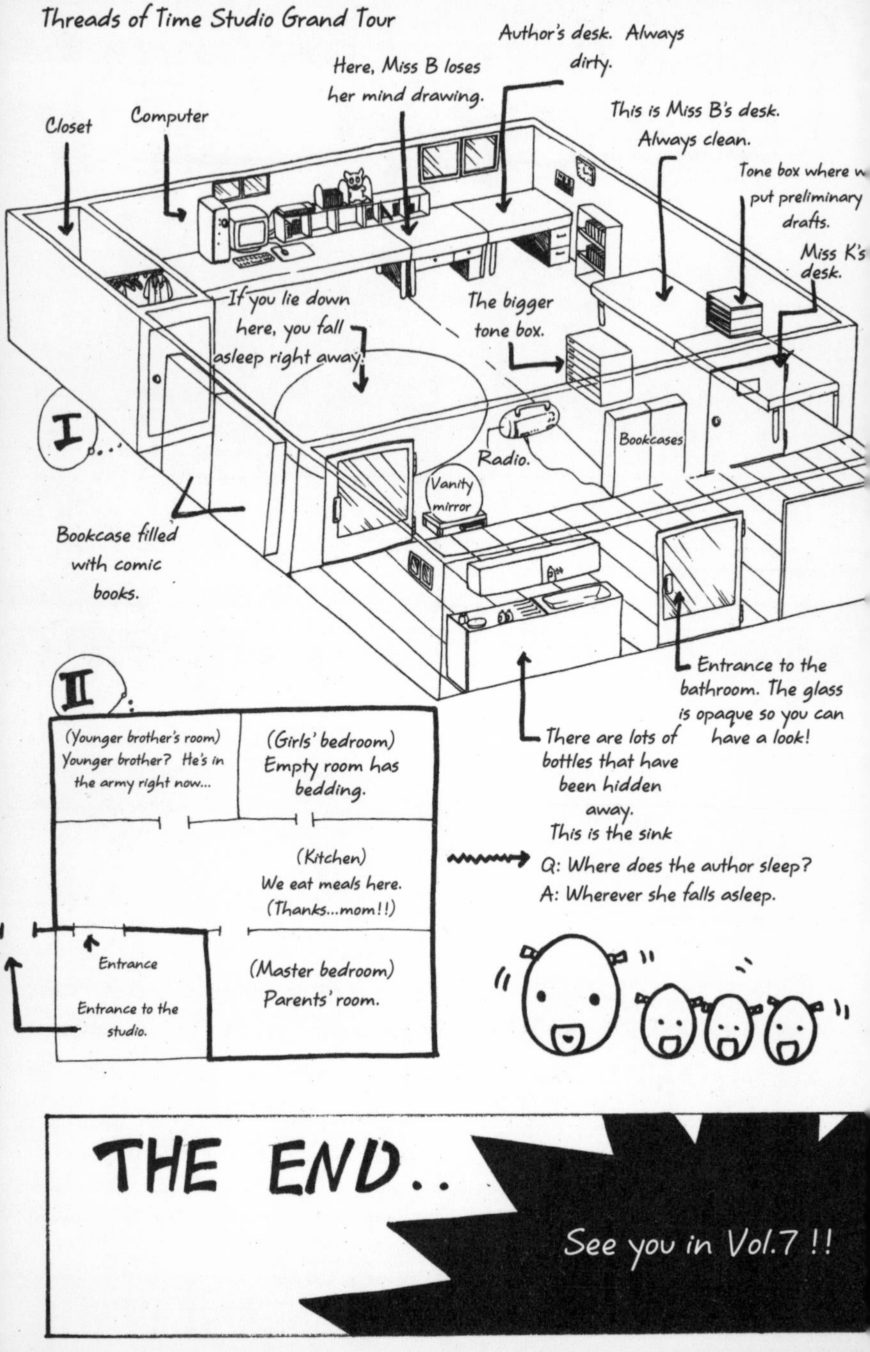

Threads of Time Studio Grand Tour
Closet
Computer
Here, Miss B loses her mind drawing.
Author's desk. Always dirty.
This is Miss B's desk. Always clean.
Tone box where w put preliminary drafts.
Miss K's desk.
If you lie down here, you fall asleep right away.
The bigger tone box.
I
Radio.
Bookcases
Vanity mirror
Bookcase filled with comic books.
Entrance to the bathroom. The glass is opaque so you can have a look!
There are lots of bottles that have been hidden away. This is the sink
II
(Younger brother's room) Younger brother? He's in the army right now...
(Girls' bedroom) Empty room has bedding.
(Kitchen) We eat meals here. (Thanks...mom!!)
Entrance
Entrance to the studio.
(Master bedroom) Parents' room.
Q: Where does the author sleep?
A: Wherever she falls asleep.
THE END..
See you in Vol.7 !!

Threads of Time™

撒神塔

In Volume 7

Flung into a Mongol military slave camp, Moon-Bin endures
arduous combat training to be part of a Shield Unit,
human fodder for enemy arrows. Orphaned, alone and now
forced to fight for his oppressors, Moon-Bin descends
into savagery, embracing the only philosophy he knows
to be true: Kill or be killed. He becomes an animal in war,
a feral beast driven only by the compulsion to survive.
His brutality catches the eye of a Mongol general, who
believes he can mold this enraged youth into a valuable
military commander.

TOKYOPOP presents a special and continuing
supplement to Threads of Time...

The Chronicles of Koryo

The Last Darugachi

Art by Morgan Luthi
Written by Brandon Montclare

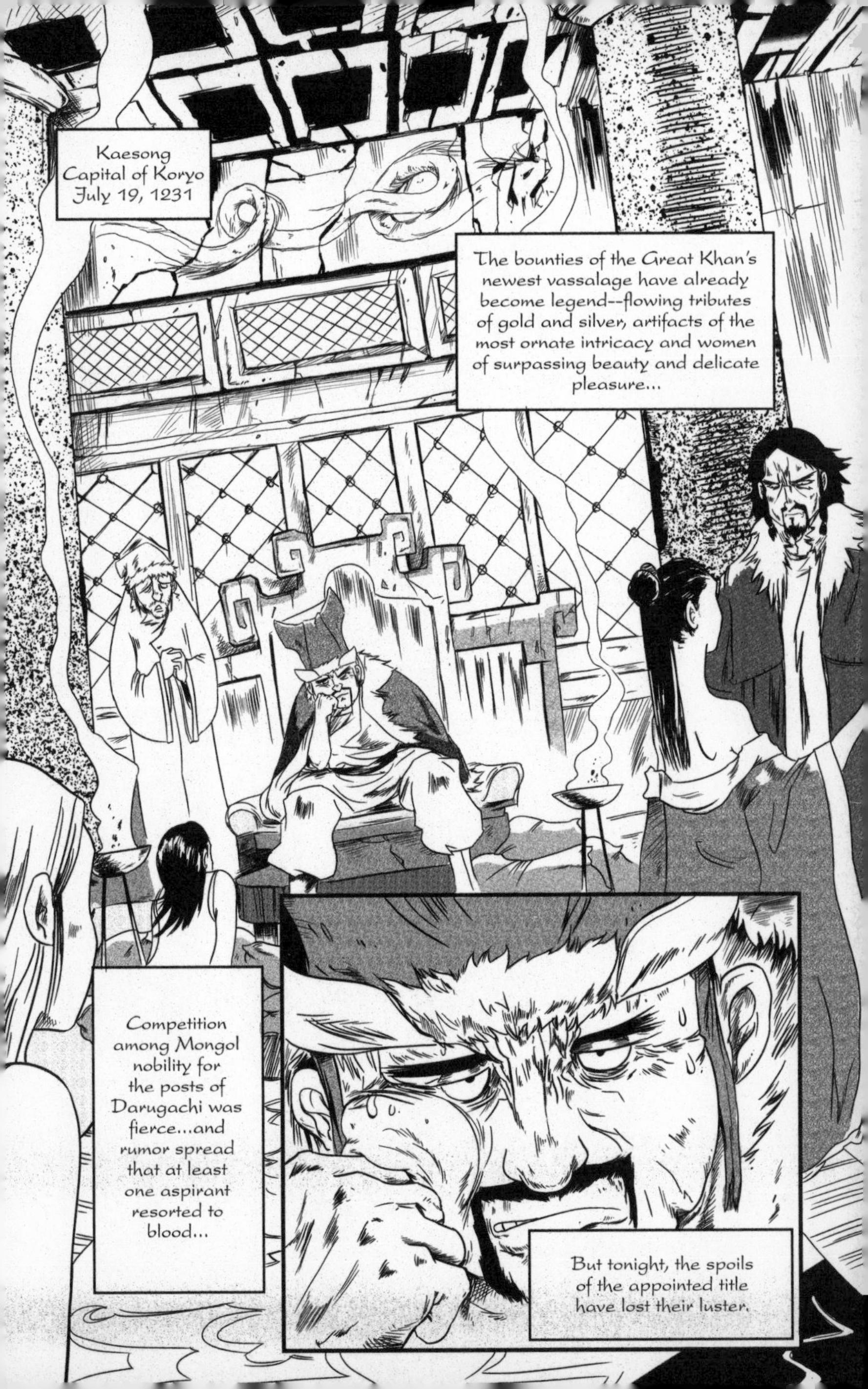
Kaesong Capital of Koryo July 19, 1231
The bounties of the Great Khan's newest vassalage have already become legend--flowing tributes of gold and silver, artifacts of the most ornate intricacy and women of surpassing beauty and delicate pleasure...
Competition among Mongol nobility for the posts of Darugachi was fierce...and rumor spread that at least one aspirant resorted to blood...
But tonight, the spoils of the appointed title have lost their luster.

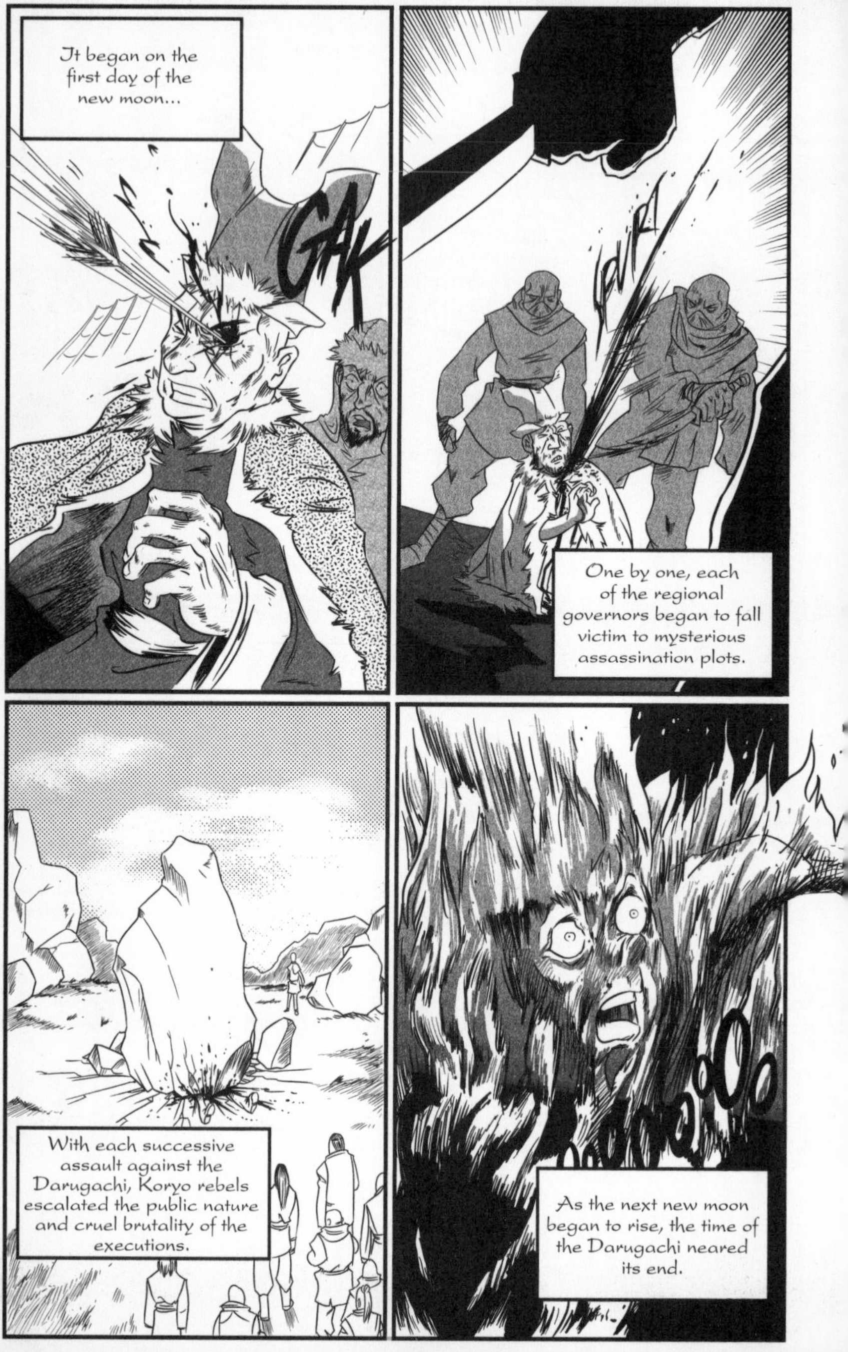
It began on the first day of the new moon...
GAK
One by one, each of the regional governors began to fall victim to mysterious assassination plots.
With each successive assault against the Darugachi, Koryo rebels escalated the public nature and cruel brutality of the executions.
As the next new moon began to rise, the time of the Darugachi neared its end.

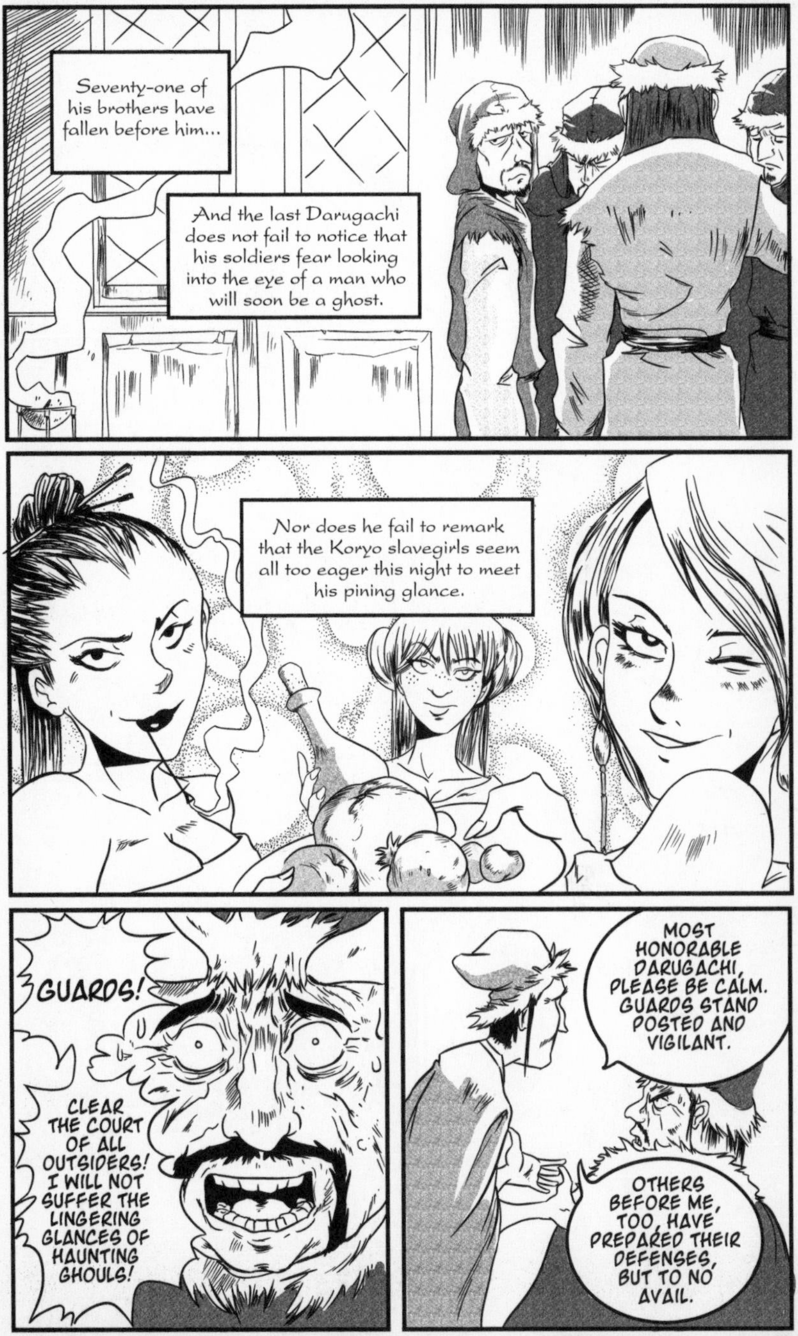
Seventy-one of his brothers have fallen before him...
And the last Darugachi does not fail to notice that his soldiers fear looking into the eye of a man who will soon be a ghost.
Nor does he fail to remark that the Koryo slavegirls seem all too eager this night to meet his pining glance.
GUARDS!
CLEAR THE COURT OF ALL OUTSIDERS! I WILL NOT SUFFER THE LINGERING GLANCES OF HAUNTING GHOULS!
MOST HONORABLE DARUGACHI, PLEASE BE CALM. GUARDS STAND POSTED AND VIGILANT.
OTHERS BEFORE ME, TOO, HAVE PREPARED THEIR DEFENSES, BUT TO NO AVAIL.

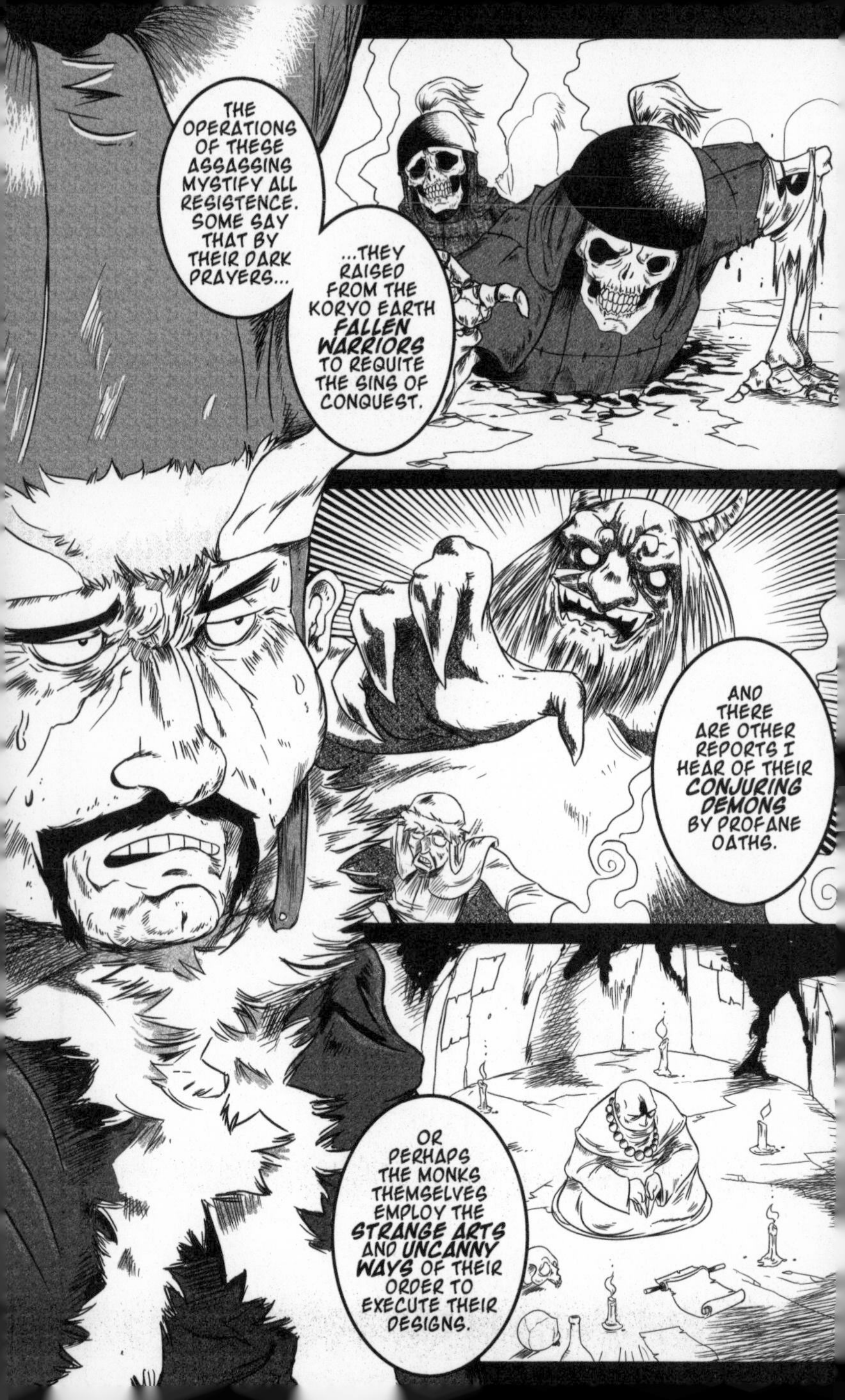
THE OPERATIONS OF THESE ASSASSINS MYSTIFY ALL RESISTENCE. SOME SAY THAT BY THEIR DARK PRAYERS...
...THEY RAISED FROM THE KORYO EARTH FALLEN WARRIORS TO REQUITE THE SINS OF CONQUEST.
AND THERE ARE OTHER REPORTS I HEAR OF THEIR CONJURING DEMONS BY PROFANE OATHS.
OR PERHAPS THE MONKS THEMSELVES EMPLOY THE STRANGE ARTS AND UNCANNY WAYS OF THEIR ORDER TO EXECUTE THEIR DESIGNS.

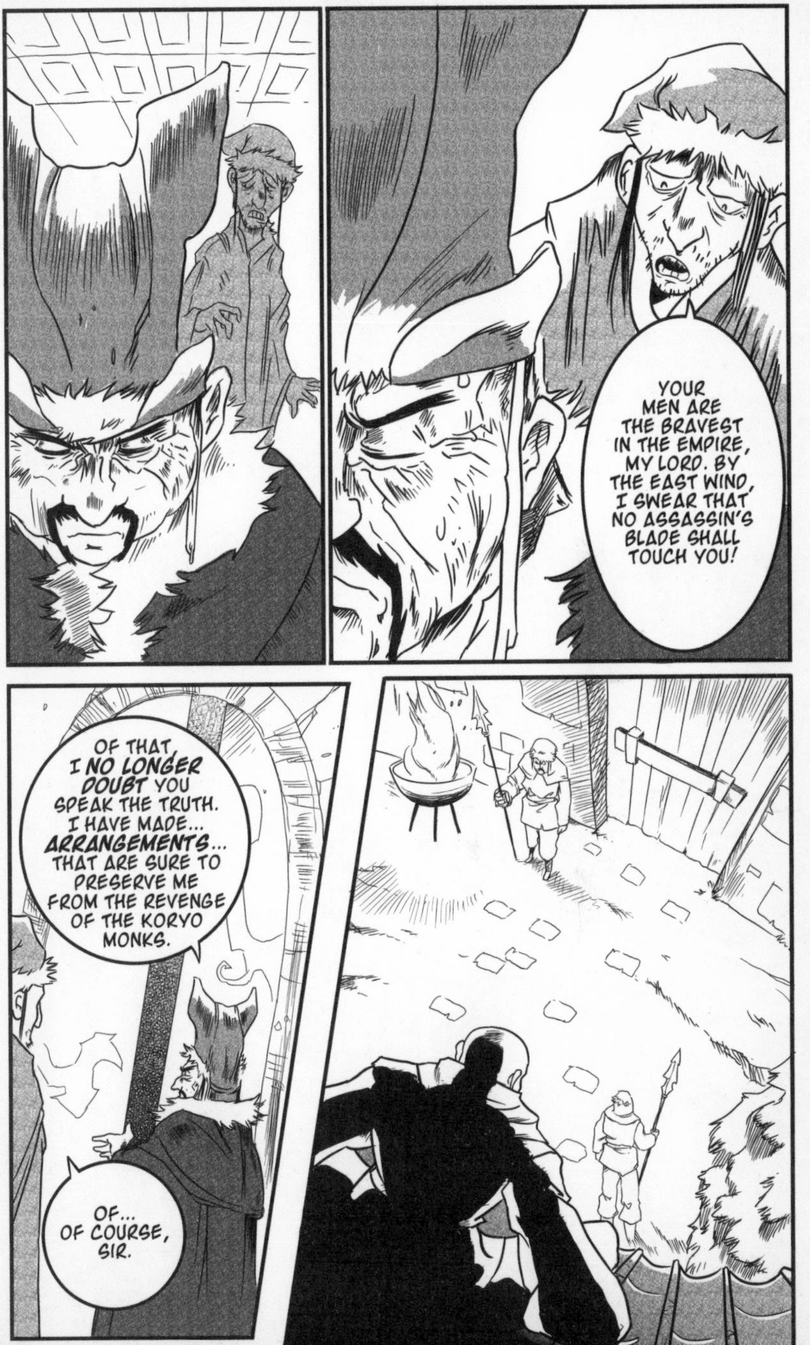
YOUR MEN ARE THE BRAVEST IN THE EMPIRE, MY LORD. BY THE EAST WIND, I SWEAR THAT NO ASSASSIN'S BLADE SHALL TOUCH YOU!
OF THAT, I **NO LONGER DOUBT** YOU SPEAK THE TRUTH. I HAVE MADE... **ARRANGEMENTS**... THAT ARE SURE TO PRESERVE ME FROM THE REVENGE OF THE KORYO MONKS.
OF... OF COURSE, SIR.

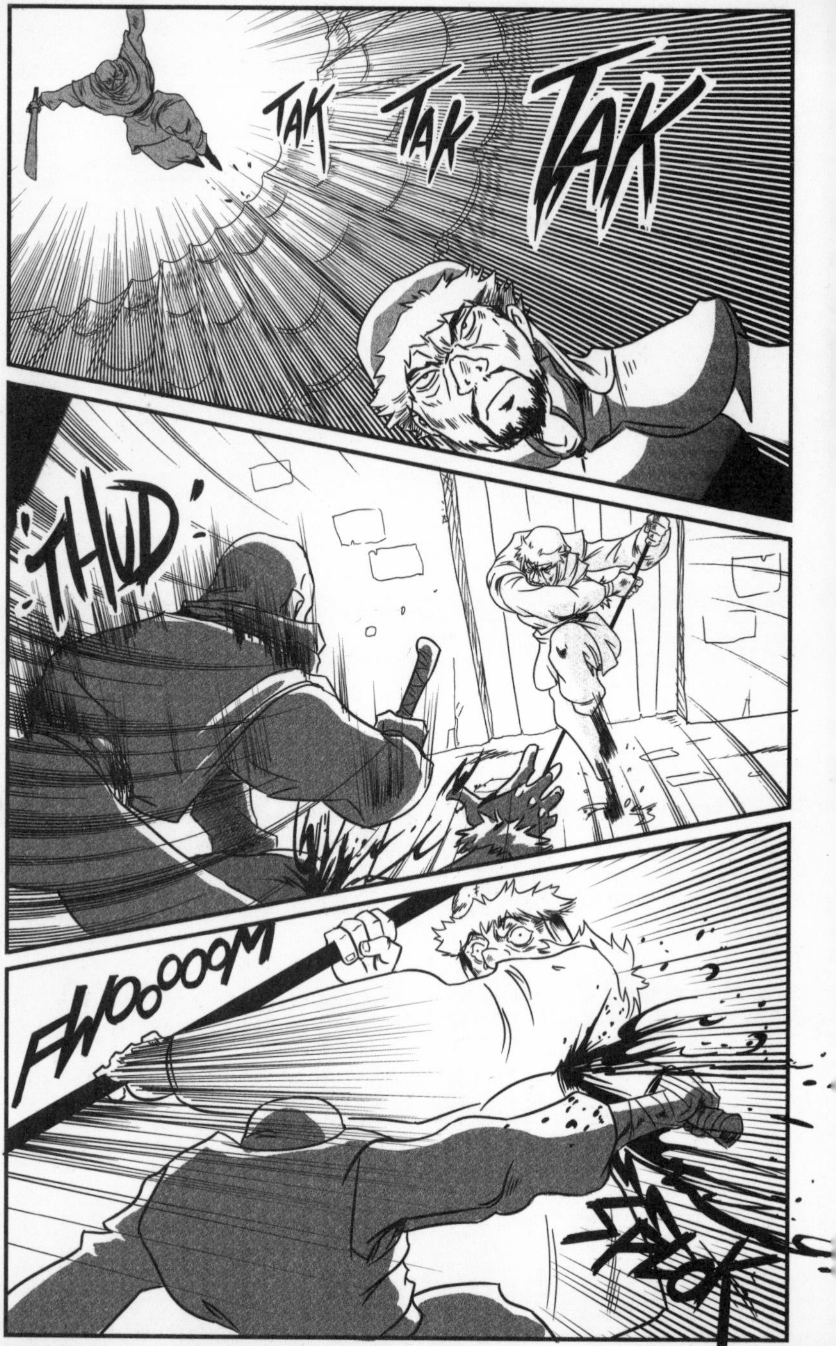
TAK TAK TAK
THUD
FWOoooOM

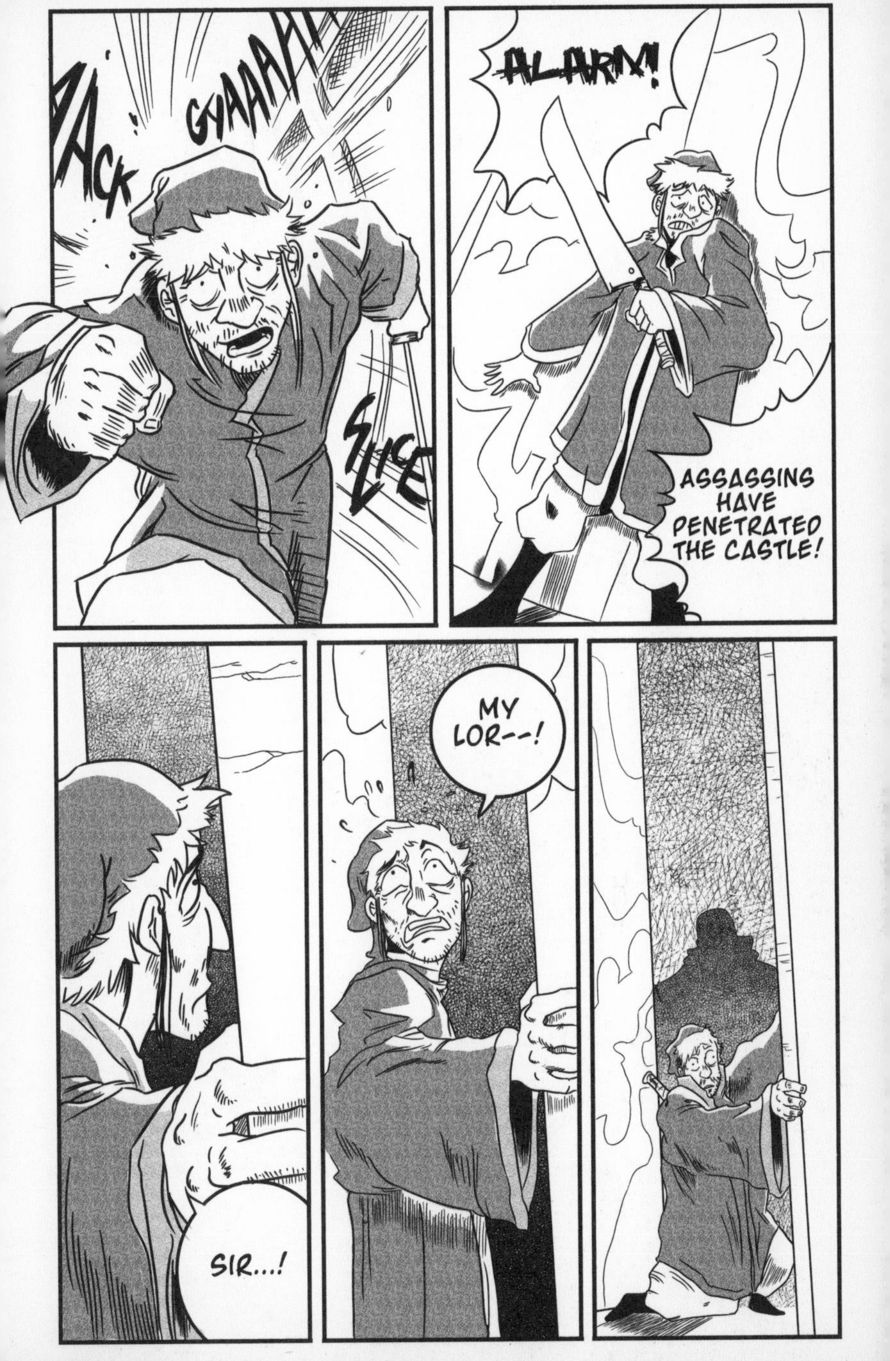

ACK
GYAAAH
SLICE
ALARM!
ASSASSINS HAVE PENETRATED THE CASTLE!
SIR...!
MY LOR--!

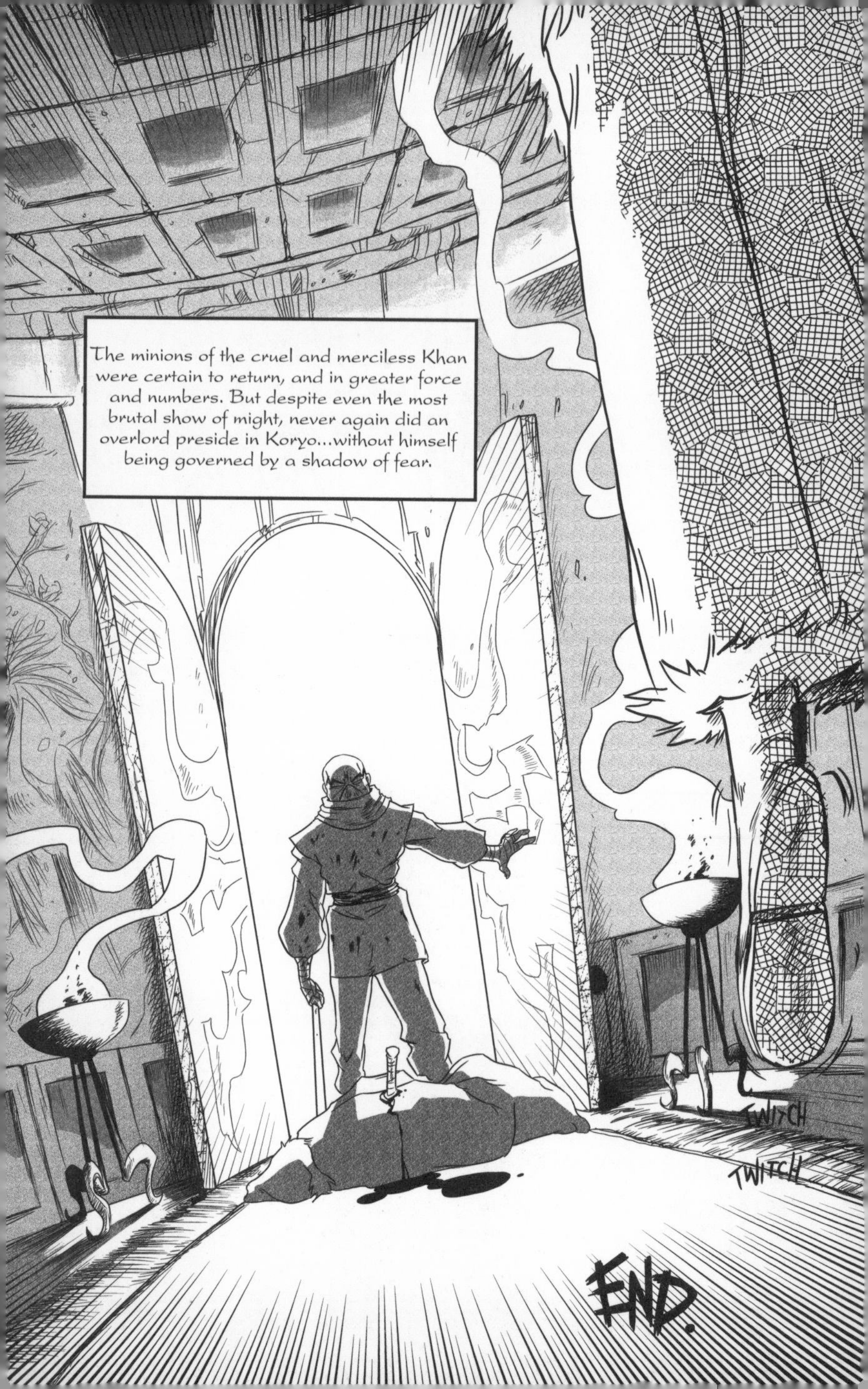
The minions of the cruel and merciless Khan were certain to return, and in greater force and numbers. But despite even the most brutal show of might, never again did an overlord preside in Koryo...without himself being governed by a shadow of fear.
TWITCH
TWITCH
END.

TOKYOPOP SHOP

WWW.TOKYOPOP.COM/SHOP

HOT NEWS!
Check out the **TOKYOPOP SHOP!** The world's best collection of manga in English is now available online in one place!

Check out all the sizzling hot merchandise and your favorite manga at the shop!

BIZENGHAST POSTER

PRINCESS AI POSTCARDS

WWW.TOKYOPOP.COM/SHOP

I Luv Halloween **Glow-in-the-Dark STICKERS!**

I LUV HALLOWEEN BUTTONS & STICKERS

- • LOOK FOR SPECIAL OFFERS
- • PRE-ORDER UPCOMING RELEASES
- • COMPLETE YOUR COLLECTIONS

I LUV HALLOWEEN © Keith Giffen and Benjamin Roman. Princess Ai © & ™ TOKYOPOP Inc. Bizenghast © M. Alice LeGrow and TOKYOPOP Inc.

LIFE
BY KEIKO SUENOBU

Ordinary high school teenagers...
Except that they're not.

LIFE™

OT
OLDER TEEN
AGE 16+

© Keiko Suenobu

READ THE ENTIRE FIRST CHAPTER ONLINE FOR FREE:

Ayumu struggles with her studies, and the all-important high school entrance exams are approaching. Fortunately, she has help from her best bud Shii-chan, who is at the top of the class. But when the test results come back, the friends are surprised: Ayumu surpasses Shii-chan's scores and gets into the school of her choice—without Shii-chan! Losing her friend is so painful for Ayumu that she starts cutting herself to ease her sorrow. Finally, Ayumu seeks comfort in a new friend, Manami. But will Manami prove to be the friend that Ayumu truly needs? Or will Ayumu continue down a dark path?

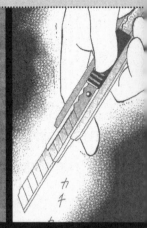

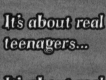

It's about real teenagers...

It's about real high school...

It's about real life.

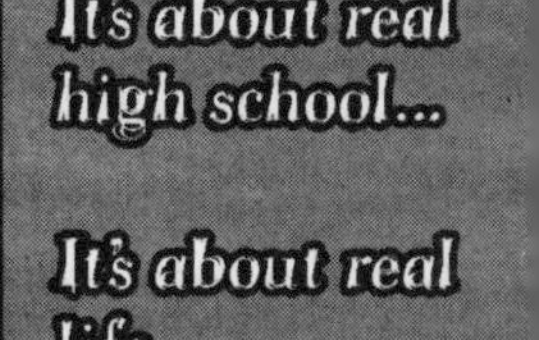

LIFE
Volume 1
Keiko Suenobu

BIZENGHAST

Dear Diary,
I'm starting to feel

T TEEN AGE 13+

Preview the manga at:
www.TOKYOPOP.com/bizenghast

When a young girl moves to the forgotten town of Bizenghast, she uncovers a terrifying collection of lost souls that leads her to the brink of insanity. One thing becomes painfully clear: The residents of Bizenghast are just dying to come home. ART SUBJECT TO CHANGE © Mary Alice LeGrow and TOKYOPOP Inc.

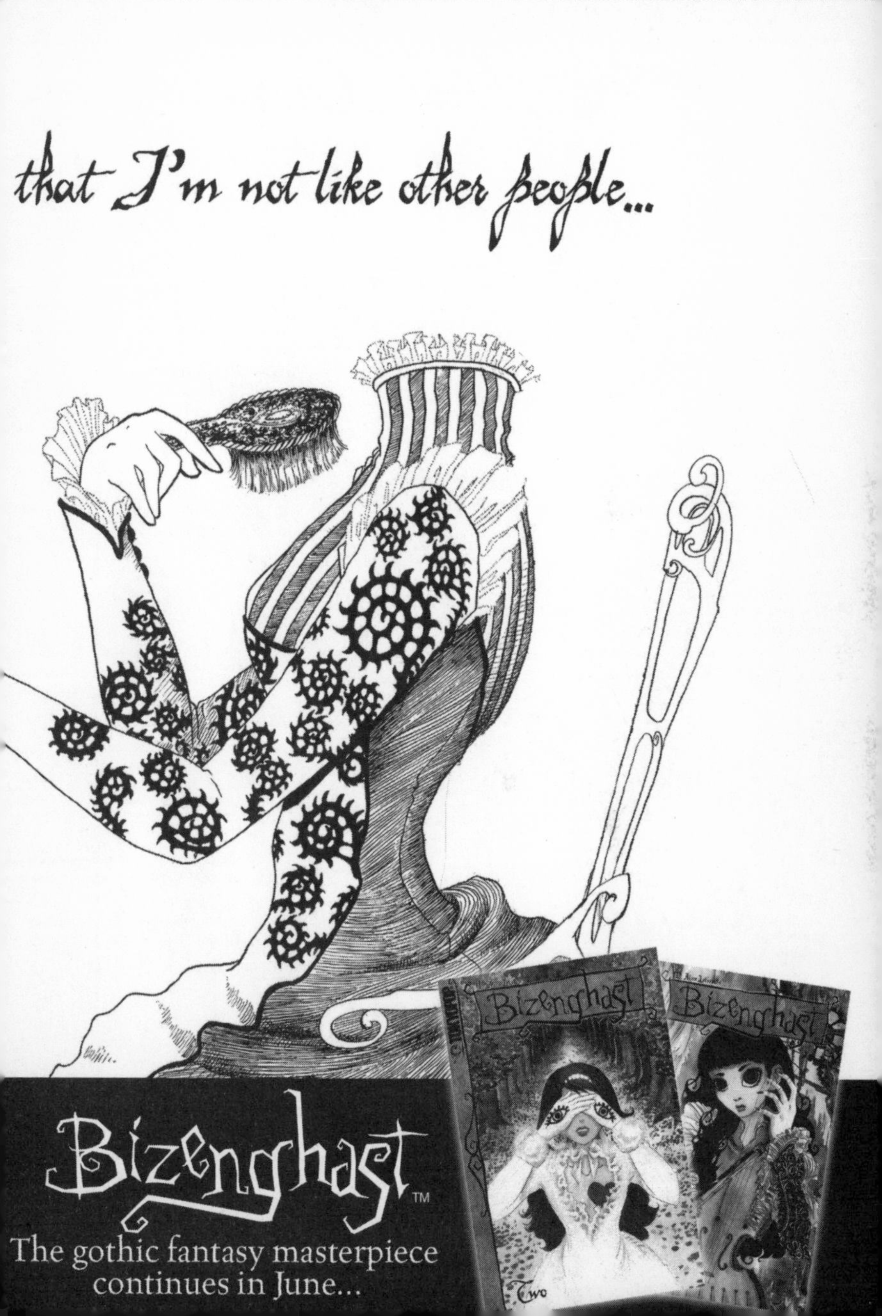
that I'm not like other people...
Bizenghast
Bizenghast
Two
Bizenghast™
The gothic fantasy masterpiece
continues in June...

POP FICTION

TOKYOPOP PRESENTS

For Believers...

Scrapped Princess:
A Tale of Destiny

By Ichiro Sakaki
A dark prophecy reveals that the queen will give birth to a daughter who will usher in the Apocalypse. But despite all attempts to destroy the baby, the myth of the "Scrapped Princess" lingers on...

THE INSPIRATION FOR THE HIT ANIME AND MANGA SERIES!

For Thinkers...

Kino no Tabi:
Book One of The Beautiful World

By Keiichi Sigsawa
Kino roams the world on the back of Hermes, her unusual motorcycle, in a journey filled with happiness and pain, decadence and violence, and magic and loss.

THE SENSATIONAL BESTSELLER IN JAPAN HAS FINALLY ARRIVED!

ART SUBJECT TO CHANGE.
Scrapped Princess: A Tale of Destiny © ICHIRO SAKAKI, GO YABUKI and YUKINOBU AZUMI.
Kino no Tabi: Book One of The Beautiful World © KEIICHI SIGSAWA.

THIS FALL, TOKYOPOP CREATES A FRESH, NEW CHAPTER IN TEEN NOVELS...

For Adventurers...
Witches' Forest:
The Adventures of Duan Surk

By Mishio Fukazawa
Duan Surk is a 16-year-old Level 2 fighter who embarks on the quest of a lifetime—battling mythical creatures and outwitting evil sorceresses, all in an impossible rescue mission in the spooky Witches' Forest!

BASED ON THE FAMOUS
FORTUNE QUEST **WORLD**

For Dreamers...
Magic Moon

By Wolfgang and Heike Hohlbein
Kim enters the enigmatic realm of Magic Moon, where he battles unthinkable monsters and fantastical creatures—in order to unravel the secret that keeps his sister locked in a coma.

THE WORLDWIDE BESTSELLING FANTASY
THRILLOGY **ARRIVES IN THE U.S.!**

ART SUBJECT TO CHANGE.
Witches' Forest: The Adventures of Duan Surk © 2006 MISHIO FUKAZAWA.
Magic Moon © 1983, 2001 by Verlag Carl Ueberreuter, Vienna.

SPOTLIGHT
TOKYOPOP MANGA SUPPLEMENT

FRUITS BASKET
BY NATSUKI TAKAYA

Fruits Basket ™

Tohru Honda was an orphan with no place to go...until the mysterious Sohma family offers her a place to call home. Tohru's ordinary high school life is turned upside down when she's introduced to the Sohmas' world of magical curses and family intrigue. Discover for yourself the Secret of the Zodiac, and find out why *Fruits Basket* has won the hearts of readers the world over!

THE BESTSELLING MANGA IN THE U.S.!

TEEN
AGE 13+

© Natsuki Takaya

FOR MORE INFORMATION VISIT WWW.TOKYOPOP.COM

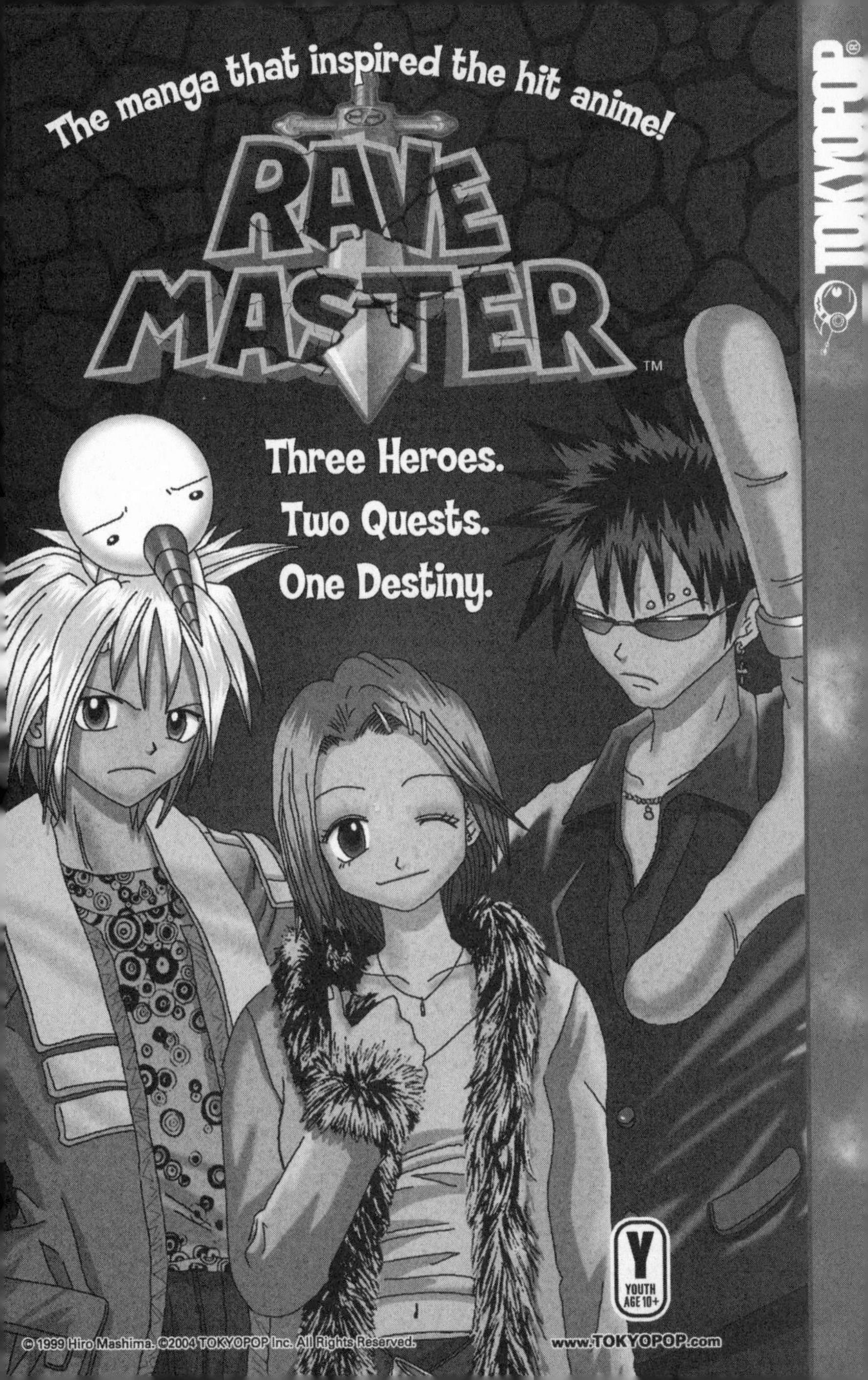
The manga that inspired the hit anime!
RAVE MASTER™
Three Heroes.
Two Quests.
One Destiny.
TOKYOPOP
Y YOUTH AGE 10+
© 1999 Hiro Mashima. ©2004 TOKYOPOP Inc. All Rights Reserved.
www.TOKYOPOP.com

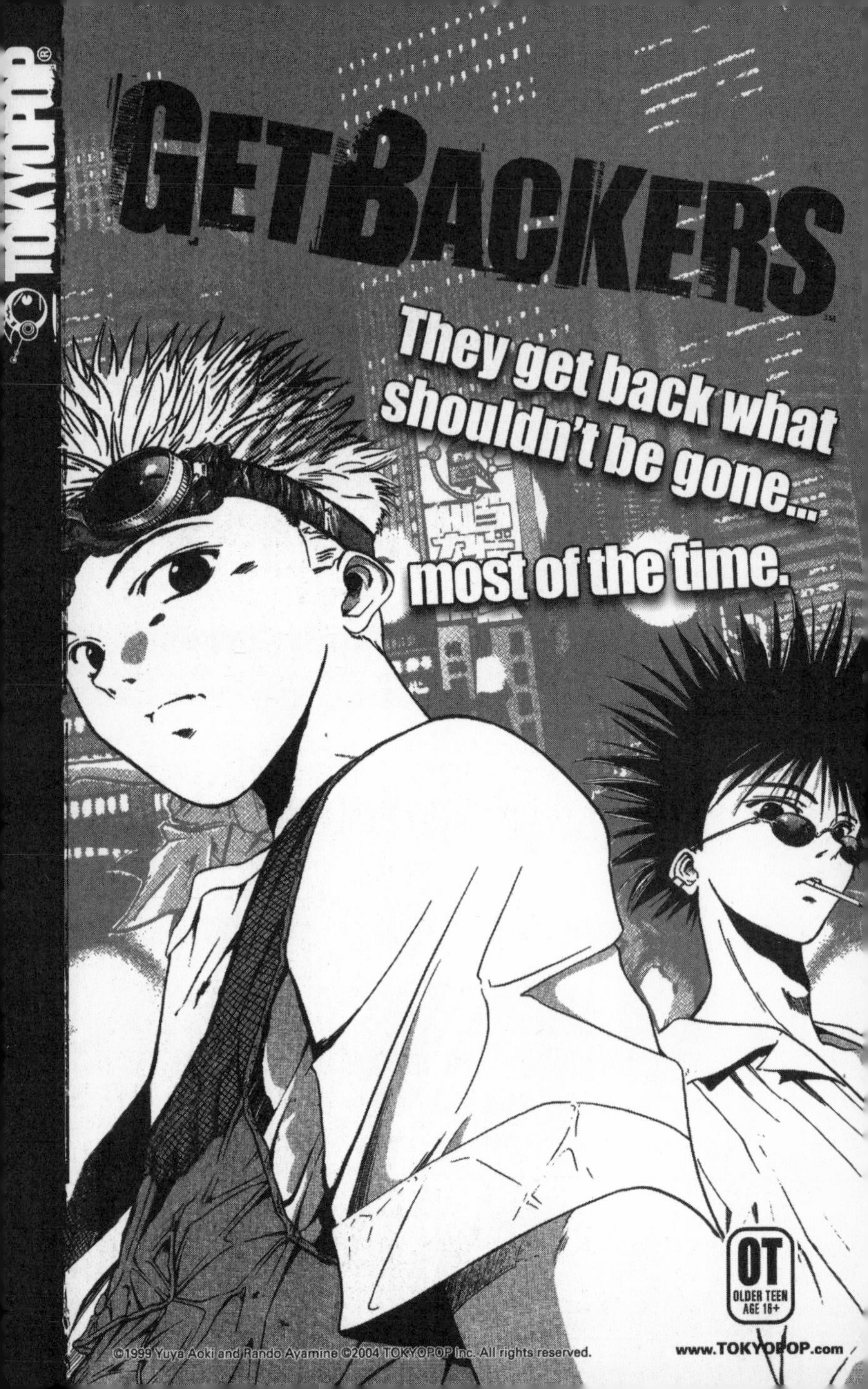
TOKYOPOP®
GETBACKERS™
They get back what shouldn't be gone... most of the time.
OT
OLDER TEEN AGE 16+
©1999 Yuya Aoki and Rando Ayamine ©2004 TOKYOPOP Inc. All rights reserved.
www.TOKYOPOP.com

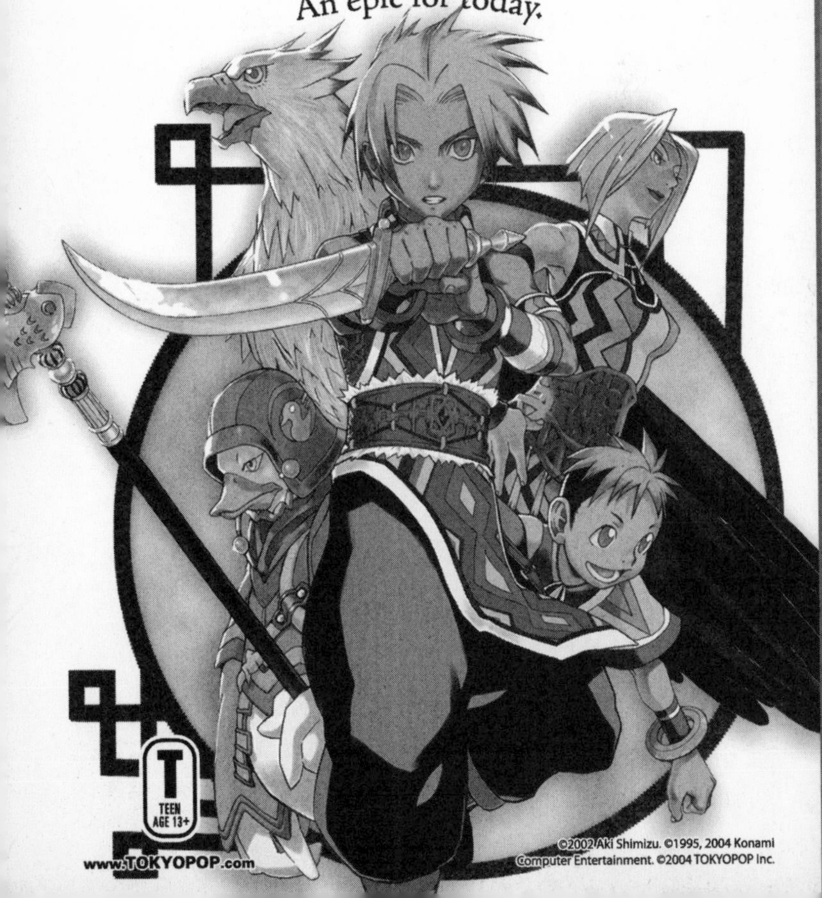
T
TEEN
AGE 13+

Dragon Knights ™

by MINEKO OHKAMI

Three warriors
with dragon blood
running through their veins

T
TEEN
AGE 13+

©1991 First published in Japan by Shinshokan Publishing Co. Ltd. Mineko Ohkami.
©2004 TOKYOPOP Inc. All Rights Reserved.

www.TOKYOP